Sir John Moore

This one is for John Sugden, who told me I should write a biography.

Sir John Moore

The Making of a Controversial Hero

Janet Macdonald

Pen & Sword
MILITARY

First published in Great Britain in 2016 by
Pen & Sword Military
an imprint of
Pen & Sword Books Ltd
47 Church Street
Barnsley
South Yorkshire
S70 2AS

ISBN 978 1 47383 394 4

A CIP catalogue record for this book is available from the British Library

Typeset in Ehrhardt by
Mac Style Ltd, Bridlington, East Yorkshire
Printed and bound in the UK by CPI Group (UK) Ltd,
Croydon, CRO 4YY

Pen & Sword Books Ltd incorporates the imprints of Pen & Sword
Archaeology, Atlas, Aviation, Battleground, Discovery, Family History,
History, Maritime, Military, Naval, Politics, Railways, Select, Transport,
True Crime, and Fiction, Frontline Books, Leo Cooper, Praetorian Press,
Seaforth Publishing and Wharncliffe.

For a complete list of Pen & Sword titles please contact
PEN & SWORD BOOKS LIMITED
47 Church Street, Barnsley, South Yorkshire, S70 2AS, England
E-mail: enquiries@pen-and-sword.co.uk
Website: www.pen-and-sword.co.uk

Contents

Author's Note

This book contains numerous extracts from Sir John Moore's correspondence and journals. I make no excuse for heavy use of these, for it is in his own words that the way he thought and reacted in various situations allows the character of the man to shine through. And for those who are as fortunate, as I have been, to see the original documents in Moore's own hand, the way his writing deteriorates in times of stress is equally telling.

I have relied on these documents rather than any of the published biographies; these range from the hagiographic versions written soon after his death, through indignant defences of his reputation published early in the twentieth century (based mainly on the previous biographies) and a mid-twentieth-century biography which includes much tangential material and much use of author's licence and imagination which frequently takes it away from the factual to the fictional. Unfortunately most of the later writings on Moore rely heavily on this book and thus the myths have been perpetuated. Those who have previously read of Moore may wonder why I have omitted some details found elsewhere; this is because I have been unable to find a credible source for them.

But I have not ignored the academic studies that deal in depth with specific military situations in which Moore was involved, or the military histories such as William Napier's and Sir Charles Oman's histories of the Peninsular War or Sir John Fortescue's multi-volume *History of the British Army*.

Acknowledgements

I am grateful to Mick Crumplin for assistance on medical matters, Nigel Lipscombe for military matters, Piers Mackesy for sending me a translation of his paper on the abortive Cadiz landing, Bob Sutcliffe for information on the transports after the Convention of Cintra, the staff at the British Library, The National Archives at Kew and the library at the Royal Military Academy at Sandhurst, and as always, my husband, Ken Maxwell-Jones, for research assistance, chauffeuring duties, his tolerance of my obsession with Moore for the best part of five years and constant provision of excellent coffee.

Maps

Illustrations

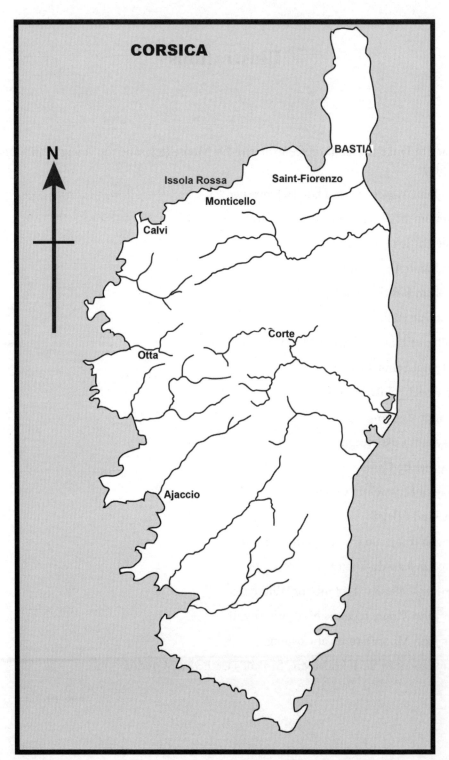

Corsica.

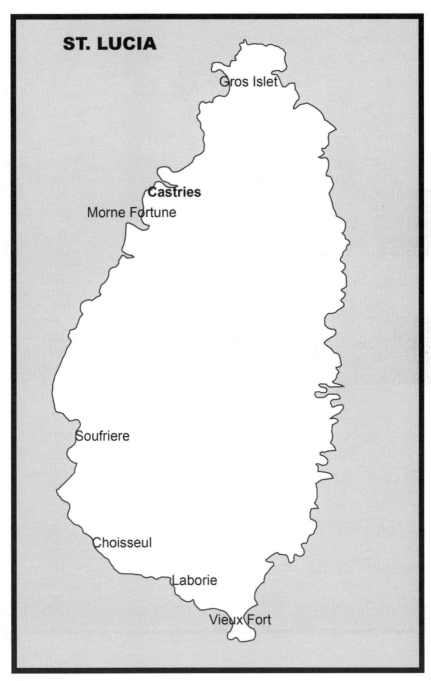

ST. LUCIA

Gros Islet

Castries

Morne Fortune

Soufriere

Choisseul

Laborie

Vieux Fort

St Lucia.

Ireland.

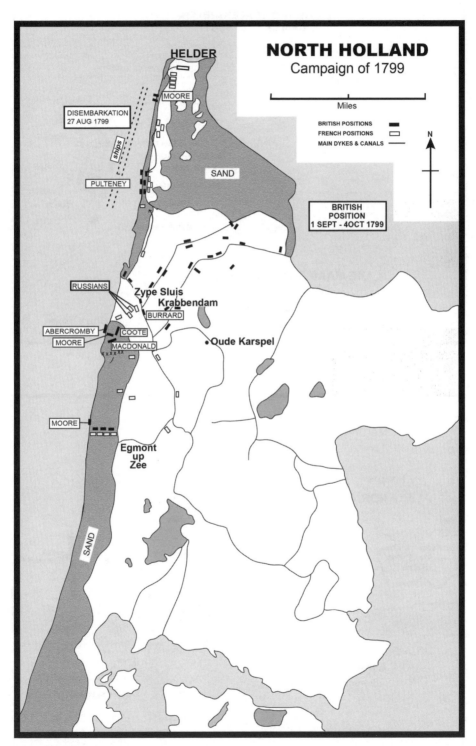

North Holland.

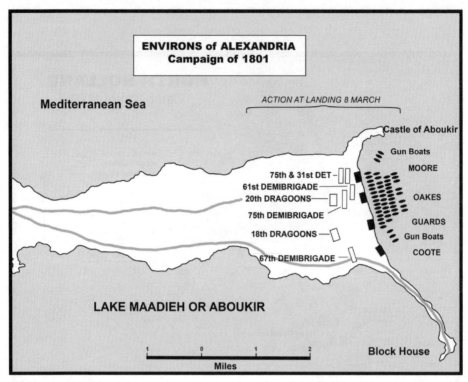

Environs of Alexandria.

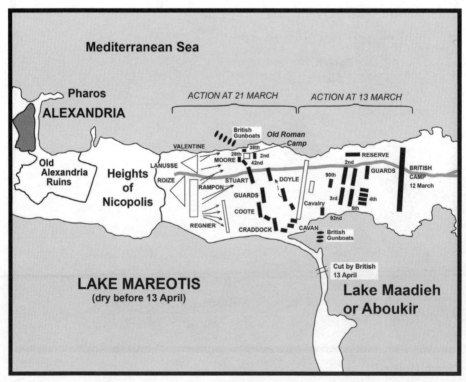

Lake Mareotis, Egypt.

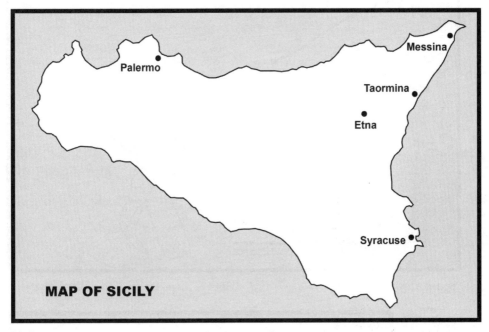

Sicily.

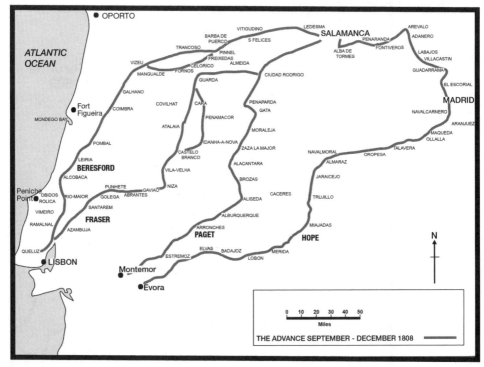

Spain – the advance.

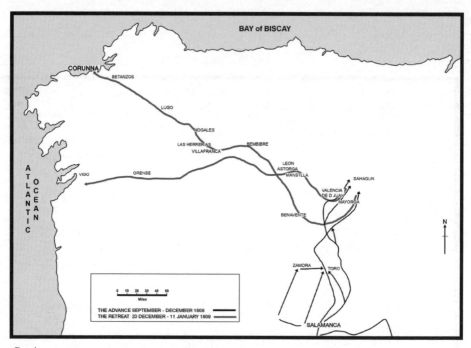

Spain.

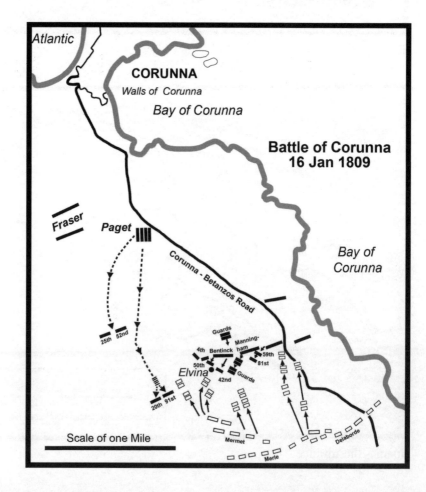

Battle of
Corunna.

Chapter 1

Early Days

Born in the Trongate district of Glasgow on 13 November 1761, John Moore had four younger brothers: James, Graham, Charles and Francis. He also had a sister, Jane, who was three years older than him, and there had been five other children who did not survive. Unlike many army and navy officers of the time, John did not come from a family with a long tradition of military service; the closest was his great-grandfather, Captain Charles Moore, who had served in William III's army. His parents were Jean Simson, daughter of the Reverend Professor John Simson of Glasgow University, and John, a successful writer and a highly respected physician; it was this latter profession which allowed him to take young John with him on an extended trip to the Continent and as a result gave John a useful patron in the early part of his military career.

In 1769, the young Duke of Hamilton, George, was travelling home from Eton to Scotland with his mother and his younger brother, Douglas; en route he was taken ill with a high fever, and by the time he reached Glasgow was too ill to go further. The family physician, William Cullen, was called in, diagnosed phthisis (tuberculosis), and since he could not stay away from his practice in Edinburgh indefinitely, recommended that a local physician should take over the case.[1]

Dr Moore was chosen and attended the Duke, accompanying him on the 10-mile journey to Hamilton House, the country house in the Clyde valley, spending most of the next three months there with the Duke until his death. Douglas now succeeded his brother and became the eighth Duke of Hamilton. Dr Moore returned to his practice in Glasgow and heard no more from the Hamiltons until two years later, the Duchess (now of Argyll as her second husband had succeeded to this title) paid a surprise visit as, she said, she wished to meet Mrs Moore. This was followed by an invitation to stay at Hamilton House; Dr Moore went on his own and stayed for a month. Some little time after this, he was chosen from several candidates to fill the post of tour guide and mentor to Douglas on a Grand Tour of Europe. This tour was to last up to three years and the emolument was generous: £500 a year and an annuity of £100 a year for life. Dr Moore promptly accepted and set out for London where the Duchess and the young Duke were staying at Argyll House, taking young John (also known to his family as Jack) with him.

They arrived on 24 February 1792 and the following day Dr Moore presented himself to the Duchess. He went alone, allowing his son to go out with a guide to see the sights of London. He came back to tell his father, and later his mother in a letter, that he had seen both the King's and the Queen's houses, and the Queen herself 'hurling in her coach, and the Guards riding after her'. Dr Moore was sure the Duchess would not object to young John joining the travelling party as a youthful companion for the Duke. His health was not as robust as the Duchess would have liked, and so she wished her son to be removed from London as soon as possible. A special travelling post-chaise was being built, but as this would not be ready for some days, she suggested that after the Duke had been presented at Court the following week they should leave London straight away and wait for the new chaise at Calais.[2]

This arrangement was welcomed by Dr Moore, as it gave him an opportunity to see his daughter, Jane, who was living in Calais with the Mollier family, and to arrange for her return home. He had already, while in London, dined with his friend the bookseller Mr Murray, who offered to put Jane up in London until his wife made a visit to Glasgow. There was also Murray's friend Mr Cruikshank, who would go to Dover to meet Jane from the boat and escort her to London. Dr Moore reported all this in a letter to his wife, ending affectionately, 'I thank Heaven with perfect sincerity for the inestimable blessing it bestowed on me in connecting me to you … Farewell my dear Soul & believe me unutterably yours'.

They did not actually leave London until the middle of April, during which time young John went to the theatre and to the place where Charles I was beheaded. He reported this in a separate page of his father's letter, starting 'Dear Mama' and ending 'your dutiful son'. At this time his handwriting was very childish and his father had had to rule lines on the paper for him. Whatever else he had learned at Glasgow Grammar School, good handwriting was clearly not a feature. Nor was good diction, for he had a broad Glasgow accent. This was one of the reasons Dr Moore wanted to take his son with him to Europe so that he could guide his son's school studies and the development of his social skills. In a further letter to his wife, Dr Moore remarked on another of his concerns about the impression his children made on the world, saying that although the Molliers had taken good care of their daughter, she had two bad habits which should be corrected: turning in her toes and 'wurbling with her fingers'. She would now return to London with Colonel Livingstone, who had accompanied the Duke to Calais.

By the end of the month they had moved on to Paris. Moore's father was also concerned lest his son should become over-familiar with the young Duke; despite the Duke calling him 'Moore', he reminded young John that he should always say 'my Lord Duke' or 'your Grace'. Not only was his father concerned with social protocol, he worried that the two youths would lead each other into trouble. He was right to worry about this; one day in their lodgings there was a loud bang followed by a shriek of pain. Young Moore, in the room next to where his father was writing, had grown bored and finding a pair of travelling pistols and not realising they were loaded, had pointed one and snapped the lock. The ball went through the wall into the next room where it hit the chambermaid. Although she was not seriously wounded, she took some time to recover and had to be generously compensated. This was not the only time the two boys' high spirits got them into trouble; a few days later, his father found young John bleeding from a wound in his side and a bloody sword on the floor. The boys had been mock-duelling, John evading the Duke's sword with skill, until he missed a dodge and impaled himself on the Duke's weapon. Although only a superficial wound, the Duke blamed himself and was filled with remorse.

From Paris they moved on to Geneva, where the Duke would remain for a year, building up his health. Their departure was delayed when young John was taken ill with what his father described as a cold, but what seems more like a violent fever, with delirious ravings. Fortunately this did not last long and after a few days he was declared fit to travel again. They passed through Dijon and Lyon where Dr Moore noted with disapproval the Duke's 'complete disregard for money' in purchasing two rich waistcoats.

They arrived in Geneva on a bright June day, staying in an inn while Dr Moore arranged for better accommodation for a long stay: a suite of rooms for himself, the Duke, his valet de chambre and two footmen, and a room in a pension a few doors away for his son. Dr Moore duly reported this to his wife, and also that they had experienced one of the spectacular local thunderstorms, with almost continual sheet lightning. He went on to say that he had received the bad news about his brother-in-law James' financial disaster. The banking house of Douglas, Heron and Co. had collapsed, and with it James' business. Dr Moore had guaranteed James's Bills of Exchange to the tune of £2,000; the doctor had been intending to use this for his sons' education, but now it had to go to James' creditors.

The rest of their stay in Geneva, and in the country house at Chatelaine to which they moved in the summer of 1773, was comparatively uneventful, although Dr Moore and the Duke made two visits to the south of France and another to see the Savoy glaciers. John remained in Geneva, a little homesick but concentrating on his lessons. He studied French and Latin, finding the latter a little difficult, mathematics, geography and writing. His handwriting quickly improved and he wrote many of his letters home in good French, addressed to 'ma chere Maman' and often signing himself Jaques. The Duke continued to indulge his extravagant habits but not exclusively for himself; on their visit to Marseilles he bought Moore an expensive knife, and later a hat, heavy with gold lace. John liked it but his father did not approve, telling his wife that if he'd known it was being made, he would have stopped two-thirds of the lace. However, Dr Moore did send two bracelets to his wife, one containing a lock of the Duke's hair and the other locks of his and John's, on a base of pale blue with a small gold chain woven round.

John was growing up fast and his father wrote to his wife that she could be proud of her son: 'his face is of a manly beauty, his person strong and his figure elegant. His mind begins to expand ... [he has] good sense and benevolence'. He was daring and intrepid, and endeared himself to everybody he met.

Their stay in Geneva lasted more than two years before they moved on to tour the principal German courts. The Duke was reluctant to leave Geneva, this reluctance probably the result of one of his unfortunately frequent infatuations. After some argument the doctor finally consented to the Duke stopping in Lausanne on his own for four days, then going on to Strasbourg on horseback. After he joined them they proceeded into Germany. Moore had decided that he was going to be a soldier and when he needed a new suit, it was made to look like a French uniform with 'a milk-white fine plush coat and blue waistcoat and breeches'. He was much admired by the German aristocracy, in particular the Dowager Margravine of Bayreuth. She liked him so much that she offered to take him with her on a tour she was about to make, and at the end would send him on to Brunswick with 'a careful Hussar'. Although flattered by this offer, Dr Moore refused as winter was coming on and he was worried about the dangerous state of the roads; they had also been warned that they would need to wrap up well in furs against the cold. A similar offer was later made by the Princess of Brunswick, and also politely refused.

They stayed next at Frankfurt-on-the-Main, with John staying in a pension during the week to concentrate on learning German. He found it a difficult language, he wrote to his mother, but would apply himself closely to it when they reached Brunswick, 'as it will be of great use to me when I am an officer, especially if I am sent into Germany, which is by far the best country to learn the art Military [*sic*]'. At Brunswick he and the Duke learned 'the Prussian exercise', achieving a firing and recharging rate of five times a minute and firing thirty-five times on the last day. John continued his study of the military arts and on a visit to Potsdam they attended a Grand Review, and Dr Moore remarked in a letter to his wife, 'If he had hesitated about being a soldier, this glorious scene would have confirmed him'. But both John and his father were concerned about the brutal discipline, soldiers being 'severely caned' whether the infringement was caused by pure accident, negligence or lethargy.

There had been some suggestions that John might enter the Prussian or Austrian armies, with patronage assured, but father was not keen. He had broached the subject of a British commission with the Duchess of Argyll, and she had written to the Secretary at War, Lord Barrington; he had replied that the King did not wish to give commissions to anyone under 16. Dr Moore resolved to declare John 16 immediately after his 15th birthday, and wrote to the Duchess from Vienna at the end of August 1775 that she could now say John was 16 as he was in his 16th year. Father was obviously unsure of his dates, and a few weeks previously had asked his wife to tell him all the children's ages. John was not even 14 at that point.

From Vienna they moved on to Italy, one of the 'must see' places for a Grand Tour by those who had been brought up on the Roman Classics. The Duke was particularly keen and had acquired more footmen and two personal servants, one Italian and one Swiss. Stopping first at Venice, by the end of November 1775 they had moved on to Rome, where Dr Moore was almost overwhelmed by the antiquities, running, he wrote, from one to the other: the Capitol, Trajan's Pillar (more familiar as Trajan's Column nowadays), the Pantheon and St Peter's almost as soon as they had arrived. From Rome, they went to Naples, where they viewed the various 'curiosities' which were then being excavated from Pompeii, and were entertained by Sir William Hamilton, the British ambassador. John and his father joined a party climbing Mount Vesuvius, which was in one of its eruptive phases; the boy, ever adventurous, had climbed very close to the edge of the crater when the volcano threw up a mass of lava and burning stones. He, and another gentleman with him, had run for their lives; Moore stumbled and fell, wounding his knee and thigh sufficiently to be laid up for several days. His father reported this adventure to his wife, continuing:

But he was well quit, for the lava and stones fell in such a quantity, on the place from which they had run with so much precipitation, that in all likelihood they would have been destroyed had they remained. Jack, on the whole, was in as much danger, and as well wounded, as if he had stood a tolerable brisk siege.

While they were in Naples, good news arrived: the Duke of Argyll had obtained an ensigncy in the 51st Regiment for John. The first task was to write for a leave of absence while he returned home and gathered the belongings and equipment he would need. As it happened, the Duke was also anxious to return home; Baron Mure, one of his guardians, had died and a packet of papers for the Duke to sign had arrived. These seemed to allow the remaining two guardians too much freedom over the Duke's financial affairs and he refused to sign them, wishing first to consult with his mother. He was also, he said, tired of constantly travelling and wanted to come home. They set out, stopping at Geneva on the way. Dr Moore wrote to his wife of one of John's more endearing traits; although always invited to dinner and parties with the Duke, he would not go if it meant cancelling a previous engagement with more humble people. When pressed to go to a particularly brilliant party at a fine villa on such an occasion, he told his father, 'They who have invited me are poor; they were kind to me when the others did not think me worth their notice.'

Having left Dr Moore in Paris, where the Duchess was expected, John and the Duke, now firm friends, arrived in London on 14 September. The Duke went to visit his sister, Elizabeth (known to family and friends as Betty), now the Countess of Derby, while Moore started by visiting Mr Murray in Fleet Street who offered him a room in his house while he was in London. While this was more conveniently located than his uncle James Simson's house, he was already committed to stay there. He wrote to his father on 19 September to explain why he was still in London instead of on his way north. It had been necessary to visit General Harvey to pay his respects and deliver a letter from his father; he had also paid a visit to Mr Drummond, the banker, who then accompanied John to visit Mr Mair, the 51st Regiment's agent. Mr Mair asked if John wanted to draw any of his pay, which had been accumulating since his commission in March, then asked when he intended to join his regiment. John did not need money immediately, and said that he would join the regiment as soon as the agent thought proper, but that since he had not seen his mother for nearly five years, he would like to spend some time with her. The agent thought this appropriate, and after receiving his actual commission (i.e. the official document), John left. He had asked Mr Drummond who would pay the fees for this document, and was told the agent would do that and deduct it from his salary.

Later that day Moore dined with Mr Drummond and the Duke of Hamilton afterwards telling his father that the Duke's sister, Lady Derby, was doing her best to turn him into a fop; she had bought a large pair of buckles for him and made him order several new suits and rich waistcoats. Whether or not he would wear them when away from London and her insistence, was another matter, said John, as the Duke was not really interested in clothes.

John had now fixed to leave London on 23 September, either in a chaise shared with two of his uncle's friends, or if the second of these could not come, on the fast stagecoach known as 'the fly'. Before he left his uncle gave him 'an excellent sword', and he had acquired a new hat. He made a mild joke about it to his father; it had gold lace, and a badge with 'a fierce regimental cock badge, which would frighten any Frenchman that ever was. This is the first time I ever knew the use of a fierce hat ...'.

Moore spent seven weeks with his family in Glasgow before joining his regiment, which was at that time in Minorca. Possession of this island was strategically important as it was located halfway between Gibraltar and the important French naval base at Toulon, as well as the larger islands of Corsica, Sardinia and Sicily. It had an excellent deep-water harbour at Port Mahon, situated at the end of a long inlet; just in from the sea was the barrack town known as Fort St Philip when the island was under Spanish control, and Georgetown when under British control.[3]

Arriving in Minorca in January 1777, Moore soon settled in and wrote to his mother from the barracks in Georgetown. He felt he had got into 'one of the finest regiments in the service'. He found the other officers pleasant, and there was neither heavy drinking nor gambling going on. He got on well with all of them. The married officers lived in one wing of the barracks, the unmarried in the other. Moore was very pleased with his accommodation:

I have got a room as big as your drawing room, and two closets, one for my servant and the other where I sleep in [*sic*]; they are each as large as the room I slept in at Glasgow ...

I was obliged to stay above a week in an inn at Mahon, which is a mile and a half from this (and where the Governor resides) till I could get bedding etc bought, for you are only allowed the four stone walls, a chimney-shovel and fender. I was obliged to get sheets and blankets, towels, chairs, etc., made, which if I had remembered I could have got most of those things in Britain, both cheaper and better, for they make you pay excessively dear for all these kind of things.

He had dined with Admiral Mann and Captain Affleck of the *Medway*, the ship Graham was assigned to as a midshipman; Graham had not yet arrived from England. He had also visited 'the subterraneans', the system of tunnels dug parallel to a defensive dry moat; the island's commanding officer, General Murray, was preparing for a possible siege and the officers of each regiment were taking it in turns to become familiar with the system.

The attack on Minorca did not happen until 1781, but by that time Moore was long gone. He had been able to transfer into the 82nd Regiment (raised by the Duke of Hamilton) as a captain-lieutenant and paymaster, and this regiment was sent to America. In the middle of July 1779 General Francis Maclean took the 82nd and 74th regiments from their base at Halifax (Nova Scotia) to Penobscot (Maine), some 60 leagues north of Boston, to build a fort. This would protect the settlement which had been created for the loyalists from New York, and also Nova Scotia generally. The Bostonians saw this as a threat, and raised 3,000 men to send to Penobscot with an armed squadron of ships.[4] On hearing of this, Maclean postponed work on the fort and concentrated instead on raising defences to protect his troops against the expected attack.

Moore wrote to his father, remarking that operations had become more interesting since his last letter home:

Upon the 23rd July, a rebel fleet, consisting of about forty ships and vessels, eighteen of which were armed, the rest carrying troops and stores, sailed up the Bay, and immediately began cannonading the *Albany, North* and *Nautilus*, three sloops of war, the only shipping we had to oppose them; they were anchored across the harbour, and supported by a battery from us; though the firing was smart from both sides, yet the [Yankees] kept at such a distance that little or no damage was done. Some of their vessels anchored opposite a wood, at one end of the peninsula, and kept up a constant fire upon the British posted there to oppose their landing. They continued this kind of play for several days, endeavouring at different times to land; but were constantly beaten back, till upon the 28th, when after a sharp cannonade from the shipping upon the wood, to the great surprise of General MacLean and the garrison, they effected a landing. I happened to be upon picket that morning under the command of a captain of the 74th regiment, who, after giving them one fire, instead of encouraging his men (who naturally had been a little startled by the cannonade) to do their duty, ordered them to retreat, leaving me and about twenty men to shift for ourselves. After standing for some time I was obliged to retreat to the fort, having five or six of my own men killed and several wounded; I was lucky to escape untouched. This affair of the Captain is only whispered, so you need not mention it. Having got possession of the wood, the enemy made roads from the shore to the opposite edge, by which they dragged their cannon and erected two batteries within about seven or eight hundred yards from us. Before their arrival, the four curtains and two of the bastions of the fort had been raised about eight feet; the other two bastions were open, but afterwards a fascine work was thrown round the well which was in one of them; the interval of the other was filled up with logs, the storming of which, at first, would have been difficult. By the addition of a cheveaux-de-frise, abatis, etc., this became a serious undertaking, and as they had been falsely informed that we were short of provisions they soon expected hunger would oblige us to lay down our arms.

But [on the 13th] Sir George Collier, with a 64, two frigates, and three 20-gun ships, was seen sailing up the Bay; the rebel fleet never attempted to make a stand, but ran up the river in the utmost confusion; two of their vessels only were taken; the rest the rascals ran ashore and burned, before our shipping could get up with them. Unluckily they had intelligence of our fleet the day before, and in the night their army got on board their shipping and took along with them most of their cannon and stores unknown to us. This is undoubtedly the greatest coup that has been done this year; it will make up for the defeat at Stoney Point.... Our regiment is to return to Halifax in about four or five weeks with General MacLean; Colonel Campbell and his regiment are to be left here.

Moore wrote a further letter to his father from Halifax, saying that he had been 'a good deal startled', confessing (since he was writing to his father) that he had been 'devilishly frightened' at the time. But now he was back in Halifax and enjoying the social life there; they had assemblies once a fortnight, at which he danced the minuet, and they dined with the army families. He was also busy with his work as paymaster, needing to catch up on the work he had been unable to do while he was at Penobscot. Another duty which was occupying much of Moore's time was sitting on courts martial; it seemed the officers of the Provincial Corps were constantly quarelling and misbehaving. Other than that he was getting bored with life in Halifax. They were expecting an attack from the French and had been working on the fortifications but he would have liked to go down to New York where he thought there was a greater chance of seeing action. This boredom had led him to gambling and although he had come out the winner by some £300 (but unlikely to see those winnings for some time, as the officers he had won from were as impoverished as he was) he stopped at that point. He had confessed this to his father, who was extremely displeased, especially since Moore had been offered a promotion to full captain and asked his father to fund the purchase. It would be many years before he was earning enough to be financially independent.

By August the following year Moore was on leave in New York where he hoped to meet the Commander-in-Chief General Sir Henry Clinton and perhaps get a post on the Head Quarters staff. This proved less easy than he hoped, for Clinton was spending most of his time meeting with Admiral Graves. Instead, he met a far more welcome visitor in his brother, James, who had joined the army as a surgeon's mate. James had news from home: Frank had wanted to be a soldier like his older brother but their father thought he would be better suited as a merchant (he actually became a civil servant), Charles was at Winchester (Dr Moore hoped he might join the Church and end up as a bishop but instead he became a barrister). Graham had changed ships to escape from a bullying captain. John and James went shopping to replace worn clothing; after a few days they rented a little farmhouse and they spent the rest of the year together. James did some part-time work at the General Hospital in New York, while John went for long walks and read. The British had suffered a number of defeats, culminating in their surrender at Yorktown and it was becoming clear that the war was almost over. A fleet for home was assembling and the two brothers managed to get passage in a transport full of sick soldiers, leaving America early in the new year. They landed at Falmouth and took a post-chaise for London, where the family were now living. Although he continued to practise medicine, Dr Moore was now making much of his living from his writing. His *View of Society and Manners in France, Switzerland and Germany, by a Gentleman, who Resided Several Years in those Countries*, published in 1779, had been a great success and he was working on another which would be published under his own name, *A View of Society and Manners in Italy with Anecdotes Relating to some Eminent Characters*. He also published three successful novels: *Zeluco, Mordaunt,* much of which was based on John's military feats, and *Edward.*

At the end of the American War of Independence, the 82nd Regiment was disbanded but Moore remained on the list as a captain, receiving half-pay. That autumn he went to stay with the Duke of Hamilton in Scotland. There the Duke suggested he should stand for Parliament, as a useful step on the route to high command. The seat for the Linlithgow boroughs was at the Duke's disposal, as the majority of voters would automatically vote for the Duke's chosen candidate. In due course, Moore was elected and took his seat in March 1784. He did not make a great impression as a politician (nor did he care for the political life) but he did vote consistently for measures proposed by Pitt. He did not stand for re-election in 1790; in the meantime he had been working to resume his army career. In November 1785 he was returned to the active list in the 100th Foot, and on the same day he purchased a majority in the 102nd. This regiment was soon disbanded, but he was left as an unattached major on full pay. In January 1788 he was able to join the 60th Royal American Foot as a major, and given the task of training two new battalions at their depot at Chatham. They used a less rigid form of drill than other line regiments, and it has been suggested that this may have been the basis for the light infantry training system he was to develop later while at Shorncliffe.

Moore's next move was back into his first regiment, the 51st, then stationed at Fort Charles, Kinsale, some 24 miles from Cork. His movements and activities over the next two years are unclear.[5] Brother James says he joined the 60th Regiment in 1787 and moved to the 51st 'next year'. After joining the regiment in Ireland, Moore soon gained a poor opinion of its commanding officer, Lieutenant Colonel Jaques, and some other officers; this left him with two career options: move to yet another regiment or persuade Jaques to retire by purchasing the lieutenant colonelcy from him. This took some time, but Jaques eventually agreed when the regiment was listed to go to the Caribbean to fight the Spanish. Jaques did not want to leave his family and go abroad; Moore described his panicky behaviour as 'stark staring mad'.

The potential move was due to what became known as the Nootka Sound Affair. Nootka was a small town and harbour on the west coast of Vancouver Island, settled by British China merchants in the 1770s. The Spanish, in an attempt to assert exclusive trading rights on the Pacific coast of the Americas, had seized some British merchant ships and taken over the harbour. The British government had not been aware of this until the Spanish ambassador informed them, and asked that the British owners of the seized ships should be severely punished to deter others. Pitt responded robustly and for a while it seemed likely that Britain would find herself at war with Spain (and her ally, France) over this situation, starting with retaliatory attacks on the Spanish possessions of Cuba and Caracas.

In this situation, Moore did not find it difficult to persuade Jaques to sell out in his favour. Moore already had an officer ready to buy his majority in the 51st; all that was needed was to obtain the necessary approvals and get his father to lodge the £1,000 he needed for the purchase with his bank. He went to Dublin to see the Lord Lieutenant, Lord Westmoreland, and then to London to acquire additional recommendations (appointments at this level required the King's approval). The Duke of Hamilton and Lord Eglinton readily gave these and he was able to return to Ireland to finalise matters with Jaques.

After a rough 48-hour crossing which made him extremely seasick, Moore arrived in Cork on 23 October. A few weeks later, Jaques, who had been with his family at the

Lake of Killarney, returned. The Nootka Sound Affair had been resolved when the Spanish backed down, and Jaques had changed his mind; with the threat of service abroad removed, he thought he would stay as he was. On reporting this to his father, Moore said, 'I told him my mind so plainly on his conduct ...', a reaction which Moore was to repeat several times during his career. Under threat of the matter being taken to higher authority, Jaques backed down and agreed to retire, saying he would give Moore his resignation as soon as the money was settled.

By the middle of December Moore had his promotion and Jaques had gone. 'He has left me enough to do, but I have the winter before me, during which it is impossible to have any communication with the rest of the World [sic], from the badness of the weather. I shall have nothing to divert my attention from my business.' Part of his business which required immediate attention was the problem of drunkenness in the ranks and the bad behaviour which ensued. Moore would not tolerate this, and severe punishments followed. Then one of the lieutenants got drunk, 'went rioting about the town and was absent from his Guard [sic] all night'. There was, thought Moore, some excuse for a man from the ranks, but not an officer, especially when they had been involved in the disciplinary process. He sent a message to the man by the adjutant that if he did not immediately offer his lieutenancy to the next ensign in line for a promotion, he would be arrested and reported to the Commander-in-Chief. The lieutenant departed; soon after, so did other officers. Moore had commented that the officers were 'very ignorant. My predecessor was so himself and of course could not instruct them', accustomed to doing 'literally nothing', on finding that they were expected to work these officers chose to leave. Among the better ones was Paul Anderson, who became a life-long friend.

Soon the only officer who needed to be replaced was the surgeon. He was also the paymaster, and Moore found him 'completely ignorant, devoid of humanity and a rogue'. By the end of March, Moore had 'shut up the channels he had of cheating, and have put the hospital upon a tolerable footing, as far as diet and cleanliness, but against his ignorance I have no remedy ...'. It took until July to get rid of the man and install a new surgeon and a new paymaster.

Moore had devised a system of training, numerous men had been drafted into the regiments going abroad and Moore worked first with the new recruits who had been sent to replace them, believing that 'by the time they are perfect the sergeants will be au fait and then the older men will want to do it too'. Many of the men as well as Moore himself suffered aching joints in the cold wet weather, an affliction which responded well to advice from Dr Moore, and by the end of winter the regiment was pretty healthy. Moore and the men were bathing in the sea early each morning and after the regiment moved to Cork there was plenty of socialising to be done. There were balls and concerts, libraries, card parties for the officers and plenty of little taverns serving good cheap porter for the men. Despite his mother's hopes, Moore was showing no sign of seeking a wife, although he was clearly a favourite among the ladies, one of whom gave him 'a very fine large setting spaniel' called Rake. Moore had wanted to change the dog's name to Soldier, but 'the lady preferred the former and was obstinate', so Rake it remained.

The situation in France was deteriorating. The King and his entourage had attempted an escape, thinking that they could do this inconspicuously with their children, the King's sister and a large entourage of servants, all in two large coaches escorted by dragoons; they were captured within 24 hours and hauled back to Paris to await their captors' decision on their fate. Although Britain going to war against France was as yet not imminent, it was becoming more and more likely to the informed observer. Not only had the new regime taken over France, their revolutionary zeal was driving them to expand into other European countries, starting with the Low Countries.

Early in 1792 Moore's regiment was ordered to Gibraltar. The men had been sickly over the winter, many of them having to be hospitalised, but were now fit enough to embark on the transports (when these finally arrived) and their colonel was convinced the sea journey and Gibraltar itself would help them recover. A last letter to his father written on the *Brunswick* transport reported that the regiment had embarked in great spirits. They had been allowed a last evening's enjoyment with their friends ashore, but were told by Moore that by 9 he 'expected every man to be in his quarters; and that at 7 next morning they should come sober to the parade ready to march'. With only a few exceptions the men complied and were 'perfectly sober' next morning. They marched down to the beach in rain and consequent muddy roads, but by the time they got to the beach it cleared up for a fine afternoon, the sun shining and the sea smooth. Moore ordered his regiment's boats not to put off until everyone was on board so they could all go together. When ready, on a signal they gave three cheers, 'which was answered by the regiments upon the shore, the band playing, colours flying, and the whole forming a lively, animating scene – in ten minutes we were rowed on board our different ships, which are the best transports I ever saw'.

After a calm eleven-day passage the transports anchored off Gibraltar on 19 March, but Moore's regiment had to wait six days before landing. Writing to his father while he waited for the start of a court martial on a regimental surgeon, he said:

everything here is so completely opposite to everything in Britain or Ireland, that we are much at a loss, and must continue so for some time, in spite of every exertion on my part. I have been up at daylight ever since we anchored, and seldom off my legs till bedtime. The weather is that of a hot July in England. Oranges, green peas, &c., are in perfection; but notwithstanding the descriptions I had of the Rock, it surprised me more than any place I ever saw.

Life in Gibraltar was quiet, and after several boring months, Moore ventured on a month-long tour of the closer parts of Spain, visiting Cadiz, Jerez and Seville. In a letter to his mother he said:

The travelling in Spain is worse than you can conceive, it even requires some degree of hardiness to undergo it. I was however fully compensated for my trouble, not for the churches, pictures, etc., for there are, I believe, few of these in Spain worth looking at, but the dress, manners, & customs of the inhabitants are very different from any I had ever seen. They are by no means the proud, distant people they are represented to be, but just the reverse. I amused myself well amongst them. This little excursion was necessary and I am returned to my duty here with fresh ardor [*sic*].

Writing on 8 February 1793, Moore had heard of the execution of the French King on 21 January but had not received the news of the French declaration of war with Britain on 2 February. He thought that the probability of his being employed was small; he actually thought that he would not be. Back in London, his father was lobbying for the 51st to be used, but this was a slow process.

In southern France, events moved on.

Toulon, situated on the southern coast of France just to the east of Marseilles, was one of the country's two big naval arsenals (the other being Brest on the Atlantic coast). There were, at this time, two centres of royalist rebellion against the revolutionary regime: one in the Vendée and the other covering Marseilles and Toulon in the Mediterranean. The British were assisting these rebels, and at Toulon the inhabitants had invited Admiral Samuel Hood to occupy the town and arsenal in trust for Louis XVII until the end of the war; in return they wanted British troops to be landed to protect them. Hood wrote to General David Dundas, asking for 5–6,000 men, moved his ships into the inner harbour and landed some 1,500 marines. The Spanish (allies at that time) arrived with some troops and promised more. Hood appointed the Spanish Admiral Gravina to be commandant of the town. At the beginning of February, Hood sent some of his ships to blockade Corsica and if possible to reduce the forts at Bastia, Calvi and St Fiorenzo. He gave no instructions on how this was to be done. Lord Mulgrave arrived from Turin and took command of the British troops, soon realising that the Spanish troops were 'utterly worthless, both officers and men, being the dregs of the Spanish army with some convicts collected from the Barbary coast'. Lord Mulgrave returned to England and his report on the situation so frightened William Pitt and Henry Dundas (the Secretary of State for War) that they issued an order to Hood that if it was not possible to hold the town, he was to destroy the French fleet and arsenal. The main difficulty came from the heights of Mount Faron behind the town, where the French had artillery batteries (commanded by the young Corsican Lieutenant Colonel Napoleon Buonaparte). Although the British troops made some successful attacks on these batteries, they were unable to dislodge them completely.

On 27 October General O'Hara with General David Dundas as his second-in-command, arrived from Gibraltar with 750 men. There were, as well as the Spanish troops, some from Naples; both showed returns of 6,000 men but produced no verified muster lists. Sir Gilbert Elliot had also arrived to take over as commissioner for the government of Toulon. All that could be considered trustworthy was a total of 3,500 British and Sardinian men, this for a task which required 25,000. Over the next two months, with French reinforcements arriving, it became obvious that the town could not be held. Plans were made for an orderly retreat, but the Neapolitans left the town overnight as did many of the Spanish. Hood finally gave up and moved his ships out of the harbour, leaving the Spanish (with the help of Sir Sidney Smith) to destroy the French ships building on the stocks and in the harbour.

Royalist counter revolutions in south-western France and then Toulon led to Admiral Hood occupying the town with an Anglo-Spanish force in July. He began to ask for army reinforcements to help hold the town. General O'Hara in Gibraltar tried to persuade the governor to send a detachment of troops, but the governor didn't wish to do this without orders from home. In September, Admiral Hood sent two ships of the line to Gibraltar asking for troops to prevent the loss of Toulon, which was under seige from French artillery positioned behind the town on the heights. Finally orders were received for two regiments (not including the 51st) and an artillery company to go on those ships; they should have left on 2 October, but contrary winds kept them at Gibraltar. Another ship arrived in Gibraltar from Hood, a frigate this time, asking for guns, shells, mortars and other ammunition, and also for General O'Hara. The governor would not name him as being in command of the embarked troops, but allowed him to go as a volunteer. It was assumed by all that he would be given the army command on arrival, and this was what happened.

Now, seeing himself as trapped at Gibraltar, without an opportunity to distinguish himself, Moore hoped that Sir Charles Grey who was preparing to go to the West Indies, would instead bring his troops to Gibraltar en route to Toulon and take Moore and the 51st with him. At the end of October Moore had a conversation with the governor who had just received dispatches from home; he seemed

> much perplexed and indeed said as much as that his instructions were indistinct – but as the conversation began by his asking me if the Regiment is prepared for going to the West Indies I take for granted that we are particularly mentioned – tho' he would not own it, but only repeated that he thought we might very possibly be sent to the West Indies – a short time will clear everything up, in the meantime I cannot help being anxious. Tho' I am persuaded we shall go either with Sir Charles Grey, or to Toulon – I shall be happy with either.... I shall write to you the moment I receive my orders, I expect them daily – the Regiment is ready – it is vastly improved since it landed here – the men both stouter and healthier.

Finally the longed for orders came through, and early in December two regiments (the 50th and 51st) embarked on four line-of-battle ships for Toulon. At last Moore was going to see some action, and on the 15th he began to keep a war journal which he continued until a few days before his death. It is these journals, as well as his official dispatches and letters to his family and friends, which give insight into his thought processes and reactions to events, and thus to the development of his character.[6]

Chapter 2

Corsica: St Fiorenzo and Bastia

Corsica, at the end of the eighteenth century, was a country of social, political and economic troubles. It had been ruled by Genoa until 1768 when it was ceded to France in the Treaty of Versailles; France had garrisons in three of the northern cities: St Fiorenzo (modern St Florent), Bastia and Calvi. St Fiorenzo lay at the southwest end of the peninsula known as Cap Corse. In order to make its bay safe to anchor in, and to capture the town, it was necessary to take two strongpoints which commanded it on the western side of the bay, both possessed of the strong defensive towers which became known as Martello Towers. One of these was at Martello Point, the other at Fornoli, which was further defended by the powerful twenty-one-gun entrenchment known to the French as the 'Convention Redoubt'.

Bastia was the largest city and held the administration centre of first Genoa and then France, but its harbour was very small, suitable only for galleys and the smallest ships. Its military citadel was in the middle of the walled town, armed with some thirty cannon and eight mortars; there were four stone-built redoubts above the town on the nearest hills, and three other posts above those.

Much of the country was rocky or mountainous, covered with dense thicket-forming shrubs known as maquis. Its major industry was coral fishing and its agriculture, such as it was, tended to be on the foothills of the mountains where a small amount of grain could be grown along with olives, citrus fruit, mulberries and grapes. Less fertile areas produced large quantities of chestnuts. There were small mules, goats, sheep and a few cattle. These animals were moved up towards the mountains in the summer, and down again for the winter; this transhumance caused a lot of ill-feeling between the peasants and the shepherds, who considered they were entitled to graze their animals anywhere, including over the peasants' crops. The peasant classes hated the monied classes, and there was much clan rivalry among the peasants. These factors, together with a distrust of the laws, led to vendetta and banditry, exacerbated by the Corsican peasants' hatred of working for someone else. Much of the seasonal agricultural work was done by Italian labourers imported for the season.

The Corsican leader was the Neapolitan Pasquale Paoli, elected in 1755 when he was 30. He was politically astute and the Corsicans soon came to love him. He drafted Corsica's liberal constitution which created an Executive Council with himself as President, which effectively made him king. This did not please the French, and after a few years Paoli went into exile, leaving the country in a British warship. He remained in England for twenty-two years, living on a royal pension. He returned to Corsica in 1790, resumed the presidency and asked Britain to assume the protection of the island.[1]

Moore and his regiment, together with the 50th, started to embark to leave Gibraltar on Sunday, 5 December. After a delay over getting boats to take them aboard the four ships of the line which were to carry them to Toulon, the men and their baggage and camp equipment were ready to leave by the Monday evening. Although the wind blew fair, they did not leave until the Thursday morning. Their camp equipment was in a captured French sloop called *La Moselle*. Intelligence had reached Gibraltar that the French had obtained a position on the south-facing slope of Mount Faron from which they could send shot into Toulon. They had been dislodged, but in the process General O'Hara had marched on into the countryside where he was seriously injured and had been captured. This hastened the departure of the little squadron from Gibraltar, and a fresh wind helped their progress, but the sloop with the baggage and equipment could not carry much sail in a stiff wind, and she held them back. On the 21st it rained and unable to take exercise on deck, Moore grew bored, writing:

> There is not a book belonging to the ship except a few medical ones of the surgeon's; our baggage is so circumscribed that we could of course bring but few, and those cannot be got at until tomorrow. The captain is so frequently called upon deck that with the assistance of a few newspapers he fills up his time. In the ward-room I believe frequent recourse is had to cards and backgammon. To such as are not fond of such amusements and have no duty to attend to, a rainy day is particularly tiresome.

After what had been a good two-day start to their passage, the weather turned 'uncommonly bad and the wind contrary' and they did not see land until the 28th. They hove to and in the late morning, a strange sail appeared and signalled that it wished to speak to *Fortitude*, one of the 74s carrying Moore's men; she sent a boat on board the stranger, which turned out to be Spanish, with news from Toulon. The town had been evacuated on the 19th and Hood was in Hyeres Bay with the army on board and had taken three of the largest French ships with him. British and Spanish frigates were cruising off Toulon to prevent French ships entering the harbour, but they were not in time to prevent *La Moselle* from going in; she was captured and the 51st Regiment was now without its baggage and camp equipment. *Fortitude* stood off in the evening. Moore commented that he:

> could not conceive why we did not immediately make for Hieres Bay the moment we were told Lord Hood was there. It was now plain we were not going to attempt it that night; we continued standing off until eight this morning, which was much longer than was necessary, if the intention is to get into Hieres today. We are not, however, so far from the land but by setting sail we might not be in in five hours, as the wind is perfectly fair. This, however, we are not doing. Captain D. seems undetermined; from his conversation and manner he seems to have no wish to go in, and I can see no military reason for his staying out; on the contrary, I should think it was his duty to make every exertion to join Lord Hood as soon as possible, both the ships and the troops may be wanted, at any rate, there can be no use in our keeping the sea. Independent of these reasons

I am naturally anxious to get in, it is impossible not to wish to know the nature and immediate cause of the evacuation of Toulon, the loss sustained, &c., and also the destination of the regiments, whether they are to return to Gibraltar or be employed in some expedition in this neighbourhood.

Hood anchored in Hyeres Bay on 20 December and stayed there for five weeks waiting for victualling ships; Dundas waited for reinforcements of men and materiel. During this time Hood decided to go to Corsica. He had already sent five sloops under Commodore Linzee to assist Paoli's national party to evict the French from the three garrisons they held at Bastia, Calvi and St Fiorenzo but the Corsicans who were 'assisting' failed at the crucial moment and Linzee had to withdraw with two of his ships badly damaged. This seriously annoyed Hood, who was already suspicious of Paoli, but when Paoli offered to put the whole island under British protection, despite having no instructions from home to this effect, Hood accepted.

Captain Dixon still delayed joining Hood for several days, to Moore's continued puzzlement; they finally anchored near Hood, and Moore and Dixon went on board *Victory*. Hood, an overbearing and difficult man at the best of times, displayed his usual contemptuous attitude towards military officers, telling Moore that he had brought fewer troops than expected and that he was late, then turning away from him to talk to a naval officer.

They remained in Hyeres Bay until 12 January, when Hood decided, without having the courtesy to consult General Dundas, to send Sir Gilbert Elliot to negotiate terms with the Corsicans, and Moore and Major Koehler (Quartermaster General) to reconnoitre the terrain and report back to him on the practicality of an attack with their small force. They arrived near the island of Rossa (now Isle de Rousse), where the people were pleased to see them and gave three cheers. They were met by Signor Leonati, Paoli's nephew; he was particularly pleased to see Koehler whom he had worked with during the siege of Gibraltar (1779–83). He escorted them to a house that Moore thought might be an inn, which was immediately filled with the local men carrying their muskets slung over their shoulders. They were given figs and oranges while they waited for the mules to carry their baggage, then went about 2 miles inland to Leonati's house. There they were greeted by musket fire from the windows and their escort also fired theirs, in the local fashion. While dinner was being prepared they went for a walk, attended again by their guard. Moore said that the countryside was 'mountainous and wild, the valleys fertile, whilst the tops of the hills are covered with snow. The only tree is the olive; oil is the staple of this part of the island.'

Leonati said that there were only some 2,600 French in the whole island: 799 at St Fiorenzo, 1,400 at Bastia and a post between it and St Fiorenzo and 500 at Calvi; there were actually more like 3,500. All that was wanted, he said, was a few cannon to drive them out.

They moved on the next morning to meet Paoli, stopping overnight at the village of Pietra Alba, at the house of one of the principal inhabitants, where the whole village poured in and 'remained in the room until we had supped and retired to bed. This was the case wherever we stopped and it seemed to be the custom of the country to enter familiarly into one another's houses without invitation.' Koehler had remained behind to study the terrain; this was perhaps fortunate because there was only one bed, which Moore and Elliot had to share. Koehler caught up with them in the morning as they moved on, arriving at Murato at 1 o'clock, where they found Paoli lodged in an abandoned convent. It was surrounded with armed peasants, who, Moore was told, came voluntarily from all over the island, carrying their provisions and the ubiquitous muskets, to guard Paoli. When their food ran out, they returned home and others took their place, all without pay.

Paoli received them in one of the cells of the convent. Although Elliot gave him a letter from Hood explaining the nature of their mission, he addressed himself to Koehler and Moore, starting a discussion on the style of attack they should adopt. Moore had to stop him and explain that although he and Koehler were indeed to be involved in the military matters, they reported in this instance to Elliot, as he was one of the King's commissioners in the Mediterranean, and that until he (Paoli) had talked with Elliot, they could not enter into a discussion of military matters. Paoli said that he was tired of ministers and negotiations; after asking some other people to leave the room, he looked at Hood's letter and remarked that it was still inexplicit, rather than candid and open. He clearly did not like Hood, referring to him as 'that man' who 'has already injured me with promises of succour which he has always withheld'. All he wanted, he said, was to see his country settled and happy.

Sir Gilbert did not interrupt him, although he used several impolite words referring to Hood; when Paoli had finished, Elliot calmly told him that Hood was not trying to take advantage, but wanted to judge the mood of the island by obtaining the assent of the people, perhaps by assembling the representatives of the states. Paoli said this would be impossible until the French had been expelled. After some more conversation they went to dinner in the refectory, where Moore had a chance to observe the old general more closely. He was showing his age since Moore had seen him in London; had recently 'suffered an attack upon his chest' and was clearly much upset by the recent death of his only brother.

The next morning, Elliot stayed to talk with Paoli while Moore and Koehler went with one of Paoli's young supporters, Pozzo di Borgo, to reconnoitre the neighbourhood of St Fiorenzo. There was a little skirmish between the French defenders and Moore's escort; only one of these was wounded and Moore was pleased with the way they had conducted themselves in occupying the different heights. While this was in progress, Koehler made a number of sketches of the different positions. Returning to the convent two days later, Moore was glad to hear that Elliot and Paoli had reached an understanding. Elliot told Moore that he was struck by Paoli's intelligence on political matters, and Moore, who had previously only ever encountered Paoli in society circles, was equally impressed with his obvious abilities as a military officer.

When they set out to return to their ship on the 20th, they left Koehler behind, as Paoli thought it might discourage his people if they all left together. At Monticello, the town just inland of the island of Rossa, Elliot went off to Elba to prepare arrangements for the refugees from Toulon; Hood was there also, having been blown off course, so Moore settled to wait for him and prepare his report on the specifics which General Dundas had requested. The first objective, he thought, must be to take possession of Martello Bay, for the security of the fleet, by taking the two stone towers which commanded the bay, and the fort of Fornoli immediately under one of the towers. The towers had two or three light guns and the fort had four, of different calibres. These were principally designed to act against shipping and were guarded by some 150 or 200 men from the garrison at St Fiorenzo. There was also the formidable Convention Redoubt, on a separate hill, some 250ft high behind the second tower.

There were heights above and behind the towers; if these could be taken and provided with guns the fort would have to be abandoned. The road up to the heights had always been thought impassable for guns, but Moore thought it possible to get light guns or howitzers up there. He attached a detailed plan, worked out with Paoli, for landing a force of 500 men at the north of the bay and marching under cover of the hills to a place called Bocca Fattojagi. The army, as soon as they had landed, would have to move into the country with a few light guns and join Paoli in driving the small force of French out of the villages of Patrimonia and Barbagio. This would not only provide a lodging for the troops, but prevent the French from moving between St Fiorenzo and Bastia, and secure the route from the landing place for transporting provisions and ordnance.

He had only been able to reconnoitre Bastia from the top of a mountain some 3 or 4 miles from the town. The inhabitants favoured Paoli, and, with others, provided information that Bastia would be easy enough to take. There was a good carriage road between it and St Fiorenzo, thus giving easy access to the fleet and ordnance stores. To the best of his information, there were just under 2,000 enemy troops (including Corsicans): 390 at St Fiorenzo, 810 at Bastia, 250 on the communication between St Fiorenzo and Bastia, and 500 at Calvi, plus the crews of two frigates at St Fiorenzo and two at Bastia. Given the current state of the French garrisons, and the promised assistance of the Corsicans, there was every chance of success, provided there was no delay, which would allow the French to frighten the inhabitants. A detailed plan of attack, and drawings of the fortifications at Martello Bay were enclosed; these had been made by Koehler, who remained with Paoli.

After several days spent on Elba, where the Toulon evacuees were landed, the fleet prepared for the landing on Corsica. One important but time-consuming task was to sort out the ordnance that had been embarked at Toulon; in the confusion there, guns and carriages had been loaded on separate ships, as had the ammunition. They also had to make carriages for the light guns. Commodore Linzee was appointed to command the landing on Corsica, with Moore in command of the Royals and the 50th and 51st regiments, which were to land first. They arrived in the morning of 7 February; Linzee was undecided whether to land straight away, but Moore persuaded him that they should, so they could get organised and start the attack the next morning. With 550 soldiers, 120 seamen under the command of Captain Cooke, one 6-pounder gun and a 5½in howitzer, Moore landed with three days provisions and their blankets.

Having lain on their arms all night, they marched to the Bocca Fattojagi at daylight, with orders to fire on the enemy from the heights, but the road soon became so difficult that the guns could not keep up with the troops; they might not be able to get them up at all. Moore halted his troops at the top of the hill, and after a while received a message from Captain Nepean of the Engineers asking for thirty soldiers to go back to assist with the guns. These were sent from the Royals, and the rest of that regiment waited while Moore pushed forward with the 51st to the place where they intended to put the guns, to reconnoitre the enemy posts.

Reaching a small plain at the foot of the hills, the regiment piled its arms and rested while Moore, Captain Pringle and Captain Nepean climbed the hill to view the enemy's fortifications at Martello and Fornoli. Since Moore had viewed them previously with Koehler, the enemy had been busy, strengthening the works and erecting some new ones; they had also added a mortar and several new guns. The attack would no longer be a 2-day affair with 500 men and 2 light guns. Moore sent for Koehler to come up, and ordered the troops to rest on their arms that night. At first light, Moore, Koehler and Nepean went up to view the enemy works, the two latter agreeing with Moore that they had insufficient troops to succeed against the French armament. Moore wrote to report this to General Dundas, saying that the whole of the army force would be needed to take Martello, but having done so, the attack on St Fiorenzo would probably be easy; he asked Dundas to come up and view the situation for himself. He had taken steps to obtain fresh provisions for his troops, and with the help of the Corsicans, felt that they were secure enough where they were.

The previous day, *Fortitude* (with seventy-four guns) and *Juno* (a thirty-two-gun frigate) had been attacking the tower, but had been unable to breach the 18ft-thick walls. In the course of this attack, *Fortitude* had lost more than sixty men killed and wounded, and had been set on fire by a red-hot shot. The ships had withdrawn, then more guns were landed and kept up a constant fire. The officer, a Garde Marine, in command of the tower had not been able to fire a single gun against this land battery, and finally surrendered.

General Dundas came up to the camp and viewed the enemy positions, staying there overnight. Moore thought he was uncertain what to do, and he and Koehler pointed out several places where batteries might be erected closer to the tower, thus saving much land carriage of ammunition. Dundas was convinced that the light guns would not do the job wherever placed, but seemed frightened of the difficulties of getting larger guns up over the rugged terrain. He left orders for Moore to stay with the 51st in its current position, but to send the Royals and the 69th, which had just joined, back to the shore as they had no tents and would suffer in bad weather. As it happened, the weather was fine and they were able to sleep in their blankets or cloaks round a large fire with no ill effect.

The general returned to the shore; Koehler went with him and discovered a good spot for a battery within 700yd which allowed them to fire down on the redoubt. With the help of some sailors and blocks and tackles, two 18-pounders and an 8in howitzer were hauled up a steep rock. At another, easier, place a 10in mortar and two other guns were mounted. Moore's troops moved into these batteries and the Corsicans were tasked with occupying the heights; they repulsed an attempt by the French to dismount those guns. General Dundas wished to storm the French redoubt as soon as it had been sufficiently battered. A couple of days later, Moore received a message from the general that he intended to attack the enemy's defences at 9 that night. Moore had been exercising his troops in the woods, but returned to camp immediately, arranged for the men to move down to where the Royals were camped at 4 in the afternoon and he went down to headquarters where Dundas explained his plan of attack: the Royals and 51st were to attack from the front, the 50th and 25th on one flank, using bayonets rather than guns, while the Corsicans were to remain on the other side to cut off the enemy's retreat.

At 8.30 the troops silently left their batteries in bright moonlight. Moore went forward a few paces to view the ground ahead, was spotted by an advance picquet and a few shots were fired at him. Returning immediately to the column, he gave the order to advance, and they went quickly down the hill to the foot of the next hill where Convention Redoubt was situated. Seeing that they were covered from the enemy's fire, they halted to gain breath and get the divisions in order, then advanced briskly up the hill and jumped into the head of the work, Moore leading. This was typical of Moore throughout his active service; he believed that 'Come on' was always better than 'Go on'. He ran straight to a traverse where he knew there was a gun, reaching it just as it was being elevated to fire on their battery. Making short work of this gun, they rushed on to the next traverse, intending to go through a passage on the left into the battery. The French fired on them and charged with bayonets; Moore's men also fired, but the French were so determined that Moore's men stepped back. While he was encouraging his men to try again, Moore heard a shout from the rear that there was another passage there, on the right, and he immediately made for that and got in. Many of the French stood their ground and fought until they were bayonetted, others threw down their arms and were given quarter. Then the 50th and 25th regiments arrived, having been delayed by the difficult ground they had had to cover; some sailors and Corsicans also came in and for a while there was much confusion. Being within grapeshot range of the other tower and redoubt at Fornoli they needed to cover themselves; fortunately at that moment Koehler arrived and gave orders to create some defensive works. They found entrenching tools and sandbags in the redoubt and quickly provided cover from the fire from Fornoli, but just after midnight they learned that the works at Fornoli had been abandoned. Their losses in killed and wounded was less than 40 men, the French more than 100. Most of the British soldiers gave quarter as soon as asked, but the Corsicans had failed to stop the escaping enemy, busily killing and plundering the wounded and dead. During the course of this engagement, Moore had a near escape when his sword bent on his first thrust at an enemy soldier; fortunately he was able to make a rapid second thrust which went right through the man's body. Dundas came to the redoubt the following morning and Moore accompanied him to Fornoli, where he thanked Moore in 'very handsome terms' and later in the day gave out an extremely flattering order to the troops employed in the assault.

The next day, the Deputy Adjutant General, Captain Hislop, was sent to summon St Fiorenzo while Moore and Koehler went to reconnoitre the enemy's position at

St Bernard and the ground near the gorge through which the road from St Fiorenzo to Bastia passed, with a view to Moore taking 500 men and the light gun and howitzer to cover the disembarkation of extra troops to attack St Fiorenzo. On their way, Moore and Koehler met General Paoli. Before supper was served there was confirmation of a rumour that the French had left St Fiorenzo and retired to Bastia, leaving the British in possession of the town. The next morning, they set out with Paoli for St Fiorenzo, where Dundas desired Moore to bring up the regiments under Moore's command. This was done the following day, and those regiments camped alongside the gorge. The rest of the troops were quartered in the town, where numerous guns, mortars and their ammunition were found, with more at the tower of Martello. Some of the French remained on the heights of Titime (now Col de Teghimé) for a couple of days, and succeeded in blowing up part of the road before the Corsicans saw them off.

The following day, Moore and Dundas went to reconnoitre Bastia. They saw that the town, which was open and close to the sea, was defended by four detached redoubts and a citadel on some heights a short distance from the town. The ground where they were standing commanded the redoubts, allowing batteries to stand about 400 or 500yd from them. Some of the redoubts lacked flanks and were generally badly built, but they were all built of stone with thick parapets. The main difficulty was going to be getting the heavy guns up to the batteries, and keeping open the road from St Fiorenzo where all supplies would come from; this was some 9 miles as the crow flies, but more than 20 on the winding mountain roads to Bastia. Bastia, now reinforced by the troops from St Fiorenzo, had some 1,300 defenders, plus another 1,000 Corsicans, a force larger than the British had available. Dundas was fully aware of all these difficulties, but by the time he had decided his next move, the French had sallied out of Bastia, attacked and burned the village of Carda and established themselves on the heights which Moore had hoped to use to batter the redoubts.

It was very cold and foggy on the heights, making for an uncomfortable night, but the position was strong and Moore made sure his troops were alert so the French could not creep up on them. Captain Alcock, who had the advanced picquet, reported that he could hear the French busy all night, entrenching on ground which the British needed to take Bastia. In the morning, orders came from Dundas to retire downhill, taking care the French did not see them. Tents were quickly struck and the troops moved back; Moore stayed with four companies to call in the picquets and cover the retreat. They camped by the gorge where the French had been, calling the place St Bernadino as the French had done. Dundas told Moore that although he intended to attack Bastia, he had realised that it would take some time to make the necessary preparations. He also said that Hood was pressing him to take Bastia as though it was going to be easy. Later Moore learned that it was more a matter of Dundas giving up the attack as being impractical with the small force at his command. Hood's experience was all of sea actions, which were much faster than those on land, but he did not realise that land actions took time to set up, especially in finding the right place to commence the attack. On a ship, one just sailed up to the enemy ships, or into a position where their fire could reach the enemy on land, and proceeded to fire; it was very rare for a naval action to last more than one day. Hood was also misinformed about the numbers of enemy at Bastia; Captain Horatio Nelson of the *Agamemnon* had written to him to report that the garrison at Bastia was only 800 strong when it was actually closer to 6,000.[2]

A few days later Moore and Lieutenant Colonel Villettes of the 69th had a visit from three naval officers, Captain Englefield (whom Moore described as the adjutant general of the fleet, but in naval terms was known as 'captain of the fleet') and two others. Englefield said he came with Admiral Hood's order to see the commanding officers of the corps, to ask for their opinion on the practicality of attacking Bastia. Dundas had said it was impractical but Hood thought differently and was willing to take full responsibility; he wanted to know what the officers at the head of corps thought. The visitors then got up and said they would leave Moore and Villettes to consider the matter. Moore replied that they did not have to wait, he was ready to give them his answer immediately, which was that he did not feel he could, with any propriety, give Hood an opinion on such a matter. If General Dundas, as Commander-in-Chief, chose to attack Bastia, he would go there with his regiment and do his duty, but if Dundas thought it was impractical and did not choose to do so, then he thought, 'it did not become me to give any opinion upon it.... it seemed to me to be a species of mutiny for a subordinate officer to pass any opinion'.

Moore dined with General Dundas that day, but did not mention what had happened.

Villettes called on Moore later that evening, and the two officers agreed the general should be told, and they did this the next morning. Dundas was surprised, but said it was typical of Hood's conduct. He then read out his correspondence with Hood on the matter. In comparison with Dundas' reasoned and sensible letters, Hood's, said Moore, were 'not remarkable for those qualities'. Dundas remarked that Hood 'was a man who never reasoned himself, nor would he listen to reason from others. He [Dundas] had always found him dogmatical and obstinate.' After some more conversation, Dundas stated that he was going to return to England.

The following day, Dundas showed Moore a letter he had just received from Hood, saying that he believed that Dundas's command had ceased with the evacuation of Toulon, after that the supreme command of the fleet and the army was his, and it had only been through courtesy that he had allowed Dundas to interfere. Dundas had replied, thanking Hood ironically for his courtesy, and asking to see Hood's commission from the King appointing him supreme commander. The following day Dundas read the letters to the commanders of all the separate corps, then told them that it was ill-health that had caused him to write home from Toulon asking for a replacement to command the land forces. Everyone agreed that Hood's pretension to command the land forces was absurd and that they should resist his attempts to take the command. Nobody seems to have mentioned this, but a significant part of Hood's desire to be supreme commander over all the forces was probably that such a command would give him a lot more prize money than he would receive as Commander-in-Chief of the fleet alone.

Colonel D'Aubant of the Engineers was given the command and made Brigadier General, until 'His Majesty's pleasure should be known', that command stated to be in the same manner as that of General Dundas. On 11 March Dundas left on a frigate, but before he left he told Moore that he had not realised D'Aubant had remained and he had intended to give the command to Moore. He asked if there was anything he could do for Moore, but he replied that all he wanted was to be employed, and feared that he would now be 'tied to so insignificant service as this was likely to become'. He said he was not concerned with emolument, but would be grateful if Dundas would recommend him for command of a more active post if the opportunity arose.

Sir Gilbert Elliot, who had been at Ferrara and Leghorn, had recently returned, and told Moore that he was very anxious that Bastia should be taken; he replied that from what he understood, D'Aubant seemed more concerned to do no more than fortify St Fiorenzo, which as Commander-in-Chief and Chief Engineer, he had 'every prospect of doing to advantage to himself'. Moore also said that he wished to make the attempt on Bastia, but did not pretend that it would be successful, and if the attempt failed, it would be best to abandon the island. There was no point in fortifying St Fiorenzo, and besides, it was in an unhealthy location.

Next morning, Moore paid a courtesy visit to the new general, to pay his respects. He found him very different to Dundas, who did not care for ceremony. D'Aubant was extremely formal, 'his language and manner having become already very official'. D'Aubant invited him to breakfast the next day, and asked for a copy of his report to General Dundas. Before that, Moore received a letter from Hood, expressing disappointment that Moore would not give him an opinion on the attempt to reduce Bastia; he had, he said, been led to come to Corsica by Moore's report, and thus had 'an undoubted right to expect my opinion'. Moore commented in his journal, 'His Lordship has perceived how much he committed himself when he sent the captains to Colonel Villettes and me as commanding officers of corps, and he now wished to give it another turn'. It was raining so heavily the next morning that Moore could not go to visit Hood, so he wrote a reply, saying that his previous response through the captains had not been intended to be disrespectful to the admiral, but he felt it would be a gross impropriety to give an opinion when General Dundas had already done so.

Moore was on his way down to visit General D'Aubant the next day when he met Koehler; he said that the general wanted them to look at the enemy positions and report back. They were unable to do this because of a thick fog, so went back down to see D'Aubant. Moore described this visit in his journal: 'He seems much adverse to the attack on Bastia, [but] has not the boldness to say so. It is difficult to speak more nonsense than he does with more gravity and decorum of manner.' After it was agreed that the reconnoitring of the French should be done the next day, Moore went to visit Elliot, telling him how much he regretted the departure of Dundas, who could be relied on to do well at whatever he tackled. He told Elliot that taking Bastia could be done, but that he thought D'Aubant was not capable of doing it and would bungle it. It would therefore be better not to try.

The reconnoitring was put off again the following day, with Moore summoned to a council of war at headquarters, called by Hood and attended by the admirals and field officers, to decide on whether to attack Bastia. Moore remarked in his journal that he could not recall all the nonsense talked by D'Aubant and that he and Koehler were the only ones to speak openly. They could not discuss the latest French positions, not having seen them, but said that if the French were driven from their current positions and the British were able to take the ground they had seen the first day they saw the works of Bastia, with the assistance of the Corsicans they could defend it from attack. Once the safety of the troops was secured, ammunition, guns and other materiel could be brought up and the town bombarded. With a simultaneous action by the fleet, this might force a capitulation; this all being dependent on the position the French had now taken. This was somewhat different from Dundas' opinion, but now that he was not there, Moore felt since he had been called on to give an opinion it should be his own opinion that he gave; he also thought that Dundas had intended to move forward once he had made the necessary preparations. Nothing was decided at this meeting, and another would be called when Moore and Koehler returned from their reconnaissance.

They set out early on 17 March and started up the hills by the great road with a large escort of Corsicans, striking off on a path which went along the high ridge and then led down to divide for the villages of Carda or La Villa, both on the north side of Bastia. There was still a thick fog on the heights so they went down to La Villa where they had a sideways view of the enemy's new position, and a full view of the town and neighbourhood of Bastia. These views showed them the absurdity of the constant statement from the Corsicans that they would be able to take the forts and the citadel by means of the town and its friendly inhabitants. Moore suspected that, like the inhabitants of most open towns, they would side with whoever seemed to be strongest. Both Moore and Koehler could see clearly that if the town surrendered to the British, they dare not take possession of it. The citadel was strongest on the side facing the town, commanding it completely. Moore's opinion that a position somewhere between the White House and the heights of Gardiola should be taken was confirmed; the French however had also seen this and moved in and erected a large redoubt about a half mile above Gardiola and in front of the White House. They had also created a chain of posts among the rocks to protect their advanced position, and to cover or support any retreat.

Moore and Koehler waited at Villa for over an hour until the fog disbursed, they climbed up again and found a spot about a half mile from the French advanced position. It was very strong, and because of the cold and constant heavy fogs it would not be possible to camp so high up until the artillery could be brought up; that meant any attack could only be made with infantry and such light guns as could be carried on the men's shoulders. With such a strong position and such rough ground around it, if an attack was successful it could only be with heavy losses; if it failed the British would probably be destroyed as there was a precipice behind them. They concluded that such an attack was beyond their present available force.

They delivered their reports to D'Aubant, describing the situation but not passing an opinion. But to Elliot, whom they saw afterwards, they did give their opinion: the French were equal if not superior in numbers, and due to the positions of their forts, they could deploy all or part of their force and could not be prevented from retreating. Much of the blame for this could be laid at the door of the Corsicans: Paoli had undertaken to cut off the line of communication between St Fiorenzo and Bastia while the British were attacking Martello and Fornoli, but his men had not done so, nor had they cut off the retreat of the fugitives from the Convention Redoubt, failing to obey the orders that Moore had given them himself. The third failure was that of Dundas. He should have moved his troops up the hill immediately after reconnoitring it, when he could have taken possession of the high ground. He had not done so but had trusted the Corsicans to keep the heights and they had allowed themselves to be surprised and driven away. He had certainly intended to move his whole force forward as soon as his artillery and stores were ready, but the enemy's enterprise in moving out and attacking the Corsicans and taking possession of the heights and the consequent difficulty of trying to move them, with perhaps a siege, were factors that had probably persuaded Dundas to withdraw and give up the idea of attacking Bastia.

'In war,' said Moore, 'an opportunity lost is never to be regained'. That report, with its tendency to prevent an attack on the enemy, was, Moore remarked, 'particularly relished' by D'Aubant, who seemed already to have made up his mind against the attempt.

Once more the council of war met, this time including admirals Hotham and Goodal and Commodore Linzee, lieutenant colonels Villettes, Wauchope, Sir J. St Clair and majors Pringle and Brereton. The reports from Moore and Koehler and another from lieutenants Duncan and Debrett were read. The latter was short, saying that batteries might be erected to the north side of the town which would 'considerably annoy' the enemy. Moore and Koehler thought it impossible to attack on that side, concluding that those artillery officers had just seen ground on which batteries could be built without giving thought to supporting and supplying them. Duncan was called into the meeting, and said that he had thought about those matters and considered that troops could also be positioned with the guns. Moore and Koehler were adamant that it would be 'perfectly absurd' to think of attacking Bastia from that direction. Going round by sea would also lead to major difficulties; once the enemy had taken the heights, which they inevitably would do, it would be impossible to bring supplies up from St Fiorenzo and everything would have to be brought in by sea. After what Moore described as 'a great deal of foolish conversation', the question was finally asked of the whole council: 'Whether it is expedient in a military point of view to attempt the reduction of Bastia with the force of the present fleet and army'. The army men were all against it, the navy men were all for it, but Moore interpreted this as meaning 'it was a desirable thing to make an attempt if possible'. D'Aubant did not want to give an opinion, but when pressed was against it. Moore was annoyed by this, stating in his journal, 'I have no conception of a commanding officer deciding an affair of such importance from the report of others when he has it in his power to see and judge for himself, but it was evident from the beginning that whatever report was made he was determined to do nothing'.

In a sour mood, Moore went on to remark on how useless the Corsicans had been and wonder if Paoli might be persuaded to make them perform, in which case the French might be driven from the heights, but with General D'Aubant it is needless to think to think of such attempts. He is unequal to them in every respect. It is difficult to paint a conduct more unlike an officer than his has been in these two councils; as for the other, Lord Hood, he enters little further into the subject than to say 'Take Bastia', as he would to a captain, 'Go to sea.', and he conceives they are both to be done with equal facility. Having taken up this idea, no reasoning has the smallest effect upon him.

Orders were given later that day for the regiments acting as marines to embark; these regiments constituted at least half of the ground forces. Hood intended to attack Bastia from the north, and demanded artillery and an engineer. Captain Collier of the Artillery produced a list of the necessary ordnance, an amount which exceeded what was in store; mortars and shells were to be sent from Naples. Moore remained unconvinced that this would be successful and Koehler was so disgusted that he asked for leave of absence and went off to Leghorn. Moore was sorry to see his new friend go, remarking that Koehler was 'a most zealous, indefatigable officer, who thinks of nothing but his profession, for which he certainly has considerable talents'. Moore might be quick to condemn the incompetent, but he was equally quick to give praise where it was due.

By 1 April various reconnaissances had been made, one of which brought a report by Lieutenant Colonel Weymes to the effect that with 400 men it would be easy to take the enemy post at Gardiola by marching at night and surprising them. Moore thought this proposal absurd, given the rough ground over which they would have to march and also the fact that there was no reason to think that the French would not be vigilant enough to spot them. Even D'Aubant saw this as impractical. Hood finally sailed for Bastia the following day, intending all but three ships to anchor to the northward of Bastia; the three other ships were to anchor on the other side, opposite the marsh. One of these was *Agamemnon*, from which Captain Horatio Nelson landed eight 24-pounders and eight 13in mortars, together with the troops who had been embarked as marines commanded by Colonel Villettes, and most of the ship's crew, commanded by himself. They built their battery near a high rock some 2,500yd from the citadel of Bastia, clearing the ground and felling trees to create an abbatis.[3]

Their first target was the small redoubt at Campanelli, although Moore had been up and seen the enemy attempting to strengthen it, it was still no more than a dry-stone wall with a single 4-pounder gun. This would easily fall from the fleet's superior fire, but since Hood had only 700–800 soldiers to take possession of it, that might not be so easy, if the enemy were to hide behind the hill and fire on the British troops as they struggled up over the difficult ground. Even if they were able to take it, Moore was not convinced that they would be able to move further as they would be exposed to constant fire. Hood was convinced that the townspeople would rise up as soon as the firing started and force the garrison to surrender, but when Moore dined with D'Aubant, Paoli, who was also there, was less confident, suggesting that mortars should be used. Moore was changing his mind about Paoli, seeing that the old general, who he had originally thought to be a good soldier, was actually completely ignorant of military matters.

Three weeks later, the bombardment of Bastia still continued, without effect. The redoubt at Campanelli had been silenced but the British could not be take possession of it, or at any rate, could not hold it if they did succeed in taking it. The suggestion that the enemy would surrender as soon as the batteries opened fire had proved to be erroneous, and it was now thought that the heights were the best place for an attack. Hood and Elliot pushed D'Aubant to assault the heights, which they assured him he could take with ease; he might also show himself up there with beneficial effect. They then threatened him with being responsible to the King for failure. D'Aubant, with Moore and artillery and engineer officers, went to reconnoitre the heights on two consecutive days, and one of these, Lieutenant Colonel Weymes, thought it would be easy to take them, but, wrote Moore, 'cannot explain how, and talks so like a boy that little weight can be given to his opinion'.

Another meeting of the land officers was called; D'Aubant read them portions of the letters he had received from Hood and Elliot and asked for their opinions on whether he should comply with their demands. Moore said that he had not changed his opinion since the meeting three weeks previously. He also thought that since a new general was expected daily, nothing should be undertaken until he arrived. He also remarked in his journal at this time that his opinion not only of Paoli but also of the Corsicans had changed; he had thought them to be an active warlike people but they turned out to be 'a poor, idle, mean set, incapable of any action which requires steadiness or resolution, and have been absolutely of no use to us since we landed'.

A few days later, Moore paid a visit to the *Victory*, where he found both Hood and Elliot were very displeased with D'Aubant; during a long conversation with Elliot, he explained the difficulty of attacking the heights without considerable loss of men, then repeated what he had said to D'Aubant about waiting until a new general should arrive. Elliot suggested that the command was going to fall on Moore. He slept that night at Paoli's quarters; on his way back to camp the following morning Moore encountered a little Corsican girl who had been to visit her father and was then going back to Bastia to her mother; she did not think there was any danger. This, he said, 'does not look as if the effect of our fire was so tremendous as is reported by the deserters'. He remarked that he did not want the command to fall to him, as he did not think the garrison would surrender unless it ran out of provisions and ammunition.

A few days later D'Aubant told Moore and Sir James St Clair that the last despatches from home mentioned that Major General Charles Stuart had received a commission, and was expected soon to take the command, but D'Aubant still seemed to hope that the command would be left to him. Hood now started a series of moves in taking possession of the army's materiel. He had asked D'Aubant for two 10in mortars, which were in a transport ship in use as a store-ship. Despite D'Aubant saying he did not think he could spare them, Hood sent an order to Admiral Crosbie to take the howitzers from the store-ship and send them to him, which Crosbie did. D'Aubant was not consulted on this.

Once more the commanding officers of the corps were assembled, this time to hear letters to Hood from the British ministers at Florence and Turin. They said that a reliable source had reported that the French were planning an attack on Leghorn, intending to pillage and destroy it, in particular the houses of the English merchants, and they requested a squadron would be sent to cruise off Leghorn harbour. They also believed that the French meant to attack Genoa before moving on to Sardinia, and asked again for a squadron to cruise there. Hood's letter, which accompanied these, urged D'Aubant to co-operate with the troops at St Fiorenzo, either by attacking the heights or at least letting the troops be seen there, which he thought would make Bastia surrender within four days rather than the two weeks currently expected. Hood went on to say that a speedy surrender of Bastia had become all the more important as events elsewhere in the Mediterranean might mean he had to withdraw the naval force from Corsica.

D'Aubant said that he was showing the assembled officers these letters to ask their opinion, not to burden them with the responsibility of a decision. Moore remarked dryly that it was pointless for him to be asked every eight or ten days to give an opinion on what ought or ought not to be done; there were many things which he could not know, perhaps no one could but the Commander-in-Chief. He still thought they did not have enough men to take Bastia, and 'with every deference to Lord Hood's opinion' he did not believe that attacking or merely showing themselves on the heights would bring about a surrender in four days. Indeed, he did not think they could reduce Bastia in a fortnight; Hood's attack had not weakened it. Blockading the harbour might work, but showing themselves on the heights would make no difference to that. He went on to write, 'much conversation then passed. It was evident from the beginning that the Brigadier was determined to do nothing.' Moore continued, 'I am anxious that he should do nothing. General Stuart may be hourly expected.'

Hood's next move was to take over the army transport containing stores and the baggage of the 50th and 51st regiments. D'Aubant refused this, as there was nowhere on shore to put the contents of that ship. Hood merely ordered the baggage to be moved to a different transport; when Moore heard of this he mentioned it to D'Aubant, who was surprised at what seemed like a repetition of Hood's annexation of howitzers. Moore suggested putting a party of men aboard and moving the transport under the guns of the garrison, but D'Aubant said that would be too violent, and that he would write to Hood. Moore returned to camp and ordered the quartermaster to move the baggage.

A few days later, after yet another reconnaissance, Moore called on Paoli, who showed him a parcel of letters which had been taken from a man going from Bastia to Calvi. These confirmed a rumour that La Combe St Michel, the Commander-in-Chief of Corsica, had left Bastia. The letters said that he was going to hasten the long-promised provisions and stores from France, and that in the meantime he had appointed General of Brigade Gentili to command in his absence and delegated all the necessary powers to him. Gentili's letters stated that he would be able to hold out at Bastia for more than a month, or even two months. All the letters spoke of the British actions as a blockade, and as if only the want of stores and provisions would force them to surrender.

On his return to camp, D'Aubant informed him that Hood had assumed power over all the vessels holding the army's baggage, stores and ammunition and would allow nothing to be landed from them without his order. He had refused D'Aubant's request for some canteens and powder, and D'Aubant seemed to have just tolerated it. There was a reinforcement of troops on the way, but Moore saw little hope of the new Commander-in-Chief arriving in time to take command of it before an attack was commenced, as he had just received a letter from his father in London dated 15 April saying that Stuart was still there.

The reinforcements arrived on 13 May, consisting of the recruits of the 50th and 51st and some of the 18th regiments, 600 men in all. The following morning D'Aubant called a meeting of the commanding officers and informed them he did not intend to wait for the additional troops expected from England, but would move forward and co-operate in the attack on Bastia. He had apparently had conversations with Captain Collier on the type of ordnance available and the practicalities of transporting 24-pounders up to the heights. He seemed to think this would be easy and quickly done, but on being informed that it would take several days to get those heavy guns up, he then said they should use 12-pounders and light howitzers. He was told that these would not carry far enough from the heights to be effective on the places he wanted to batter, and that before those batteries could be established, the troops would have to build sandbag fortifications, operations, said Moore dryly, that 'evidently required combination and arrangement, qualities of which he is devoid'. D'Aubant then seemed to give up that idea, and said that since guns would take so much time, he would just order the reinforcements to land immediately; the enemy must know they had arrived but not how many there were and would think there were more than there actually were. He saw no difficulty in moving the new troops up to the heights that night and attacking the entrenched posts at daylight, but gave no explanation of how the attack was to take place and seemed to think there was no more to it than for the troops to leave their encampments and the town of St Fiorenzo at midnight, arrive at the heights and attack at dawn.

Moore remarked that before D'Aubant finalised his plan of attack, it might be wise to ask Hood about the enemy's situation, since there was information that they were on the eve of surrender for lack of provisions. It would at the least seem odd to commence any operation against Bastia without consulting the person who had been before it for six or seven weeks. D'Aubant said he would write to Hood saying in general terms that he was ready to co-operate with him. After being asked for an opinion on this letter, Moore said that by the time the letter had been sent and answered, they would be no further forward than before, it was better to do such things face to face. Adjutant General Erskine and Moore were sent to wait on Hood. Moore delivered D'Aubant's message that he now had reinforcements and was ready to co-operate if Hood so wished. Hood replied that if D'Aubant had shown himself on the heights as he had requested ten days ago, the town would have surrendered, now he need not give himself the trouble, as surrender was expected within seven days at the most. He wished all communications between himself and the general to be in writing; spoken words are often misinterpeted, he said, there would probably be a hearing in due course and all the letters between them had been sent home. He could thus give no answer to the message. He also expressed his disappointment that a full regiment as well as the recruits had not been sent.

Moore and Erskine stayed to dinner, during which Hood was very polite, but this made them so late back to camp that Moore's report had to wait until the morning. On receiving this, D'Aubant stated his intention of moving troops up to the heights in case there was not an immediate surrender. As before, he seemed to have no idea of how to carry this out, especially getting the heavy artillery up there. Moore wrote in his journal that since the operation would be fraught with difficulties, he had every hope that General Stuart would arrive 'before we can possibly strike our tents'.

He had received another letter from his father, dated 25 April, in which he said that people at home were surprised Dundas had left his command, as had been Moore. He had spoken to Elliot about this, but he replied that matters between the two men had come to the point where one of them was going to have to go home, and it clearly could not be Hood. Elliot was glad that Dundas had gone, as it had become clear that he was not going to do anything, and because Elliot was convinced that the army should do something, he was not inclined to consider the reasons why they could not do anything without considerable losses.

At Moore's next meeting with D'Aubant, he told Moore that he had accepted the command on the condition that if an officer senior to him came out he would go home, as he did not want to serve as second where he had been first. He had received permission to go home, and had asked Hood for a ship to take him to Leghorn. The command would then devolve on Moore. Did he approve of the idea of moving the troops up to the heights, and asking Hood for assistance to drag up the guns? Moore replied that since Stuart was daily expected and his command thus only a short one, he wished to do nothing, but would not anyway decide on anything until he had seen Hood and knew the situation at Bastia. D'Aubant asked him to call again the next day, when he intended to hand over the command, but when he did so, he learned that Hood had said he could not spare a frigate to take D'Aubant to Leghorn, so his departure had not been mentioned in orders. Later that morning Moore was informed that the Royal and Royal Irish regiments were on the march to Titime; at the same time he received on order to move the 50th and 51st at daylight to the spot marked by the Quartermaster General above the French advanced posts. Everyone was surprised by this; it was thought that since Hood would not spare a frigate the only alternative was a tartane* which D'Aubant did not think was safe enough, so he had decided to stay and felt that in those circumstances he should not be inactive.

On 19 May, Moore was informed that a white flag was flying on *Victory*, the batteries had ceased firing and a negotiation was in progress. Moore's orders were to march with the regiments but the mules for the baggage had not arrived; D'Aubant's response on being informed of this was that they should march as soon as the mules did arrive. They had not arrived by noon, so Moore ordered the men to cook their food and put the tents up, as even if the mules did come that day it was already too

---

* A tartane was a single-masted merchant vessel, usually only used in coastal trade.

late to get to their ground before dark. The road to Bastia was solid with troops, guns, wagons and finally D'Aubant himself with a party of dragoons on the way to Titime. His intention was to summon the town next day if he did not receive official confirmation of the surrender that evening. After all his dithering of the previous weeks, D'Aubant was suddenly keen for action. No confirmation arrived, so Moore's regiments started moving. Keen to save them a tiring march over the mountains and hoping to be able to camp on or near the place they had previously occupied, Moore pushed forward to see D'Aubant, but 'he who is proud of his absurd march' said they must go to the ground marked out for them. This was some 3 miles off the great road over a very steep and craggy mountain; numbers of the men 'fell down' as a result of the excessive heat and bad road; as if this was not enough, when they reached their allocated ground a thick fog arrived, followed by cold, hard rain. They were exposed to this, shivering from the cold, for over 3 hours before their baggage and camp equipment arrived, and they could get under cover. As soon as the provisions arrived, Moore ordered a glass of raw spirits for each man. The fog and rain cleared up during the night, but the following morning the fog came down again, even thicker.

On 22 May, an aide from the French General Gentili arrived to see Moore, saying his orders were to give up the post immediately in front of Moore's outposts and asking for troops to go and take possession. In subsequent conversation, he said they had 6,000 men under arms, 4,500 of whom were fully trained, and that they had never feared being forced, knowing the British force was small. They still had plenty of ammunition but little food and knowing there was little chance of any arriving from France, were obliged to surrender.

Hood then made another attempt to take over command of the army for the next phase. St Clair arrived early to see Moore with an order for the Royals and Royal Irish to embark immediately on an expedition, and the 50th to move to the vacated camp. St Clair said this was by requisition from Hood, and that D'Aubant would leave in a day or two for Leghorn. Hood's purpose in asking for these two regiments was to give the command of the attack on Calvi nominally to Villettes but in reality to himself, and to prevent the army from having any share in it. The commanding officer of the troops was not to go on the expedition nor any of the staff. Thus the small part of the army involved would be lumped with the seamen and marines, and the capitulation, as at Bastia, would be to Hood alone. Moore remarked in his journal, 'General D'Aubant had the weakness to consent to this slur being thrown upon himself and the troops under his command'.

Moore was rather inclined to stand on his dignity in such situations. And he went immediately to see D'Aubant, telling him that since he meant to leave the island, the command would fall to him (Moore) as senior officer and that as such he thought he had a right to be consulted on measures which would affect him, not D'Aubant. It would be disgraceful to him and to the army to be left unemployed at Bastia or St Fiorenzo. This was a situation in which he had no right to put Moore. If D'Aubant chose to stay until the arrival of Lieutenant General Stuart, then he (Moore) would submit in silence to this disgrace, but if D'Aubant intended to go home he should give up the command entire. After much discussion, during which D'Aubant affected to be angry, he finally agreed that there was some justice in Moore's opinion, 'but what could he do? He had already consented to give the regiments, and they were at that instance paraded and ready to march.' Hood had much influence at home, their discussions had often made him miserable and he did not want to suffer any more. Moore told him that the first thing he had to do was to stop the regiments and order them to pile their arms until further orders, then give Moore a letter to take to Hood saying that as he was about to depart, the command of the troops would devolve on Moore, who had come with the letter to consult on the steps needed for the attack on Calvi. D'Aubant duly did this and Moore set out for *Victory* with the letter in his pocket.

He was prevented from getting to *Victory* by the weather, but had prepared his arguments while he waited. He intended to be mild with Hood, but would insist that if any troops were go to the attack on Calvi he would have to go with them to command them in person. If this did not bring Hood round, he intended to tell him that he should not have the two regiments, nor anything else from the army. The following day he was able to get to *Victory*, where he found Elliot and General Stuart, who had arrived the previous night. He told Hood that he no longer needed to bother him with the business that had brought him, thus saving himself from the inevitable wrath that this would invoke in Hood. Instead he told Elliot and Stuart his story at full length. Stuart told him he had acted properly; Moore replied that he hoped that all *tracasseries** were at an end and that he was the happiest man in the world in the thought that Stuart's arrival meant the service would be properly conducted. They went ashore together, accompanied by Moore's old friend Major Oakes.

A week later, having moved their camp from Titime, Moore walked over the ground which had been occupied by the French. Their advanced post on the heights at Campo Ventoso was strong, the ground between it and the mountain which the British troops must have crossed to advance on the post was so rough with thorny brush that they could only have moved in single file. He could see that the land attack which Hood had attempted was impossible and he had actually never advanced; it was only the French failing to take advantage of the situation that prevented total destruction of the troops. Moore wrote in his journal that no doubt Hood would gain credit for it at home, and had hurried the negotiations of capitulation in a hurry in case the troops from St Fiorenzo had arrived and thus gained a share of the honour. Certainly the army had little to do with the surrender of Bastia; this had been achieved by the naval bombardment and blockade of the harbour.[4]

---

* Chicaneries.

Chapter 3

Corsica: Calvi and After

Calvi is situated on the north-west side of the island, at the north end of a rocky peninsula overlooking the Bay of Calvi. It was much stronger than either St Fiorenzo or Bastia. To the west, commanding the north coast were two batteries of six and three guns, a little to the south of the western battery was Fort Mozzello, built of stone in a pentagon shape with a heavy gun on each face. About 1,000yd south of that was Fort Monteciesco, also on a steep rock with one heavy gun and five or six field guns. This, with the aid of two French frigates in the Bay of Calvi, could command the approaches to the town from the south.

* * *

When the British first arrived, Calvi had two French frigates in its harbour; once these were removed the harbour could be blocked by frigates and gunboats while the rest of the fleet and the army were busy elsewhere. This blockade would 'subject the garrison to such inconvenience as to render it unwilling, perhaps incapable, of much resistance'. Paoli's 'patriots' were in sufficient numbers to prevent enemy land communication, and he believed that 2,000 could be brought together to serve permanently with the British army. In order to organise this he said he needed £4,000, a hundred barrels of powder with a proportion of lead and flints and, if possible, 1,000 stand of arms. Paoli also suggested that the Regiment of Dragoons should be landed; although the terrain was not really suitable for cavalry, nor was much feed available, some cavalry would be helpful in preventing enemy communication. The partisans would be particularly useful to surround the British posts to prevent surprise attacks, and take possession of high spots. They were excellent marksmen and could be housed in the villages, only the batteries and outposts would need tents. With four days' notice, mules could be provided, but would have to be paid for; their owners would feed them. The ordnance belonging to the army would be sufficient, but they might on occasion need some landed from the fleet; if there were not enough shells for the attack on Calvi, Moore presumed they could be got in time. There was plenty of material available for building platforms and fascines, but tools and nails would have to come from the engineers' stores.

After making a detailed inspection of the stores, ordnance and hospitals, and inspecting the regiments, General Stuart went off to reconnoitre Calvi. Moore was to have accompanied him, but Hood said that the ships to take the troops round would be ready in two days, so Moore stayed to embark the troops and accompany them round to Calvi. Theoretically they should have left on 2 June, but still had not done so when word came on the 8th that a French fleet of nine ships of the line with frigates and other smaller armed ships had come out of Toulon and was heading for

Calvi, and that Admiral Hotham, with seven ships of the line, was in pursuit. Hood departed with his squadron to intercept them, saying he would send back a frigate for Stuart when the situation was clearer. The transports were left to convey the troops, and the stores were already loaded. Stuart, who had returned from Calvi, told Moore that Hood had asked him for powder; this had surprised him as there was little on shore and he was depending on what he needed for Calvi to come from the fleet, which, it seemed, had very little itself. After the indecisiveness of Dundas and D'Aubant, Moore was delighted with Stuart, 'General Stuart is indefatigable.... it is a principle with him that a general should [reconnoitre himself], in order to form the better judgement of what he may order others to perform'.

On the morning of the 12th, word came from Hood that he had not seen the French fleet and that they had not put any reinforcements into Calvi. The troops from Bastia sailed the following day, arriving in Martello Bay on the 16th. General Trigge with 700 or 800 recruits from England had arrived, as had ammunition from Gibraltar. Trigge went to take command at Bastia and the recruits went on to Calvi, where they all arrived on the 18th and camped on the heights immediately above the plain of Calvi, at a point concealed from the French posts, especially Fort Monteciesco which was well within reach of the British guns when the battery under construction was finished.

The next week was spent getting materiel on shore and up to the battery, the heavy work of dragging the guns and their carriages uphill being shared by sailors and soldiers. Hood was back in Martello Bay, having left nine ships of the line to watch the French. Instead of coming to help with the siege against Calvi, he had demanded 140 soldiers from the 60th to embark as marines, this demand being made to General Trigge. He had not written to Stuart, who was surprised by Hood's conduct, and wrote to him in stong terms. Hood did not reply, but sent 250 sailors with 3 26-pounders to act on shore under Captain Nelson.

Delays were caused by two days of severe weather, and despite some of the necessary sandbags being ready, work had still not started on the batteries by 28 June, but they were well on the way to completion by 4 July, when they were able to fire their three 26-pounders against Monteciesco first thing in the morning. That night they planned to move a howitzer and another six 26-pounders closer, but it transpired that the Chief Engineer had not made the necessary arrangements or circulated his orders. At 10.20 the work had only just begun, and Stuart arrived saying he was afraid the battery would not be ready by daylight. Moore replied that they had either to decide whether to make every effort to complete it, or give up and retire for the night. They decided to do the latter.

In the morning they saw that the French did not seem to have registered what was going on with the British battery but were busy enclosing their own battery. The day was spent in bringing up stores and the night in moving sandbags, shot and shells to a rock some 60yd from the place planned for the new battery; it was evident that they could not have done all that was necessary to build the new battery in one night. Moore commented scathingly in his journal that the Engineer was 'perfectly incapable of his business. The commanding officer of Artillery is also a man without method or arrangement'. The plan for finishing and manning the new battery was for the reserve to move forward to arrive at about 9 o'clock, finish the battery by 3.30 and start firing at 4. The Corsicans created a diversion on the right, which drew the enemy's full attention, and as planned, by 4 o'clock the last of the six guns was being dragged into the new battery. The French did not notice it until much later than they might have done, their attention being focused instead on a smaller battery of two 26-pounders and a mortar constructed on the heights well to the rear of the British. But at about 6 o'clock they opened fire from three batteries; all that the British were ready to fire at first were the 26-pounders on the heights, and three 13in mortars. Before they were able to use the bigger guns, ten men had been killed or wounded, but once those guns were able to start firing the French fire was considerably checked.

After a quiet night the French started firing again at daybreak; the sun was in their favour and their fire was very accurate, hitting the British battery with almost every shot. As a result three of the British guns were hit, two were damaged. The French were using two mortars and two 10in howitzers; the British armament was four 26-pounders and two 24-pounders at the advanced battery, two 26-pounders and a mortar on the heights and three 26-pounders at the old French battery. The French fire varied in intensity, and during the night the British were able to repair their advance battery and construct some traverses. During a quiet period on 10 July, Stuart took Moore to see a spot where he intended to place a battery of four heavy guns. On the following day the French withdrew from one of their batteries, but then started firing from the town where they had five or six guns. Moore spent the night and the following day in the trenches with the Grenadiers; they suffered a few injuries, but Captain Nelson was struck in the face by stones thrown up when a ball hit a heap of them. 'It is feared he may lose one of his eyes,' Moore wrote.

The guns in the advance post of Mozzello were silent, and plans were made to breach it. There had been some fires in the town, and by the 18th it was thought practicable to storm Mozzello. 'Lord Hood,' wrote Moore, 'continues to hover around us eager to have his name in the capitulation. General Stuart, by his firm behaviour, keeps him in order'.

In the early hours of 19 July the British moved off, one corps under Lieutenant Colonel Weymes with the Royal Irish was to attack the half-moon ('sans culottes') battery, Moore's corps was to attack Mozzello, with the 50th and 51st regiments to support where necessary. Moore formed the Grenadiers and Light Infantry in a column of companies, and sent the Royals to a height in his front, in the rear of two field pieces sent ahead. Each man carried a sandbag, and they also had fourteen ladders to get them over a stone wall; as it turned out they did not need these. The enemy had placed shot, hand grenades and live shells on the rampart, and rolled these down on the attackers, but the Grenadiers advanced intrepidly with their bayonets and the French gave way and ran from the fort. Captain McDonald and Moore attacked the breach on the left, and as he went to it Moore was struck on the head by the splinter of a shell. 'It turned me round and made me senseless for a moment,' wrote Moore, 'I however recovered and went on.' Soon after this Captain McDonald was severely wounded in the face and had to retire; a few men were killed outright, but Moore got into the fort with the rest and soon the place was filled with five companies of Grenadiers. Two companies of light infantry had been ordered to move round the foot of the fort and get between it and the town, but the Grenadiers stormed so briskly that the light infantry could not get there in time and most of the enemy escaped. General Stuart, who had been close to the action throughout, was so delighted that he ran up and took Moore in his arms.

Now the town began to fire on them but soon stopped. The British had gained a strong position within 600yd of the fortress and were poised to storm the walls. Stuart sent Moore and the light infantry, who had been out for two nights, back to camp to rest, and soon Major Oakes came back with a message that Stuart had summoned the town. It refused to capitulate, but had not fired again. Ten days later, the enemy had not fired a single shot, and the British had been occupied in bringing their stores and ammunition forward and in erecting batteries. By daylight on 20 July, the reserve were in the trenches and the batteries were completed. These consisted of one at 600yd from the citadel, with seven 26-pounders and two 10in howitzers on the left, one of three 13in mortars and one 18-pounder in the Mozzello, one 26-pounder and two 32-pounders on the right of the Mozzello and another with two 26-pounders. The old six-gun battery erected on the night of the 6th and that of three guns erected on the 19th continued with two 26-pounders and one 13in mortar remained on the heights. This totalled thirty-three pieces of ordnance. On seeing this, the French manned their batteries but did not fire. Stuart received a letter from the commander of Calvi asking him not to fire on the lower town where their hospital was; Stuart replied politely that he would not, and asked if the commander had any terms to propose. This opened negotiations, with letters passing back and forth. The French demanded a twenty-five day cessation of fire, while they waited to see if relief arrived, offering to surrender at the end of that time if it did not. Stuart felt this was too long and offered them twelve days.

It had now become extremely hot, and both officers and men were falling sick with more than a third of the British force being listed in the sick reports. When no better response had been received from the enemy, the British started firing on the town again. There was a weak response and on 31 July a flag was sent out with a letter to the general. Moore went out to receive it and waited with the French officers while a reply was written. They told him that the letter was a complaint about a shot that had gone through their hospital, killing or wounding three men; they hinted that their people were extremely sickly and seemed surprised that the British force stood the sun so well. The town was set on fire in several places that night and on the following day another flag was sent out, on which the firing ceased and was not resumed. Stuart told Moore confidentially that the enemy had agreed to accept the terms he had offered them before, he had refused this but agreed to give them until the 10th. All communication between the two sides was forbidden.

Moore moved the reserve camp to a place higher up, hoping that this location would be healthier. Contrary to what the French officers had thought, more than two-thirds of the troops were in the hospital, and more, as Moore said, 'tumble down daily in the most melancholy manner'. He thought they could not have continued the siege another week. He went on to praise Stuart's ability, 'conspicuous during this service'.

On 7 August Stuart called on Moore; saying that he had received letters from Secretary Henry Dundas; he wanted Stuart to let Sir James Erskine go home, on the condition that he should give up his position as adjutant general. Stuart believed that Erskine would agree to this, in which case Moore could have that position if he wished. Moore was uncertain; he did not see any further action in the island, Stuart would inevitably go home and he would be left as adjutant general in a peace establishment under a stranger. The extra pay would only be enough to support the additional expenses of the position, and, worse, he would be 'tied by the leg' in Corsica. After some more conversation, during which Stuart pointed out that the appointment might bring him the rank of colonel, Moore finally accepted the position, noting that it would mark Stuart's approval of his conduct and might bring him the promotion earlier than it would come otherwise.

On 10 August at 9 o'clock, the reserve, and detachment of artillery, some sailors, some royalist French gunners and Corsicans assembled and at 10 o'clock moved forward and formed up some 300yd from the gate, where General Stuart joined them. Soon after, the garrison, led by General Casabianca and Arena, the Commissioner of the Convention, moved out and formed a line 50yd from the British, then moved across the British front, laying down their arms as they went. They went into the low town to embark on the transports provided for them. Moore took possession of the citadel, commenting later in his journal that the damage caused by the British fire was inconceivable, 'there is literally not a house which has not been damaged by shot or shell. The whole is a heap of ruins.' The men had to be housed in the Palais, the officers in what had been Casabianca's house. In both places, there were no beds and all had to lay on the floor, the men with their blankets and the officers in their cloaks. This was no hardship for Moore himself; Elliot had remarked in a letter to his wife, 'He is in love with his profession, and as all services one renders to a mistress are pleasant, he enjoys all discomforts'.[1]

Hood, meanwhile, bitter because he had not been named in the capitulation, wrote to Henry Dundas' under-secretary to complain of Stuart's actions: he had, said Hood, sacrificed his men in the process of delaying the capitulation. The town would have capitulated two weeks earlier if it had been heavily bombarded for two days; he gave as evidence a statement by a French officer on the lack of shelter and ammunition in the town. The amount of stores captured in the town proved this to be untrue. Next, Hood demanded four complete regiments to man his ships, which were short of crews. Stuart let him have a few, but needed all the rest; there were less than 800 fit for duty, the rest were in the hospitals.

Of the 600 men of the reserve, only 216 were in a fit state to move from their camp to the town, and many of those were convalescents, many of whom promptly relapsed.* Moore's servant, William Hillows, who had been with him for four years, died in

---

* Moore only ever refers to the illness his men suffered as 'fever'; it was probably malaria.

Bastia of the fever, having been sent there to recover. Moore wrote to his mother, 'He was my valet, cook, groom, and without him I am helpless. I had other business to attend to and left to his fidelity and assiduity the whole of my private affairs.' He went on to comment on his head wound, 'you have heard how the thickness of my scull saved my life. The last plaister fell off today, and as soon as the hair, which was shaved, grows, there will not remain any trace of the hurt.'[2]

General Stuart was moving all but the Royal Irish regiment, which was to remain and garrison Calvi, back to Bastia. The sick embarked first, then the others. Moore remarked in his journal that he would be returning to the command of the 51st Regiment, which had fewer sick than any other regiment. This he attributed partly to its excellent surgeon, M'Cleish ('a diligent and intelligent man'), and partly to his own insistence on maintaining the regimental hospital in good order, which was one of the things he organised as soon as he took command of the regiment. The result was that he now had three times the number of men fit for duty than any other regiment there.

Embarking on the *Helmesley* transport on 19 August, they were off Cape Corse the following day, but due to bad weather and contrary winds, did not reach Bastia for another four days. Hood and the fleet had departed as soon as Calvi surrendered, so for lack of hands they were unable to dismantle the batteries or remove the stores. Stuart had wanted to make an immediate distribution of the prize money from the captured frigates and ordnance; he had asked Hood how the navy wanted to share, but Hood, awkward as ever, replied that it must be referred to the King, which would cause an inevitable delay. Stuart had given his share to the troops and the widows of men killed during the siege.

They took a few days to settle into the barracks at Bastia, then Stuart wanted to make a tour of the island, so he, with Moore, St Clair, captains Nepean and Duncan, set out on 31 August and returned on 24 September, having visited Calvi, Ajaccio, Porto Vecchio and Corte. Baggage space was limited, and Moore had been unable to take his writing case, just making occasional notes in pencil and writing up his journal when they got back to Bastia. They had made a trip to the island of Rossa in a tartane but the winds were uncertain and they decided to do the rest of the trip by land. Stuart had some arrangements to settle with Major Montressor at Calvi, which took two days; Moore spent these walking over the ground and looking at the various British positions above the town, reflecting that the ground was so favourable to the enemy that it was only their lack of spirit and ability that allowed the British to take the town. He also realised that if the siege had continued for another ten days, sickness would have made them give up. When they moved on down the west side of the island, they spent a night at the village of Otta, where they stayed with Signor Benediti, the chief of the village and a long-term adherent of Paoli. The chief's house was in the village, there being no country houses in Corsica. Such a man's status depended on the size of his family, and these were also in the villages, the safest place from attack. The hills round this village were provided with supporting walls which were planted with vines, olives and figs, demonstrating what could be done in the rest of the island if the inhabitants were industrious, but unfortunately they were not, preferring to wander around carrying a musket in the hopes of finding some game.

As they moved on, they found that the Corsicans were convinced they must have some foreign power over them, being unable themselves to ensure the laws were kept. Moore made a comment about the native Corsicans: they were small, and both men and women 'uglier I believe than in any other part of Europe'. Moving further south to Ajaccio, they found the Gulf of Ajaccio beautiful and the harbour good; the area round the town was less mountainous and fertile. The chief product was an excellent wine. Moore found the people better looking and hospitable; they danced every evening. The general opinion was that the best form of government for the island at that time was a military one, what Moore called 'the sensible people'; they were somewhat ambivalent about Elliot, he was thought to be much influenced by Pozzo di Borgo 'who is universally disliked and generally thought to be a scoundrel'.

From Ajaccio they went on to Corte. This small town is in the rocky centre of the island, it had always been thought of as the capital. The barracks and the House of Assembly were the principal buildings, and there they dined with the members of the provisional council. Moore remarked that they were originally 'the creatures of Paoli: the choice does him no great honour', being, as Moore thought, 'a set of vulgar, low-minded men without talent'. It seemed the country was already dissatisfied with them, impatiently waiting for the return of the deputies from England and the organisation of their new government. The French had built a good road between Bastia and Corte, and had intended to continue it to Ajaccio. Stuart and his party arrived back at Bastia on the evening of 25 August. Moore was disappointed to find little change in the sick list; there had been a considerable number of deaths.

On 3 October a courier arrived from England with Sir Gilbert Elliot's appointment as Viceroy; the actual commission was to follow. The title caused some curiosity, seeming to suggest more powers than would pertain to a governor. It surely could not have been intended to give him the same powers as the Lord Lieutenant of Ireland, although Elliot seemed inclined to make him his model. General Stuart told Moore of a conversation he had with Elliot; Elliot mentioned he wished to visit the hospitals, Stuart was rather surprised and asked if someone had told Elliot the hospitals were not in good order. 'No,' said Elliot, 'but I like to visit hospitals'. The general replied, 'Why have you not done it, then?' and Elliot said he would like to visit them with the general, and even to see some returns from them. Stuart replied that if he wished to see them as Mr Elliot and have information about them, he would be happy to give it, but if he meant that as Viceroy he had any authority over them or any part of the army, and that this was to be the first act of his reign, he would not consent to it. Elliot had no authority whatever over the army. Elliot replied that he was totally of a different opinion and the general assured him that he had none, and reminded Elliot that his (Stuart's) commission was not just to command the troops in Corsica, but as Commander-in-Chief in the Mediterranean; and that Elliot should consider it as a fortunate circumstance. As a friend, said Stuart, 'I advise you never to interfere with the army until your powers are explained to you by your commission; you will otherwise involve yourself in endless difficulties.' Stuart went on to comment that the only law in the island was martial law, over which, as Commander-in-Chief, he presided, and that until such time as Elliot's commission gave him the powers of a Commander-in-Chief, he should not attempt to interfere in military matters. Elliot agreed that these were difficulties he had not foreseen.

Moore commented in his journal:

> It might have been as well, perhaps, if the name of Viceroy had not been mentioned without first consulting the administration at home. This would probably have been the case had personal advantages not interfered. Peraldi and some others at Ajaccio said that they were surprised when it was inserted in the constitution; that the idea had not originated with the Corsicans, who were all equally surprised [as General Stuart] at it. Government will find out perhaps when too late how much they have allowed themselves to be committed from the confidence they have reposed in the good sense and moderation of Sir Gilbert; qualities which perhaps he does not possess in so great a degree as is imagined. He has been infinitely dazzled by the splendour of aides-de-camp, general ushers, &c. &c., and I fear he will involve his country in difficulties. It is particularly fortunate that a person of General Stuart's manly, liberal understanding happens to be at the head of the army. He will undoubtedly prevent much mischief. I dread his departure.

The 9 October was fixed as a day of public rejoicing in Bastia; *Te Deum* was sung in the churches and there was a ball in the evening. It was also the appointed day for introducing the principal officers of the army (commanding officers of corps, heads of department) to the new Viceroy; Stuart took them to Elliot as a group and Stuart and Elliot made brief speeches before the army officers were introduced.

This was all very civilised, but Elliot was not finished with his claim to command the army. Stuart showed Moore correspondence between them, which began with Elliot again asserting his rights to the command of the army. It was, he said, incompatible with the newly established constitution that any armed force remained on the island over which he did not have complete control. Although he had presently yielded, Elliot wished it to be understood that he did not give up the right. Despite the conversation they had had, matters of such importance should be dealt with in writing. Moore thought Elliot's letter tediously long and mean, but artful with too much forced flattery for the general. Stuart's replies were concise, positively denying the government of Corsica the smallest power over the British troops, while Elliot continued sending what Moore thought were childish responses, though it was obvious that Elliot's purpose in this correspondence was to send it home, although this might not have the effect he intended: 'The high footing upon which he [Elliot] puts Corsica will surprise and stagger people at home. It will appear evident that he can have no motive for it but his own aggrandisement. How little are people known whilst in the private walk of life!'

Elliot spent much time ingratiating himself with the Corsicans, including Paoli's right-hand man, Pozzo di Borgo. Elliot found him well-mannered and intelligent; his ability to speak good English was an added bonus. But it transpired from conversations between the Corsican gentry and the army officers that he was not liked by his countrymen, 'a scoundrel' several of them described him vehemently.

Elliot soon found an opportunity to interfere again. It had been thought expedient to raise a body of Corsicans; Stuart's plan was for 3 battalions of 500 men, each of 5 companies, 1 battalion each to be quartered at Bastia, Ajaccio and Corte, under the command of British field officers, with the whole under a British officer as inspector. Great care was to be taken in selecting the officers, on the basis of character and merit. Elliot soon changed the plan, with a view to increasing his patronage: he had already named the principal officers and made each battalion consist of 10 companies of 50 instead of 5 of 100. In order to pay for the increase in officers, he had reduced the pay of each rank; the end result was that instead of useful military units, Elliot would exploit them to forward political views. This, thought Moore, arose from Elliot's character which lead him to pursue his ends by intrigue and management, instead of by bold, open and manly conduct. Stuart, once he saw how things were going, declined to have anything further to do with it.

Stuart told Moore that Admiral Hood had told General Trigge that he (General Stuart) had ordered only sick or invalid men to serve as marines. He had written in detail to Secretary Dundas about Hood's behaviour and this may have contributed to Hood's recall and the order to strike his flag and go ashore; on 17 March 1795 he gave up his seat on the Admiralty Board. Hood went home in *Victory* when a frigate would have done equally well; this last sop to Hood's dignity deprived the British fleet of a large battleship, when they already had two less than the French fleet.[3]

Moore, meanwhile, was mourning the loss of his friend, Captain Tourle, of the Light Infantry:

> [Tourle] was seized with fever towards the end of the siege of Calvi. He has continued more or less ill ever since, but a few days ago he was taken with an inflammation in his stomach, of which he died this morning. I have been occupied all day in giving directions for his funeral, which is to-morrow, and I am just now returned from one of the last offices of a friend, seeing him placed in his coffin. When I reported his death to General Stuart and asked his orders respecting the funeral, he said he would walk as chief mourner. The General, who is full of heart, thinks this tribute due to a person he had remarked as a gentlemanly, spirited officer. Tourle was undoubtedly that, as well as a worthy, cheerful companion. We all feel his loss, but nobody more than myself, as from my first coming into the regiment we had lived on the most cordial and friendly footing.

At the beginning of December Moore wrote to his mother, commenting that her letter had arrived by the good offices of Major Stewart. His promotion had come through while he was in England, where he had paid a visit to Mrs Moore. This was a common feature of Moore's life: that he would encourage his friends to present themselves to the Moore household and make friends there. It also had the advantage that the visitors could give a better account of Moore's own health and adventures than could easily be conveyed in a letter. Moore also commented on the news of some family friends, including Mr Murdock, who had fallen on hard times in his old age, and what may have been a misguided attempt at matchmaking by his mother:

> Since Peggy Coates has the prospect of an independent fortune she need not so soon look forward to being an old maid. I should think it not so difficult to find a man she might both love and esteem, if she puts fortune out of the question – as for me I should like to inspire a lady of such fortune with those sentiments, who was, as well disposed but not quite so fat as my friend Peggy.

The first of two other events in the Moore household was that brother Frank got married. This was not, however, a matter of rejoicing, as for his bride Frank had chosen the disreputable Lady Eglinton, divorced by her husband as the result of an affair with the Duke of Hamilton. She had two daughters, the second of which may not have been her husband's, and the year after their marriage produced a son. If her reputation had not endeared her to the Moore family, her flighty character added to their distaste. It was several years before the family was prepared to acknowledge her. The second event was that brother Charles, the brilliant lively barrister, was suffering from a bout of what Dr Moore sadly had to accept was insanity.

At the beginning of January the long-awaited clarification of Elliot's position arrived: his powers were to be similar to those of the Lord Lieutenant of Ireland, and thus gave him command of the army. This meant that General Stuart's command ceased immediately, Moore's appointment as adjutant general had arrived some weeks previously, but had not yet been put in orders as St Clair remained in Corsica. He went home with Stuart, and Moore took over his post. Elliot wrote a long address to the troops, which was put into orders. This concluded by appointing Major General Trigge as Commander-in-Chief; Elliot then appointed him a lieutenant general. Moore remarked sardonically that he had understood such appointments were only made by the King.

Stuart had promised to pay another visit to Ajaccio before he left the island, and decided to go there even though he had given up the command. A large party set out, including Colonel Oakes, St Clair, Colonel Wauchope, Dr Robertson, two of the general's aides-de-camp and Moore himself. Their route took them through Bocognana and Vivario and they arrived at Ajaccio the following night, where Peraldi visited them immediately and extended an invitation to them to attend his daughter's wedding dinner the next day. Although they accepted with delight, they were unable to go as Stuart was seized by an attack of gout overnight. There was then a very heavy fall of snow which continued for several days; the symptoms of Stuart's gout wore off and he began to worry about getting back to Bastia. Despite warnings from the locals about the dangers of attempting to reach Bocognana in the snow, Stuart determined to try it. They set out and reached Bocognana at the foot of the mountains the first night and despite more dire warnings from the inhabitants, they continued the next day through snow which was 5 or 6ft thick in places; they had to dismount and lead their horses. Moore wrote that they had undergone 'as much fatigue as I ever experienced'. They finally reached Vivari that evening, and stayed with the curé who provided them with dry stockings. The curé told them that the

Corsicans were sorry Stuart was leaving as they had a high opinion of his military ability; they also appreciated his justice and believed that he did not act from blind veneration of the 'great people'. The curé told them that Paoli had offered to arm the local inhabitants but that he had refused on their behalf, saying that they could be armed if they were recruited to go to war, but otherwise, if armed, would become idle and stop cultivating their lands. The British party found the locals equal rogues with the rest of the population; they extorted high prices for everything, setting these on what they thought the British would pay.

They arrived at Corte the next day and Basti the day after that. They found that the meeting of the Parliament at Corte had been postponed because of the bad weather, and that it had been fixed for 6 February at Bastia, causing much discontent. It was felt that Corte was the most proper place, as it was in the centre of the island, and that the Viceroy had moved it to suit his convenience rather than that of the rest of the Parliament.

General Stuart fixed his departure for 7 February. He gave two balls for the officers of the garrison, and they gave a dinner for him. Moore accompanied him to St Fiorenzo, where he and St Clair embarked in the frigate *Juno*. Moore wrote in his journal of Stuart, 'It will be long probably before I serve under an officer for whom I have so much esteem and attachment.'

Two days later, Moore and all the field officers and heads of department were summoned to meet the Commander-in-Chief to attend the Viceroy at the meeting of the Parliament; the streets were lined with troops and the Viceroy and his party processed to the Parliament, all with hats off except the Viceroy himself. Once there, he read a speech in Italian before returning to his house where the principal officers dined with him. On the following day the Parliament set about electing their President. Paoli was not there but was chosen by acclamation which alarmed the Viceroy; Moore was told by a Corsican member of the Council of State that with Paoli as President the Viceroy's position would be reduced to that of merely 'a pageant with authority'; he had even thought of going home. The Viceroy need not have worried, as Paoli declined the presidency, and an elderly man called Giafferi was chosen instead.

Before this was announced, the Viceroy's concerns showed themselves by an order to stop the 51st Regiment leaving Bastia. Their baggage was already on wagons and ready to leave for Corte when a messenger arrived with orders to follow it if it had already left and bring it back. Trigge told Moore the next day that the reason for the change of plan was the fear of being left unprotected. Moore remarked sardonically that if the Viceroy's government could only be supported by 1,500 or 2,000 troops, the sooner he left the better. In fact, the baggage was not that important and there were numerous reasons which could have been given for the retention of the troops which would not have alarmed the Corsicans. There was, however, no public demonstration of this alarm, and it was thought that if they showed too much dislike of the Viceroy they might lose the protection of Great Britain.

The next event was the inauguration of a bust of Paoli in the Parliament. Once the Viceroy was seated, the new president uncovered the bust, to great applause. Speeches were made by three members, then the Viceroy got up, walked over to the bust, read the inscription, took off his hat, made a low bow to the bust and walked on to applause. The Viceroy was fond of such occasions, but did not reciprocate with equally grand events at his own house, which was open twice a week. The only refreshments were lemonade, and there were cards, a sort of cross between a drawing room and a *conversazione*, not much to the English taste. The Viceroy may have been guided in this by Pozzo di Borgo.

Pozzo di Borgo was originally an attorney and found a niche with the French in the first National Assembly in Paris. When he returned to Corsica he attached himself to Paoli which was when Elliot had met him on his first visit to the island. After the taking of St Fiorenzo he spent much time in Moore's camp and was responsible for accepting money for the Corsicans and managed this for Paoli very badly. His mismanagement meant the Corsicans did not get the essentials they needed, and this led to accusations of his having pocketed it. Moore was not impressed with him: 'he is a low, mean-minded man, with some cunning and intrigue, but totally devoid, in my opinion, of talents. The Viceroy, whose friendships are passions, is completely blinded by this man, who has already led him into several scrapes.'

It seemed that the Viceroy's government's main plan was bribery and faction. Moore had been told by a Corsican gentleman of his acquaintance that he had gone to the Viceroy hoping to get a place in government service. He was told that if he were of the party that was against the Viceroy's rule he could expect nothing but if he was of the other party he might obtain his wishes. Another young man was told by Elliot's niece that he could expect nothing unless he was a friend of Pozzo di Borgo. Moore continued, 'several [people] have told me that Sir Gilbert's government is the completest despotism ever exercised in Corsica. I expect daily a revolt in some part of the country.'

Elliot's next move was to appoint a Major John Drinkwater to be Secretary of the Military Department. General Trigge seemed to think that the reason for this was to have someone to make out warrants; Moore saw it as putting someone between the Viceroy and the Commander-in-Chief, thereby lessening the importance of the latter. When Elliot ordered a party of the Corsican battalion to clean the streets of the citadel, Trigge did not see why those soldiers would object, but when the party was assembled and told what they were to do, they said they were employed as soldiers, not scavengers, and refused to do it. This battalion was already rather troublesome and this incident made them worse.

On the evening of 8 March news reached the Viceroy that the French fleet was off Cape Corse. The following morning the news was confirmed by the master of a transport which had been sailing for Leghorn with the line-of-battle ship *Berwick*; they had fallen in with the French fleet, were attacked by two French ships and the *Berwick* was taken. The transport had been a long way behind and despite being fired on managed to make the shore of Cape Corse and escape. A frigate arrived the same day with news that a large convoy for Corsica and other British bases in the Mediterranean was about to leave Gibraltar under convoy of two ships from Hood's old fleet; messages were sent to delay them. The Viceroy was reported to be very alarmed and Moore remarked that he could see no effectual measures being taken to defend the island, 'as if it were impossible that we should ever be attacked'. He thought that the island was defendable if proper measures were taken. As was normal in a situation of neglect, there was a total lack of intelligence; the last from Toulon was that the French fleet was unfit to put to sea and it seemed that this was incorrect. The French were clearly sanguine about attacking the British fleet in the Mediterranean; they would be aware that any action forced on the British fleet, unless the result was total destruction of the French fleet, would result in the British needing to go to Gibraltar to refit, and leaving the Mediterranean open to the French.

By the 16th they had heard nothing of the fleet, it was thought that the French would have taken *Berwick* into Toulon. The general opinion was that the French were about to move against Italy, having loaded 140 transports with men and materiel and headed towards Genoa. The Grand Duke there had ordered a two-week quarantine for ships from Corsica, which would cause much inconvenience as most of the British supplies came from there.

That same day a soldier from the 69th Regiment was to be hanged for robbing a house, having been found guilty at a court martial, a sentence which the Viceroy had announced before the court martial was held. General Trigge sent a message to Moore to the effect that he was going to see the Viceroy. He was back within half an hour; this was far too short a time for the Viceroy to have read the minutes of the proceedings, nonetheless he had signed them, but Trigge told Moore to put it in orders. They could not fix a day for the execution as the hangman was at Corte and had to be sent for. Moore recalled a similar occasion when Stuart was Commander-in-Chief. A court martial had found several men guilty but only one was sentenced to be hanged, the rest to corporal punishment, but General Stuart had taken over an hour to read the court martial minutes, asking questions as he did so. He had then said he would announce his decision in a few days, and when he did so had clearly given the matter a lot of thought. Moore remarked that although it would not be right to reach conclusions without good foundation, he could not help but think that there were other motives than the fact that the man no doubt deserved to be hanged: first that the theft had been from a Corsican ('everything yields to what is Corsican', Moore noted), and secondly, that it demonstrated the Viceroy's power over the army.

News came that the two fleets had met and fought. As a result, two French ships, *Ca Ira* and *Censeur*, had been captured and two others were thought to have sunk while the rest of the French fleet was dispersed. The only British damage was that two ships were dismasted. It was thought that the French were going to land troops in St Fiorenzo Bay. The captain of *Ca Ira* said there was a large body of men embarked at Toulon for the Bay of Rosas and from there to besiege Barcelona; *Ca Ira* carried artillery, camp equipment and a quantity of small arms.

On 25 March, Pozzo di Borgo gave a speech in the Parliament, announcing the victory, and proposing that the House should give thanks to the British officers who had been instrumental in freeing the island from the French. He named admirals Hood and Hotham, General Dundas and Colonel Vilettes. When he had finished his speech, a member stood and remarked that Pozzo di Borgo had forgotten General Stuart, and went on to praise him. Pozzo di Borgo rose again and said that it was true he had forgotten him, an obvious lie. Moore believed this act of meanness brought more honour to Stuart by having him named by the House rather than by the Viceroy's agent. He went on in his journal to villify the Viceroy:

> The fact is that the Viceroy, led by Pozzo di Borgo, allows himself to be actuated by the little, mean, illiberal, revengeful passions of that fellow and his adherents. I can hear of no action of the Viceroy that is not subject to criticism. There is a degree of harshness and want of feeling in them too frequently, which one would not expect who had only a superficial acquaintance with him.

Moore, in the following weeks, continued to describe several more mean actions taken by the Viceroy. Many of these consisted of punishments which would not have been made had the offender not been Corsican, and smacked of offences against Pozzo di Borgo rather than against the State. He did, at least, have the confidence of General Trigge, who shared his view that there was little they could do against the French. There had been a report that the French fleet had been reinforced by five or six ships from Brest which gave them complete superiority in the Mediterranean. Trigge asked Moore what he thought they should do to guard against French attempts to invade. He seemed to take it for granted that St Fiorenzo and Bastia could not be adequately defended with the troops they had available, and asked if, given that they could not be defended, it would be better not to attempt to do so. Moore replied that he thought it most important that they should try and prevent, as long as possible, the French from landing in St Fiorenzo Bay. Although the French would probably come in such numbers that they would eventually succeed in landing, if they saw the obvious posts defended, they would be cautious and slow to move, and might commit blunders which could perhaps be taken advantage of by the British; and at the least it might be possible to prevent them getting to Bastia. Moore then took the liberty of remarking that the Corsicans, seeing that no steps were taken for their defence, were losing confidence in their British allies. Moore knew this from conversations with his Corsican acquaintances, who spoke more freely to him than they would to the Viceroy or the general. It was most important to regain this confidence by taking measures to defend the island, and also by the general showing himself to the militia when they were assembled, making himself known to them, and in their presence giving general directions to their chiefs. Whatever opinion they might have of the Viceroy's abilities in non-military affairs, they certainly had no faith in his military talents, and did not like to see him interfering in those matters. It was also important that Trigge should examine the ground around the Gulf of St Fiorenzo and acquire the thorough knowledge of it that he could not get from mere descriptions.

Trigge agreed to go with Moore and examine the ground round St Fiorenzo. He and the Viceroy went to St Fiorenzo on 17 April by request from Admiral Hotham; Moore followed the next day to find the fleet under way. The admiral had decided to go and wait off Toulon, where he might be able to stop the French coming out, and also would be in position to join any ships arriving from England.

What had been intended by the general as a quiet inspection of the ground turned into a major expedition. After breakfast with the Viceroy, Colonel Green, Captain

Nepean and several others, the whole party set off in two boats and were rowed to a small bay just beyond the one where they had landed in February the previous year. A battery was being erected in that bay to command the first one. Moore wrote, 'When we got ashore much absurd conversation took place, as is always the case in these sort of field councils.' The Viceroy wanted to erect more field batteries along the coast; Moore did not agree, saying, 'You may in this manner go from bay to bay till you get to Calvi ... but with the small force we have, considerable detachments cannot be risked at such a distance from the main body.' It would be better, he thought, 'to guard the bay of St Fiorenzo and the hills which command the towers of Martello and Farinole, the Convention Redoubt'. He pointed out that those hills were extremely inaccessible; if the French landed by the Martello tower it would be to secure the bay for their shipping and they would see how easily the British could oppose them, so they were more likely to attempt a landing on the eastern side of the gulf, somewhere between the tower at Farinole and the town of St Fiorenzo. The moment they appeared, the heights should be occupied by a large body of militia commanded by a trusted British officer.

All this was stated in a firm tone. No one offered to contradict it, few being sufficiently knowledgeable about the terrain to have any real opinions. Nepean, of the Engineers, agreed with Moore, 'and Colonel Green, who had been looking very wise the whole morning, began to look more so than ever'. The Viceroy was not happy that anybody should deliver their thoughts without 'the smallest deference to his opinions'. Moore finished by writing, 'Upon the whole, the scene was rather diverting.' The following morning Moore rode back to Bastia with Trigge, turning off to have a look at part of the eastern coast. Trigge said he had been disturbed by the crowd and suggested returning for a quiet look in a couple of days. They had much conversation on their ride, and Moore remarked later that although Trigge was 'a worthy, even-tempered man', despite between thirty and forty years' service he seemed never to have thought of military matters beyond his own regiment. He lacked confidence and firmness, and was so unused to action that he was not able to execute the actions suggested by others. He disapproved of the Viceroy's interference but had not the manliness to tell him so. Moore feared that between the two of them, they would 'cut a very poor figure' in the event of an attack.

At the end of April there was still no clear news of the French fleet; one day they were said to be reinforced, the next they were not. Despite the imminent danger, the Viceroy had no clear source of intelligence from Toulon. The measures to strengthen the defences of Corsica were proceeding very slowly and Moore thought the only real safety was in a reinforcement of the British fleet. Meanwhile the Viceroy had appointed Lieutenant Colonel Weymes of the 18th Regiment as governor of Calvi; this without consultation with Trigge. Moore rode over the ground between St Fiorenzo and Bastia, and later returned with Major Collier of the Artillery, 'an officer of great zeal and judgement'. They agreed that the country around Murato was the likeliest for the enemy to penetrate. Collier discovered an iron foundry and thought they might be able to cast balls for the artillery as ore was plentiful round Farinole.

Paoli had had two private meetings with the Viceroy but they had been unable to agree. By 16 May, Paoli was speaking openly against the Viceroy. He told Moore he had written home; no doubt the Viceroy had done the same, misrepresenting Paoli, commented Moore.

Towards the end of May, the British fleet continued to cruise, mainly near Minorca. The French had come out with eighteen sail but went back in on hearing the British fleet was about. They had sent two fast gunboats to reconnoitre but these were captured by British frigates. The weather was getting into what they called the sickly season; the Viceroy had brought his wife and children out, but sent them off to Leghorn for their health.

In the middle of June, Moore and Trigge took a two-week tour through the island, visiting the places they had been to before. Calvi had been tidied up and the defences strengthened. Their route took them through the middle of the island, and Moore remarked on the beauty of the scenery:

> Nothing can be more romantic or magnificent … Mountain, wood, water, and rocks are beautifully intermingled. The trees are chiefly pine, evergreen, and white oak, and the chestnut. The produce of the latter is the chief food of the inhabitants of those mountainous regions. We were everywhere received with great hospitality, though we had no recommendations [i.e. letters of introduction]. In the middle of the day we stopped to refresh ourselves and our horses at the village[s], riding up to the house to which the guide directed us, generally that of the podesta or curate. In the evening we did the same, and had everything the houses or villages could afford produced for us. It consisted sometimes of a little mutton, oftener of cheese, milk, bread, wine, and excellent water. The good air and water is what they seem most to value themselves upon, and never fail to tell how much better these are than in the towns or lower parts of the island. Their greatest want is corn; very little grain is produced in the mountains; but the villages of those interior parts all own land, in the plains upon the coast, twenty-five and thirty miles off, which they descend to cultivate, also for the harvest, and return with the produce to the mountains to pass the summer. It is impossible to give a greater proof of the want of population. This want of hands, together with the natural indolence of the inhabitants, is the great cause of the island being so unproductive.

Soon after they returned, the general said he would like to see the locations round Calvi where they had fought the battle for the town. They duly 'refought' the battle before going on to St Fiorenzo where they found Admiral Hotham and the fleet, reinforced by six ships. The 100th Regiment (Gordon Highlanders) had also arrived. The admiral informed Trigge that he had had to arrest a lieutenant of the 11th Regiment, serving as marines on the *Diadem*, for seriously bad behaviour towards the captain of the ship; he was to be tried by court martial. After they had returned to Bastia, the general received a letter from the lieutenant, claiming the general's protection and requesting an army, rather than a navy, court martial. This subject was the source of endless disputes between the two services, particularly in the

Mediterranean, where the fleet's marines were provided almost entirely by men from the army. It was not just the matter of courts martial, there were frequent squabbles between the officers of the two services. Moore had heard of three recent duels and there were other stories of disputes; Moore thought the problem was caused by the haughty behaviour of the naval captains when on their ships. The general wrote to the admiral to stop the court martial, as he thought it would serve to stir up even more disagreement. However, the admiral replied that although he had done what he could to prevent the situation escalating to its current state, now the order for the court martial had been issued it could not be revoked. Moore attended the court martial to which Lieutenant Fitzgerald sent a badly written paper which denied the legality of the court and refuse to plead. Despite this protest, the court called for witnesses for the prosecution. Moore was not able to stay for the full proceedings, which had ended with a sentence of dismissing the lieutenant from the ship and rendering him incapable of holding any military employment. The admiral then requested another army officer to replace him. The general declined, on the grounds that there was no other officer from the 11th Regiment who was not particularly employed, and that he knew of no law, order or precedent that authorised naval courts martial to try officers of the army. He therefore could not consider Lieutenant Fitzgerald dismissed from the service and ordered him to rejoin his regiment. He told Moore that he intended to write home about the proceedings.

At the beginning of August there was more trouble. The Viceroy had been touring the island and at Ajaccio the officers of a battalion of Corsicans decided to hold a ball in his honour. The municipal hall (where the bust of Paoli was displayed) was chosen and the officers met to decide on how to decorate it. The Viceroy's aide-de-camp, Captain Colonna, pointed to the bust saying 'What business has that old charlatan here?' He then threw it in a small closet where some of the officers destroyed it with their stilettos and, as Moore wrote, 'It was pissed upon'. The story of this act spread rapidly through the town and surrounding countryside. The bust was replaced by another belonging to a Mr Peraldi, and by order of the Viceroy, Pozzo di Borgo wrote to Paoli, saying that the story was a calumny: no affront whatsoever had been offered to the bust. This story was not believed and indignation grew; it was thought particularly offensive that the person who had given the affront, not only to Paoli himself, but to the whole Corsican nation, was not punished but allowed to remain in the Viceroy's close service. People began to gather round Paoli; he said he laughed at the incident as it related to himself, but warned Pozzo di Borgo that he should do something to justify their conduct as it related to the whole of the Corsican people. In the meantime the Viceroy returned to Bastia where his entourage affected to know nothing of the story, despite it having been the subject of much conversation and correspondence throughout the island.

Moore had been paying a long-promised visit to Paoli with his friend Colonel Oakes and Colonel Giampietta from Rostino. Paoli received them with great kindness, but while they were there they heard that Pozzo di Borgo and Colonna had been burned in effigy in several local villages. The anger that was manifesting itself in all the towns and villages Moore passed through was aimed not at the Viceroy but at Pozzo di

Borgo. It seemed that the Viceroy was trying to raise a party of those who did not like Paoli, and Moore wrote, 'He would have done better to have governed through [Paoli's] influence. Through him we were received into the country, and to break with him seems to me perfect folly.'

Returning from a social gathering at the citadel, Moore was surprised to see the 100th Regiment getting under arms. On enquiring the reason, he was told that the Corsican battalion was suspected of disaffection and the British regiment at the barracks had been told to be ready to turn out; five cannon were ready loaded with grape and canister. The governor was convinced there might be an insurrection and had ordered guards to be posted at all the gates ready to fire on any body of men coming in from the country. Major Murati of the Corsicans went to see Moore, saying 'all the English are under arms against us. Our people are asleep in their barracks!' Moore thought the Viceroy and his close faction were behaving like children, and told Murati he hoped the Corsican officers would behave like men, keep quiet and take no notice of what they saw.

On the morning of 4 August, General Trigge gave Moore orders for the Corsican battalion to march to Corte; Moore thought they had been very forbearing, and remarked, 'Few corps would have suffered their barracks to be surrounded as theirs were with sentries, more especially as they knew that if they had sent out into the country they would have been supported by whatever number of men they chose'. Their lieutenant colonel and major dined with Moore, and they had seen the Viceroy who, they said, seemed confused and agitated. He had softened matters by asking them to dinner, but said he was determined to support Pozzo di Borgo at all risks. Moore thought that if he had dismissed his aide-de-camp, Captain Colonna, for 'a very foolish mean action, he would have prevented all this uproar. By a series of rash, absurd actions he committed the troops … had the Corsicans been equally intemperate, and one shot been fired, we must have been driven out of the country.'

Although the Corsican battalion marched quietly to Corte, and the situation seemed to have quietened down, the Council advised the Viceroy to dismiss Pozzo di Borgo and to call the Parliament together to quieten the people, he refused to do so, saying he would rather die than give up his friend. From several of the councillors, Moore learned that they thought the Viceroy would stick to Pozzo di Borgo regardless of all advice; they thought the Viceroy was directed by Pozzo di Borgo like a child.

Moore wrote to his mother at the end of August, entrusting his letter to Captain Paul Anderson of the 51st, a young man who was to become one of his closest friends. This letter was brief, hoping that such a visitor would give pleasure to his family in Clifford Street, and commenting, 'I am tired and disgusted with this place' and that if General Stuart had got the command in the West Indies he would have liked to go with him.

There is a small gap in Moore's journal here, with no entries between 11 August and 1 October. By the events he recorded then it is clear that the threat of uprising continued. He was called to see General Trigge, who informed him that the Viceroy had directed him to tell Moore that his support for the people of the island who opposed the Viceroy's views made it impossible to carry on governing if Moore remained on the island. He had written to the Secretary of State that Moore was an exceedingly good officer who could be beneficially employed or promoted elsewhere, but that he could not remain in Corsica. The secretary's answer empowered the Viceroy to send Moore home. The Viceroy intended to do this, unless Moore broke off his connections with those who opposed the Viceroy, and supported the Viceroy's government. Trigge said he was extremely sorry and that he had known nothing about this until the previous night.

Indignant, Moore said that the Viceroy had, by representing falsehoods to the minister and the King, done him an injury: recommending him for promotion and employment elsewhere was absurd. Trigge suggested he thought about it for a while before giving an answer. After several hours of consideration, Moore returned to the general and asked him to say to the Viceroy that he was surprised and felt much injured by his having made such a representation to the King. It was not true and before taking such a step he should at least have told him or the general what he intended. He went on:

> As to the last part of the message, being conscious of no crime or impropriety of conduct, I could promise no change; but I expected before he took any final determination that he would point out more distinctly what he meant or alluded to, that he would allow me an interview, and before the General hear what I had to say.

The following day, Moore went with the general to see the Viceroy. He repeated his surprise at the message he had received, then said that during his whole service he had done his duty to the utmost of his power, that his ambition had always been to distinguish himself and establish his character as an officer. He added that the Viceroy must have been misinformed, for his opinion was unfounded, and that he was at a loss to understand what was meant and asked for more explicit detail. The Viceroy replied that Moore had for a long time appeared to have some personal enmity against him and felt this had affected him severely and thus had found it necessary to ask the Secretary of State to remove him from the island, that he had orders to do so, but would postpone this if Moore would promise to sever all connections with those who opposed him, cease expressing his opinion on the Viceroy's measures and give the government his full support.

Moore replied that he could not promise to approve of measures until he knew what they were and that he believed that as long as he performed his military duties, he was at liberty to give his opinion when these happened to be the subject of conversation and:

> I always had in common with other officers given my opinion upon what was going on, sometimes approving, sometimes disapproving; that neither he nor any other man had any right to extract from me a contrary conduct; and that I would not allow any private interested motive to extract from me a promise which I thought was unbecoming of me to give.

The Viceroy said that he should, in that case, feel himself obliged to execute His Majesty's orders. Moore said that he might send away every officer of the army, but he could not stop officers expressing their opinions of his measures. He felt that the Viceroy's conduct was highly arbitrary and oppressive. He denied the assertion that he had ever taken any part in the politics of this country, and challenged the Viceroy to point out any specific action that authorised the representations he had made. He was not prepared to allow any private interested motive to extract a promise which Moore thought was unbecoming of him to give.

The Viceroy then read part of his public despatch, which stated that Moore had taken part in the politics of this country and that he disapproved of the generality of this, but still more when it was against himself. Moore was so indignant that at times during the half-hour-long meeting he was brought to tears and could not speak. He got up, saying that he supposed Elliot would communicate his determination through the general.

A few hours later Moore received the following two letters:

Bastia, 2nd October. [to Thos Trigge]

Sir, I have the honour to acquaint you, that I have received a despatch from his Grace the Duke of Portland, one of His Majesty's Secretaries of State, commanding me to intimate to Lieutenant-Colonel Moore 'that it is His Majesty's pleasure that he should quit the island in eight and forty hours, or as soon after as a passage can be obtained for him, and that he should come directly home, when his Majesty's further pleasure will be signified to him.'

I am, therefore, to request that you will communicate the same to Colonel Moore in order to his compliance therewith. I have the honour to be, &c. (a true copy),
Signed   Gilbert Elliot.

Bastia, 2nd October 1795. [to Lieutenant-Colonel Moore, Adjutant-General, &c.]

Sir, I enclose the copy of a letter I have received from his Excellency the Viceroy. I have only to say that I am extremely sorry that anything should have occurred to deprive me of so able, and so pleasant an assistant in my military business. I have the honour, &c.
Signed   Thos. Trigge, Lieutenant-General.

Moore settled his business as quickly as he could, and paid a last visit to his regiment in Corte before leaving on 9 October. Paoli had written to him saying that he was also leaving, and proposing that they should travel together, but Moore declined. He landed at Leghorn and set out for Florence, where he wrote briefly to his father while he waited for a carriage to take him and a Mr Barnes overland to Cuxhaven:

If you have received the letter which I wrote to you from Bastia some days ago it will prevent your surprize at the date of this. I have reason however to doubt if you will receive it. In consequence of a representation from Sir Gilbert Elliot to the Secretary of State, that I had taken part in the politicks of Corsica, hostile to him, I received the King's order to return home, there to receive His Majesty's further pleasure. I left Bastia accordingly upon the 9th, landed at Leghorn the 10th, and arrived here yesterday. I hope the day after tomorrow to be able to proceed to Cuxhaven & expect to be in London the first or second week in November.

I can enter into no particulars in a letter which goes by post. I have written to General Stuart – be so good as to call upon him – but endeavour to be quiet till I see you – do not commit me for my line is already determined upon. I do not think in my life I ever did an action unworthy of you, or myself, and least of all does my conscience tell me I deserve blame in the affair which occasions my return – I can say no more – remember me to my mother.

As always, Moore was concerned that his father was not disappointed in him, and that his behaviour was that of a gentleman. With hindsight, however, we can see that his conviction that he was in the right, and his stubborn refusal to change his stance, was likely to make personal enemies.[4]

Chapter 4

West Indies

The island chains of the Antilles were both strategically and economically important. They were 'owned' by the British, the French, Spanish and Dutch, and there was a constant battle to take over islands. As well as the risk of hurricanes and revolt from the slaves, who outnumbered the whites, there were considerable health risks, especially mosquito-borne fevers such as yellow fever and malaria. The islands were of volcanic origin, and were, to a large extent, mountainous with deep ravines, interspersed with flat areas which were cultivated almost entirely with sugar cane. The island of St Lucia is oblong in shape, some 15 miles across at its widest point and a little over 30 miles long, and edged with numerous small coves and bays called 'ances'; the heights between the ravines were known as 'mornes'.*

The sugar was the source of immense wealth for the European planters and their families, and those families wielded great political power. This made for an influential West Indies lobby in Parliament, both in terms of applying pressure on Members of Parliament and family members holding seats in Parliament. When the French Revolutionary War broke out in 1793, it provided a legitimate reason for attacking and taking over certain islands; it also caused great trouble on the islands themselves, as French revolutionary advocates of freedom encouraged the black slaves to rise against their masters, and gave them arms.[1]

* * *

It took Moore a month to get to Cuxhaven; unfortunately he arrived there an hour after the packet had left for England, and was delayed a further ten days until the weather settled and he was able to sail. General Paoli arrived on 17 November and Moore had two long conversations with him, during which Paoli railed against Elliot, calling him the meanest of mankind. Moore asked him why he had agreed to a union and a Viceroy. He replied that he knew the British ministry regarded Corsica as a convenience and intended to abandon it at the peace. He knew Elliot's vanity gave him the desire to be Viceroy, and by flattering him made him commit England to the protection of Corsica. Paoli was now leaving Corsica for good.

Moore finally arrived in London on 25 November and spent the next couple of weeks attending various ministers to whom, he said, it was important he should explain his conduct. Pitt told him that ministers could not refuse to acquiesce with Elliot's request to have him recalled; nobody had done so without regret and he would be happy to hear that Moore was able to justify himself. Moore responded that having been forced to leave Corsica, he could do no more than flatly deny Elliot's accusations. He would feel himself injured unless employed immediately or given some other mark of the King's favour. Pitt told him to see the Duke of Portland, the

Secretary of State, whose business it was to express the King's pleasure; warning him to remain calm when with the Duke and avoid 'the language of passion'.

The Duke repeated what Pitt had said: that it was impossible for ministers not to comply with Elliot's request, but that it had by no means affected Moore's military character. Moore responded that it was difficult for people to make that distinction, and that he felt it somewhat cavalier to dismiss an officer on such grounds without a trial. He felt it as an insult and expected to be employed immediately as a mark of the King's approbation. The Duke said nothing useful on that front, and Moore thought he was embarrassed by the situation. Seeing that he was not going to get anything specific from the Duke at that time, Moore retired. Despite this stance on the part of the ministers, Moore knew that the Duke of Portland was surprised at Elliot's behaviour and was determined to speak to the King and get Moore employed. He remarked wryly that 'Sir Gilbert's character is not altogether unknown in this country. General Stuart and some others of my friends assist in justifying me. On the whole, he will find he could have done nothing less politic than to send me home'.

A few days after seeing the Duke of Portland, Moore paid a visit to Henry Dundas, who gave him a good reception, listened to all Moore had to say and remarked that Elliot had on several occasions displayed a degree of jealousy. If he wished to be employed, he would.

Shortly after this Moore was given the temporary rank of Brigadier General in the West Indies, and was attached to a brigade of foreign corps assembling in the Isle of Wight. He paid a brief visit to Bath to see the Duke of Hamilton, of whom he said tactfully that he was much altered, and in 'a most deplorable state of health', so bad that Moore actually wondered if this might be the last time he would see him. The Duke had succumbed to the addiction of alcohol.

Moore arrived on the Isle of Wight on 23 December and moved to Newport the following day, where he fixed his quarters. His first official act was to get the two regiments of his brigade landed from their transports and quartered ashore. The regiment of Choiseul (Hussars) was already in Newport. This regiment of French émigrés were extremely good, officers and men alike, and was commanded by the Baron de la Chassague, an old officer who knew his business perfectly. From this regiment Moore acquired a servant who was to remain with him for the rest of his life: François David. A few days later Moore ordered the Uhlans Britanniques, a corps of light cavalry commanded by Comte Louis de Bouille, to land. Moore thought the officers of this corps a set of the most gentlemanly and handsome men he ever saw. After living with those two regiments he wrote that he could not be happier with any British regiments. The Uhlans were not attached to Moore's brigade, and they soon marched off to Lymington. Lord Cathcart was appointed to command all the foreign corps assembled at Newport and Southampton.

There was little society in Newport. The lieutenant colonel, Major Compte des Vieux and Capitan Compte de la Rochefoucault usually dined with Moore at the Gun Inn; Moore often invited some of the other officers to join them. They had given some balls, which were attended by the local families. The women in the island were generally good looking, as were the young French officers, who were also polite and fond of dancing, which, although they spoke little English, endeared them to the local ladies.

He wrote to his mother to bring her up to date. He was sorry to have missed Christmas dinner with the family, but hoped to be able to do so the following year. He had, however, found their friends the Minchins at Cowes and dined with them and also met them at a ball in Cowes: 'the youngest Minchin, in spite of her teeth a pretty girl, was the chief Belle ...'; it seemed he was somewhat pickier than his optimistic mother when contemplating prospective wives. He then asked his mother to organise some domestic supplies for him: a dozen hand towels and eight or ten tablecloths, half a dozen to cover a table such as was used at Clifford Street, and the same number for a table of eight people for dinner. Later he asked her to arrange for his trunk to be sent to him care of Harlands Hotel, Southampton, and to get brother Charles to send any letters which had arrived at Clifford Street to Frank, who would be able to send them on free (a privilege given to some government servants).

In November, part of the expeditionary force left for the West Indies, led by Admiral Christian. This consisted of 8 sail of the line and 10 lesser warships escorting 12 navy victuallers, 11 ordnance storeships, 4 hospital ships and 110 transports carrying 18,742 soldiers, plus many merchant ships taking advantage of the naval protection. They got as far as the Scilly Isles when a major storm struck; a few ships managed to gain the shelter of Torbay, but many were dispersed up the Channel, even as far as The Downs (the anchorage off the east coast of Kent). In the morning less then 100 ships were still together. Christian ordered the fleet back to Plymouth; on 12 December they set out again with 218 ships, only to encounter a further violent storm just west of the Scilly Isles. Many of these ships were damaged and had to put in to Plymouth for repairs; only 177 were fit to carry on.[2]

This was not the first time a military expedition had gone to the West Indies. In 1793, a combined force headed by Admiral Jervis (later to be the Earl of St Vincent) and the 64-year-old General Grey had taken several of the islands, but had then blotted their copybooks by parcelling out various lucrative positions to their relatives and close friends. This created such a scandal that when General Abercromby was given his instructions as Commander-in-Chief of the 1795–6 expedition, they contained a clause expressly forbidding such nepotism.[3]

During February, Moore was directed to move with all the foreign regiments to a site near Southampton, vacating space on the Isle of Wight for part of General Abercromby's troops.[4] The worst of Moore's regiments were embarked under Brigadier General Perryn, to Moore's relief, but he was pleased to be on the mainland, as this made it easier if he wanted to visit London. This was not to be, as just as he was setting out from Portsmouth, he received the order to embark with the foreign troops, expected to sail immediately. He had nothing with him but his portmanteau and seven shirts; although he had asked for his trunk to be forwarded from Southampton, it would not arrive before he sailed. He hoped to be able to buy 'a dozen or two shirts for the voyage', and asked his mother to send a message to Rymer the shoemaker in Cockspur Street to finish his short boots as soon as possible, and send them to Portsmouth by the coach, enclosing his bill which he would pay immediately. The following day he wrote to his father adding a further commission for his mother: saddles from Gibson in Coventry Street, in the Haymarket.

He had not been allocated a ship for his passage, but found one for himself, on the *John and James* transport, where in preference to joining some artillery officers who were strangers to him, he accepted an invitation to join the captain and an agent of transports to share their mess. He remarked in another letter to his mother on the 28th, 'We shall do very well, and I feel as if I should cut no despicable figure, presently, on a piece of roast beef which I heard the Captain order.' He added that he had been able to buy fifteen shirts, some stockings and bedding, then asked for messages to be passed to his sister, Jean and, if his father should visit him, General Stuart. They were, he finished, going through the Needles with a fair wind and hoped to reach the trade winds in ten or twelve days. However, there had been no transports ready for Moore's 'foreign' regiments, and they were thus going to be delayed six weeks or two months. So when he arrived in the West Indies he would find himself without an immediate command.

They reached Barbados on 13 April, anchoring in Carlisle Bay mid-afternoon. Admiral Cornwallis was not with them, his ship having run down a transport in the Channel, sinking the transport; more than 100 soldiers were drowned. Cornwallis' ship received a little damage, and had to return to Portsmouth. Moore dined with Abercromby (he called him 'Sir Ralph'), telling him he wished to be employed and would accept whatever command Abercromby wished to give him. Abercromby said he could depend on being employed.

The assembled troops were beginning to depart for other islands. The troops for St Domingo were ordered to be ready to sail immediately under Brigadier General Howe, with Moore listed in Howe's orders as commanding the foreign cavalry. He believed this was a mistake, as Abercromby had not mentioned this to Moore. He went to see Abercromby who confirmed that it was a mistake; Abercromby later that day told the Adjutant General that he intended to send Moore as second-in-command to St Vincent. On hearing of this, Moore went to see Abercromby again, thanking him for the opportunity of employment, but stressing that he would prefer to serve under Abercromby himself. He thought this would give him better experience than going to St Vincent. Abercromby replied that his purpose had been for Moore to assist General Hunter who had been unwell, but principally to give him experience of the country before he arrived with the rest of the army. But since he preferred to go with the main army, Abercromby was happy to agree to it. His intention was to go to St Lucia and after taking that island, he would divide the army between St Vincent and Grenada to take those islands also.

While he waited for his instructions, Moore wrote a long letter to his father, bringing him up to date with his movements and prospects, and adding a warning: 'Any of your friends who have West Indies property had better dispose of it; for whatever our success, that property must be finally annihilated.'

On 19 April Abercromby sent for Moore, who found him with the various generals, giving them their dispositions and instructions for the attack on St Lucia. Moore was attached to Major General Campbell's division, which was to land first. The whole army was to go to St Anne's Bay, Martinique, where arrangements were to be finalised before sailing for St Lucia. This plan seems to have come from Admiral Laforey, and

Abercromby was not so keen. Moore sailed on the East Indiaman *Valentine*, having been invited to do so by the quartermaster general Brigadier General Knox; he was accompanied by his friend Captain Anderson, who he had named as his brigade major.[5] Just as they left, there was a signal for an approaching admiral; this turned out to be Admiral Christian, in a frigate. He was bringing the remainder of the troops in a convoy, but had shifted his flag to the frigate soon after sailing from England and come on alone.

The fleet arrived in St Anne's Bay on the evening of 23 April; some ships had missed the bay and were carried away to leeward, an ordnance sloop was lost and the seventy-four-gun *Minotaur* had run aground. Moore, with several other officers, could not understand why it had been necessary to go to Martinique, nor, given that Admiral Christian also disapproved, why he had not changed the plan as soon as he had the overall naval command. Once all the final arrangements had been made, Moore moved to the seventy-four-gun *Ganges*, in order to be with Major-General Campbell and his command of the Grenadiers, 14th, 42nd and 48th regiments. They were to land at Ance le Cap, advance to Longueville House with two light guns and a howitzer, then to move on in two columns, one to the right along the coast to the village of Grosislet, the other to the left to Balman. They were then to reunite on the Chemin Royale and destroy the batteries at Trouillac and Brelotte which commanded the anchorage in Choc Bay where Abercromby was to land the rest of the army. General Morshead was to fall down to the southward of the island with 1,800 or 1,900 men, to land his men in Ance le Raye, occupy the heights north of the river Mascarries and if possible to establish himself on the Morne Petit. In the event, the ships carrying the 14th and 42nd regiments arrived first. The other ships were some way off, but as no enemy appeared, it was decided to land the two available regiments immediately, before the enemy had time to assemble and resist. Moore accompanied the regiments, and on reaching the shore took a position favourable for defence and to cover the rest of the landing troops. Longueville House was ¼ mile to his front and he ordered 150 Jägers to go and occupy it as it was a strong place for an advance post.

Several enemy skirmishing parties appeared and attacked the Jägers, killing one and injuring seven. General Campbell arrived, saying he saw no possibility of moving on until the next day, as the Grenadiers, 48th Regiment and the artillery would all be late reaching shore. Then a letter arrived from Abercromby, saying that the Admiral was not ready to co-operate, so he wanted to defer the landing. Since it was already partly done, it would be dangerous to re-embark, as would be deferring their march to Trouillac, especially since the enemy was aware of their presence; 'they might therefore assemble, attack and tease us upon our march, perhaps completely impede it', said Moore. As they were certain to be joined that evening by the Grenadiers, 48th and artillery, he gave a strong recommendation to Campbell that they should post picquets at sunset as though they intended to stay the night, but to get everything ready and march when the moon rose. The general had written to Abercromby for orders, a letter carried by Captain Hay who would suggest the night march to Abercromby.

Hay returned with authority to march whenever Campbell wished; Campbell was extremely ill, and asked Moore to give the necessary orders for the march. The other corps had landed and joined them and they began the march at 3 am. The Grenadiers led off, followed by the howitzer; Moore remained in the rear with the 14th and some Jägers. About a mile from their starting point at Longueville the Grenadiers encountered a small force of the enemy, which fired and fled. No other shots were fired. At about 11 o'clock they were informed that the batteries at Trouillac and Brelotte had been abandoned. The fleet came into the bay and the Admiral and Abercromby landed immediately followed by some of the troops that evening. The enemy could be seen at Angiers House; Abercromby ordered the Grenadiers and a gun to advance and the enemy promptly retired. Abercromby and the staff and some of the principal officers assembled there; he and Moore went forward to reconnoitre after which Moore posted some picquets on the heights.

Soon after he returned, Moore was presented with the following order:

G.O. Angiers House, 27th April 1796.

A detachment of 500 rank and file of the 53rd Regiment including their two flank companies, 280 of the 57th including the light company, 100 of Lowenstein's corps, 200 of Malcolm's, will be ready to parade this night at 12 o'clock. One division, consisting of the 53rd Regiment, 50 of Lowenstein's, and 100 of Malcolm's, under the command of Brigadier-General Moore, to march as soon as they are ready after twelve o'clock. The 2nd division, consisting of the 57th, 50 of Lowenstein's, and 100 of Malcolm's, under the command of Brigadier-General Hope, to march half-an-hour after the first. The object of this attack is to drive the enemy from Morne Chabot, and as any communication between the columns in this country is difficult, the column under Brigadier-General Hope will not begin to act till the attack on the left has commenced; when the troops are masters of Morne Chabot 500 men will be posted there, and the remainder of the force will extend themselves towards the left of La Feuillay's, or farther if possible. Messrs. La Feuillay and Babinet will accompany the first as guides, Bravet and La Force the second.

(Signed)   John Hope,
                                                                Adjutant-General.

Not surprisingly, Moore was very tired, but before he could rest, he had to see Abercromby, talk to the guides and pass on orders to the junior officers. They began their march at midnight, with a bright moon. Lieutenant Colonel Ross of the 21st Regiment was acting as aide-de-camp to Abercromby; they accompanied Moore on the march. The path was so narrow they could only march 'but one man in front', as Moore put it; this meant they could only go slowly with frequent halts to prevent the column from separating. The guides had said they would get out of the trees about half a mile from the Morne Chabot, from there the going would be easier, and close to the Morne it should be quite smooth. Moore's plan was to wait at the edge of the wood for dawn. Just before 4 am, while still on the narrow path in the wood, the small advance party of an officer and six men were challenged and fired on by a sentry; five or six other sentries challenged and fired. The advance party fell back, as instructed. Although this would prevent the planned meeting with Brigadier General Hope, Moore did not want to stay where they were in country that was unknown to them but familiar to the enemy, so gave the order to push on and attack.

As the path widened, a picquet of some forty or fifty men at the edge of the wood fired on them; some of Moore's men fell but they advanced and drove the picquet back. Moore ordered the Grenadiers to form up at the front, and the Light Infantry to cover them, then 'desired' Ross to stay and form up the other companies as they arrived. The guides had left at the first fire, leaving him uncertain on the ground to attack; a guide was found and brought up to point out the best way to go. The ground was fairly smooth in front and sloped away to the left; on the right was a thick hedge which Moore feared might be lined with the enemy. Telling the Grenadiers not to fire but to use their bayonets, they advanced again, following the hedge for a couple of hundred yards. They came up to a wood in front, then found a fence in the hedge; beyond that was the road, according to the guide. The fence was too strong to pull down so Moore ordered the men to jump over it and gave them a lead by getting over it himself. When they were all over and reformed, they found the enemy in front of them drawn up on top of the hill. Their fire was very effective, killing or wounding some seventy or eighty men and officers, including Brigade Major Anderson who was shot as they reached the summit. Despite Moore's repeated efforts to induce them to use the bayonet, his men began firing; but when they did reach the summit the bayonets were used on those of the enemy who had not fled. There were seventeen or eighteen dead enemy, as many laying wounded and probably as many wounded who had crawled off into the woods. The routes of escape were littered with discarded arms.

After the attack, Moore commented on the men's performance:

In this attack the men showed no want of spirit; no man ever offered to show his back, but [they] showed great want of discipline and confidence in their officers, and against an enemy of experience we must have failed. A failure would have been destruction. Through such a country there was no retreat. The men of our regiments are mere recruits, the officers young, and without either zeal or experience. With such troops success must ever be doubtful, and, upon this occasion nothing but the great exertions of a few officers at the head of the column caused the attack to succeed.... The consequences of failure were strongly imprinted on my mind; besides it was my *coup d'essai* in an army where I was unknown, and upon success my character would be judged.

He also commented that at one point providence had thrust a Grenadier into his arms just in time to receive the ball aimed at him 'I do not think ... I ever ran more personal danger'.

He sent a party forward to warn Hope that they were in possession; he had pushed forward when he heard the firing and was at the bottom of the hill wondering how to move when he had heard the firing cease. Moore ordered a drum to beat the Grenadiers' march, and they gave a cheer. As day broke, Hope joined Moore. His original orders were to leave 500 men on Morne Chabot, and press to the left with the rest, but he and Hope saw a commanding hill called Morne de Chasseur which would give a communication with Major General Morshead on Morne Petit, and facilitate the approach to the Morne Fortuné. Moore decided to attack it immediately, before the enemy recovered from their panic and saw its importance. He sent Ross back to Abercromby, to report events and to explain why they were attacking before the agreed time. Asking Hope to accompany him, they set out. The road was so bad that it took 3 hours to cover the 3 miles but on reaching their destination Moore saw that the position was even better than he had thought. Below the Morne de Chasseur was a ridge extending towards the Morne Fortuné: on one side was the Valley du Grand Cul de Sac and on the other, Castries. He left most of his force on the ridge, and put advanced posts up to within 1,200yd of the Morne Fortuné. In the evening, the enemy put advance posts within 700yd of Moore's.

Despite his tiredness from four days of strenuous activity, due to the undependable officers, Moore and Hope had to patrol the whole night; Moore even found one picquet asleep, not a desirable situation with the enemy so close. That morning, Moore received a note from Abercromby, praising their efforts. On the whole, said Abercromby, the conduct of the troops had been commendable, and he asked Moore to give them his thanks publically. General Morshead had landed, and Abercromby intended to move the 55th and 42nd regiments to Morne Chabot straight away, with the rest of the 53rd and 57th following. He intended to open up enough of a road to Morne Chabot for a few light field guns, and would endeavour to send the wounded to a hospital ship. The messenger also said Abercromby was at Morne Chabot and wished Moore to go and see him. He then went back with Moore to see the post; from there they could see Morshead's troops on the Morne Petit. Abercromby was anxious to destroy the enemy batteries which commanded the bay of the Grand Cul de Sac, so the fleet could anchor there and help complete the investment of the Morne Fortuné.

This was not a speedy affair, but Moore's men were housed in wigwams, providing shelter from the sun and some of the rain. They could find plenty of vegetables and had no means of obtaining alcohol apart from the regular allowance and thus were perfectly healthy. Moore continued to stay up all night going round the picquets; the enemy fired at them occasionally and two Jägers had been killed by shell. A long skirmish at Grons ended with several officers and forty or fifty men killed or wounded. On 7 May, the 3rd and 42nd regiments joined Moore, and with them came an order to hold the light company of the 57th and 200 of Colonel Maitland's corps to be ready to march. That evening Hope arrived and said that a combined attack was fixed for that evening on the enemy's batteries on the side of the Cul de Sac. He and the troops listed above were to attack the Seche battery and spike the guns. Morshead in two columns was to attack the battery Ciceron; if successful the two groups were to join up and take a position between Morne Fortuné and the sea.

Hope moved out at midnight; at 3 am Moore commenced firing on the enemy's picquets to attract their attention. After an anxious night, dawn brought the sight of the British troops retreating through the valley of Cul de Sac, under attack from all sides. The country was woody, which exposed the troops to harassment, but Hope got to his place before full daylight and sent Colonel Malcolm to attack the battery. He was killed before he reached it, but his men got in and managed to turn the guns on the enemy. They had no spikes with them and so could not spike those guns, and were soon driven from the battery. Colonel Riddel, with one of Morshead's columns, gained one of the batteries he was ordered to attack, but since he was not supported by the other column, which had failed to cross the river, had to retire. Morshead's column, which was supposed to have supported the other two, had been given to Brigadier General Perryn, as Morshead had the gout. Perryn, seeing that the men were tired from their march to the river, had not crossed, leaving Riddel and Hope in the lurch. They had all retired to Morshead's camp, with a loss of more than 100 officers and men. Of this, Moore reported laconically, 'The Commander in Chief is, I understand, infinitely displeased.' Displeased, but probably not surprised, as he had previously referred to Perryn as a madman.[6]

General Perryn was ordered to hold himself in readiness to sail with the foreign troops to St Domingo; General Graham was sent to command the left wing at Morne Petit, Hope commanded the right of the right wing and Moore the left. Large bodies of soldiers and seamen were busy making roads and bringing up mortars, with the intention of creating batteries for ten guns and two mortars. It was hoped that with such an amount of ordnance playing on them, although at a considerable distance, the enemy might surrender or at least be so fatigued that an assault might be successful. There was also to be a chain of posts set up to surround them in case they tried to escape, but this required reinforcement by the troops newly arrived from England, who were expected hourly from Barbados.

With little of a military nature going on, Moore had time to comment on other matters. Abercromby, he reported, was very short-sighted, needing a glass to observe the terrain. Although 60 years old, he had 'the zeal and eagerness of youth, and much activity both of mind and body'. As for the country, he thought the parts he had seen were very beautiful; they were mountainous and heavily wooded. He considered the position of his post to be 'very romantic' and from its height, much cooler than he had expected. The ground produced, with no or little effort, a variety of vegetables 'of the potato kind' and greens 'as delicate as spinach'; fruit was in great abundance, especially pineapples. The plantations were mainly deserted, only a few occupied by women. He was surprised that no one from the enemy had joined them, despite their having been on shore for two weeks.

The regiments from Barbados arrived on 9 May, the howitzers on the 11th. Batteries were erected for them in advance of Moore's position. The enemy had a 6-pounder, from which they fired grape; one of Moore's men lost a leg to this. The enemy continued skirmishing, but only at a distance from Moore's post. On the 14th, Abercromby came up and was not pleased to find that the line of communication with General Graham was not completed. This surprised Moore as he had reported that all that was needed was a properly directed working party. Abercromby also found fault because the Royal Étrangers were, he said, 'huddled' on the plain; what he could not see with his poor eyesight, was that the plain was covered with impenetrable vegetation, including sugar cane. He was just in a bad mood. Moore went with Captain Hay to visit General Graham's post. He, too, was discontented and full of arguments, none of which related to his having failed to go lower with his troops; worse, the comments were expressed at the dining table, which was not the accepted place for such matters. Before he left for this meeting, Moore had ordered the sugar cane to be burned.

The road which had been started the day before should be finished, the batteries were finished and firing commenced, but it was badly aimed and had little effect; the enemy fired back with three mortars and seven guns. Similar events went on for two more weeks: advance and retreat, spiking guns, a near 'friendly fire' incident. Colonel Count d'Heilimer exceeded his instructions and first sent a reconnoitring party to Morne Fortuné, which got too close and fell in with a party of the enemy who killed or wounded four officers and twenty men, then that same evening d'Heilimer not only sent out picquets as instructed, but also sent a company to take possession of the height which was already occupied by another British picquet. Fortunately the officer in charge of this picquet, Major Inglis, who was about to fire on a group of the enemy, held his fire until the enemy were closer, otherwise the Count would have found himself in between two fires. When Moore went to see if it would be possible to retain the ground they had gained, he saw that trying to hold it would only mean more loss of his men, so he ordered them to retire.

News came, with a visit from Abercromby, that an attempt on the Vigie by the 31st and Grenadiers had failed with the loss of some 170 men. This attack had been planned in a hurry and carried out without, as Moore said, 'spirit or judgment. The regiments in general are extremely bad; it is hard to say whether the officers or men are worse.' Abercromby and other officers were disappointed that the efforts of the Artillery had not been greater. Moore pointed out to them that when posts cannot be assaulted but only taken by cannon, it took more time. At Calvi, where the terrain was more difficult than where they were, it had taken more than two months, but the ordnance there were 13in mortars, 26-pounder guns and 10½in howitzers. The difference in labour to bring such armament up was trifling, but the effect was very different. Moore added to Abercromby that another major difference would be made if he stayed at Moore's post as he would be able to see events as they happened and give appropriate orders; it would also inspire zeal in the men. Abercromby replied that it was not personal convenience that had kept him away, but a desire to be near the admiral, but he would move up straight away. Moore responded that taking the Morne was the greatest objective, above all other considerations. Although it was supposed to be a combined operation, all the admiral could actually do at that stage was land 1,000 soldiers or sailors, and keep his frigates cruising to prevent the enemy landing supplies, which, they had been told by a prisoner, were running low.

On 19 May, a road had been made under cover from the battery Moore had taken the day before to one of the advanced howitzer batteries. Abercromby arrived, took Moore aside and told him that Captain Hay had told him he had wished Brigadier General Knox to join him; Abercromby did not intend to supersede him, but thought he might be fatigued and in need of rest. Moore replied that he was by no means fatigued and did not wish to be relieved, but as they were about to move some men to the left, an officer needed to be appointed to direct it, as he could not be in two places at once. Knox was a good sensible officer, which was why he had mentioned him to Hay, and there was certainly no jealousy involved. A couple of days later Knox appeared in orders to command the advanced posts. Some found this strange (those who could not understand why anyone would apply to have a senior officer put over them), but Moore felt that in times so lacking in zeal and talent, it was better to serve under him than to lose him to a post elsewhere. Moore and Knox soon got to know each other and carried on in harmony.

They had planned to attack and carry the enemy's outposts on 22 May. Everything was ready, but they had no powder for the batteries, so had to postpone the attack. Then it rained hard, destroying the road and making it impossible to bring up the 24-pounders. Finally on the 24th, they were ready and commenced firing on the Morne. When they had fired sufficiently to dislodge whatever troops were there, Moore and Lieutenant Colonel Drummond with the Light Infantry and Grenadiers advanced. They had not expected any resistance, but were fired on by thirty or forty men at the *flêche*.* Moore saw that the other parts of the fort could not fire on it for fear of hitting their own men so he ordered the two companies to attack it. The enemy abandoned it as they advanced, and some of Moore's men worked rapidly to reverse its direction. Other work teams were busy clearing a road for cannon.

Moore went to hurry up the Engineer work parties and to report to Abercromby. He found him in one of the batteries, and as they spoke they saw a body of the enemy marching out of the fort towards the post he had just taken. Orders were sent to the most commanding batteries to fire on them; Moore ran to the post which was attacked almost immediately. He sent a detachment to reinforce a party he had posted on the left flank, but they they had been unable to occupy the ground he had directed. The enemy had cover and were clever in using it; their fire was brisk and well directed and the British men were falling fast. He ordered the Grenadiers and Light Infantry to charge; Colonel Drummond led them, cut down an officer with his sword and drove them back with bayonets. He had only just returned when the enemy reinforced their party and attacked a second time. Moore ordered another company to advance and line a hedge to his left but they did this rather badly; their fire from that position should have been able to scour the dip which would give cover to the enemy, letting them advance as close as 20yd. They took advantage of the hedge not being properly lined and attacked boldly, and being in superior numbers to the British, knocked down so many Moore began to dread they must give way. He knew the general was watching close by, and expected a gun to arrive, or a movement of troops from the left. This did not happen, and he begged Brigadier General Hope, who happened to be with him when the attack started, to go back to tell Abercromby of the dangerous situation they were in and begged for more troops to at least show themselves on the left.

After Hope had left, matters became more serious. The Grenadiers and Light Infantry had suffered too much to charge again, so Moore told Colonel Gilman that

---

* An arrow-shaped outwork on a fortification.

two companies were needed to charge again or the post would be lost. Two were duly ordered in and performed gallantly, being obliged to advance in file and then form up under fire. Captain Dunlop at their head was wounded almost instantly and Major Wilson was killed while making the charge. The enemy, although superior in fire power, could not stand the bayonet and took off. Gilman took two companies from the rear and went to line the hedge on the left, sending back the companies which had been there before and were badly cut up. Moore then called back those who had charged as they were exposed to the guns of the fort. The enemy retreated to the fort, leaving many dead, some of whom they dragged away, as they did their wounded. Moore ordered the houses in front of the fort to be burned, and asked Captain Hay to take advantage of the moment to dig trenches and make abattis in front of the post, without these defences they could easily be overrun in a third attack.

The grape from the fort gradually slackened, and after a while parties began to come out with stretchers for the killed and wounded, demonstrating that they had no intention of an immediate attack. Moore went back to see Abercromby and to enforce the need for trenches and securing the safety of the post. The general thanked Moore for his exertions, Moore replying that saving the post was due to the gallantry of the 27th Regiment, but they had lost 120 in killed and wounded, including 8 officers.

At dusk an officer came from the fort with a letter stating that they had written to the general and admiral, requesting a cessation of activities until noon on the following day to allow them to assemble a council to consider their affairs. Previously they had sent a letter asking how they would be treated if they surrendered. Moore understood that the answer had been 'as prisoners of war'. The cessation of activity was granted and the general and admiral awaited the answer with impatience. Moore thought the attack of the previous day was a desperate last effort and that as it had not succeeded and they realised that batteries would be built even closer to them, the enemy could do little but capitulate. After some negotiation, they did so.

Abercromby gave Moore the honour of taking possession of the fort on 26 May at the head of the 14th, 27th, flank companies of the 53rd, detachments of the Royal Artillery, Navy and Lowensteins Jägers. They formed a line from the gate and the garrison of some 2,000 men (mostly black or men of colour) marched out, laid down their arms, and were taken to Vigie and put on board transports.[7] Moore met with General Cottin and Representative Goyrand; Cottin, formerly a saddler in Guadaloupe, was, he thought, 'a hot-headed, insolent blackguard' but Goyrand a plain military man risen from the ranks.

Abercromby sent a message to Moore by Brigadier General Knox, saying that he intended to recommend strongly to the King those officers who had exerted themselves on the expedition and Moore in particular; he was at a loss for a proper officer to leave in command at St Lucia and 'would take it as a particular favour' if he would remain, as governor and commandant of the island. Some flattering comments were added, and Abercromby said he would leave Moore 3,000 troops. Moore had suspected a few days previously that this was coming and had mentioned it to Hope, asking him to prevent it if possible 'and state how disagreeable it would be', adding 'of all things I dislike a garrison'. He did not wish to remain in the West Indies after the war, preferring to stay with the army. He repeated all this to Knox, who said that Abercromby was so eager for Moore to remain that he would be disappointed if he did not. Moore saw that it would be pointless to refuse and thus accepted. At their next meeting Abercromby thanked him for his efforts, and granted all his requests, including a company for Brigade Major Anderson.

By 3 June, the general and the admiral sailed, initially to the island of Carriacou and then to St Vincent. They left two line-of-battle ships and some frigates, as well as some 4,000 or 5,000 men fit for duty, besides officers, sergeants and drummers. These consisted of the 31st, 44th, 48th, 55th York Rangers, O'Meara's black corps, 100 Royal Artillery, two engineers and their assistants. They also left, as well as all the guns mounted in batteries, quantities of ordnance and ammunition which were intended to have been embarked with the army. The ammunition and provisions for Moore's current post were left in Castries and had to be brought up; this was made more difficult as the rainy season had commenced. They lacked cover for some two-thirds of the troops, and although the fort at Morne Fortuné had surrendered, Vieux Fort had yet to be taken. There were many armed blacks in the woods all over the island and the prisoners were still in transports in the Carenage. To add to all this, the men were falling sick and there was no room in the hospitals for them. Moore was not pleased, writing:

> The General and Admiral think they have cleared themselves from all trouble by running away from it. They have, however, hurt their character as military men. The moment the fort had surrendered large detachments under proper officers ought to have been detached to different parts of the island to encourage and support the proprietors and disarm the blacks. A week or ten days would probably have done this; in the meantime the rest of the army might have been employed in dismantling the batteries we erected, destroying roads, and embarking the stores and artillery with method. All this could have been done, and the expedition to Grenada and St. Vincent not retarded ten days. These ten days would have secured a conquest which it took an army of 11,000 men a month to make. As it is, the island is left in the most precarious state. I wrote to the General before he went, stating the situation in which he had left me, that I should not be deterred by difficulties, but, should however any misfortune happen, I desired he would recollect my situation and shame me only in proportion to my deserts.

One of his first acts as governor was to issue a proclamation of pardon for all people who would come in with their weapons. He issued passes to encourage all the inhabitants to return to their homes, assuring them of protection if they stayed quiet and attended to their personal affairs only. He announced that there should be no aspersions cast against those who had been republicans and that he would not tolerate ill treatment of Negroes, nor further disturbances. It was, he said, better to leave the ownership of the island to the negotiations at the end of the war than to try to bring about change by arms, which he would resist to the full strength of his power. The government remained a military one, and the administration of justice was vested in the commandant.

On 2 July Moore reported that he had been too busy to keep his journal. He had a large force, but a lack of good officers meant that the size of the force was actually an embarrassment. It had rained solidly for the whole month since Abercromby left, and that, combined with a lack of proper accommodation and proper regimental care and economy, had left a force so sickly that the three regiments on the Morne Fortuné had only between 600 and 700 men fit for duty. He had written a long private letter to Abercromby:

> giving him my opinion fully respecting my situation and the character of those under me, showing the necessity of a change in the departments; that in particular the person immediately junior to me, instead of being an assistance, was a man so completely absurd and wrong-headed that I dreaded leaving the fort, though my presence in the country was necessary.

There were 200 engineers, under the command of Major Shipley, at work on the fort, enclosing it and securing it against a sudden assault. This, together with removal of baggage and the sick, as well as the usual garrison duties, had kept the troops busy. However, they still needed more hands for the work, and ideally 150 more black pioneers. There were also problems with the custom house, which, wrote Moore to Abercromby:

> gives me a great deal of trouble owing to the want of people conversant in the business. Mr Duthie who was not appointed collector from his supposed knowledge of that branch, or with one idea that he should be required to do the duty of it is however the only person who acts at all. Mr McLean the Comptroller is incapable, a Naval Officer & Searcher are indispensable. I beg leave to recommend Mr James Barclay as Naval Officer & Mr Jno Woolsey as Searcher. Those gentlemen are upon the spot and from necessity are employed in those capacities, which they are in all respects capable of filling.

Moore had been receiving daily reports of the damage being done by the escaped slaves in the south-west of the island, in the woods near the towns of Soufrière* and Vieux Fort. The inhabitants were demanding troops, which Moore thought they hoped would help them tyrannise the blacks, something he was not prepared to allow. He spent a week visiting these areas; remarking that the country was less mountainous and much more beautiful and fertile in the north near Castries and the Morne Fortuné. The four coastal towns (Soufrière, Choisseul, Laborie and Fort Vieux) were neat and healthy. He spoke to many of the locals who had left their homes for the safety of the towns, reassuring them that he would place troops to protect their plantations, and urging them to return; he told them that they would be safer if they treated their slaves with more kindness, reminding them that men who had been free would not wish to return to slavery and hard labour. But if they did so, and were treated decently, the others who were still in the woods would be more likely to join them.

He expressed these opinions at public meetings as well as privately, which did not please the French émigrés. He found them insolent and treated them no differently

---

* Not to be confused with the volcano of the same name on the island of Monserrat.

than any others. 'I observe,' he wrote, 'that those people, instead of profiting by their misfortunes, seem only to have increased their prejudices, and in their banishment pant for the moment to gratify their revenge and tyrannise over their fellow-creatures.'

At Vieux Fort Moore found that Rupez Roche, who had been supporting the brigands, had been arrested. He owned property on the island and was considered clever but of an ambitious temperament; Moore sent for him and he started to justify his conduct, mainly by protestations of innocence, delivered in a theatrical manner. Moore was not impressed, told him he would be tried, and sent him off to the naval commodore at Castries to remain prisoner on the ship. There were still many brigands infesting the land between Vieux Fort and Soufrière. Known as the plain, it was only a plain in comparison with the mountains, consisting of irregular ground with ridges and steep ravines. It was generally fertile, growing sugar, cotton, coffee and cocoa, which were easily taken to the coast and its many small bays where it could be embarked. The 'plain' was generally about 5 miles wide, and the houses extended right up to the wooded mountains which provided cover for the armed Negroes who sallied out to murder and plunder. Moore set up a line of posts, with patrols going between them. They were to be occupied by two separate detachments; Major Lindsay with five companies of the 55th at Vieux Fort and Laborie, and Major Wilson with the rest of the 55th and a detachment of the black corps. Their orders were to guard the plantations from the brigands, and the coast from boats landing from St Vincent with arms and ammunition. He returned to Castries pleased with his tour, having seen both the country and the character of the inhabitants. He ordered several people who had no business being on the island to be shipped off.

The ship which had been sent with Moore's letters to Abercromby returned having been unable to find him. One of those letters had been Moore's response to one of Abercromby's asking for O'Meara's black corps to be sent to St Vincent explaining why he would detain them until further orders. He sent the ship back out with orders to follow Abercromby until they found him. Meanwhile accounts were arriving of the depredations of the brigands on the eastern side of the island. Major Lindsay reported that he had been attacked 3 times by some 300 men, only half of whom were armed. Lindsay had killed or wounded some twenty or thirty of them, having two of his men wounded in the process. Moore was concerned about the possible arrival of men and arms from Guadaloupe and felt it was necessary to put a stop to this sort of insurrection, so he accompanied a reinforcement of 190 men to Grosislet and sent ships with provisions to Dauphin and Denérie. They marched by night to Acquarts estate near Dauphin, having left orders for Major Campagne to bring 200 of the black corps by a shorter route. The house at Acquarts had been burned and some of the culprits were still in their huts. One was taken and hanged and on threat of the same, the others offered to lead the soldiers to their camp in the woods. This consisted of 'bowers' in the deep woods, but these were empty when Moore arrived; the brigands were supposed to have gone up the mountain of la Sorciere. There was plenty of what Moore called 'ground provisions' (presumably root and other vegetables) and some groups of brigands had rounded up some cattle, but ran off when the soldiers arrived.

This guerrilla warfare continued for some time and many more houses were burned, but not the sugar houses and mills. These made good barracks for the troops. Reports of Major Lindsay's activities were disappointing; he had lost several good opportunities of routing the brigands. His letters to Moore showed that he was frightened of the brigands and did not known how to deal with them, but treated them with as much respect as though they were a regular disciplined body of troops. He had been attacked three times and repulsed the attackers, but Moore thought he should have counter-attacked. Moore went to see the situation for himself and after dinner on the day after he arrived, set out with an escort of twenty men for a Mr Rigby's plantation. Half-way there, on passing a river they were fired on by a party of brigands. Moore formed the men up but as there was a village on his flank where there might be more brigands, he continued his march. The brigands took this for flight and followed with loud shouts. Seeing some open ground a little way ahead, he continued the march to encourage the brigands to approach. When they came close, he ordered the men to halt and turn, firing and then charging with bayonets. The brigands ran off, leaving their box of ammunition behind, which was picked up and emptied and the march continued unmolested.

After making some more dispositions of troops, it had been Moore's intention to return to Vieux Fort but on hearing that Abercromby was at Morne Fortuné he went there, only to find that Abercromby had been there for just a few hours before returning to Martinique. Disapppointed at having missed him, Moore wrote him a long report of the situation: he had found that the negroes on St Lucia were 'to a man' attached to the French cause; neither hanging, threat nor money had provided any intelligence from them. Those still on the estates were in league with those in the woods; any landing from Guadaloupe, even if only a few men with substantial numbers of arms, would, he thought, force him to abandon the country and retire to the Morne Fortuné, which was inadequate in cover and all conveniences, as well as being an unhealthy spot. If the British really wanted to retain the island, the present troubles needed to be stopped, and a body of 800 or 1,000 black troops sent to scour the woods while the British troops who lacked the experience to act in the interior, could then occupy positions in the coast. He still, as he had said before, needed some better officers. He added a sardonic comment, 'our commanders now seem to think of nothing but a flourishing [report in the] Gazette and then to get off'.

Admiral Christian had been superseded and it was said that Abercromby was going home. Moore continued to moan in his journal about the quality of the troops and the officers and added, 'However flattering command is to a military man, I would give the world to get quit of mine, or even to get home. I conceive I may lose my life and reputation and without a possibility of doing good. With such instruments it is impossible to work.'

More days passed in the same manner, burning brigand camps and trying to capture the brigands. Then, finally, on 11 July, there came a letter from Abercromby. He would not let Moore have any more black troops, and generally avoided the things Moore had told him of the situation on St Lucia, or 'misunderstood' them, dealing instead in general advice and observations. Moore saw this letter as a put off, but answered it promptly, restating the situation on the island and the impossibility of restoring tranquillity to it. He reminded Abercromby that it was against his inclination that he had accepted the post. The assistance which had been promised at that time had not been forthcoming and he now found himself in exactly the opposite situation to what he had been promised. He begged Abercromby to relieve him of the command which he found very irksome; he had not one officer whom he could depend upon to command a district. Instead he had to go from post to post himself, and had the constant worry of arms being landed from Guadaloupe. Indeed a vessel under American colours had attempted to land a cargo at Esperance but fortunately Moore had a detachment there and the landing was prevented.

On the 21st Moore received a reply from Abercromby. He was not pleased. His letter was short, complained of Moore's impatience, said it was his duty to struggle with difficulties and desired to hear no more on the subject. He considered possession of the Morne Fortuné as securing the sovereignty of the island. In the light of this, Moore could do no more than carry on, and justify himself in his journal: 'I continue my endeavours to quell the disturbances, conscious of having done everything in my power for the good of the service.'

He continued to attack and burn the brigand camps whenever he could, and ordered the 'ground provisions' to be destroyed. Without those, they could no longer remain in the interior, but they remained committed to the cause, going to death with indifference; one man having persevered in denying any knowledge of the brigands, cried out the moment before he was shot 'Vive la Republique!'. Their cruelty was shocking, even in the ways they murdered women and children. Moore wrote:

This I attribute to the people, black and white, who have hitherto directed them. These have been vagabonds from France, of the Robespierre faction, or blacks and men of colour devoid of principle, but with a little education, and some more cunning than the rest. These have led them to commit every excess, and have succeeded in making them perfectly savage; but the blacks have naturally many good qualities. The cause in which they fight is praiseworthy did they not disgrace it by acts which disgrace human nature. These acts make us feel less remorse in ordering them to be put to death. I do it, however, with pain, convinced the poor fellows are misled.

After a five-week absence spent traversing the island in all directions, Moore returned to Fort Charlotte (the new name for Morne Fortuné in honour of the Queen). Two weeks before that, Abercromby had sent him a reinforcement of 300 black troops with a very kind letter before he returned to Europe. With these additional troops, Moore was able to step up his actions against the brigands and, he said to Abercromby's successor, General Graham, 'have so tormented them, that many have returned to the estates and have delivered themselves to their masters'. He continued to complain about his junior officers: 'I have few who execute my orders, and the regiments are literally dying for want of care. One has not a man fit for duty. Two others are little better. The want of zeal for the service is dreadful. I really believe many of them wish their men to die that they may get home.'

By the end of August reports were coming in that the brigands were disheartened. In an attack on one of their camps by Captain L'Aureal and the Black Rangers over 100 were killed and wounded. Moore continued to worry about 'succours' from Guadaloupe, and wished the navy would do more on the windward side of the island. Meanwhile, sickness raged among the troops; those going sick at Fort Charlotte were some sixty or seventy a week. Moore knew that a great deal of those were the result of the climate, but also, he was sorry to find, from:

a total want of discipline and interior economy in the regiments. The soldiers in the W Indies should be well fed, well dressed, and great attention paid to the cleanliness of his person, his barracks, etc., but he should also be eternally exercised and moved about; and tho' it is done occasionally in the sun, it will not hurt him. The troops at St Lucia which have been in the out-quarters and constantly moving and exposed, are the most healthy. They were then generally well-fed, besides the ration; where they found cattle they were allowed to kill them. They had frequent opportunities of washing their bodies and clothes in the rivers ...

Quite apart from problems caused by the brigands and junior officers, Moore also had others of a domestic nature. Mr Ewing, the agent of the contractors, was meant to supply the troops with fresh provisions but failed to do so despite repeated orders from Moore, and such beef as he had delivered to Morne Fortuné was bad. Moore wanted, he told Graham, to enforce the terms of the contract and to replace Ewing. Graham approved of his having got rid of Ewing, and a successor was appointed, but was awaited at the end of August. In the meantime two hospital ships had arrived and those who could be moved were embarked on them. The sickness on Morne Fortuné and its neighbourhood was, in Moore's words, 'dreadful', even the medical staff were themselves sickly. The windward side of the island was more healthy and he was sending the convalescents there but many of the sick were too ill to be moved.

He was disappointed to find that only one prison ship was coming and that it was a small one, with space for only 200; he had hoped to be able to embark at least 700, including some 20 white people who he thought were the principal fomenters of the disturbances. These would have to be embarked with the blacks; Moore would have preferred to separate them, and ideally get them off the island. He asked Graham for more prison ships.

Other 'domestic' tasks included replacement of officers. The Regiment of York Fusiliers needed two and the two oldest lieutenants, St Laurent and Layonski, had asked to be considered and Moore was happy to recommend them as 'deserving and active officers'. That regiment had no men fit for duty, but the fault was not with those lieutenants. A week later he received an application from one of the majors of that regiment to be permitted to sell his commission. Other irksome questions which had to be resolved included the matter of the allowance in lieu of green forage, whether it was to be paid for the effective horses only, as the general order stated, or for the numbers allowed on the establishment as the regiments claimed was the custom. He also asked Graham how he should treat the expenditure of monies for

Secret Service, negroes' mules, guides, boat hire, and pilots; he had already paid out some £400 and needed to know how this should be shown in his accounts.

There was a backlog of courts martial, including one on the quartermaster of the 48th Regiment. This had built up from the sickness of officers able to hold such courts, including over twenty being held for desertion to the enemy. The most recent on the list was a request from Major Campagne of the Royal Rangers. Moore had a letter from Lieutenant Colonel O'Mara with some details, which he passed on to General Graham: the officers of that regiment were extremely dissatisfied with Campagne's conduct towards them. He had even gone so far as to strike one of them on parade, and they accused him of 'some dirty practices' respecting plunder and of cheating the soldiers. O'Mara had warned him about this, but had put him under arrest initially for disobeying orders and disrespect to himself. Then, at a meeting of all the officers, they resolved that his conduct was unbecoming an officer and therefore unfit to remain in the corps. Moore commented that as an old and reputedly brave officer, it might be best if some situation could be found that would allow him to retire. He was still under arrest and in the current circumstances unlikely to be brought to trial for some time.

Apart from all these administrative problems, the situation on the island at that time remained much the same. Moore was so busy that it was the end of August before he was able to write to his father. He brought him up to date with military events, but confessed that his journal was not going well as he was just too busy and the events so numerous. This comment suggests that a large part of the reason for keeping such a journal, though many officers of the time did so, was to demonstrate to his father that he was doing his best and sticking to the principles that his father had instilled in him as a young boy. He wrote again on 11 October, having just received a packet of letters from home dated 19 July, which had obviously been delayed at the Post Office, for he had already received others dated 2 August. Father had obviously had something to say about excessive spending, as Moore remarked:

Your lecture upon economy shall not be despised tho' I assure you it was unnecessary. The sentiments you express are exactly my own. I am not at four and thirty what I was at four and twenty – my mind is made up upon that subject, and you will never, be my income what it may, hear of my owing a shilling again. The hurry in which I left England was the cause of my not paying Rymer and some others, & the affairs I was immediately engaged in prevented me from remitting money to James which I have since done – but of all men he, Rymer, has least right to be clamourous – in 12 years that he has worked for me he has been most regularly paid.

My appointment as Commandant is 30/- a day. General Abercromby promised to recommend to Mr Dundas to make it £1200 a year – if he does, and he ought to do it I shall have the difference to the good. I think luxury out of character with a military man. My table, which it becomes me in my station to keep, is plain and without ostentation, & no excess of any kind prevails at it. My occupation will not admit of my looking narrowly into my expenses. My brigade major, who knows my sentiments, regulates them and they are always within my income as Brigadier & Commandant. In time of peace I could not live under the £1200 – and I rather suppose, from what Brownrigg said to you, that Dundas has agreed to it – at present I have my Lieutenant Colonel's pay only, ...

He sent a couple of Bills of Exchange, one for James to pay off the debts he had left behind when he sailed in a hurry, and another for Anderson, for father to invest for him. He had also bought and sent two cases of noyeau (a brandy liqueur flavoured with bitter almonds or peach kernels) for his father, but due to an error they were not put on the ship he had intended, and had to be transhipped at Martinique.

After some more news of the situation on the island, he commented that he had been 'attacked with the fever'; he believed this was more due to the constant fatigue he suffered than the climate. The treatment he received was immersion in tepid baths, bleeding, purging, blistering and doses of 'bark' (quinine), and after two weeks of this regime was recovering from 'the weakness produced by all these remedies'. And then he remarked, perhaps presciently, 'I am determined that if I fall it will be by a good round cannon or musket shot, not by an ignominious fever.'

Early in the New Year (1797) Abercromby went back to the West Indies, landing at Martinique, where Moore paid him a brief visit. He was received kindly, and Abercromby said that while it would be just to relieve him of the command at St Lucia, he did not know who he could send there in Moore's place. He then suggested a couple of other posts Moore might like: the governorship of Grenada, or the office of Quartermaster General of the whole army. This latter post was vacant, and it would be a permanent position, retained even after the peace. Moore did not wish for either; he did not want to stay in the West Indies indefinitely, nor for the post of Quartermaster General, which was a post he did not like. What he really wanted, he told Abercromby, was to be employed in military situations until the peace, then to return home.

He went back to resume his duties as governor of St Lucia. A return to home was to come before the peace, but in the meantime things went along much as before on the island with the brigands making forays from the woods and being beaten back and their camps destroyed. They were, unfortunately, receiving arms and intelligence from outside. The British regiments were still losing men to the fever – there were only 531 fit for duty, including engineers and artillery, the 31st had only 16, the York Fusiliers 27, but these were mainly occupied in looking after the sick. Other regiments were better off, but the sickness continued unabated. He reported to Graham that of the 4,000 men left to him by Abercromby just after the surrender, he had no more than 1,000 fit for duty and just under 1,500 sick. Even the medical officers were falling sick and dying, including Mr Grant, the surgeon of the hospital.

During February word came from Abercromby that he was going to attack Trinidad, and although he regretted it, could not take Moore. As it happened, there would have been little of interest to be done if he had, as the Trinidadians surrendered without a shot being fired. Abercromby arrived in St Lucia on 20 March; he was about to take an expedition to Puerto Rico, but again could not include Moore as he had no one else to whom he could trust the island. However, he intended to give Moore a large reinforcement that would enable him to finish the business of the brigands before the hurricane season. He could not do it straight away as he did not wish to be detained, but he did send the 38th Regiment, consisting of just under 300 men, of whom 200 were fit for duty; he also sent a small detachment of artillery.

At the beginning of May Moore was struck with another bout of fever; at the same time he developed a large abscess in his right hip, and described the pain as excruciating. Eventually it was opened up and discharged a great deal of matter. He was confined to his bed for over three weeks, and it was some time before he was able to sit up. Extremely weak, he wrote that he was more shaken by this illness than any other he had had. He wrote to General Hunter, telling him that his officers could carry on the general business without him, but that he was incapable of doing anything himself. Hunter sent Colonel Drummond of the 43rd Regiment to assist, and to take over if Moore was to leave the island, which he urged him to do. But he was determined to stay, unless it became absolutely necessary to save his life.

In the end, it was, if not actually to save his life, on the strong advice of the doctors for the recovery of his health that he left. He had suffered another severe bout of the fever, and had it not been for the determination of Anderson and François he might easily have died. He moved first to Martinique and then to Tortola via St Kitts where he and Anderson stayed for a couple of days before leaving for England. They landed at Falmouth on 9 July after a passage of thirty-one days, moved on to Plymouth and finally on London and the family home in Clifford Street on the 14th. He wrote to his mother from Falmouth when he landed on 9 July:

> [as you know] I had another attack of fever.
>
> I was told by everybody that if I remained during the hurricane months, I would probably die. The campaign in the West Indies was completely over; I had no scruple, therefore, to ask permission to quit that country [which Sir Ralph gave and I landed here today] not an invalid but in perfect health. The sea air has done more than pounds of bark[8]
>
> Major Anderson is with me. I wish you could take a lodging for him in the neighbourhood of Clifford Street; the nearer the better, Maddox Street, for example – a second floor will answer his purpose as well as a first.

Moore paid a visit to the Duke of York, who received him kindly, and after a couple of attempts to see Henry Dundas, the Secretary of State for War, he met him at a levee and as requested paid him a visit the next day. Dundas asked many questions about St Lucia, mainly about its usefulness, and the force needed to garrison it. Finally he asked Moore to put his thoughts in writing, and two days later he sent the paper.

Moore wrote that the island might be valuable when fully cultivated, but currently it was most valuable for its harbours and anchorages, and military position with respects to other islands, specifically Martinique, St Vincent and Grenada. The Carenage was a deep harbour where ships of war could moor safely during the hurricane season and the bays of Choc and Grosislet were good anchorages. Possession of the island deprived the French of the only harbour fit for war ships in the West Indies.

The most important post on the island was that on Morne Fortuné with its close dependencies, which protected the Carenage harbour. However its size required a large body of men to defend it, and its height and distance from the sea made the carriage of stores and provisions difficult. It was also an unhealthy spot. There had been a suggestion that it could be abandoned if some ships were sunk across the entrance to the Carenage, defences were concentrated round Grosislet and Choc bays and other posts were fortified, this would require only a modest garrison; this plan was a point for consideration at the peace rather than immediately.

Previously the blacks had been under the control of the whites, but by freeing the blacks the French had inspired them with energy and 'excited them against us'. He thought the white population should be overawed, the black population kept in subjection and both prevented from communicating with the enemy. Detachments to secure this state were necessary in various places round the coasts. The island required a garrison of 1,500 to 1,800 effective troops, two-thirds of which should be Europeans; circumstances would direct where they should be stationed, but in general there should be 500 or 600 Europeans on Morne Fortuné, 100 on Pigeon Island and the rest divided between Soufrière and Vieux Fort.

Moore does not say in his journal how Dundas received this, but at that time Abercromby's conquest of St Vincent and Grenada had effectively finished his West Indies campaign, as he did not have a large enough force to deal with Guadaloupe. His losses from enemy action during the campaign were comparatively few compared with those from disease, especially yellow fever. Accurate figures are not available, but are reckoned to be in the region of 44,000 troops and between 19,000 and 24,000 sailors between 1793 and 1797.[9]

Chapter 5

Ireland

I reland had been a problem to the English for many hundreds of years, dating back to the twelfth century when Pope Adrian IV gave Ireland to Henry II. There were numerous attempts at insurrection, but after each had been put down, the lands of the Irish nobles who had been involved were confiscated and given to Englishmen who the King wished to reward. After an attempted invasion of Ireland by the Spanish and an associated revolt, Elizabeth I ruthlessly crushed both and made a vast seizure of estates. She also introduced the Supremacy Laws which barred Catholics from public office and service as officers in the British army and navy.

After the loss of America, some of the laws against Catholics were rescinded and in 1782 internal independence was given to the Irish Parliament; this was little more than a gesture as most members of that Parliament were Protestants. In 1793, the British Prime Minister Pitt passed an Act giving the vote to all Catholics (providing that the other requirements were met), but the Lord Lieutenant (Viceroy) refused to implement that Act. As a result the United Society of Irishmen came into being, with Wolfe Tone at its head. It believed the Viceroy had usurped power and saw the only chance of regaining this was to seek the aid of the French in forming an Irish Republic. The south and west coasts of Ireland were comparatively easy to reach from the French naval base at Brest, and thus the British government was concerned that these might be used as a base for invading the mainland.

* * *

In October 1797, Moore spent two weeks touring the coastal areas of Essex, Suffolk and Norfolk with his friend Major Hay of the Engineers. They made a quick survey of those areas to consider their defence in case of a French invasion, Moore making brief notes in his journal on every town they passed through. Back in London, he learned that Sir Ralph Abercromby had been appointed Commander-in-Chief in Ireland and had asked that Moore be put on his staff as brigadier general, which was duly done. He attended Abercromby at a levee on 15 November and kissed the King's hands. They left London on the 24th, reached Holyhead on the 28th, sailed on 1 December and landed in Dublin the next day after what Moore described as 'a most boisterous, disagreeable passage of thirty hours'.

They were received by an aide from the Lord Lieutenant, with a message that apartments were prepared for Abercromby and his suite at the castle, where the Lord Lieutenant hoped he would stay until the previous Commander-in-Chief, Lord Carhampton, had vacated his quarters. Abercromby felt he could not refuse this offer; rooms were also offered to Moore, but he declined and got himself rooms at the Kildare Hotel, where he thought he could be his own master. He did not expect to be in Dublin for long, but would soon be detached to the provinces. He and Abercromby dined with the secretary, Mr Pelham, and the Lord Lieutenant, when Abercromby introduced Moore to him.

He remarked in his journal that it was now nearly five months since he had returned from the West Indies; there was no prospect of any service other than in Ireland (or idleness at home, of which he was already tired). The north of the country was quiet at that time, probably because of the strong military presence there. There had been some disturbances in the south; it was generally thought to be 'the lower class of inhabitant' which was disaffected throughout the kingdom. Despite this belief, the government had armed a considerable number of the inhabitants under the heading of militia and yeomanry. There had been little discrimination when setting up those bodies. Over 56,000 of the total of nearly 77,000 troops were militia and yeomanry, and between 18,000 and 20,000 were thought to be cavalry.

Abercromby kept Moore in Dublin while he made his arrangements. Lieutenant General Sir James Stuart, who had not yet arrived from England, was to command the southern district, extending from Limerick to Waterford and everything south of those ports. Moore was appointed to command, under Stuart, the forts of Cork harbour, Kinsale and Middleton. Abercromby gave him various papers on the defence of the south to read and take notes to pass on to Stuart. This was Moore's chief occupation in the mornings of his month-long stay in Dublin. He left there on 6 January and arrived at Cork two days later. While he had been with Abercromby they had discussed the defective state of all the military posts and preparations. None of the artillery was in a condition to be moved and in most cases there were no horses to move it. There were no magazines for the militia regiments, little discipline and the troops were generally dispersed to protect certain individuals.

As had been the case in Corsica, the Commander-in-Chief was subservient to the Lord Lieutenant, by whom even the most trifling decision must be made. In peacetime the Commander-in-Chief was not listened to, and the army was considered no more than, as Moore put it, 'an instrument of corruption in the hands of the Lord Lieutenant and his secretary'. Even though the country was currently in a state of alarm, it required all Abercromby's moderation to get anything done; the method which had been employed to quiet unruly districts had been to let the military loose, encouraging them in acts of great violence. This, with the practice of arresting people on suspicion and sending them out of the country, may have quelled the disturbances but did not reduce the disaffection felt but tended to increase it. 'The gentlemen in general,' wrote Moore, 'still call out aloud for violent measures as the most proper to be adopted, and a complete line seems to be drawn between the upper and lower orders'.

By 1 February, Moore had inspected the forts and defences of Cork harbour, as well as the troops of his district, then moved on to Bandon. He thought the harbour of Cork should be strongly fortified; money had been spent on this before but on badly conceived works and thus it was still in a precarious state. Abercromby came down for a two-day visit during which he inspected the garrison at Cork and the forts round the harbour. The command at Bandon was vacant (General Coote who had held it was about to return to England) and Moore was appointed to it. He went with Abercromby to Bandon where Coote handed over the command, then on to Bantry which was part of his district. Abercromby continued on his tour towards the Shannon and Limerick while Moore returned to his new station. He had over 3,000 men, including 12 companies of militia light infantry: 'very fine men indeed ... considered as the advanced corps of the south'. The batteries erected at Bantry since the previous invasion attempt by the French would, he thought, 'throw some impediments in the way of an enemy, but nothing but a considerable corps of troops could possibly prevent his landing'. The bay itself was too large to be completely defended by batteries alone. The country around the bay was wild and barren, lacking resources, and if troops were brought up quickly from the south an enemy could at least be prevented from penetrating and at best, beaten. Moore resolved to look more closely at the road to Bantry than he had been able to do before.

He was still at the Bantry garrison two weeks later. There had been a conspiracy the previous summer among the militia, some of whom planned to murder their officers, seize the cannon and march to Bantry. Several of the conspirators had been shot. Moore was hopeful that the spirit of rebellion had been squashed, but he noticed that the men did not respect their officers, which worried him more than mere disaffection. He thought that transfers to regiments of the line and better officers might help solve the problem, but accepted the inherent dangers of armed men who were not properly subordinate to their officers.

Abercromby had gone back to Dublin, writing to Moore that he thought the Shannon River was the easiest means of landing for an enemy, and tempting because of its richness of produce. Moore wrote back, urging completion of the old regiments as all they had to face an enemy accustomed to war was the militia. If, when they had been first formed, pains had been taken to provide good officers and introduce proper discipline, they would, by this time, have made good troops, but like everything else in Ireland, the choice of officers was tied to political influence and electioning purposes. The officers, he wrote, were 'in general profligate and idle, serving for the emolument, but [without] a sense of duty or military distinction'.

At the beginning of March a plot was discovered in the Sligo regiment at Macroom; three men had deserted and several had been arrested. Moore went immediately to Macroom and examined them but could get no more from them that that several meetings had taken place and improper toasts drunk, such as 'The French Republic' and 'Hell to the King and Duke of York' and that an oath of secrecy had been taken by some. It seemed that a soldier from Dublin was thought to be the instigator. Moore ordered them all to be tried by regimental court martial, and after punishment to be sent abroad. He thought the problem stemmed from the fact that the militia in Ireland were only raised to serve a fixed number of years and not for the duration of the war. That number of years had recently expired, and thus the greatest number of the militia were recruits, and worse, recruits from a mass of people who were disaffected. The discipline learned in four years had been lost and with it the advantage of keeping them separated from the rest of the population. An Act had recently been passed to enlist future militia men for the duration of the war. The militia officers were generally Protestants while the men were Catholics and the old hatred between them was still alive and the officers lacked the sense to hide their prejudices. All the plots that had been discovered had been confined to the Catholics and the object was the murder of officers.

When General Stuart arrived a few days later Moore went to Cork to meet him. He had suffered a recurrence of what Moore described as 'his nervous complaint' which 'completely unfitted him for business'. Stuart said he should not have accepted a command for which 'he said he was unequal to when well, much more so when under the influence of this complaint, to which he was ever subject'; he seemed determined to resign. Moore tried to talk him out of this, but to little effect. They then went for a walk which cheered Stuart up; in high spirits he returned to dinner with an appetite but the following morning he was again in low spirits. He agreed to tour Waterford and the Blackwater if Moore would go with him, having already obtained Abercromby's permission to take him. Although he was reluctant to leave his district at that moment, Moore agreed to go, hoping, if not to cheer Stuart up, at least to judge whether it would be proper to encourage him to remain in the command. He went to deal with some business at Bandon, promising to return in two days to begin 'our jaunt'; he also wrote to Abercromby with full details of Stuart's state of mind and what they had discussed, promising a further letter from Waterford. But before he could return to Cork he received disturbing news by letters from Skibbereen and Bantry and by a visit from the High Sheriff of the county; there had been outrages committed in those areas by 'united men' and that a general rising was expected. The High Sheriff was very worried and Moore tried to reassure him that there was unlikely to be a general uprising unless the French landed, but if there was it could be immediately crushed; he believed the majority of the militia were faithful and that they had never yet refused to act when called on. He then said that he would postpone his visit to Cork, which cheered the High Sheriff; he would set out the following day for Clonakilty and be with him the following day at Skibbereen. There was some apprehension among the people at Clonakilty, although it seemed the lower class had been quiet. However, several of the respectable inhabitants were disaffected, calling themselves Democrats.

He inspected the three companies of the Westmeath Militia, and shortly after received two anonymous letters complaining of injustice from their officers, and that their money had been withheld from them. He ordered the regiment to parade the next morning and told them that if they had complaints they should not make them by anonymous letter, which was unbecoming to soldiers; they should either make them openly by letter, or by deputing a man to speak for all, and added that men who were conscious of doing no wrong should not be afraid. The articles of war directed soldiers to complain when they thought themselves aggrieved, and it was the duty of general officers to investigate and act as necessary. He asked them to choose two men from each company to come to him and state their grievances. He also directed the captains of companies to attend with their account books. The men who came were, he thought, decent, intelligent men; he found their grievances to be just and ordered a regimental court martial to state them. It seemed it was the colonel, Lord

Westmeath, who was at fault and had retained their money. Moore waited for the proceedings of the court martial and sent them on to Abercromby.

From there he went to Skibbereen, where the gentlemen of the neighbourhood had come to meet him. They were alarmed and fearful of a rising but nothing seemed to have happened except a few trees had been cut down; this was presented as being for pike handles, but Moore thought it was more likely to have been for fuel or farming implements. Although alarmed at the prospect of an uprising, the gentlemen had taken no steps to protect themselves, always relying on the army or militia. Moore told them that he could not fight phantoms, and if they could produce evidence of improper meetings he might be able to prevent them, or if there was a rising he could do something to quell it. He could not act if there was nothing to act against.

That evening a soldier of the Westmeath Regiment came to see him and said some people of the country had asked him to drill them. He was somewhat drunk, and Moore told him to go to his officer the next day. Nothing he had said seemed important enough to prevent Moore continuing his visit along the coast. When he returned he received the soldier's deposition; this accused thirteen or fourteen inhabitants and more than forty soldiers of the two companies of swearing to join the French. The whole thing was incoherent, and Moore doubted its veracity, but he did send a detachment of cavalry and directed the major of the regiment to go and take command there. However, although there was nothing on which he could act, he did think that the whole of the regiment was disaffected and that if the country had risen or the French landed, they would have joined them. At the time, though, because of the strong conviction everywhere that there would be an uprising on St Patrick's Day, he felt he should remain at headquarters.

St Patrick's Day and the day after, which were usually quite riotous, passed quietly. The garrison was perfectly behaved with the exception of one captain on picquet who got drunk. When Moore heard of this in the morning he had the man arrested and reported the circumstances to the Adjutant General to pass to the Commander-in-Chief. Understanding that such things had happened before he had warned the officers that it was such a disgraceful practice, he still could not ignore it. Soldiers were flogged for drunkenness, so he must equally punish drunken officers. They might call it harsh, but he considered that having a worthless officer dismissed would have more effect than flogging fifty other soldiers.

When he returned from his tour of the coast, he reported to Abercromby that he thought the only harbours in his district fit for a large invasion force were Cork and Bantry. By the end of March, Abercromby had visited the different areas and observed and received reports of the abuses which existed in the regiments, particularly those of the militia. These had risen to a disgraceful height, disgraceful to those who permitted and connived at them, and were subversive to discipline and order. As the colonels and principal officers were men of rank and many were members of Parliament, no one had previously dared to check them. He had issued an order at the end of February, remarking that the army was 'in a state of licentiousness which must render it formidable to every one but the enemy ...' and went on to demand that all generals commanding districts and brigades should compel the officers under their command to pay strict attention to the discipline, good order and conduct of their men.

This did not please those principal officers, who could not bear this expression of the truth, and they raised a public outcry about what had been intended as for their private guidance. Abercromby wrote to Moore that it was possible he might be forced to resign, he certainly did not intend to retract the order which had caused the trouble. He urged Moore to take no hasty action on his own position.

Moore received a visit from Robert Longfield O'Connor, one of whose two brothers was in the Tower for high treason and the other in Cork gaol, who said he had positive information that 300 pikes, some muskets and eight-hundredweight of ball cartridges were concealed in the garden of the latter. It was, he said, unpleasant to have to give such evidence against his own brother but he felt it was his duty to the country. He agreed to meet Moore the following morning and, as a Justice of the Peace, authorise the search. Moore went with the search party himself to avoid any irregularities by the troops. After meeting on the road, Moore went forward to inform Mrs O'Connor what was happening so she would not be frightened by the sudden appearance of dragoons. She was not at home, having gone to visit her husband in the gaol; her children were there in the care of a young lady called Miss Beamish. The garden was searched but no arms were found.

At the beginning of April a proclamation was issued from the Lord Lieutenant and his Council to the effect that the whole kingdom was in rebellion, and directed the Commander-in-Chief to take the most effective means to quell it. It included an order that the troops were to act without waiting for the authority of a civil magistrate. Abercromby issued the necessary order because he did not wish to be accused of having disobeyed, but he promptly wrote home asking to be recalled. The Council and Parliament seemed to be in disorder. Moore also wrote home to Colonel Brownrigg, the military secretary at Horse Guards, asking to be recalled. He was worried that not only would the measures adopted be most odious, but there would be no one to direct operations if there was an invasion attempt and no advance preparations had been made. He wrote in his journal, 'the scene will be disgraceful, and I wish to retire from it'.

Abercromby issued an order in April that the countryside should be not have arms and instructing the people to deliver their arms to the local magistrates or officers commanding the troops. Moore then issued a similar order in his district, giving 2 May as the date by which arms should be handed in. This had no effect, and he reluctantly ordered in the troops to conduct searches; they were to treat the people with as much harshness as possible (but in word and manner only) and to take whatever provisions they needed to allow them to live well. On the second day after this operation commenced, having previous denied having any arms, the people started handing them in; after four days they had collected sixty-five muskets. One party of soldiers had had to burn several houses before a number of pikes were handed in. This went on, parish by parish, until after 3 weeks Moore had collected some 800 pikes and almost 400 muskets.

Abercromby returned to Dublin, from where he expected to return to England. He said that if Lord Cornwallis were to come as Lord Lieutenant and Commander-in-Chief, he would stay, but not otherwise. Cornwallis was appointed, but Abercromby still went home at the end of April, and spent the next few months as commander of the forces in Scotland.

On 26 May, no mail arrived from Dublin at Bandon; this was unusual but raised no worries until none came the next day either, and reports were received that Dublin and the surrounding countryside was in insurrection. Sir James Stuart then wrote to Moore asking him to go to him at Cork. Letters had reached him from the general officers at Waterford and Kilkenny saying that the insurgents were in control of the country between Naas and Kilkenny and had completely stopped all communication. There had been several attacks by the insurgents on the army but these had terminated with great slaughter of the insurgents. A week passed without any communication from Dublin, then some letters arrived by sea from the Lord Lieutenant and General Lake, saying that Dublin was quiet, the troops had been successful there and wanting to know the state of the south. Sir James had sent troops to Clonmel and Kilkenny to help Sir Charles Asgil, who commanded there, to open the communication with Dublin. Sir James Duff had marched from Limerick with a corps of cavalry, infantry and artillery to Maryborough. The different generals had acted according to local circumstances and independent of each other, so little effect was created. Everywhere was in great alarm and a rising was feared in Cork, and indeed everywhere. Moore stayed with Sir James for a couple of days then returned to Bandon. His district, although quiet and getting over its initial panic, needed to be watched, and he was fearful of what he described as 'a visit from the French'. He set about establishing better lookouts on the coast and gave them detailed instructions.

After a couple of days he received another summons from Cork, where he found the same confusion and indecision. General Fawcett had detached some small parties from Duncannon Fort against the insurgents at Wexford, and two of these were cut off and two guns captured. Retiring to his fort, Fawcett feared an attack. Sir James had sent Major General Johnstone to march immediately with about 1,200 men to Waterford. It was understood that General Eustace had arrived at New Ross with 800 men from Dublin, but the town of Wexford and the surrounding country were in the possession of the insurgents. Moore suggested to Sir James that he should go himself to Wexford to direct operations, but Sir James replied that Wexford was in General Dundas' district. Moore then suggested that he might go by post to Waterford, where he would arrive in the morning, could deliver to Johnstone whatever instructions Sir James chose and otherwise help him, especially as he was short of officers to lead the troops if it came to action. Sir James refused immediately, saying that he had already detached too many men and must keep some; so Moore returned to Bandon. Lord Edward Fitzgerald and other leaders of the uprising had been seized, and the uprising, which they had planned to be general, was in fact only partial, being confined to the counties immediately round Dublin. Dublin itself had been prevented from rising by lack of arms and stores, the troops having opportunities of attacking different bodies of insurgents and killing many of them without loss to themselves.

This situation having been quieted, the troops could be turned against Wicklow and Wexford, two counties where there were normally few troops. Moore was concerned about the consequences if a French force had arrived; however the superiority of the troops against what was no more than a rabble without discipline or arms had allowed success. After a few days, Moore received an order to take the Light Battalion to Cork, which, with accounts of poor success in the county of Wexford and disturbances near Cork, created much uneasiness in the neighbourhood of Bandon. Arriving at Cork with the Light Battalion and two 6-pounders, Moore found that Sir James intended them to remain there instead of moving on to another trouble spot. Then a letter arrived for Sir James from Lieutenant General Lake, ordering him to send Moore on to Clonmel with the 60th and Light Infantry; it also found fault with Sir James' failure to send on troops as he had been directed. He had not done so, being concerned about the tranquillity of Cork and the safety of the magazines on the Blackwater.

After pausing overnight at Fermoy, orders came to move on to Clonmel and then to Waterford to await orders from Major General Johnstone, who was at New Ross. There was such a large force of rebels in the county of Wexford that it was necessary to wait until a larger force had been assembled to attack it. News came of disturbances in the north, and although these had been quelled, Moore began to see a regular war as inevitable. He was concerned about the discipline of his troops, especially the militia and was spending much of his time instructing them and trying to get the officers he regarded as dilettantes to exert themselves. Leaving Fermoy at 3 in the morning, they arrived at Clogheen at 10 am, where they found the High Sheriff, Mr Fitzgerald, conducting a major interrogation. His method was to seize and flog a man until he confessed and gave the names of other rebels. He had, by this process, found several people who confessed to holding rank in the rebel cause: generals, colonels, captains and so on. This went on all morning, and although some who confessed were probably innocent, it was generally felt that Fitzgerald was a good magistrate, and was expected to restore calm.

Moore moved on to Waterford, leaving at 3 am for New Ross, arriving about 8 am on 18 June. Moore had mentioned in his journal that the roads were dusty and that the heat was debilitating, which was presumably the reason for these early morning marches. The morning of the 19th was fixed for attacks on the rebel posts; Moore found it difficult in the confusion to find what his role was to be in these attacks, but finally established that he was to lead the right column of the three that were to march out. This was supposed to be at 2 am, but due to heavy rain was postponed until six. Moore had command of the 60th Jägers, 900 Light Infantry, fifty Hompesch Cavalry and six guns. They could see the rebels posted on a hill about 1½ miles from Ross, looking, Moore thought, as though they intended to fight, but when his march brought his troops within range of the cannon, they retreated. General Johnstone, with the centre, was moving forward to attack from the front, and pursued the rebels, killing sixty or seventy of them.

They moved on to Old Ross and Carrickburn, which had been evacuated, then Moore was ordered to proceed to Fookes Mill, where he would be joined by the

Queen's and 29th regiments, recently arrived from England. He took post that night at the house and park of a Mr Sutton, having passed through rich and beautiful but completely deserted country. During the early part of that march, some of the soldiers had left their divisions and set fire to many houses; he had managed to put a stop to this, and the later marches were calmer. The following morning he sent a strong detachment under Lieutenant Colonel Wilkinson out to patrol, hopefully to communicate with the troops he was expecting from England, and on return to forage cattle for the camp. Wilkinson reported that he had found some straggling parties of rebels, many of whom his men had killed. The inhabitants were gone, and he had seen nothing of the troops Moore was expecting.

Moore's orders were to move on to Taghmon, 7 miles from Wexford. He waited until 3 pm for the troops from England, but heard nothing of them so decided to make a start. He had 1,000 men and thought this enough to hold his ground against the rebels, and as part of the general plan was for him to be at Taghmon that day he did not wish to disappoint. They had not gone more than a mile when they saw a cloud of dust moving towards them and realised that it was a large party of rebels. He had reconnoitred the ground that morning, so knew where to place his men, with part of the Light Infantry on the right and left of the road, and two guns at a commanding situation at the crossing of two roads. While this was being organised, he ordered the Jägers to advance and skirmish.

The attack began; the Light Infantry were not used to fire and hesitated a little so he dismounted and put himself at their head to jump over a high ditch and advance on the rebels. They drove them downhill over a bridge, and Moore directed Wilkinson to post himself at this bridge and prevent their crossing it again, then ordered Major Aylmer with three companies of Light Infantry to march against a large body of rebels which was seen going round to the left. He sent back word that they were in a wood, but there were so many that he was afraid to advance on them. Moore sent him two more companies and a field gun under Major Daniel, with instructions to advance cautiously and see how many there were, but follow them if they moved away from him. Moore was reluctant to leave the front, which was opposite great numbers of rebels who seemed to be waiting for the right moment to fall on him. The fire from the left grew hotter and messages for reinforcements were coming. He sent Brigade Major Anderson to go and see the exact state of the left. He returned and told Moore it was absolutely necessary for him to go to the left immediately, so he set off at a gallop, leaving Anderson to stay and watch the movements at the front. He met the Infantry, Jägers and some Dragoons all mixed up in the road and retreating, while the enemy were following closely and firing. He managed to stop some of them and got the Dragoons to jump out of the road and make a front on either side of it, encouraged the rest to halt, then to advance and when he saw they were ready, he took off his hat, pushed his horse into a trot, gave a huzza and they all pushed forward. The tide turned immediately; they drove the rebels before them and killed a great number.

The rebels attempted twice to make a stand but failed. Moore was surprised later to find that there had been some 600 muskets, there were also numerous pikes, in a force numbering some 6,000. He had lost ten men killed and forty-five wounded. He pursued the rebels until they disbursed, during which a messenger arrived with the news of the missing two regiments under Lord Dalhousie. By this time it was almost 8 o'clock, too late to carry on. Moore took post for the night on the ground where the action had begun. He reflected on the great courage of the Light Infantry, and the confidence they seemed to place in him, and the turn which his arrival gave to the action, but from want of officers and experience to form quickly they fought at a great disadvantage.

On the 21st he continued his march to Taghmon; while on the road, two men, one in red with a white handkerchief in his hand galloped up to them. They proved to be from Wexford, one a militia officer who had been taken prisoner some time before. They delivered a letter from Lord Kingsbury, who was also a prisoner of the rebels, stating that the inhabitants of Wexford offered to lay down their arms on the condition that their lives and property were safe. They had already delivered many arms to him and the mayor of the town. A letter to the same purpose was also delivered from Mr Keogh, the rebel governor. Moore made no answer to these proposals, having no authority to treat with the rebels. He decided that instead of stopping at Taghmon, as per his orders, he would carry on to Wexford, and without entering the town, take a position outside to give him the command of it until General Johnstone or General Lake arrived.

The road from Taghmon to Wexford led along the side of the Forth mountain and Moore could see, with his glass, crowds of armed people. Suspecting a trick, he halted and sent on a strong advance guard with orders to gain the top of the mountain and stay on it until the main body and baggage had passed on the low road. He followed with the column at a distance that would allow him to support the advance guard if necessary. The people on the top ran off, and the whole British party passed unmolested. As they came up to the town, they could see crowds of people running out of it in all directions; a house on fire made him suspect the rebels intended to burn the town and even the prisoners in it. He advanced close to the town and took his post, then sent Lord Dalhousie into it with 200 men, with orders to release any prisoners and leave a strong enough force to keep things quiet. As soon as he had settled the regiments he went into the town himself and saw 'the most affecting scenes': fathers greeting their wives and children who they thought had been killed. Forty prisoners had been shot or piked and the rebels had intended to shoot the rest (some hundred persons of the best rank in the county) that evening if he had not come.

In the morning he wrote a report of the whole incident for Major General Johnstone, and ordered the troops to retire half a mile as he thought he was in a bad position. Just after he had taken this new position Generals Johnstone and Lake arrived with their columns from Enniscorthy, where they had jointly attacked the rebels on Vinegar Hill. They had killed a great many rebels with little loss to their own men. Moore dined with General Lake and met his brother Graham, whose ship lay off the town; he had to go back to his ship, so the two brothers had only half an hour together.

Staying in that camp a few days, they had no real information on the rebels, although it was said they had retired westward. Moore took a small party of Dragoons and rode through the district, returning by a different road. He saw no sign of the enemy; the number of visible inhabitants was, he thought, small for the number of houses but he was assured they had all returned, though afraid to go near the soldiers. He spoke to several, and distributed notices promising pardon if they would give up their arms and the rebel leaders. He collected several pikes, although he thought their owners sullen and dejected. It was, he wrote, the finest country he had seen in Ireland, enclosed and well cultivated, and the farmers' and peasants' houses were in good condition and clean; a pity that a place which showed so much industry and comfort should be the most disturbed.

The rebels fleeing Wexford had been met by Sir Charles Asgil and some 400 were killed. General Roche, and Mr Keogh, rebels who commanded in the town, had been hanged by sentence of a court martial. Roche was a priest, 'a great fat, vulgar-looking beast', while Keogh had been in the army and had the appearance, Moore thought, of a gentleman. He asserted that he had exerted himself in the defence of Wexford but when the rebels (some 20,000) entered the town, they had forced him at the point of a pike to be their commander. Affected by this story, Moore ran to the officer who had charge of the execution and asked him to hang Keogh last, then ran to General Lake to tell him the story. Lake thanked him, and said it was natural for him to be affected by Keogh's story, but he had himself seen correspondence of a most violent and horrid kind between Keogh and other rebel chiefs and that he was well known to have been a rebel leader.

Moore marched back to Taghmon on 27 June, with the 2nd Battalion of Light Infantry, fifty dragoons, two 6-pounders and a howitzer. On arrival, he found the 4th Battalion of Light Infantry under Lord Blaney, which was also attached to his brigade. The whole made between 1,600 and 1,700 firelocks. The Commander-in-Chief was on his way back to Dublin. It was intended that Moore's corps would be ready to move as needed. He was having some difficulty keeping his troops under control and preventing them plundering and ill-treating the inhabitants, especially as he wanted to show the residents the difference between troops chastising them for rebellion and living among them as their countrymen for their protection. Thus he commanded his troops to behave kindly towards the locals and to take nothing without paying for it. He rode out several miles into the countryside and wrote how melancholy it was to see most of the habitations deserted and the fields full of weeds. He noted in his journal that the leaders of the rebellion had almost all been seized and executed, several of them being men of considerable property. A week later he was still waiting for orders, and had seen no newspaper or received any other communication from Dublin to tell him what was happening in other places. Another week passed and the people were gradually returning to their homes.

On 8 July Moore remarked, without any fuss, that he had been promoted to major general, and continued on the Irish staff as such. This was a permanent rank, that of brigadier general being a brevet rank and only for certain periods.

News came that the rebels were assembling in the mountains of Arklow and Wicklow; a larger force was needed to subdue them and prevent them carrying on a sort of brigand war, which was thought to be their intention. Major General Sir James Duff's health now prevented him carrying on an active role, so his brigade, as well as most of the troops in Arklow and Wicklow, were put under Moore's orders. The mountain passes to the north and west of Arklow and Wicklow were guarded with troops and about 2,500 remained to act offensively as needed. Two more regiments joined from Waterford but they brought no provisions with them; Moore left one of them at Taghmon and took the other and the rest of the troops from that post and marched first to Enniscorthy and then Ferns, where he expected to meet Lake, who had advanced to direct Moore's operations. The town had been burned by the rebels, and plundered by the army. He visited Vinegar Hill, which, he wrote, 'stinks with half-buried bodies'.

Having joined up with Lake, a combined attack of four columns was planned for when the rebels were reliably located. Moore's was to ascend to the top of a high hill then descend into Glenmalure; two 6-pounders and the baggage were dragged to the top with considerable difficulty. He saw no sign of the rebels, but as the route before him consisted of a ravine, with bog everywhere except the actual road, and as he thought it would only take a few rebels to stop his progress, he decided to get down and through the glen before the rebels spotted him and assembled a force to obstruct him. He had intended to march at night, but having brought up the guns and baggage, and the men having eaten and rested by 6, he moved on and reached the end of the glen by 11. There were a few people visible just before nightfall and two shots fired at the column, but that was all. He sent a report to Lake, who came up and they moved on together to Seven Churches where they met the other two columns. None had seen the rebels.

It had rained heavily for two days and was cold; they had no tents with them but slept as best they could. In the morning they marched on, seeing no rebels but much evidence of their passing, with all the villages burned. A few people were seen on foot and on horseback, scattering up the hills. Moore took up a post in the park of Lord Tyrone; it was a good position and the house was intact, although very small. Moore took a room to eat and write in, but slept out in the bivouac with his troops, having put a guard on the house. Some of the militia, as soon as they had piled their arms, went off plundering, until the exasperated inhabitants killed three of them. Moore took advantage of this to make the men believe the rebels were close and thus managed to keep them within the camp. Once again, Moore wrote of the bad behaviour of the militia and their poor officers.

By 19 July they were at Blessington, close to Dublin, where Moore saw Lord Cornwallis. He repeated that he wanted Moore's corps to be a moving body, ready to be despatched to any place where commotion threatened. He also asked for any intelligence Moore might receive so that they could keep the mountains of Wicklow clear of rebels. He dined with Cornwallis that day, noting that the style was very different than that of the Lord Lieutenant; everyone in uniforms and boots, and the meal without ceremony.

A week later he wrote that the weather had been so bad, with constant rain, that it was impossible for the troops to act; the officers had taken advantage of this pause to refit their men. Moore had encouraged the local residents to come in and surrender their arms: over 1,200 had done so and others were still coming. It looked as though tranquillity was returning but he was still having to reprove the gentry and yeomen farmers for the violent attitudes which prompted them to take revenge on the poor inhabitants. He thought it was probably these attitudes which drove the peasants to revolt. There were still rumours coming in of forces of rebels assembling in Tipperary and areas around it. Having received positive information of the rebels, he marched out at 1 am with 500 men, and after 4 hours came up with the rebels. There were less than 500 of them, and on Moore's force advancing, they retreated to the mountains and dispersed.

A Mr Bryn, who had been a rebel general before surrendering himself to the government, was sent to Moore as someone who had influence with the people and now wished to use it to restore calm. He stayed for twelve days, a shrewd and well-behaved man; his presence did some good, though not as much as he had expected. He said that the cause for which the rebels had risen up had been abandoned and now they were just murdering and pillaging, which he disapproved of as it was ruinous to the country. The good behaviour of the troops and the pleasant manner of the senior officers were bringing the people back to their homes but there were still bodies of armed men in the mountains. Moore had refrained from sending detachments after them while he still had hopes of bringing them in by fair means, but when he saw that this was not working he made plans to send detachments to the glens and other habitable parts of the mountains. After going to Dublin to lay these plans before Cornwallis, who approved, he started sending out detachments of about 500 men. Some of these took possession of the glens, others patrolled the mountains, keeping the rebels on the move with no means of subsistence. They soon dispersed and threw away their arms, and most of them came in for the protections they had been offered. Moore stayed in Wicklow for three weeks, during which time the country was completely quieted and the people had returned to their work. Back in Dublin he found that Lord Cornwallis had made his troop dispositions and was anxious that they should go to their assigned stations. Moore's was to be Clonmel with a corps of up to 4,000 infantry and cavalry and some light artillery, all ready to move as circumstances required. But he was suffering from fever again, as a result of fatigue and exposure to the wet; weakened, he was confined to his tent for a week. Lord Cornwallis kindly sent his own physician to care for Moore. Anderson was also unwell as the result of fatigue, and had been ordered to Bristol to recover.

Meanwhile Wolfe Tone, one of the major instigators of the rebellion, was in Paris repeatedly begging for help, until at the end of July the French agreed that several small expeditions would invade Ireland. The first of these, consisting of 3 frigates and about 1,000 men, anchored in Killala Bay in County Mayo and landed their troops on 22 August. (They had been intended for Donegal Bay but prevented from getting there by contrary winds.) Having overpowered a small party of about fifty Yeomen and Fencibles, they occupied the buildings round the bay. These troops, commanded by General Humbert, were veterans of the armies of the Rhine and Italy but they found little enthusiasm for their cause among the peasants of Mayo until they produced some gaudy uniforms for recruits and then a few hundred peasants joined them. Mayo is one of the counties of the province of Connaught, which had previously taken no part in the rebellion. Major General Hutchinson commanded in Connaught and as soon as he heard of the enemy's landing, he collected two regiments of Irish militia, a detachment of Fencible Infantry, a few cavalry and four guns and set out towards them, having asked for reinforcements.

Cornwallis sent for Moore as soon as he heard of the French landing, and Moore found himself so busy and his movements so great that he did not have time to write up his journal until 17 September. He found Cornwallis pondering the map of Ireland; he immediately told Moore that the French had landed, and showed him several letters he had received with intelligence. These were none too clear on numbers; it did not appear that there were many, but they had received a kind reception from the country people. Troops were already on the march to locations previously chosen by Cornwallis, but it was necessary to assemble an army large enough to march against the enemy without denuding the countryside of troops to protect the inhabitants. General Nugent was directed to assemble a force at Sligo, while Brigadier General Taylor, already at Sligo, was directed to feel out the enemy to gain intelligence, but not to risk himself and his troops. General Lake was ordered to assemble a force at Galway but warned not to risk any action until he had a sufficient force to ensure success. The principal army was to assemble at Athlone or Longford; Lord Cornwallis intended to command it himself. Moore was to assemble his corps at Blessington and march to Sallins where boats would take them along the canal to Athlone.

When they reached the canal the boats were late, not arriving until after midnight; while they waited the troops rested with their arms in their hands. They finally got to Kilbeggan in the afternoon and camped. They had been joined by some English militia, and now a brigade of English artillery joined. The whole were put under Moore's command. Cornwallis was concerned to hear that General Hutchinson had advanced to Castlebar; he thought this was too near the enemy. They all marched to Athlone on the 27th and camped. During the night an express arrived telling of the defeat of General Lake at Castlebar. Lake had reached Galway to find that Huchinson had already moved towards the enemy, so he went on to Castlebar; arriving just before midnight, everybody very tired from the constant movement. At 5 am news came that the French were approaching and 2 hours later they attacked. After a heavy British cannonade, which caused the Irish allies of the French to run and killed about 100 of them, General Humbert ordered a bayonet attack, on which most of Lake's men fled in panic. The few who stayed were made up of the Artillery, about 100 of the 6th Foot and a small body of Fencible Dragoons; those who ran were the Longford and Kilkenny Militia, some of Fraser's Fencibles, some Galway volunteers and the 6th Dragoon Guards. Many of the Longford and Kilkenny Militia deserted to the French side after the action, and others went over to them after being taken prisoner.

Cornwallis was concerned for Athlone, and thought his position on the Leinster side of the Shannon was poor. He had a badly inflamed foot and had been travelling in a carriage, but he could wear a cloth shoe and managed to ride to accompany Moore to view the ground on the other side of the river. They found no good ground to camp his small force and decided to wait until the reinforcements he was expecting arrived from Longford but directed Moore to place strong picquets. More troops turned up overnight with generals Campbell and Weymes and they all moved to a camp closer to Athlone. Generals Lake and Hutchinson and the remainder of their troops arrived and joined the camp. They could get no sure news of the enemy's location, and Lieutenant Colonel Craufurd was sent out with a detachment of cavalry to patrol towards Castlebar and hopefully get intelligence of the enemy. While they waited, the army was brigaded: Major General Campbell commanded the first brigade and General Hutchinson the second, both under General Lake. Moore's corps, called 'the advance corps', consisted of the first and second flank battalions, the 100th Regiment and flank companies of the Warwick and Bucks, Roxburgh Fencibles, some cavalry, a detachment of the Hompesch and some artillery, and directed to report to Cornwallis only.

More reinforcements arrived from England and Cornwallis, with the troops at Athlone, began his advance westwards on 30 August. The following night they moved forward again, and Moore camped half a mile in front of the rest of the army. As they were striking tents just before daylight, Moore's brother James arrived. He had heard of his brother's illness in Wicklow and that John (now known to the family as Jack) had moved with the army before he was quite recovered; James had decided to go over to Ireland and look after him but was delighted to see he was fully recovered. He brought good news of his own affairs: he was engaged to be married to Harriet Henderson, the daughter of a widow. Although he longed for the day when they would be married, he hoped that his mother-in-law would not think she should move in with them. Jack was delighted with the news, and sympathised with his hopes of seeing a battle. He gave James a horse and he joined the march. At least one member of his family would see how much they moved around; he had already told his father that it was useless for them to try to trace his movements, as most of the places he went through were so small they would not be marked on any map they might have.

Moore received a note from Cornwallis saying that he should move his camp. As he did not quite understand what was wanted, he rode over to headquarters and visited Cornwallis at his bedside. He said that he had had a sleepless night and did not want to spend another night in such a camp. He explained what he wanted Moore to do, and said that the rest of the army would change positions during that day; they needed to postpone movement for a day as the 2nd and 29th regiments, which had just joined, needed a day to rest after marching non-stop from Wexford. The whole army then moved forward to a position which was only marginally better than the previous one as it was more spacious. Late in the day on 3 September, Cornwallis sent for Moore; Craufurd had returned and reported that the French were camped near Castlebar and had put out picquets less than a mile from the town. A later report came in that the French and rebels had moved early in the morning towards Swineford but as no one had followed them long enough to ascertain their direction, cavalry patrols were sent out to observe their route and

Craufurd was sent out again with a detachment of dragoons to follow the enemy. As information on the enemy's movements came in, it was sent on to Lake with orders to follow and harass them, but not to risk an action.

Cornwallis started to move north-east, to the disapproval of several of his generals who thought he should be going directly north, but he explained that he was concerned that the French might turn his right flank, cross the Shannon before him and move towards Dublin through the counties of Longford and Leintrim, which were believed to be much disaffected and thus might rise and join the French.

Then on the 6th word came that the French were heading for Sligo and that Lake was following them; Cornwallis saw that nothing Lake could do would save Sligo so he sent Moore to reinforce him with about 2,200 men of Light Infantry, the 100th Regiment and some Artillery. On the road he received a letter from Lake saying that he was about to march towards Colooney and watch the enemy. Moore replied that he would follow as fast as he could, but that since his men had had long marches on the two previous days he doubted they would be able to do more than 19 miles that day. The next day, while on the road, he received a further letter from Lake saying that the enemy were now on route to Manor Hamilton and that they had thrown five English 6-pounders and one tumbril into the river at Drumahaire and abandoned three more and another tumbril on the road. A further letter, received on the 7th, said that the French were now heading for Balintra on the Shannon.

Moore continued his march after Lake, but soon an express arrived from Cornwallis ordering him to march to Carrick-on-Shannon to join him there. While on this new march, he received news of an unfortunate action between the French and 300 of the Limerick City Militia, who had marched out from Sligo to attack them. Their information on French numbers had misled them, and their choice of ground was poor. They fought bravely and it took the French an hour to beat them but they lost their two guns and sixty men were taken prisoner. Humbert took this little corps to be the advance of a larger force, and changed the direction of his march several times in an effort to evade it. News was coming of rebels deserting the French and seen heading for Mayo. Some of the Yeomen brought in several prisoners they had found with arms. The French tried to destroy the bridge at Balintra but were stopped by Craufurd with the cavalry of Lake's advance guard. James Moore missed the battle he had wanted to see, for he had already left for London.

Cornwallis rested his corps for some hours, then moved on at 10 pm and met up with the French; after a short action on 8 September Humbert and his remaining force of 800 men surrendered. Cornwallis sent word to Moore that he was going to Lord Longford's house, Packenham Hall, near Castle Pollard and would like to see him as soon as possible. Moore rode on to Mohill, where he was able to get the good bed he hoped for after sleeping on wet ground the previous night. In the morning he rode through the ground where the action had taken place, it was covered with the bodies of dead rebels. Arriving at Packenham Hall in time for breakfast, he found Cornwallis ready to discuss plans. He had received information from the Duke of Portland that an armament was readying at Brest to sail for Ireland. He sent

General Trench to the Mayo coast and Moore to the central plain, ready to move in any direction.

Moore settled his troops under canvas a mile from Moate, 10 miles east of Athlone. Although the weather was fine, he decided to indulge himself by sleeping in a house in Moate village. There, on 23 September, he heard that another rebel agitator, Napper Tandy, had landed with a small party of French soldiers and marines. One of the ships that had chased him was *Melampus*, commanded by his brother, Graham. Tandy issued what Moore referred to as 'a ridiculous proclamation' but this was not received with enthusiasm by the local population, so Tandy set sail again. Two days later Moore received information from one of the frigates cruising off Brest that one line-of-battle ship and eight frigates had put to sea and were thought to be en route to Ireland. On 14 October he wrote that although there was no firm news of the French ships, they were not expected to go to Ireland. He had recently heard of Nelson's victory in Aboukir Bay and thought this might discourage the French relish for naval expeditions and persuade them to spend a calm winter.

It had not done so, for the following day he was informed that two French ships had anchored in Donegal Bay and were attempting to land troops, while other ships were waiting their turn in the offing. Admiral Warren captured half this fleet (one French ship, *La Resolue* was captured by Graham Moore in *Melampus*) and dispersed the rest.[1] This squadron was carrying what Moore believed to be 6 or 7,000 men with arms and stores for the Irish country people. Although grateful that they had not succeeded in landing those troops, Moore wrote that while they would have given the British some trouble, Ireland was no longer likely to be subdued by such a force. Cornwallis himself was a powerful presence and additional troops had been sent over from England. Part of Moore's brigade was already in Athlone, the rest were cantoned in nearby villages until the barracks in Athlone were ready for them; the weather had turned too bad for them to remain under canvas. Moore's next task was to reorganise his troops; he had felt for some time that the 1st and 2nd flank battalions were too large, and his proposal to form a third battalion from them had been approved. He gave the command of the third battalion to Lieutenant Colonel Nightingale. These new battalions each consisted of about 500 men.

Moore was summoned to give evidence before a court of enquiry on 6 November. Cornwallis invited him to stay with him while he attended this court and having accepted this invitation he stayed there for three days. Cornwallis lived like a general officer with his aides-de-camp without the ceremony of a Viceroy; he took breakfast at 9 am, then retired with his secretary to attend to business. He saw the Adjutant General first, and then the different civil and military officers, continuing this business until 2 or 3 o'clock when he rode until 6 pm. Dinner followed at 6.30 or 7 pm, and when Moore was there it was generally laid for ten or twelve people. Cornwallis conversed freely on whatever topics were started, although he preferred the military ones. Dinner took about 2 hours, when all moved to another room, the newspapers were brought in and the conversation continued to about 11 pm when he went to bed. Moore thought him 'a man of plain manly character, devoid of affectation or pretension, displaying great good sense and observation'.

The day before Moore left Dublin, Wolfe Tone was brought in as a prisoner, having been taken on board the *Roche*; he was tried by court martial at the barracks the day after his arrival. As one of the principal organisers of the United Irishmen, he was found guilty and sentenced to death. He was found to have tried to kill himself that night, being found with his windpipe cut across. His execution was postponed, and never rescheduled; he died of his self-afflicted wound on 19 November.

At the beginning of December Moore received a letter from Colonel Brownrigg saying that General Charles Stuart was sailing with troops from Lisbon and Gibraltar to take possession of Minorca, that reinforcements were being sent and that Stuart had asked that Moore should command them. Brownrigg's letter also said that Stuart's operations would probably include Italy and asked if he would like that command. Moore replied 'in the most pressing terms' to accept it. He only said that since Cornwallis had always been kind to him that he would be sorry to disoblige him, and thus asked that the order for his change of command would be sent without any hint that he had been asked if he wanted it. Waiting impatiently for the order, Moore then heard from Brownrigg that after talking over the arrangement with the Duke of York and Mr Dundas, Dundas had said that in his private correspondence with Cornwallis, the latter had laid such stress on the esteem he had for Moore that he did not think he could be removed without causing umbrage. The change of command was given up for the present. Moore was extremely disappointed, as he was convinced that there would be no more action in Ireland, he considered it a mere loss of time to stay in Ireland any longer. Of Cornwallis, he wrote that he had 'behaved so remarkably well to me, and has treated me on every occasion with such kindness and distinction that I should be sorry to do anything that would appear ungrateful ...'.

He was correct about the lack of activity in Ireland. There is a long period with no entries in his journal, then on 17 June 1799 he wrote that in April there had been an alarm following the report of a French fleet leaving Brest which soon faded when that fleet turned south and entered the Mediterranean. He asked Cornwallis if he might have a couple of months leave to go to England. This was granted, but before he set off, he received a letter from Cornwallis' secretary informing him that he had been chosen for a secret expedition. He left on the 18th, preceded by the 92nd, 2nd and Guards regiments, who marched for Cork to embark for Portsmouth. Moore took with him a gift for his sister, Jane: a dog called Paddy who, from his description, was like a modern deerhound, or a slim Irish wolfhound: tall and thin with a coarse iron-grey coat, an ideal companion for the country walks near the cottage his parents had taken on Ham Common. He was worried by this development as he thought his father would be unhappy away from all his London acquaintances; a letter from James, although removing the immediate worry, told him that his father's heart was beginning to fail.[2]

Chapter 6

Holland

The country known in the late eighteenth century as North Holland incorporated much of what we now call Belgium. Politically Holland (the Netherlands) consisted of several small provinces. Revolutionary France declared war against Holland in 1793, and it became part of the 'first coalition' against France, the other members of which were Austria, Prussia, Spain, Portugal and Britain.

North Holland was very flat, and a large proportion of its territory consisted of low islands on the estuaries leading into the North Sea. The greater part of the terrain over which the Allied troops were to serve consisted of sand or flat land broken by ditches, dykes and bridged canals. For 4 miles south from Kamp to Bergen, the sand hills rose to a greater height, and from a width of 200 or 300yd to 4 miles as they approached Bergen, with these latter rising to 150ft high with ridges 400 or 500yd in length; these were covered with dense scrub and birch coppice, the lower hills with low creeping shrubs, patches of stunted birch and heather. In some places the seaward side of these sand hills rose like cliffs, some 80ft sheer from the beach.[1]

Britain had traditionally helped to protect the Netherlands from invaders, and when parts of it were overrun by the French, its reaction was almost automatic. Previous unsuccessful attempts had been made on North Holland in 1793 and 1794, both by forces led by the Duke of York. In 1799, the first wave of troops went out under the command of Sir Ralph Abercromby, with instructions which defined his purpose as being 'to rescue the united provinces of Holland from the degrading tyranny of the French Republic, and to restore them to their independence, under the authority of the Prince of Orange and their lawful government …'.[2]

* * *

Although referred to at the time as a 'secret' expedition, its purpose was no great secret. When a grand parade of the army was held in Kent, reviewed by the King, the Royal Princes and the exiled Prince of Orange, standing with his father next to the Duke of York (the Commander-in-Chief of the British army), the newspapers could see that this was more than just a review. The planned invasion of Holland was no longer a secret, although what did remain secret for some time was that a treaty was being drawn up with the Czar of Russia for Russian troops to assist (at Britain's expense). The main objective was to gain possession of the Dutch fleet, which was under the control of the French as the occupying power. If it could not be captured, it was to be destroyed. Once this was achieved, the next objective was to land reinforcements and free Amsterdam; a secondary secret was the negotiations with the Prussians to assist in pushing the French back.

Sir Ralph Abercromby was called to London and informed that he was to take command of the first part of the expedition; they did not tell him until later that the Duke of York would bring reinforcements and take over as Commander-in-Chief. Abercromby was not entirely enthusiastic; he had been in Holland before and was not convinced that the Dutch people were ready to rise against the French. He had a low opinion of the Prince of Orange, and of the Russians, and did not approve of either of the places suggested for his landing: the open beach of Scheveningen, north of the Hague, or the coast of Groningen province.

Moore, now named Major General under Abercromby in the expedition, crossed from Ireland on the regular packet, arriving at Holyhead on the morning of 23 July 1799, and went on to London with Paul Anderson, arriving there on the 28th. His mother joined them from Ham Common and stayed for the ten days he remained in London. His father and Graham were at the London house, and he also took the opportunity to meet James' wife.

The troops for the expedition were assembling in a camp at Shirley, near Southampton. Moore went to join them but had only been there three days when orders came for the troops to march in four divisions by two routes to camp at Barham Downs, on the Kent Downs, south-east of Canterbury. Moore's command was the fourth brigade, consisting of the Guards, the 21st (Royals), 25th, 49th, 64th, 69th, 79th and 92nd regiments.* Moore was pleased with the Guards, and the 92nd (Highlanders), next best were the Royals and 25th; the 79th were, he thought, weak but not bad, the 49th had not been established long enough to make a good judgement and the 64th Regiment was not, he thought, fit to go on service. Abercromby inspected the brigade and told Moore they were to march to Sandwich and embark the following day at Ramsgate. The 69th Regiment was taken from Moore and given to General Coote. They embarked on the 8th, but then it poured with rain and a strong wind kept them in harbour until the 10th. They sailed from there to The Downs where the whole expedition gathered to set sail together, some having embarked at Margate.

Moore went ashore and dined with Prime Minister Pitt and Mr Dundas at Walmer Castle. They were, he thought, in very good spirits, but anxious for the expedition's departure. Its original destination had been the island of Walcheren but this was changed to Goeree and Voorne. Goeree commanded the entrance of the Meuse and Voorne and its fortified harbours of the Brielle and Hellevoetsluis, but information on the force on these islands and their state of defence was thin. It seemed, Moore wrote in his journal, that the expedition had been 'hurried beyond reason, but the country having been put to the expense of assembling it, it is necessary that we should be sent to attempt something. We are now upon a voyage of adventure.' The underlying objective was to get possession of the Dutch fleet, and Holland itself, with 17,000 Russian troops joining the equal number of British. The first attempt was to

---

* This list is from Moore's journal; Fortescue omits the 64th.

be by General Coote's brigade, on the island of Goeree; if he succeeded on landing, he was to push on to occupy the point opposite Willemstad.

The weather continued to be stormy and they were not able to sail until the 13th and unable to get close enough to anchor until the 21st. They hoped to begin the landing on the 22nd but on the night of the 21st it blew up again and became dangerous at anchor, so the fleet put to sea again and were unable to land until the 26th. These difficulties over landing caused a change of plans, and Goeree and Voorne were given up and it was decided to attack the Texel, further north.

They finally landed on the morning of the 27th, in great confusion. Moore was put on shore with no more than 300 of his men, a mixture of all his regiments. The enemy did not oppose them; if it had, Moore wrote that they would have been beaten with little ability to resist. There were a few enemy picquets which retired as he advanced; most of the rest of his brigade were put on shore in the next half hour and he was able to take up his position fronting the Helder without opposition. On his immediate right, Sir James Pulteney with the reserve and part of Coote's brigade also landed without opposition but fell in with a body of the enemy as soon as they began their advance. They drove them for some distance, but at the end of the sand hills they encountered a large body of cavalry and infantry with guns, who began what Moore termed 'a very hot action' which continued until 3 o'clock. Abercromby had to take the grenadiers of the Guards to Pulteney's assistance, when after a while the enemy retired. The British loss in killed and wounded was 452 men and officers, including Moore's friend Lieutenant Colonel Hay of the Engineers (Abercromby's aide-de-camp) and Colonel Smollett of the Guards, both taken by cannon balls as they stood at Abercromby's side, and the Adjutant-General Colonel Hope was wounded in the leg. While this action was going on, Moore pushed his advanced posts forwards towards Kuyck-Duinen where some riflemen emerged and skirmished for a while.

Abercromby came over when the main action was over; he agreed with Moore that their situation was not good, with the enemy on both flanks, and they were in an extremely bad position, although it had looked more promising on the maps. Abercromby directed Moore to attack the Helder that night and gave him part of the Guards to assist, but it was clear that if this attempt failed, they would need to re-embark immediately. Then a cutter arrived with news that 6,000 men commanded by Major General Don had sailed to reinforce them, a material change to their benefit. But the attack on the Helder should still be undertaken; some enemy deserters had come in and all had said that there were 2,000 men defending the Helder. That evening, Moore went to his advanced posts and saw much movement among the enemy troops at the Helder which he thought was just taking up positions for the night, but when it was nearly dark they marched off along the coast towards the road to Alkmaar, obviously retreating. He immediately pushed forward his patrols and followed with the Royals; they met a man with a white flag from the town, who reported that the enemy had spiked all their cannon and marched off. He carried on, and at 10 pm arrived at the enemy's defences, where he posted himself and sent a detachment into the town. The 92nd Regiment joined him in the night and at daylight he took possession of the batteries and the town. The Dutch ships were at anchor close to the batteries but departed on seeing the British. As soon as the British fleet was able to come in and receive the news, it followed the Dutch fleet; in the middle of the following night an officer came to Moore with the news that the Dutch fleet had surrendered without firing a shot. He wrote in his journal that 'the greatest stroke that has perhaps been struck in this war has been accomplished in a few hours, and with a trifling loss'. He put this down to Abercromby's perseverance in the attempt, when the enemy must have known they were coming. The main enemy force on the right was thought to be some 5,000, which, having been joined by the 2,000 from Helder, had retired to Alkmaar.

Moore was given the two battalions of the 20th Regiment in lieu of those he had left behind at Oude Sluys. His position was behind a high dyke by the canal, while the cantonments were on the other side of the canal. Four bridges crossed the canal, and four more were being constructed of boats; Moore's picquets were on the dyke, which they were strengthening by cutting places for guns and fortifying some of the villages. They were to wait in their position until the Russian reinforcements arrived, when they would instantly move forward. In the night of 9 September, some of the picquets heard the noise of gun carriages and drums beating, meaning the enemy were obviously moving. Moore sent a patrol of dragoons between 3 and 4 in the morning with orders to patrol forward as soon as it was light. He rode to the picquets on the dyke, where they reported that the noise had ceased some hours previously. He started to move on to the villages where he had sent the dragoons when a dragoon overtook him with a message from Lieutenant Colonel Smith reporting a large force marching to attack Krabbendam. Sending Captain Anderson on to the outposts, he turned towards Krabbendam and heard a gun and some musket fire on the right where the Guards were posted and a few shots from Krabbendam. He rode to Zype Sluys and sent orders for all regiments to move to their alarm posts; it was still not quite light when he got there and he found that Lieutenant Colonel Smith had gone to Krabbendam. This eased his mind somewhat as he had confidence in Smith who was charged with the immediate defence of Krabbendam; it had not yet been attacked but a smart fire began from the picquets to which Anderson had gone. He was more concerned about the part of the dyke in the rear of the villages of Haring's-Karspel and Ennigerburg where there was a good road on the dyke which the enemy would find easier to use than what Moore called 'the impediments of the country'.

He galloped to the alarm post of the Royals and 92nd Regiment and saw that the enemy intended to attack there; it was sufficiently light to make out large bodies of the enemy marching towards Haring's-Karspel. The regiments were nearly at their alarm posts and the picquets from the villages were falling back; Anderson had got the bridges on the canals lifted, which retarded the enemy's advance. The attack on the Guards continued and another had started on Krabbendam; orders came from there from Abercromby to Moore to detach a regiment and go there himself. He sent a reply saying that he would send a regiment if Abercromby desired it, but the enemy were in force behind the villages and preparing to attack. He thought his presence was essential where he was but less so at Krabbendam since Abercromby was there himself.

A number of the enemy's Jägers and light troops started firing, as did some cannon, providing cover for a large column to attempt to charge the small British contingent they could see, with shouts and drums and bugles. Most of the British troops, hidden behind the dyke, then sprang up and threw a galling fire from the muskets and field guns situated on the dyke, which made the enemy retire in some confusion. They appeared to support a feint attack on the village of St Martin, but this was merely to cover their retreat. As they retired their numbers could be seen to be between 12,000 and 14,000, and they had, as was learned later, lost 2,200 men. The British losses were very small, due to the protection given by the dyke. At the beginning of the attack, Moore was struck in the index finger by a shot that his spyglass turned, preventing it going into his body. With a broken finger and the arm in a sling, Moore was unable to write, and his next few letters home were written for him by Paul Anderson.

At about 3 o'clock he retook the village in front; a couple of hours later the troops returned to their cantonments. The enemy had driven the British from Krabbendam and a redoubt on the right of it, but had not been able to penetrate further. Lieutenant-Colonel Smith and six officers of the 20th Regiment were wounded; this regiment was formed of drafts from the militia, and Abercromby told Moore that they had performed with great gallantry. That evening the Duke of York arrived and over the next two days reinforcements of Russians and English landed, bringing the Allied force up to between 30,000 and 40,000 men.

On the 14th Moore was ordered to take his brigade and a squadron of the 18th Dragoons to occupy the villages of Winkel and Nieudorp. This new position was in front of the left of the rest of the army and well secured by water: the broad canal of Lange Keyz protected Moore's front and right flank, the Zyder Zee his left flank. The enemy's advanced posts were close to his on the right. His patrols were pushed to the gates of Hoorn and forward towards Rustenburg; the bridges were broken near there but the only enemy was one battalion at Rustenburg. On the morning of the 18th Moore moved his whole brigade to Winkel and Nieudorp to make room for Lord Chatham's brigade and the reserve. Abercromby arrived with orders for Moore to march that evening with his brigade, Lord Chatham's, Lord Cavan's, the Reserve, the 18th Dragoons and a considerable portion of artillery; about 10,000 men in total. A general attack was planned for daylight; two columns of Russians under General Herman would advance on the right and a third column under Sir James Pulteney, consisting of General Coote's and General Don's brigades, was to attack Lange Dyke. The corps under Abercromby was to turn to the right of the enemy and take advantage of whatever success the other columns had achieved.

They marched at 8 in the evening and arrived 5 hours later at Hoorn where 200 Dutch troops laid down their arms after some parley. The morning was very wet and windy but they could hear from the guns on the right that the attack had started. The men were very tired but since Abercromby could make no decisions until he received reports of the success ahead, the men were directed to lie on their arms on the road.

At about midday Lord Charles Bentinck arrived with a letter from the Duke of York's secretary with news that the attack on Wannenhuizen had been successful, that the Russians and Guards were advancing on Schorldam and that word from Sir James

Pulteney was still awaited. With this remaining uncertainty, Abercromby did not feel he could make a move and sent Moore to find a good place to remain overnight. At about 4 pm Captain Fitzgerald (another of the Duke's aides-de-camp) brought news that after considerable resistance and some loss Pulteney had carried the village of Oude Karspel, but that the Russians had advanced bravely as far as Bergen but were repulsed. The Guards and other troops had been ordered to their assistance, and Abercromby should march immediately to join the Duke. Fitzgerald said that from the firing he had heard he thought that the enemy was being driven back. As the people of Hoorn had shown great goodwill to Abercromby's troops, he did not want to leave them without some protection, so he ordered the 55th Regiment to remain. The rest of the corps, in two columns, began their march at dusk along the same roads they had used the day before. En route Abercromby received a letter saying that the two columns on the right had been completely repulsed; General Herman and numerous Russians had been taken prisoner and there had been considerable losses among the Russians and British in killed and wounded. The Duke had retired to his previous position behind the dyke and wished Abercromby to go to him as soon as possible. Leaving Moore to bring on the column, Abercromby rode on to the Duke; at about 2 am the column took its position in the same place they had been before the march.

On 28 September, Pulteney was ordered to leave the village of Oude Karspel, and this was done in such a great hurry that he had to leave the guns and batteries as he had found them. Moore thought that the order for this was 'certainly the effect of panic in consequence of disasters upon the right'. The Russians had taken the village of Bergen, but had preserved no order in their advance, nor in their precipitous retreat. They had lost two of their generals, one as a prisoner, the other dying of his wounds; their total killed and wounded was in the region of 3,000, and they had lost another 3,000 or so as prisoners. These were chiefly Dutch. The British losses were between 1,500 and 2,000. Moore thought the whole attack was launched before the generals had perfectly understood their part and before the leaders of the different columns had managed to communicate; also that detaching Abercromby's large column before the general attack was 'ill imagined'. Moore wrote that he thought that without a general rising of the Dutch people it was unwise to hope to conquer it. It would have been better to have withdrawn all the troops after the Dutch fleet was taken. The Duke of York's arrival with reinforcements had made it a point of honour that they should make another attempt to force the enemy out. If this was successful, they would be able to take up winter quarters in North Holland, if not, they would have to re-embark.

Another attack was planned for 29 September and the preceding ten days were spent in preparations. Abercromby, with 9,000 British troops, was to march along the sands from Petten to Egmont-op-Zee and try to turn the enemy at Bergen, while 8,000 Russians attacked it in front. Lieutenant General Dundas with a column on either side of the canal would protect the left of the Russians attacking Schorldam. Pulteney with a reserve would watch Oude Karspel and protect the left. Information on the nature of the country was poor but they trusted in the gallantry of the troops and the judgement of the generals to take advantage of circumstances as they occurred. It was clear that they could not rely on a diversion and must have a real battle with the French or give up the point, but Moore was sure that they would prove completely successful if the Russians did their duty.

It had been intended to assemble Abercromby's column on the evening of the 28th, but it was so wet and windy that it was thought better to defer this until the morning of the 29th. Moore commenced his march at 3 am but he had gone barely ¼ mile before one of Abercromby's aides-de-camp brought an order to return; although it was a fine day, the surf was still so high from the previous day's storm that it impossible to march along the beach. This disappointed the troops but they got back to their cantonments just at daybreak and before the enemy could see them. Moore was also disappointed; he had been feverish for two days, and although he thought he could have gone through the day, he realised that if he had done so he would probably have been unwell for the rest of the campaign. When he returned to the camp, he took some tartar emetic and went to bed; after a quiet day he was, he wrote, 'perfectly recovered' the following day. Abercromby called on him and told him that the attack would now be in daylight; they had found some quicksands between the camp and Petten which made it impossible for artillery to pass other than at low water and in good weather. A thousand British were to act in the sand hills on the right of the Russians, while General Dundas was to move in their rear, extending to the right through the sand hills, and hopefully be able to communicate with Abercromby's column.

The captured Russian general, Herman, was boastful and pretentious, 'His action fell short of his talk as much as it generally does with men of that description', wrote Moore, and it was even suspected by some that he had deliberately allowed himself to be captured to hide his misconduct. His replacement, General Essen, seemed to be as cautious as Herman was imprudent; whether he would be adequate in their current situation was yet to be seen.

The attack was then scheduled for 2 October, with Abercromby's column assembling at Petten at 3 am. There were 10,000 men under Abercromby to form the right column, which was intended to move along the beach to Egmont-op-Zee and turn the enemy's left. The 8,000-strong Russian force, under General Essen, was to march to Bergen. Lieutenant General Dundas with some British troops was to follow the Russians and act as a reserve to them, Major General Burrard with the 2nd Brigade of the Guards was to move on Wannenhuizen; Pulteney, with a reserve made up of the brigades of generals Don, Manners and Prince William, was to watch the left, especially the enemy's positions in Oude Karspel and Lange Dyke. Major General Coote's brigade was to act in the sand hills on the right of the Russian column and support Colonel McDonald. 2,000 Russians were left at Petten as a reserve. The whole was dependent on the success of Abercromby's column while the others, until he had turned the enemy's flank, were merely to keep the enemy in play and prevent their detaching to reinforce their left. Abercromby's column was made up of the 1st Brigade of Guards under Major General D'Oyley, the 5th Regiment under Lord Cavan, the 4th Regiment under Moore, the reserve of about 1,100 Dragoons under Colonel McDonald and a troop of mounted artillery under Lord Paget, with ten guns.* These were disposed with Moore at the front, followed by D'Oyley, then Major General Hutchinson with the 6th Brigade and Colonel McDonald with the Reserve.

The success of this plan depended on the Russian columns advancing boldly towards Bergen so that Abercromby could move forward safely. Abercromby's infantry were to move in a column of companies from the right at half distance with the artillery on the right of the column opposite the proper intervals; the cavalry were also on the right. Colonel McDonald with the Reserve plus a battalion of Grenadiers, one of Light Infantry and 3,000 Russian Jägers were to drive the small picquet of the enemy from the height of Camperduyn then move in the sand hills on the left of the main column and flank it during the march. The column was to move along the beach, depending on the tide; at 6 am it was low enough and the advance towards Petten began, watched by the Duke of York. There was no resistance from the enemy picquet on Camperduyn, but Colonel McDonald, who should have stayed to his right, went left and joined Coote's brigade, leaving the main column exposed on its left flank. There were bodies of the enemy on the beach in front and in the sand hills on their flank. The sand hills which separated Coote and the Russians from Abercromby's column were at least 4 miles wide and difficult to cross. McDonald had gone out of sight and no word of him was received for some time, when finally a note from McDonald said he was at the village of Groet on the far side of the sand hills.

Abercromby ordered Moore to organise part of his brigade to oppose the enemy in the sand hills and keep them from the flank of the main column. At this time the enemy's Light Infantry and Hussars started skirmishing with Moore's advanced guard and he had only just formed the 25th and 79th regiments when they were attacked. He gave orders to the regiments' commanding officers to charge as soon as he gave the signal, which he did as soon as he thought the enemy close enough. The regiments advanced boldly and drove the enemy back for a considerable distance, but with some losses. Moore received a wound in the thigh during this phase, but this did not prevent him from carrying on. The Royals and 49th were ordered to join the 25th and 79th, and then, after a while, the grenadier battalion of the Guards. As they advanced, the enemy continued to retreat but stopped every time they came to favourable ground then moved on again. This encouraged the column on the beach to move forward and they continued this fight and retreat pattern for over 5 hours until they were within a couple of miles of Egmont-op-Zee where they met up with a fresh enemy corps who advanced on them 'with considerable intrepidity', as Moore wrote.

Moore's brigade were very tired from this constant movement and fighting and they were dispersed; some of the regiments on the left had not been able to keep up in the broken terrain and this had let the enemy strike on the flanks of the

---

* There were two Pagets with Moore at various places: Lord Henry (later the Marquis of Anglesey) who was with him in Holland, and in Spain under General Baird; and the Hon. Edward, who was with Moore in Egypt, Sicily and in Spain with the Reserve.

25th Regiment, which was forward of the rest. Moore sent three companies of the 92nd to support the 25th but the fire was so hot they, and the rest, began to give way. Moore sent Anderson to fetch the rest of the 92nd which, although belonging to Moore's brigade, had continued with the column on the beach but before they could join, the enemy advanced briskly and Moore's men were forced back. Moore saw he was almost surrounded and turning to get back could see that it would be impossible to rally his men in such a hot fire; they were falling in great numbers in every direction and he decided to let them fall back and then rally them to bring them back. At that point he was hit by a shot which knocked him off his horse, entering behind his ear and going out through his left cheek just under the eye. Stunned and thinking his wound was mortal he did not try to get up but he heard a soldier say to his companion 'Here is the General, we will carry him with us'; they helped him to get up and assisted him off the field to the rear where his wounds were dressed and he was got on his horse. With his groom leading the horse, they got him back to his quarters in the Ragge Wey, a journey of nearly 10 miles which with his loss of blood and general fatigue he managed, he said, 'with difficulty'. In the morning the Duke's surgeon Mr Knight came and dressed his wounds; he had no bones broken in his face, and said that the wound in his thigh was superficial. By 3 October he was able to write his own letters.

Before he left the field Moore was pleased to hear that when the 92nd Regiment arrived, those who had been retiring turned and returned to charge and made a spirited attack on the enemy, repulsing them with great slaughter but not without great loss. The killed and wounded of Moore's brigade were 44 officers and more than 600 non-commissioned officers and men. There were no more advances, the rest of the day being occupied in skirmishing. As dusk approached, the enemy, who had brought some guns to the beach, made a cavalry charge and took two more guns from the British column; they were instantly repulsed by Lord Paget, Colonel Erskine, Sir Robert Wilson and half a dozen other officers and a few mounted dragoons who happened to be with him at the time; the rest of the Dragoons ran and got mounted before joining the fray. It had been a hard day; as well as his own wounds, Moore had had a horse killed under him, and Abercromby had also lost two horses. When McDonald returned with his corps, they were too late to be effective in Abercromby's plan.

Although the fighting continued, there were many casualties on both sides and it was finally accepted that the Allies could not win. On the night of 7 October the whole army retreated to their previous position behind the Zype Dyke and after a few days an armistice was agreed, followed by a treaty signed by the Duke of York on 18 October, in which he was to evacuate all his troops by 30 November.

Moore returned to his quarters and as soon as he could be moved he went to Helder where he got on the frigate *Amethyst* and arrived at the Nore on the 24th. He arrived in London, staying at a lodging in Grosvenor Street taken for him by his mother and sister. His brother James cared for him and his wounds were completely closed in about five weeks, when he moved to his parents' house in the country. However, there had been one incident during his convalescence which nearly killed him: feverish and with a constant thirst, the army surgeons had told him he could drink as much whey as he liked and a supply of this had been placed where he could reach it. Unfortunately someone had left a quantity of sugar of lead for bathing his wounds by his bedside, and before he realised what it was, he took a deep draught of it. He immediately realised his mistake, and snatching up a quill pen, thrust it down his throat to induce vomiting, while Anderson ran to fetch some vinegar. These rough and ready remedies did the trick and Moore resumed his convalescence.

He was able to rejoin his brigade in Chelmsford on 24 December. His brigade was now called the 8th and consisted of the 1st and 2nd battalions of the 52nd, 79th, 85th and 92nd regiments; all were in the barracks except the 85th which was detained in Norfolk by sickness. It was intended to send troops to the Mediterranean under Sir Charles Stuart, who had asked for him. He was delighted to accept, but soon after that he was ordered to London to sit on a board of claims; expecting that to take until the expedition was to sail, he dismissed his establishment (i.e. his personal servants) except his batman François. Stuart told him that there were to be 15,000 troops from England and that another 5,000 would come from the garrisons in the Mediterranean. This corps of 20,000 men would act in the Maritime Alps, cutting off the French communication with their own country and make a useful diversion for the Austrians. There was some hope in the government that they would be able to get into southern France.

Typically the troops returning from Holland had not had the necessary attention paid to their discipline; their quarters had been frequently moved and the officers had been allowed to be absent as though the country was at peace. When the troops were collected up for this service in the Mediterranean, they were found to be lacking the necessary equipment. There had been little recruiting, and it the regiments allotted to the expedition had insufficient numbers, so that instead of the 15,000 promised, they had only 10,000 effectives. It was the middle of March 1800 before the first division of about 5,000 men under Major General Pigot was embarked. Although Moore did not know why, there had been a change of plans by the government; it was said that some of the Cabinet had been against it from the start. None of them had the faintest idea of the preparation required for such a large army to get to the Mediterranean and enable it to act. General Stuart, with the division already embarked would go alone to the Mediterranean.

There had been a report that the Spanish were marching for the Portuguese border; Sir Ralph Abercromby was sent for to take command there and Moore was named as one of the major generals to serve with him. The news about the Spanish turned out to be wrong, and at about that time, Stuart quarrelled with the ministers and resigned his command. Abercromby was appointed to serve in the Mediterranean and Portugal; Moore, Hutchinson and Pigot were appointed to serve under him. Pigot, with his division of 5,000 men, sailed first, followed by the rest a few days later.[3]

Chapter 7

Egypt: Preparation

E gypt was important both to the French and to the British because it allowed comparatively easy access across the desert to the Red Sea and on to India. After Nelson's failure to catch the French fleet in 1798, the French got into Alexandria and had penetrated down the Nile beyond Cairo and taken over the country. The British government was anxious to oust the French and make friends with the Turks, so removing the threat to India.

Most of the country round the city and port of Alexandria was desert, but the Nile Delta was fertile, as was a strip of the country either side of the Nile itself. To the east of the city of Alexandria was Aboukir Bay, where Nelson had finally caught up with the French naval fleet and destroyed it; to the west was a long narrow bay with a sequence of islands giving some protection from storms; this was known as the Old Harbour. The city itself was built round the neck of a T-shaped peninsula; it had its water supply from an ancient canal.

* * *

Bad weather and contrary winds forced Abercromby's fleet into Portland Roads and they did not arrive at Gibraltar until 6 June; the 28th Regiment and 100 artillery were embarked on the 11th, arriving at Minorca in the morning of the 22nd. Letters from Admiral Lord Keith at Genoa awaited Abercromby, urging him with his troops to lose no time going to Genoa. He sent two battalions of the 35th Regiment under Major General Pigot to Malta, keeping two divisions with him. They sailed in the afternoon of the 23rd, but calms and contrary winds prevented them from reaching Genoa until 30 June. Here they learnt that Genoa had been evacuated and Keith with the fleet was waiting for them at Leghorn Roads, where they arrived on 1 July.

Abercromby and Moore went on shore to meet Keith. The Austrians, commanded by Melas, had been defeated by Buonaparte at Marengo, an action which was immediately followed by a convention in which the Austrians had agreed to give up the fortresses in Piedmont and the Milanese, keeping only Mantua and some other areas ceded to them by an earlier agreement. This had yet to be ratified by the Austrian Emperor, but the evacuation of Genoa and the fortresses had already taken place. At any rate, Tuscany was declared neutral with just one road left for the French to march into lower Italy. Keith regretted that Abercromby's troops had not reached Genoa earlier, believing that they could have saved the city. Moore thought it was fortunate that they had not arrived sooner as this could have meant the sacrifice of up to 5,000 men.

Abercromby paid a formal visit to Maria-Carolina, the Queen of Naples, who was at Leghorn at that time. She had pushed hard for him to undertake the defence of the kingdom of Naples. Keith also wished for this, but Abercromby had refused, stating that his force was not large enough for such a task. To attempt it would involve great expense and sacrifice of a corps that should be saved for better purposes. A formal written application was then made to Abercromby and Keith by the Neapolitan Minister, to which a joint answer was given stating the impossibility of complying with their wishes.

Abercromby avoided further contact with Maria-Carolina by remaining on board the *Sea Horse*. He had offered a regiment to garrison Messina, or even to undertake the defence of Sicily if the French attempted an invasion, but refused to do anything else until he had heard from England. In the meantime he decided to go to Malta and to send Moore back to Minorca with the troops. Moore moved into the *Alkmaar* troop-ship and arrived at Minorca on 14 July, his troops arriving over the next few days. Keith was still at Leghorn when Moore left, but intended to follow Abercromby in a few days. Moore wrote that Sir William and Lady Hamilton were there, attending Maria-Carolina. He then added, somewhat sardonically, that Nelson was also there 'attending upon Lady Hamilton. He is covered with stars, ribbons and medals, more like the Prince of an Opera than the Conqueror of the Nile. It is really melancholy to see such a brave and good man, who has deserved well of his country, cutting so pitiful a figure.'

Abercromby had left orders for Lieutenant General Fox to place the troops returned from and about to return from Leghorn under Moore's command at Mahon. Other dispositions were that Brigadier General Doyle with the first division had the lazaretto (hospital) and the second with Brigadier General Oakes had Fort George, Georgetown and Mahon. More troops came in: on the 18th Lord Dalhousie with 3,800 men and Colonel Lawson with 3 companies of artillery who landed but left their stores on board. The ships that brought these men also brought despatches for Abercromby; he had directed that all despatches should be held for him at Minorca, but a ship was sent immediately to Malta to inform him of the arrival of the reinforcements. Moore expected orders from England to recall the whole of the troops but in the meantime they all had to remain on board their ships until Abercromby returned.

While they waited for his return, applications had arrived from General Melas for troops in Tuscany. Keith seemed to agree with this idea but Moore remarked that not only did he expect Abercromby to land no troops until he had heard from England, but that any application from Keith for troops would not be complied with. When he last saw Abercromby, Moore had expected something of this sort to come, and had begged Abercromby to be explicit in his instructions to General Fox, the Commander-in-Chief in the Mediterranean. The expected request for troops was received on 29 July and was shelved for Abercromby's return. He arrived on 3 August, and on the following day he sent Brigadier General Hope (the Adjutant General) to General Melas' headquarters; he was not happy with the situation of the Austrians, as reported by Keith and he did not think that Melas realised that it was to him, not Keith, that requests for troops should be made. Once the last of the troops arrived, the army was rearranged into two divisions: the first, under Major General Hutchinson, with the first brigade under Brigadier General Doyle and the second brigade under Lord Craven; the second division, under Moore, was made up of a third brigade under Brigadier General Oakes and the fourth brigade under Colonel Paget. While Abercromby was away, Moore inspected the regiments; when Abercromby returned he also inspected them. They were generally in better shape than most of the troops left in England, with those who had been in the Mediterranean for a while being better than they had had in Holland. Those who had recently come from England, being made up of drafts of militia, were unformed and some of them were extremely bad. It was too hot to train them with field exercises, but they were improving interior discipline and learning to adapt their equipment for light movement. Abercromby was determined to keep the army free from camp baggage and to reduce officers, and men's personal baggage to what was absolutely essential.

Despatches finally arrived, brought by Major General Cradock. The regiments to be left as garrison on Minorca were named, the rest were formed into three brigades and a reserve, this under Moore. This was not considered a permanent disposition, but merely to ease the immediate embarkation. Their destination was supposedly kept a great secret, but Moore was sure that they would stop at Gibraltar and meet up with a large force under Sir James Pulteney which was ready to sail when Cradock left England. Pulteney's force was 13,000 or 14,000, Abercromby's at least 10,000. This latter force began its embarkation on 28 August, the regiments taking their heavy baggage, but leaving their women behind. Despite all this, the Austrians had agreed to an armistice everywhere and there was a possibility of a peace.

Abercromby's force sailed from Minorca on 1 September, first to the south, then, when the wind turned to come from the east, they went west, leaving no doubt that they were headed to Gibraltar. They arrived there on the 14th and Moore went on shore with Abercromby to see the governor, who showed them the *Spanish Gazette* with an account of Pulteney having landed at Ferrol. He did not seem to have achieved anything there as he was not opposed and his troops were back on their ships a day later. Abercromby told Moore that they would wait for Pulteney, probably meeting in the Tagus, and, Moore understood from this conversation, it had been intended that they would attack Cadiz and destroy the naval arsenal there. Abercromby had changed his mind on this, perhaps because a severe outbreak of the plague or a similar fever was raging in Cadiz.

At this point Pulteney's fleet was seen in the west; it sailed for Gibraltar Bay, while Keith's fleet sailed across the Straits to Tetuan Bay, partly to avoid the strong westerly winds and partly to water. On the 27th *Ajax* arrived from Gibraltar and made the signal to weigh anchor; the whole fleet sailed out of Tetuan Bay and made for Gibraltar. The wind dropped and stayed calm and they remained almost motionless in sight of the Rock for two days. Captain Alexander Cochrane of the *Ajax* and Colonel Maitland paid a visit and from Maitland Moore found that they were going to Cadiz. He had no communication from Abercromby or Keith. During the night the wind blew fresh from the west; with the wind from that direction it was impossible to get out of the Gut.* On Cochrane's signal they turned to make for

---

* The Gut is the very narrow strait of water between Gibraltar and the Moroccan coast.

Tetuan again, but left there on 2 October, meeting the *Foudroyant* with Keith and Abercromby on board. The wind had changed again, now coming from the east, the whole fleet of almost 150 sailing together as they passed through the Straits and out into the Atlantic. The following morning they were in sight of Cadiz and later in the day the signal to anchor was given. A signal was made for general officers to go on board the *Foudroyant*, where they received their orders for the landing. Moore's Reserve and the Brigade of Guards were to go first and land in a bay north of Rota; his orders were to land and destroy the Carraccas arsenal and shipping, if it could be done in a way that would ensure the re-embarkation of the troops. Abercromby had been unable to obtain much information about the force likely to oppose them, or how ready they might be, but he did know that the Spanish had been expecting such an attack for some time, so his orders to Moore were very general. If his attack was successful, Moore was then to move carefully towards Rota to get intelligence.

On 5 October, a naval captain and two engineers reconnoitred the coast, while *Foudroyant* stood in. While they waited, a letter addressed to the admiral was brought out from the Governor of Cadiz under a flag of truce. Moore went on board the flagship and heard the letter read out:

> That at a time when the town and neighbourhood of Cadiz was suffering under so severe a calamity as the plague, he saw with surprise the force under his Lordship's command upon the coast, with a view no doubt to take advantage of their present state to destroy the town and arsenal; that a conduct so inhuman was unbecoming a nation like Great Britain; that he still hoped his Lordship would desist; that if he did not, he was not to expect an easy conquest; that the force collected was sufficient to baffle him, and that the garrison and inhabitants, however, reduced by sickness, would prefer an honourable death, in defence of their country, to that which was at any rate awaiting them from disease. We should, by persevering in our unmanly and inhuman design, be held in execration by all Europe.

An answer from the admiral and Abercromby was sent:

> That if the governor would deliver up the ships of war in the harbour, the officers and crews should be immediately sent back and the British force should be withdrawn; if not, as the force was sufficient for the destruction of the town and arsenal, the troops should be instantly landed.

Some information was got from an American vessel leaving Cadiz and then a captured fisherman: there were 8,000 troops on the Isle of Leon, two regiments of cavalry at Rota and a corps at St Mary's; that the fever still raged at Cadiz and in the countryside and towns around it. Each day 200 or 300 were dying in Cadiz and the fever had reached the troops, killing most of the officers in some regiments.

Moore stayed on the flagship for dinner. In the afternoon, Abercromby told Keith that it was necessary to come to a decision; he had no doubt that the troops could achieve the landing and fully perform the service required. What he needed to know was whether Keith could guarantee the re-embarkation of the troops afterwards.

Keith had a copy of Abercromby's orders, which were to land and destroy the arsenal, if he was satisfied that he could re-embark the army afterwards. But all he could get from Keith was that he would be answerable for landing the troops, he could not be answerable for the winds, if the weather was fine he would re-embark the troops but if a south-west wind blew, the fleet must put to sea. Keith remarked to Abercromby that he had heard the opinions of other naval officers as well as his own: they were more averse to the operation than he was, but he had no objection to trying if Abercromby chose. Moore reports that Abercromby replied that it was true that he had heard the opinions of Sir Ralph Bickerton and other naval officers, but did not feel himself competent to judge of them. He repeated that his orders were to land if he could be assured of re-embarking his troops, but it was for Keith to form his own opinion from his own knowledge and that of the naval officers under him, and give a specific answer. Abercromby did not wish to take more than his share of the responsibility; he would take the whole of the responsibility of the land action and half the responsibility of the naval. If Keith would say that it was worth the risk, he was willing to undertake it and to share with Keith the merit or blame which might attach to the issue; if Keith would say it was not worth the risk he (Abercromby) was also willing to share the merit or blame of that, but he must have a determined answer one way or the other. Keith was not willing to do this, repeating that if, during or after the landing, a south-west wind got up, from that moment there could be no communication between land and fleet and that it was possible that most of the transports would run on shore.

When Moore left the *Foudroyant* no conclusion had been reached. When they were at Gibraltar, Keith had said that as soon as Fort St Catherine had been taken, the fleet could anchor in security; it was on this assurance that Abercromby had agreed to undertake the expedition. When they had arrived off Cadiz, Admiral Bickerton and other naval officers who were acquainted with the coast gave their opinion that the anchorage was not safe against a south-west wind, on which, said Moore, Keith became frightened. Moore wrote his opinion of the whole thing:

> taking into consideration the chance of bad weather at this late season, in which case the army must be lost or subject to a difficult retreat to Gibraltar or to Portugal leaving everything behind them, also the probability, or rather certainty, of catching the fever at present raging, I have not a doubt upon my mind that the undertaking should be given up. The object is in no degree equal to the risk.

The following morning the fleet got under way, standing off and on in a light wind. On 6 October the signal was made to prepare to land, on which Moore went on board the *Ajax* and spoke to Captain Cochrane who had the direction of the landing; he said he would take Moore on shore in his barge. The second signal was made for the troops to get into the flatboats, and the other captains who were to superintend the landing under Cochrane asked him for directions. Cochrane was very busy, but confessed that he knew no more than they did. During all of this, the fleet was under way some 7 miles from the shore. Many flatboats were assembled alongside and astern of the

Ajax, all full of troops, but there were not as many boats as were expected. Moore begged Cochrane to go to *Foudroyant* and tell Keith there were not enough boats and ask if more could be made available; he returned no better informed than before. The signal was made to know if they were ready to land and Moore replied 'No'. He told Cochrane that his orders were to land with his whole brigade, some 5,000 men, and since he could not do so he could not take it on himself to land without particular orders from Abercromby, especially since the whole fleet was still under way so far from the shore and there was no probability of the boats, having landed the first division, being able to return and land the second division before nightfall.

Abercromby had gone inshore to the *Phaeton* frigate, so Moore went to *Foudroyant* to explain his position to Keith. He found him in great confusion, 'blaming everybody and everything for the situation, but attempting to remedy nothing'. Keith made the signal for the flatboats to row to the *Phaeton* to get fresh orders from Abercromby. He said he could not help the shortage of boats and that his orders had not been obeyed. Moore left him, determined to go himself to Abercromby but as he was about to leave the ship he encountered one of Abercromby's aides-de-camp with a message for Keith from Abercromby. Moore went with him to Keith to hear the message: that Abercromby understood that only 3,000 men were in the boats, and since it would be dark before they could return for the rest, so he wished them to be re-embarked, for the ships to anchor closer to the shore and a proper arrangement made to land all the men in the morning. Keith said it was impossible to anchor closer in or make a better arrangement; he then, Moore said, 'went on repeating much more incoherent nonsense'. Moore had some difficulty persuading him to make the signal for the troops to re-embark; he would not do so until Moore said, several times, that Abercromby must be a better judge of the propriety of risking 3,000 troops on shore without the possibility of support for 6 or 8 hours, perhaps until the morning, and that it was the first time anyone had tried to land an army from a fleet under sail.

Moore went to the *Phaeton* and informed Abercromby of the complete lack of organisation and the confusion and the state Keith was in, taking the liberty of adding the opinion given to him by every naval officer he had talked to, of the danger of the fleet remaining in their anchorage and the impossibility of having any communication with the shore in case of a south-west wind. Before he returned to his own ship, he suggested that Abercromby, if he could not get a positive opinion from Keith, should insist on having one from the naval officers. That evening an order came to prepare to land at daylight, stating that the ships of the first division were to anchor near the *Phaeton*; it gave no further detail, and Moore anticipated similar confusion. Then, at about 1 am an order came to hoist in the flatboats and launches and to prepare for sea at daylight. Soon after this, it began to rain and blow from the south-west. At daylight a signal came to annul the landing and be ready to weigh. Abercromby went back to his own ship, the *Diadem*, and all indications were that the expedition was given up. Whether because of the weather or some other decision, by then the surf on shore had made it impossible to land and the officers of Moore's ship said that if he had landed with the Reserve on the previous day, the weather would have made it impossible to offer any support.[1]

The south-west wind blew hard until midday on 8 October when it calmed, with scarcely any wind. It took them until the 12th to reach Tetuan Bay where they received orders to complete their water. On the 13th, a heavy swell came from the east, indicating wind from that direction and Keith gave the signal to weigh. His ship (with Abercromby on board) got off, as did a few others, but the others had to trust to their anchors and ride it out. This left them in an unpleasant position, as there was no close safe harbour where they could anchor safely, and until they completed their water at Tetuan and provisions at Gibraltar, they could not go any distance. This wind soon built up to hurricane force, scattering the fleet, most into the Atlantic and some down off the west coast of Africa.

In his conversations with Bickerton and other naval officers, Moore learned that they were all displeased with Keith's conduct; they could, they said, hardly believe that he intended to carry out the landing on the 6th, and they thought Abercromby was perfectly right in ordering the troops to re-embark. All the army officers were incensed by the incident; Moore wrote to his father, 'You must have heard of the ridiculous figure we cut before Cadiz'. He went on, 'Lord Keith was frightened of the opinion of the officers, and somewhat ashamed of what he had before asserted'. Others made similar comments to the effect that Keith had left the army 'the scorn and laughing-stock of friends and foes'.[2]

Moore's ship, the *Wassenaer,* had some damage and went into Gibraltar for repairs. While there, he dined with Keith and saw Abercromby that evening when his ship came in. Both Keith and Abercromby thought they should go to Lisbon, where there was a secure anchorage, and where fresh meat could be got for the troops and sailors. Finally, on 24 October, orders came from England. Sir James Pulteney was to take 6 battalions to Lisbon, the rest, some 15,000 troops, were to go with Abercromby to Egypt where they were to work in collaboration with Turkish forces. Moore belonged to Abercromby's force. It was thought wise to sail in different divisions, meeting at Minorca; Moore's division went first. This consisted of seven troop-ships, eight transports and six victuallers; Abercromby was to follow in a few days with the rest. They were not to land the troops at Minorca, but to procure fresh meat and vegetables (very necessary as some of the troops were beginning to show signs of scurvy from their long time at sea), to land the sick and obtain other necessaries to keep the troops healthy and comfortable. Moore inspected the troops and found that only seventy-three sick had to be landed; at that season the weather was cool and pleasant. He remarked, 'Means had been taken to procure vegetables for the whole whilst we remain here'. This would have been comparatively easy on Minorca, as the British navy's Victualling Board maintained depots at Port Mahon, as they did at Gibraltar.

Letters from home suggested that the Emperor of Austria and the French had made peace but there were no hopes that England was to be included. It was thought important that the French should be forced out of Egypt, and to that end a force from India was to assist Abercromby's force by attacking, and hopefully dispossessing the French of their ports on the Red Sea. Keith appeared off Mahon on 15 October and made the signal for Moore's division to weigh and join him to sail for Malta; they arrived there on the 22nd after a rough passage. A two-day gale had strained Moore's ship and opened her seams so that she let in water. Abercromby had arrived at Malta four days previously.

Moore was very impressed with the sight of Malta, enough, he said, to repay them for all the inconvenience they had suffered during the past six months.

> The fortifications, the public and the private buildings, prove the former magnificence and grandeur of the ancient Order to which they belonged.[3] The state in which many of them are now marks the gradual decline under which the Order has been suffering for many years past – a decline not of substance or revenue, but of spirit and morals. The money which had formerly been laid out with so much judgement and taste in strengthening and ornamenting the town and neighbourhood has, for more than half a century, been wasted in sensuality and luxury. The fortifications for many years have had no repairs, and in some places the defences have been injured and converted into gardens and orange groves; yet, even as it stands, La Vallette and its dependencies may be considered as the strongest place in Europe. The town is well laid out and paved; the houses built of a very fine stone, and their fronts handsome. Buonaparte robbed the churches and public buildings of whatever was valuable, and considerable contributions were afterwards raised upon the people by Vaubois, whom he left in command.[4]

While they waited for Keith and the rest of the fleet, the sick of all the regiments were landed, the troops from some ships which needed repair or to have their hulls cleaned were landed and lodged in the town; the other troops were landed frequently for exercise. The *Wassenaer* was surveyed and reported unfit to go to sea again, indeed, if the gale had continued a few more hours, she would have sunk; many of the other troop-ships were in little better condition.

Abercromby had obtained an intercepted report of the French Chief Engineer to General Kleber on the defences of Alexandria. Although the report had been produced twelve months before, it was thought unlikely that conditions had changed materially, and that the defensive works were not in a state to resist a large force for any length of time. It was suspected that the French had received supplies of stores and arms as little attention had been paid lately to blockading the port of Alexandria. Two vessels going there and containing officers, arms and ammunition had been taken. Moore remarked in his journal that if they could force a landing at Alexandria and take over the port, 'the business would soon be done', but if they had to land at Damietta and move first on Cairo, it would take much longer and it was not the best season for such operations. The north-west winds that blew strongly directly on the coast made it dangerous for a large fleet to approach, and very difficult to land.

On 30 November, Moore received a written plan of the campaign from Abercromby. Starting with a comment to the effect that the weather off the Levant and Egyptian coasts was known to be unfavourable for navigation between November and April, it stated that there were many days during the season that were clear and moderate and not adverse to landing troops on the coast of Egypt. Even in blowy weather, ships could ride at anchor off the coast without danger, and the gales were not generally violent or long-lasting. If after further enquiry, it was found that a landing might be effected without too much risk, it would be advisable to attempt it for four reasons: first, Alexandria was the only port on the coast of Egypt where ships could remain in safety; second, once the British were in possession of the port of Alexandria, all communication between France and Egypt would be cut off; third, they would avoid the fatigue of a long blockade; and fourth, after leaving a garrison in Alexandria they would be able to detach large forces to reduce Rosetta and Damietta, or to assist the Turks in expelling the French from Cairo and Upper Egypt.

If they could not take Alexandria, they could always take Damietta, where there was safe anchorage for ships of war and transports, although further from the shore than at Alexandria. In that case, the plan of campaign would have to be changed. They would ascend the Damietta branch of the Nile, with or without the Turks, and after reducing Cairo, descend to Rosetta, cut off all communication with Alexandria and prevent the annual supply of water from the overflowing of the Nile from reaching Alexandria, which would have to surrender without a long siege. By acting in conjunction with the Turks, they would profit from the services of their cavalry, be supplied with horses and camels, gunboats and other craft for navigating the Nile, and benefit from the effects of terror and fanaticism on the minds of the inhabitants and the Bedouin. If the Turks had advanced from Jaffa towards Damietta there would be no resistance to landing and, at any rate, the French forces were not sufficient to oppose the British without abandoning Alexandria or Cairo.

Moore received a further memorandum from Abercromby on 2 December with more information on Alexandria: Aboukir was 6 leagues from Alexandria and 4 from Rosetta. Aboukir Bay gave some shelter, there was water and the surrounding country was cultivated; there was a castle reduced to ruins by the French before the occupying Turks surrendered. The cisterns which supplied Alexandria with water were within but not well covered by the French line of fortification; these were supplied with Nile water by means of a canal. The Nile began to rise between 17 and 19 June and continued to rise for two months. Some modern travellers had reported that this canal was never dry, although the water was not as good after the overflowing of the Nile. Rosetta was 10 leagues from Alexandria on the left bank of the left branch of the Nile, which rushed into the sea with such violence that sweet drinkable water could be dipped from the surface of the sea. The eastern branch of the Nile was protected by the projection of the Delta, as the winds in winter generally blew from the west; the coast of Caramania and the island of Cyprus afforded good shelter for shipping. The coast of Caramania had good harbours at Marmaris and Makri; and in Cyprus Lanarka and Limasol, where there was plenty of water, wood, wine and provisions.

The road from Rosetta and Aboukir was heavy sand, except on the beach. Troops would have to leave their ships 4 or 5 miles from the shore near Alexandria. The fleet had boats for 4,000 men and it was probable that small craft could be found locally for 3,000 more, so nearly 7,000 men could be landed at almost the same time. Eight artillerymen and twenty sailors would have to land with each gun. It would then take two more trips to land the rest of the army. With care and proper arrangement 7,000 men could be on shore 3 hours after the boats and small craft left the rendezvous,

The 8th Duke of Hamilton (centre) with Dr Moore (left) and the young John Moore (right).

Monument to Sir John Moore in Glasgow.

Sir John Moore by Sir Thomas Lawrence.

The Battle of Alexandria.

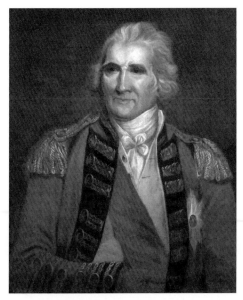

Sir Ralph Abercromby .

William Pitt the Younger.

Pasquale Paoli.

Gilbert Elliot, 1st Earl of Minto.

Admiral Samuel Hood.

Frederick, Duke of York.

Sir David Baird.

British troops on the retreat to Corunna.

Nicolas Jean-de-Dieu Soult.

Arthur Wellesley, 1st Duke of Wellington.

Sir John Moore receives his death wound.

Sir John Moore's tomb at Corunna.

Monument to Sir John Moore, St Paul's Cathedral, London.

and the rest in another 7 hours, assuming the weather was favourable. All this, of course, was subject to a degree of uncertainty.

The memos continued:

In a country like Egypt, and in an army without cavalry, the order of battle and march ought to be compact with the flanks protected by movable columns composed of steady troops and commanded by judicious officers. The troops should be taught to throw themselves quickly into squares or oblongs, and when time or circumstances will not admit it, the column ought to close into a mass and face outwards. Some instructions on this head will be given. The General Officer commanding the reserve, to whom the advanced and rear guards, and the most important services of the army may be entrusted, is requested to turn his mind to the different situations in which he may be engaged.

The order came from Dundas in England; they were to go to Marmaris, meet with and negotiate with the Turkish government, take delivery of the horses purchased for them by Lord Elgin, the Minister at Constantinople, and purchase others as needed, as well as top up water and provisions and make other necessary arrangements. Elgin had reported to Grenville at the Foreign Office that there were no horses available near Jaffa, so it would be best to get them from the region close to Constantinople; they needed 1,000 for cavalry and some draft horses for the artillery. Elgin started acquiring these, but then lost the services of his translators and had to stop. It was not easy getting large numbers of the right sort of horse; the local cavalry was composed of individuals who provided their own horses, always stallions as using geldings was considered unmanly, but he had managed to get 400.[5] These should have been good horses, as Elgin had seen them himself and was considered a good judge of a horse, but when they arrived at Marmaris they were found to be too small, weedy and sickly. They were too small for the Dragoons, many of them were suffering from sore backs or lameness and many had to be shot or sold. After modifications of the harness for field guns and howitzers were made, to lighten them, about 130 of these poor beasts were trained to work in harness, but even so it took a much larger team than usual to draw the guns: 10 or 12 horses to drag the 6-pounders through the heavy sand and shingle. It was obvious that the original good animals had been exchanged en route. Purchasing parties were sent inland to find better animals, and they did eventually manage to find 450 good spirited stallions, but these were no bigger than ponies, useful for patrols and mounted sentries, but not for charges. Another 1,000 horses had been sent by the Grand Vizier at Jaffa, but these were also poor animals and almost a quarter of them had to be rejected as not fit for service.

The expedition was to sail on 13 December, but as so often happened, contrary winds delayed them until 21 December. Moore's division finally reached Marmaris Bay on 1 January (1801), Abercromby, Keith and the first division having arrived a few days earlier. Moore described the bay as 'a circular basin of several miles diameter, surrounded on every side by hills covered with wood the sight is romantic and beautiful'. They were to wait there for at least a fortnight until the horses and other equipment and provisions could arrive. The Turkish government was friendly and promised co-operation and assistance; their fleet was in the Gulf of Macri but was to join them and bring 5,000 of their best troops.

The day after he arrived at Marmaris, Moore was despatched by Abercromby to go to the Vizier's (effectively Prime Minister and Commander of the army) army near Jaffa, with these orders:

Instructions for Major-General Moore.

Headquarters, *H.M.S. Kent*, Marmaris Bay, 3rd January 1801. Major-General Moore is to proceed to the Turkish Army near Jaffa, where he will endeavour to make himself master of the real state and condition of the Ottoman Army. He will ascertain, as far as he has an opportunity, the means that army has of acting in the ensuing operations, and what resources the British Army may receive from their co-operation. A review of the whole circumstances attending the proposed disembarkation near Alexandria has led to the determination of preferring Damietta as the point towards which the first effort of the British arms will be directed. Major-General Moore will therefore state that, influenced by this consideration, by a deference to his Highness the Vizier's opinion, and by a desire to accommodate his plans to those of the Porte, it is Sir Ralph Abercromby's intention to endeavour to effect his disembarkation at or near Damietta, form such magazines as may be most immediately necessary, and, having equipped a flotilla upon the Nile for the purpose of commanding that river and bringing forward supplies of all kinds, march directly upon Cairo. As soon as the British Army is in a situation to commence its operations, it will be necessary that the Ottoman Army should be put in motion and should advance to Katseh. Major-General Moore will therefore come to a clear understanding on this point; he will likewise propose that, when disembarkation is effected and the two armies are in a situation to move, the Vizier shall advance by the route of Salahih, and make himself master of that place, whilst the British Army on his right will so far take the lead of the Ottoman forces as to cover the head of his Highness's march and be in a situation to afford him assistance, should it appear to be the design of the enemy to make a separate attack upon the Turkish Army.

Should these operations succeed, and the enemy retire upon Cairo with an intention of maintaining himself there, a more immediate plan of operations will be concerted, which must depend upon local circumstances, to be ascertained upon the spot. In opening to the Vizier this plan of the campaign, Major-General Moore will endeavour to enforce the great importance of leaving the army in the persuasion that our operations are in the first instance to be directed against Alexandria, and may state that in all probability a part of the fleet may be detached after the disembarkation is completed to keep the enemy's force there in check. While Major-General Moore endeavours to engage the Turks to enter heartily into this plan and to execute punctually their part of it, he will assure them of the most cordial co-operation on the part of the British commander, as well as of his readiness to communicate on all occasions in the most unreserved manner every circumstance that may be interesting or important to either army.

It must be established that the armies are to form distinct corps, acting, however, towards one common point and connected by one common interest. At the same time Major-General Moore will state that in the first instance it may be necessary that a corps of Turkish cavalry under an approved officer should join the British Army, and if circumstances allow him to point out any particular corps, he will pay more attention to the quality of the troops than to their numbers. He may, on the other hand, state that, should any particular service require it, a small corps of British troops will occasionally be detached to act with the Turkish Army. Major-General Moore will endeavour to ascertain the nature and extent of the Vizier's intelligence respecting the force and situation of the enemy, and will encourage his Highness to carry on any useful correspondence he may have established in Egypt. The preparations on foot here render it difficult to state any precise time for commencing operations, but Major-General Moore may venture to say that it is hoped the army will leave the coast of Caramania about the end of this month, and may repeat the assurance which Sir Ralph Abercromby has already given the Vizier, that an officer will be despatched to the Ottoman camp previous to our departure, when it is expected the Turkish Army will be put in motion. An immediate communication of the success of the disembarkation will be made to the Vizier from Damietta. If it is agreeable to his Highness, a Turkish officer of confidence shall be resident with the British Army for the purpose of carrying on the correspondence. Major-General Moore will endeavour to ascertain the practicability of procuring a sufficient number of horses for mounting a body of cavalry to the extent of one thousand, and, should it appear that such a number or any considerable proportion of them could actually be brought forward with the Turkish Army on eligible terms, so as to join us soon after the disembarkation, he will enter into a contract for that purpose in the name of the Commissary-General. Another object of attention will be the possibility of procuring at Jaffa, or elsewhere on the coast of Syria, a number of small craft for the purpose of aiding in the disembarkation of the troops and for the navigation of the Nile; the latter to be vessels not drawing more than four and a half or five feet of water; and on this subject he will collect whatever information may be in his power. Should the subject of future arrangements be touched upon, Major-General Moore cannot enter further into it than to state it to be the object of Great Britain to expel the common enemy from Egypt and not to interfere with internal concerns. Major-General Moore will communicate and act with Brigadier-General Koehler in the most confidential manner. The service performed, Major-General Moore will join the Army here as expeditiously as possible.

(signed) Ralph Abercromby.

Moore landed at Jaffa on 9 January. The first thing he heard was the death of Koehler, who had died on 29 December after three days illness of 'a putrid fever'. Moore went immediately to the Vizier's camp, about a mile from the town, where he met Major Holloway, now the senior British officer. After telling Holloway of his mission, they went first to the Reis Effendi (the Turkish Secretary of State for Foreign Affairs) and then the Vizier. They lived in high splendour, and were seated cross-legged on sofas with numerous attendants on each side. Moore and Holloway were presented with pipes, coffee and sherbet; these were compliments served out according to the rank of the visitor or the amount of respect they wished to show. The Reis Effendi was secretary to the embassy in England and spoke French, which was unusual for a Turk. Conversations were generally carried out with the aid of a dragoman (interpreter). This first visit was to pay mutual compliments only; a further meeting was fixed for that evening to discuss business. Moore told the Reis Effendi that his business was not such as should be trusted to the common interpreter, so that second meeting was confined to Moore, the Vizier, Kaia Bey and the Reis Effendi, who translated. Moore stayed for 3 hours, and fully explained Abercromby's plan and everything else in Moore's instructions. Kaia Bey and the Reis Effendi discussed this in Turkish; the Vizier made a few minor objections which Moore answered. On the whole he seemed very pleased and said the sooner operations commenced, the happier he would be. The next morning Moore wrote out the heads of a plan which he thought would meet the Vizier's wishes without deviating from Abercromby's instructions. Taking it to the Reis Effendi, he asked for it to be shown to the Vizier, and if he approved, Moore would write it out in full for himself and the Vizier to sign. He was told to go back in the evening, but when he did, was told the Vizier was indisposed, but would send for him the next day.

While he was at Jaffa, Moore lived with Major Holloway and the British officers of the mission; he had a good tent, and his dinners came from the Vizier's own kitchen. He occupied his time in studying the Turkish camp, their soldiery and manners, all very different from his previous experience. It was unfortunate that Koehler had died as he had known about the state of their magazines, and the organisation and administration of the Turkish army; Holloway did not. As Moore felt he could not rely on the conversational assertions of the Reis Effendi or the Vizier, he wrote to the latter and asked for information on the effective force under his command, the extent of his magazine, what means he had of forwarding this to the advancing army and what steps he had taken to keep the magazines complete. He also asked for whatever information had been received by the Vizier on the French. In their next conversation the Vizier said that he had sufficient ammunition and biscuit for his army at Jaffa and El Arish, but no barley for his cavalry or other beasts. This, of course, was essential to cross the desert and had been ordered long since; he was hourly expecting the ships that were to bring it. He stated that he had 7,500 cavalry and 7,500 infantry, with 50 field pieces. Moore asked to be given written confirmation of this information.

Moore reflected in his journal that this meant the advance of the Vizier's army was dependent on the arrival of barley; he had also found out, by discrete enquiry, that they did not have enough biscuit to sustain them any length of time on the Egyptian frontier. He had seen the composition of their troops and their discipline and was not impressed with either; he thought they were nothing more than 'a wild ungovernable mob, incapable of being directed to any useful purpose ... while their chief, the Vizier, was a weak-minded old man, without talent or any military knowledge ...'.

Despite the Vizier's having signed the plan for a joint operation, he concluded it was therefore pointless to expect any co-operation from them or to change any plan to include them, as he reported to Abercromby on his return.

He thought that his five-day stay had been a waste of time. The Vizier had given him very little information on the French in Egypt despite people constantly coming from there; they seemed ignorant of the importance of intelligence and of the means of obtaining it. There was always plague in their camp and even while he was there numerous people died of it and the loss in the camp was up to 200 per day. The Vizier's 'family' were particularly sickly, nine of them dying while Moore was visiting the camp. They had no idea of hygiene, auctioning the clothes of the dead to people who wore them without washing; nor were they in any hurry to remove the bodies of dead horses, dogs and even men, which lay about the camp. Not surprisingly the Turkish army had lost some 6,000 people to the plague in the past 7 months. Moore had to evade the customary present of a pelisse, which the Vizier threw round the recipient's shoulders on leaving. He did not wish to risk the plague by wearing it before it was fumigated, so asked that it be sent to him instead.

On his return to Marmaris, Moore reported to Abercromby and Abercromby duly passed on his findings to Dundas in England.[6] The state of the Grand Vizier's army was not encouraging, he said, but he had written to Lord Elgin to ask if he could find 7,000 to 8,000 Turkish infantry from Constantinople to join the Capitan Pacha, the High Admiral of the Ottoman navy. The British army was, as yet, unable to leave Marmaris for want of boats, and were receiving varied reports of the numbers of French in Egypt, from about 30,000 (Sidney Smith's estimate) to only half that number; but even so, if the British government really wanted to 'extirpate' the French from Egypt, more troops were needed.

Soon after Moore's return to Marmaris, what Moore described as 'a sort of council of war' was held on *Foudroyant*, with Abercromby, Keith, Bickerton, General Hutchinson, the Adjutant General Hope, the Quartermaster General Anstruther, Moore and naval captains Hallowell and Sir Sidney Smith. Smith had been in the area for some time, and his brother Spencer Smith had worked in Constantinople alongside Elgin with the Levant Company. Sidney Smith had, without any authorisation, drawn up a convention at El Arish with the French General Kleber, part of which involved returning the French troops to their home towns in France. This convention was repudiated when the British government heard of it; it was typical of Smith to go off and do such things off his own bat. Although brave, he was over confident in his own abilities and importance, and took to boasting of his 'triumphs' whenever he could get an audience to stay still long enough.

Abercromby stated his preference for landing at Aboukir Bay and wished for a naval opinion on the safety of this. This bay, to the east of Alexandria, was some 2 miles in length from north to south and at its northern edge there was a castle on a horn-shaped projection. This castle was strongly armed, with eight 24-pounders, two 12in mortars and several smaller guns, all of which allowed it to enfilade the beach for just over a mile. On the southern horn of the bay was a blockhouse with at least one heavy gun.

Captain Hallowell, who had some experience of this coast, was certain that it would be possible to land a two- or three-week supply of ordnance, ammunition, provisions and water. From there, since the march to Alexandria would be within a mile of the coast, boats with water and provisions could bring these to the army, and if the surf should rise dangerously, the boats could be hauled on shore and protected by the army. Hallowell said that there was no point on the coast that was too rocky to land provisions; other captains said it was very rocky for the last 5 or 6 miles to Alexandria and that no boat could approach it.

It was decided that the landing would be at Aboukir, and although it was 18 miles to Alexandria, all supplies, even water, must be brought ashore there and conveyed to the army as it proceeded and during the siege. While they were waiting at Marmaris for the horses and other supplies to arrive, equipment was rationalised and in some cases manufactured: the fleet's coopers and carpenters made casks, buckets and pumps for water, and sledges, carts and barrows for moving equipment.

The French had had plenty of time to complete the fortifications at Alexandria and it was sure to be very strong. A plan was drawn up for the landing: Abercromby did not want a disorganised debacle, as there had been at Cadiz. Captain Cochrane was appointed beach-master, and the landing plan was practised until it went smoothly. The first wave of troops would get into their boats and, sitting in complete silence with their muskets in their hands, be rowed to their allotted rendezvous ship, from which they would wait for the signal and go on to the shore, where camp colours would be raised so the men could run straight to them and commence the line. Of the total 200 craft, 58 were flatboats which had a very shallow draught, a mere 9in, which allowed them to run up almost on to the beach.

The intention had been to go on 18 February and everything was ready, but once again bad weather and contrary winds delayed their departure and they did not go for another four days. The Reserve and Guards, about 5,000 men, with 10 field guns, formed the first wave, followed by the brigades according to their rank. Before they left, they received news that two French supply ships had got into Alexandria, and British cruisers had taken two more, laden with medical staff, medicines and more bullets. They set out with 180 ships, but on 1 March Moore could count only 140; that same day they came within sight of Alexandria, close enough to see the ships in the harbour. They stayed there for a while, then at dusk made sail to the north-east; the weather was still unsettled, too much so to allow disembarkation. On the morning of the 2nd they received orders to cook three days' worth of provisions (i.e. meat) and to prepare to land. Coming into Aboukir Bay, they could see the castle and the vessel that had been sent in during the night to mark the anchorage. Moore thought it was too boisterous to attempt a landing; Abercromby was going in a cutter to reconnoitre and Moore accompanied him. The ships were about 7 miles from shore, in 6 to 9 fathoms; they took the cutter in to where it was only 2 fathoms but this was still 3 or 4 miles from the shore. The land appeared to rise from the beach; it was sandy with groves of palm trees dotted about, and from such a position the enemy could be covered from fire from gunboats and thus able to oppose a landing. They could see a couple of enemy gunboats anchored close in and some small detached camps between the castle and the entrance to Lake Alexandria; after fixing on a place for the landing, they returned to *Foudroyant*.

By that time it was nearly 2 o'clock and too late to start the landing, so orders were given for the Reserve and Guards to be ready to get into the boats at 4 the next morning. Moore stayed to dine with Keith; Cochrane was there also and they discussed the final details of the landing, but after a windy day it became windier during the evening and the sea got up. Unless it moderated during the night, it was clear that it would be impossible to land. That was the case, and was not until the 7th that the wind abated and the order was given for the Reserve, Guards and two regiments of Coote's brigade to get into the flatboats and launches at 2 the next morning. While they were waiting for the wind to die down, they had been able to see the French at work, on a sand height opposite where the British right was to land, and in other places. While they were eating dinner on the 5th, a French vessel arrived and anchored under the guns of the castle; it would have been easy for British vessels to prevent this, but when it was reported to Keith, he said he could not spare a vessel to go after her. She then moved so that her guns could rake the beach.

Moore went over to the *Kent* for a conference with Abercromby who sent him inshore with Colonel Lindenthal to see what the French had been doing and the state of the ground. They went to a bomb vessel which was anchored in 17ft of water about 1½ miles from the shore but could see no defensive works. The ground to the left was uneven and woody, on the right was a 60ft-high sand hill with a steep front; the distance between these features was about a mile and that was where the landing would be made. Lake Maadieh (sometimes referred to as Lake Aboukir) was behind a sea wall which formed a boundary on the left and the right of the sand hill but was in range of the guns of the fort. The ground was favourable to the French, who had means of concealing themselves, although Moore saw none. He could see a line of their picquets and constant movement of individuals and small parties between them. The captain of the bomb concluded, from the increased activity, that more troops had joined.

The ships which contained the first wave were all troop-ships anchored 6 or 7 miles from the shore. During the evening of the 7th two small vessels were anchored closer to the shore, one to mark the right of the landing, the other at an intermediate point on the same line. The boats, once their cargo of troops were on board, were to rendezvous alongside these vessels, where the naval captains, under the direction of Cochrane, arranged the boats of the respective divisions to the order in the plan: brigades, regiments and companies, as stated in the army's order of battle. During the evening the second wave of troops were moved from the large ships to some smaller ones with a shallower draft, which anchored further in to give better support to the first disembarkation. The majority of the boats were at the rendezvous soon after daylight, but it took considerable time to arrange them. Moore was in the boat with Cochrane, with the reserve on the right aimed at the centre of the high sand hill and the others taking their dressing from them. The sand hill commanded the ground on either side, it could be either the centre or the left flank of the enemy position; in either case it was desirable to possess it and Moore was determined to take it with the regiments on the right of the reserve as soon as possible.

Just as the signal for the boats to move was about to be made, General Hope arrived with a message from Abercromby, who was in one of the bomb vessels with Keith. This said that if the enemy fire was so great that the men could not bear it, he would make the signal to retire and that they should keep an eye on the ship he was in. Hope said that Abercromby wanted to know if Moore was still determined to go to the landing point on the right, or whether it might be better to extend their line a little more to the right of the hill, as it seemed very steep. Moore replied that he did not think it was too steep for them to get up it.

The instructions for the captains commanding the divisions on landing the troops were quite detailed: the boats were to keep to the line, with at least 50ft between them. The first line was to consist of the flatboats and the launches carrying the artillery, these towed by cutters. The second line was to be cutters only, to attend the flatboats and render immediate assistance if it should be needed, doing this without waiting for an order. A third line of cutters towing launches was to follow; all boats belonging to each ship should keep in the wake of the boats in front of them. The boats carrying the grenadier companies of each regiment would carry the camp colours of the regiment and the rest of the boats with that regiment would dress to the left, taking care that the companies were embarked on the boats in the order they should be when landed. Each flatboat should drop a grapnel from their stern a little distance from the shore so they could haul off as soon as the troops were landed. If it became necessary for the flatboats to turn, they should all do so at the same time and in the same direction; they should look for a signal on which way to turn, and if none was made, then they should turn to starboard.

The captain of the divisions should repeat all the signals made by the commanding officer of the disembarkation, and each should have a rowing boat in attendance to carry his orders to the boats of his division. A musket would be fired from the commanding officer's boat to draw attention to the signal, this to be repeated by the captains of each division. The boats carrying signal flags were to be issued with stretchers (tall poles) to ensure that the signals could be seen in calm weather; the signals were to be made from a flag staff in the centre of the boat. The troops were not to stand up until instructed on landing, as this might endanger the safety of the boat. Each flatboat should be provided with four or five breakers (small casks) of water in case the troops needed it on landing.

When the first landing was complete, the boats should go to the ships carrying ensigns on their fore-top-gallant-masthead; afterwards to those having their ensigns at the mizzen, until all the troops were on shore. For this second landing, the captains of each division should take their boats to specific ships, to ensure the regiments were landed in a collective body, this being observed until all the troops were on shore. The launches that landed the artillery were to go to a specific ordnance ship, to land the light artillery and stores. The captains of the divisions were to pass on copies of these, and any following, instructions to the lieutenants under their orders, and others were to be given to the midshipmen commanding the flatboats.[7]

There were also orders aimed specifically at the troops and their officers: each man was to land with sixty rounds of ammunition and two spare flints; the ammunition which would not fit in their pouches was to be carefully stored in their packs. They were not to load until on shore. Each man and officer was to carry three days' bread and three days' pork (ready cooked); a further three days' worth was to be landed, but not issued: it was to be in kegs under the charge of the quartermaster of each regiment. Each man was to carry a full canteen of water. Three days' barley was to be carried for the horses of the cavalry and of the staff and field officers. The staff and field officers were to carry forage sacks.

The men were to carry an entrenching tool and the following necessaries: two shirts, one pair of shoes, two pairs of socks or stockings, neatly made up in their packs, their camp kettles and blankets. Regiments having both blankets and greatcoats were to leave the latter on board their ship. Officers were not to take on shore anything that they could not carry themselves; their servants were not only to be under arms with their corps, they were not to carry anything more than any other soldier, and were to mount guard and picquets with their masters. Mounted officers only were entitled to batmen.

The musicians and drummers, and men less fit for actual service, were to be selected for all regimental duties, not purely military, and officers in command of corps were to be held strictly responsible for their being in the most effective state at all times. A proportion of the general hospital staff must be attached to each brigade and were to be allowed only essential orderlies; regimental surgeons were to be allowed one orderly each, and these were to carry the field case of instruments. The spare arms, tents, horses' appointments of the dismounted cavalry and all spare baggage were to be left in charge of a careful non-commissioned officer on each ship.[8]

On the morning of 7 March the army's return was 14,965 men, of whom 2,808 were in the Reserve, under Moore, the rest under major generals Ludlow, Coote, Cradock and Caven, and brigadiers Doyle, Stuart and Finch. The general commanding the French army in Egypt was Abdullah (previously Jacques) Menou, who had taken command by seniority when General Kleber was killed. He was 50 years old, paunchy, lacked any experience of an independent command and was thought by his contemporaries as no better than third-rate. He had converted to Islam and taken a native wife; this did not encourage his officers to view him with respect, but he had been a favourite of Buonaparte while the latter had remained in Egypt.

Menou's army consisted of some 22,000 field troops and 8,000 auxiliaries: native and Coptic infantry, marine artillery, seamen, sappers and administrative troops; these were mostly in the garrisons, thus freeing the field army for mobile operations. Of the field army, there were seven cavalry regiments and fourteen demi-brigades, the cavalry were almost 40 per cent down in numbers and the demi-brigades 30 per cent; after two-and-a-half years in Egypt, many men had been lost in battle and to disease and those who were left were tired of Egypt's filth and disease, hostile inhabitants and their squalid villages. This large force was spread throughout Egypt and Menou had to defend himself against both a Turkish attack from the Sinai and British attacks from the Red Sea as well as the Mediterranean.[9]

Chapter 8

Egypt: Action and Aftermath

Finally, early in the morning of 8 March, a rocket was fired from *Foudroyant*, the signal to go, and the boats began the long haul to the shore, arriving at about 8 o'clock. The enemy had been watching them for over 2 hours, and had drawn up their cannon. Some of the British gunboats started firing at them to draw their attention, but as soon as the boats were within reach of the shore fifteen guns began to fire on them, first with round shot, then with grape, and finally the French infantry joined in with their muskets. The boats continued to row in, and some men were killed and wounded from the severe fire, and several boats were sunk. As soon as the boats touched land the officers and men sprang out and formed on the beach. Moore gathered up the Grenadiers and light infantry of the 40th, 23rd and 28th regiments in line and scrambled up the sand hill. They held their fire until they got to the top, where they charged the French and drove them back, taking four cannon and some of their horses. Moore and his men followed them, the French firing as they retired to the edge of a plain, where Moore halted while he checked what was happening on the left, where there was still a very heavy fire of musketry.

Brigadier General Oakes, with the Corsican Rangers and the 43rd and 58th regiments, had landed to the left of the sand hill where the enemy were waiting to receive them. Forming up rapidly, they were attacked by artillery, infantry and cavalry, which they drove back into the plain, taking three guns. The Guards, who should have been on the left of the reserve, had become confused on landing and were at first in the rear of the 42nd and 58th, but soon fell into place as the others advanced. The lack of artillery (it was some time before what had been landed could be dragged through the sand into position) prevented the British from pursuing further and destroying the enemy who made good their retreat, although with considerable loss. The British losses at this stage were 102 killed, 515 wounded, 35 missing and 5 seamen killed and 20 wounded.[1] Moore remarked that the French had had eight days to prepare and that the ground was favourable for defence. 'Our attempt was daring, and executed by the troops with the greatest intrepidity and coolness.'

Abercromby had landed at the stage when the British infantry were gone from the beach, pursuing the French over the dunes. The wounded were attended to before being sent back to the ships and the empty boats were heading back to the fleet to pick up the rest of the troops, the horses, the guns and more ammunition. This time the boats did not go to assigned ships but headed towards any ship with its ensign still flying, the signal for 'we have troops on board'. The castle of Aboukir was besieged and the British attempted to summon it, but the defenders fired on Lieutenant

Colonel Murray and refused every communication; Abercromby directed that heavy artillery should be landed and then fire on the Castle.

The French defence at this stage was led by General Friant, who had been a ranker in the pre-Revolution French Royal army. He had some 1,600 infantry, 200 cavalry and 15 guns lined up on the isthmus between the sea and Lake Maadieh, and sent reinforcements to Aboukir castle before the action began; this castle surrendered on 18 March.

The following day Moore pushed forward with the Reserve a couple of miles in front of the rest of the army, and there they waited for ammunition and provisons; some of the horses were arriving, straggling into Aboukir between the 10th and the 14th; they were on vessels hired in the Greek islands, and these could not keep up with the fleet.

The British army was now on a narrow strip of land about 40 miles long, between Aboukir in the east and the Arab Tower in the west, which divided Lake Mareotis from the sea. The ground consisted of an irregular sandy surface dotted with palm trees. Sidney Smith knew water could be found near those trees, so the men dug and found water, to the immense relief of Abercromby, who had been worried about having to depend on the fleet for water. On the morning of the 10th Moore went out to look at the ground in front of him, but soon met up with the advanced guard of a large body of cavalry escorting some French generals who were also reconnoitring. A brief skirmish followed in which the Corsican Rangers had several men wounded and an officer, a surgeon and ten men taken prisoner.

On the 12th, the whole of the army then moved forward in two columns, headed by the Reserve as an advance guard. A corps of French cavalry, which had been opposite Moore for the two days while they waited, retired skirmishing, but a body of infantry could be seen at some distance, moving towards the British. The line was quickly formed and advanced; the enemy halted and retired and the British took up their ground. The enemy on their front was in a good position; both sets of picquets and sentries were close to each other during the night, and it was clear that neither army could move without an action. As Moore's men had been almost continuously on duty, they were allowed to rest during the night and were replaced by the 90th and 92nd for the night, still under Moore's command. He divided them into three bodies, spread out to cover the front of the army, and ordered each group to put one-third of their number forward as sentries in front, changing them over every hour.

The main action commenced on 13 March; they marched in two columns from the left, covered on the right by the Reserve in one column. The intention was to attack the French right, and hopefully turn it. The main army formed in two lines, the Reserve remaining in a column. Moore's objective was a square tower with a flagstaff. The guns soon fell behind, as the sailors dragging them could not move any faster in the heavy sand; the French artillery was numerous, and having as many as sixteen horses to a gun was able to move easily. They set up a tremendous cannonade, knocking down many British men, but 'nothing could overcome their cool intrepidity, discompose their order or prevent their advancing', wrote Moore to his father.[2]

The French gave way and were pursued by the British despite the fire from the fortified position the French had prepared in front of Alexandria. General Friant had brought 1,850 of his troops up to join those of General Lanusse, and was now under his orders. The French now numbered 3,950 infantry rank and file and 520 cavalry. Preparations were immediately made to attack but on examining the position it was seen to be so strong, well-provided with artillery and reinforced by two forts beyond it that Abercromby decided to wait until his own heavy artillery was brought up. During that time Lake Maadieh had been surveyed and found to be deep enough for small boats to a point about 4 miles from Alexandria, so supplies and provisions were brought up by that means. Three days' provisions were delivered to the troops and in the evening orders were given for the march the following morning.

Abercromby had imagined they would be fighting on open level ground, but it turned out to be uneven sand hills and numerous palm groves. Much of the surface was loose sand, not only almost impossible for the crews hauling the guns, but also hard work for the marching infantry and dismounted cavalry. These groves of palms also made life difficult for the British attack, as they provided cover for groups of French troops who dodged between them. The normal order of advance was for the divisions to split into brigade and then battalion columns before they swung into line; here, the left columns did not have room for such a deployment until the ground widened out at the head of the lake and gave them room on the left. Only Hutchinson's brigade was able to spread out and close with the enemy until the ground opened out and the battle developed. Columns might be useful for manoeuvre but presented a dense target for artillery; with no cavalry to threaten them, the French were able to open up on the columns, their shot bouncing through the columns. Colonel Paget's 28th Regiment lost two captains and thirty or forty men in this way, but continued to march on in perfect order and in perfect silence.

The Reserve was to attack the enemy's right and to turn it if possible. The 90th and 92nd regiments formed the advance guard, but had got too far ahead of the column, were attacked by the main body of the French and suffered badly until the columns could come to their aid. However, they held their ground and defeated a body of artillery which tried to charge them. The action then became general along the whole front; the French were forced back, retreating under the protection of numerous guns, halting and firing whenever the ground was favourable to them. Moore kept the reserve in column, covering the right flank of the main army. They advanced rapidly, exposed to a heavy cannonade from the front and musketry from hussars and light infantry until they finally reached some rising ground which overlooked a plain over which the enemy was retreating in confusion. He saw that the British right was in advance of the rest of the army and that following onto the plain would expose them to the guns on the fortified heights in front of Alexandria. He asked Major General Cradock, whose brigade was next to his, to halt until the rest of the army came up.

The army came up and continued its advance; Cradock and Moore joined them. Seeing that the enemy had halted and formed up on strong ground in the middle of the plain, the British also halted. At a meeting with Abercromby it was decided that Hutchinson, with some brigades of the second line which had been less engaged and was thus less tired, would attack the enemy on their right and Moore with the reserve supported by the Guards would attack the enemy's left near the sea. As Hutchinson had to make a circuit to get up with the enemy, Moore would regulate his movement and attack by Hutchinson's, but when he got closer Hutchinson could see that the enemy's ground was so strongly defended by numerous artillery that he halted and sent a message to Abercromby. He explained that the heights could not be carried without great loss and as the heights were exposed to the fire of the fortified hills they would not be able to hold them without entrenching, for which they lacked the tools. He asked for further orders; Abercromby sent Hope up to see the ground and then went up himself. This took many hours, the day was getting late, and the enemy had had time to recover its spirits and organise its disposition. Abercromby saw that what might have been attempted was no longer advisable. The attack was abandoned and they retired to the point where the right had halted in the morning. While in the plain they had been exposed to the guns of the enemy; some 1,300 officers and men had been killed or wounded, far more than the enemy's loss, Moore thought.

The enemy's superiority in cavalry and artillery had done great damage to the British troops, but undaunted, they continued to advance and gained ground, which, said Moore, 'is the great object in action [we] drove the enemy back tho' with loss superior to his. Every attempt the enemy made, ... was defeated, and at last the whole retired under cover of their artillery'. He thought that if they had committed any fault, it was advancing too far before they had decided to attack the heights. Halting in the plain had exposed them to the guns on the heights and led to a retrograde movement which 'was mortifying to troops who had displayed such spirit, and who had been successful'.

Alexandria was no more than 5 miles; they had found that the boats could come up the lake to within half a mile from their camp, and were there landing stores, ammunition and provisions under the protection of gunboats. The enemy were about 1½ miles in the front and their sentries and videttes (mounted sentries) were close to one another. The French had spent two days trying to drive the British videttes in; this led to some skirmishing which killed a few Frenchmen before they desisted. Abercromby wrote a polite letter to the French general in command, suggesting that it was pointless to 'aggravate the calamities of war, which, without benefit to the general cause, tended only to distress individuals'. The French general replied politely, agreeing with Abercromby's sentiments.

The British position was weak, with the sea on its right and with its left on the lake and the Canal of Alexandria. They were building some field works along the whole of their front and some of the heavy cannon placed along these defensive works would make their position quite secure. The camp equipage was being landed and the officers were now permitted to have some of their light baggage. No deserters had come in, and the local Arabs, who had brought some provisions, could provide no reliable information. They did not know what General Menou was doing, whether he was still in Cairo or assembling a force halfway between there and Alexandria at Demenhur. All they knew for sure was that the enemy was 6,000 or 7,000 strong on the 13th; that their current position was extremely strong and studded with artillery;

and that when they had taken it, they still had to besiege Alexandria, which was defended by one army with another army on their flank and rear. Moore thought that they lacked enough men to defeat the French at that point.

On the 14th Moore was general of the day again; in the night they had lost Lieutenant Colonel Brice who was in command of the Guards' picquet; he had strayed past his sentries and was wounded and taken up by the French and carried into Alexandria where he died the next day. By mutual agreement, the dead of both armies were buried on that day. The British were finding plenty of water by digging near their camp, but lacked fuel to cook their meat or provide warmth after dark, which was necessary on the cold, damp nights immediately after their landing. Until the tents arrived, officers and men alike huddled on the ground under their blankets; Abercromby had intended to sleep under the stars, but his servants made him a bivuoac with palm leaves, which the rest of the army copied. When they stood to under arms in the cold hour before daylight, Abercromby looked at the men's cold faces and ordered an issue of rum.

The marks of ancient buildings were all around them and in digging for water they had found some aqueducts, one of which was full of good water. There was also a ruin of what had been a substantial building near the redoubt on the right: the French called this 'Caesar's Camp'. These were Roman ruins which dominated the valley close to the sea; the broken gaps in the masonry were manned by the experienced 58th Regiment, which had thrown up breastworks of loose stones across the gaps.

On the 17th, Moore rode along the canal between the lakes for 2 or 3 miles. Lake Mareotis was mostly dry, there was no deep water and the bottom was a firm sand which could be used by cavalry and artillery. Moore encountered a French patrol and returned to camp. The following day a detachment of dragoons patrolling at the place where he had been the previous day was driven back by French cavalry. A stronger detachment was sent out from headquarters, attacked the French and beat them, but pursuing, they tired their horses before falling in with a body of French infantry which killed and wounded a great many of them and took three officers and sixteen men prisoner. Worse, they lost forty-four of the irreplaceable cavalry horses. Colonel Archdale, who had commanded them, lost an arm. Some 'severe animadversions' were posted in the next day's general orders on the imprudent conduct of the cavalry and warning others against advancing without proper support, and 'pursuing advantages beyond what the occasion demands or prudence warrants'.

On the 20th, Moore was the general of the day again; he had a visit from Abercromby. It was now believed that Menou was at Demenhur, but this information was not sure. Abercromby was well aware that his army was in a critical situation; from faulty information and erroneous intercepted letters, the government had sent him on the expedition with inadequate numbers of men. The French had superior numbers, even 'the greatest gallantry must fail when opposed to superior numbers protected by position and by fortifications', wrote Moore. There was no information on the distance of the fortified hills of Cretia and Caffarelli from the current position of the French, or what benefit could be obtained from this should they commence a siege. Abercromby said that as soon as the heavy cannon was brought up and entrenching tools brought forward, he thought they should make an effort. He wanted to push the artillery forward in the night, form up the troops in whatever cover they could find and advance to attack both the French flanks at daylight. If this failed, they could still retreat to where they were and stay there until another position could be prepared to cover a retreat and finally their embarkation. He regretted having been put in a position where he had to throw such a fine army away, adding that he believed nobody would envy him his situation.

After visiting the picquets Moore remained with the left picquet of the reserve until 4 am on the 21st. The enemy had been quiet during the night, except for throwing up a few rockets, which was not unusual. Moore left orders with the field officer to retire his picquets at daylight and rode on to give the same orders to the other picquets; when he reached the left picquet of the Guards he heard some musketry on the left. Since all was quiet on the right and from the style of firing, he thought it was a false alarm, which didn't surprise him since he had formed an adverse opinion of the officer who commanded the picquets on that side. He trotted on to the left when he heard firing commence from the Reserve's picquets. Turning to his aide-de-camp, Captain Sewell, he said, 'This is the real attack, let us gallop to the redoubt'. This was at about 4.30 am. All the picquets were falling back and by the time he reached the 28th regiment in the redoubt it was under what he described as a warm attack. It was still dark, and this darkness was exacerbated by the smoke of the guns and small arms.

The French plan of attack was for General Lanusse's division of about 3,000 men to surprise and assault the Roman Camp (the British name for Caesar's Camp), killing all its defenders and gaining ground, then to fall on the British right flank and rear of the British centre, while the cavalry would pursue and disperse the remainder of the British right wing. To Lanusse's right, but a little behind, General Rampon's division would attack the British centre as soon as Lanusse had gained some advantage. On Rampon's right was Regnier with the strongest division of the French army, some 3,500 infantry. Regnier was to give the signal by sending 100 of his Dromedary Corps and 300 dragoons to make a feigned attack on the extreme left of the British position. They did make an attack surprising the redan on the isthmus and made its defenders prisoner; it was this attack which had been heard by Moore and made some officers think this was the real attack, on the British left flank. In fact this attack, as well as giving the signal to Lanusse, was intended to occupy the British left wing and prevent them going to the support of their right, and finally to assist Rampon on forcing the British centre. They hoped that the whole of their army could then wheel to their right which would drive the British in confusion into the waters of Lake Maadieh.

The arrangements for receiving and repulsing an attack had already been organised. Moore and Brigadier General Oakes agreed that the redoubts and old ruins in front of the right of the army, where the 28th and 58th were posted, must be supported, and that this was the ground for the reserve to fight on. If the enemy carried these positions, the army would have to fall back. The general orders were for the troops to stand to their arms an hour before daylight, and fortunately they had done this before the attack commenced. Colonel Paget, with the 28th, manned the redoubt and had two companies in reserve; he formed these on the left of the redoubt, which was open to the rear. The 58th manned the old ruins, which were some 20 or 30yd behind the right flank of the redoubt and swept the ground between it and the sea. As had been agreed before, Oakes brought down the left wing of the 42nd to the left, and Moore sent Captain Anderson to the right wing with orders for the 23rd and four flank companies of the 40th to support the ruins. They were able to feel the effect of the enemy's fire, but could not yet see what he was doing. His drums were beating the charge and they were shouting to encourage each other to advance. Moore's horse was shot in the face and became unmanageable, forcing him to dismount. While he was speaking to Paget on the platform of the redoubt, Paget was knocked down by a shot in the neck; he said he was killed and Moore agreed with him, but then he recovered a little and was put on his horse.

The left wing of the 42nd arrived on the left. At that moment someone told Moore that a French column had turned the left; he thought that in the dark they had mistaken the 42nd for the French and said so. He could see the 42nd forming exactly where he had ordered, but at that moment Colonel Paget, much recovered from his wound, rode up saying, 'I assure you that the French have turned us and are moving towards the ruins'. Moore looked to where Paget pointed and saw a battalion of French completely in the British rear. The right wing of the 42nd arrived at that moment and Moore ran to them, ordered them to face to the right about and showed them the French, who were driven into the ruins where everyone was killed, wounded or taken prisoner.

Moore then led the regiment back to the flank of the redoubt, meeting another column of the French which had penetrated the British front. Moore received a shot in the lower left leg in the process of repelling them. The 42nd and part of the 28th drove the French column, but went too far and were attacked by cavalry. The French cavalry were in among Moore's men, but although the latter were in some disorder, they rallied and brought down so many men and horses that the rest retired. Shortly after this Moore met up with Abercromby and told him of the encounter at the ruins; Abercromby had received a shot in the thigh, but typically made little of it. Moore was still on foot at this point, but had difficulty walking from his wound and was lent a horse by Major Honeyman. The French were keen to gain the redoubt and made another effort but the 58th Regiment in the ruins allowed them to get within 60yd before firing so effectively that a great number were brought down and the rest went off.

On the left the 42nd and 28th, having repulsed what was in front of them, was charged by a large body of cavalry, which penetrated their line, got into the redoubt and behind where Moore and Abercromby were. Abercromby was actually seized by a French dragoon, but a man from the 42nd shot the man and freed him. Moore, who said, 'I was obliged to put spurs to my horse to get clear', galloped to the ruins to bring some of the troops from there. The 28th, which was lining the redoubt, turned around and killed the dragoons who had got in there. This earned them the right to wear a badge on the rear of their caps as well as on the front, and they became known as 'the back and front boys'. The line of the 42nd had broken, but the men were fighting individually, so Moore ordered the flank companies of the 40th to pour a couple of volleys at the French, even though there was a risk of hitting their own men. The French cavalry was destroyed, riderless horses galloping about; every attack they had made was repulsed. The British men had gone boldly up to the French wherever they appeared even where there was inevitably some confusion in the dark. Wrote Moore, 'even the cavalry breaking in had not dismayed them'.

As day broke Brigadier General John Stuart brought up his Foreign Brigade from the second line to give 'spirited' support. At this point the British guns had fallen silent for lack of ammunition and even the musket cartridges were all used. The French were also low on ammunition for their muskets, and at one point both sides threw stones at each other. Daylight gave them the chance to reorder the troops, and as the French continued to pound them with artillery, Moore got as many men under cover of the redoubt as he could. There they had to wait an hour until cartridges came up, and Moore remarked that if the French infantry had advanced again the only way to fight them would have been with bayonets; his men would have done it, 'I never saw men more determined to do their duty', but the French had suffered so much that their men would not make another attempt. They remained where they were until ammunition for the British guns was brought up, when they soon retreated.

The main effort of the French was against the British right, opposite the reserve, but another column had attacked the Guards, which were on the left of the reserve; both attacks were repulsed with considerable loss. The French also suffered from the firing from the gunboats in the sea to the north. At this point Moore did not know the British losses but hoped it would not be more than 800. He estimated the French losses at between 2,000 and 3,000, remarking, 'I have never seen a field so strewed [*sic*] with dead'. The horse that he had borrowed after his own was shot in the face had been killed in the last minutes of the battle, but as the wound in his leg was becoming stiff and painful, he managed to find another horse. After getting Colonel Spencer to take command of the reserve, he returned to his tent, accompanied by Oakes, who had received an almost identical wound. Moore wrote to his father on 25 March, of this wound, adding, 'Having lost so many men, it was but decent to get a lick myself', and of Abercromby's wound, 'the ball is lodged … he has, however, still a degree of fever; and will, I fear, be incapable of taking any further direction this campaign'. Abercromby, who had remained in the field until the French had retired, at about 9 am, had been pacing within the Guards' redan when he stopped and collapsed. Having recovered a little, he did not wish to leave the field and was propped against the parapet until Menou withdrew his troops, when he allowed one of the Guards' surgeons to examine his leg. The surgeon said he should be taken to *Foudroyant* for treatment. He was lifted on to a litter and Lieutenant John Macdonald of the Queen's regiment folded a blanket and laid it under his head for a pillow. Abercromby asked, 'What is that you are placing under my head?' 'Only a soldier's blanket', replied Macdonald. 'Only a soldier's blanket!', said Abercromby, 'A soldier's blanket is of great consequence, and you must send me the name of the soldier to whom it belongs, that it may be returned to him.' It was clear that he would not return for many weeks, and Major General Hely Hutchinson took over as Commander-in-Chief.

Moore and Oakes had their wounds dressed by the surgeon, who reported that in neither man had the bullet touched the bone. Not being in immediate danger, they returned to their ship where as well as being quieter it would be more comfortable and they would make a speedier recovery. Captain Anderson, Moore's aide-de-camp, had also been wounded in the arm; he had been in the hands of some French hussars who were shot at the same time as he was. He fell and they made off.

Moore believed there had seldom been more hard fighting. The French made three separate attacks, their numbers were superior to the British, they had the advantage of cavalry and a numerous well-served artillery, but the British troops had no idea of giving way, 'there cannot be a more convincing proof of the superiority of our infantry'. The losses on both sides were higher than Moore had thought: 1,436 British, of which 451 were of the Reserve and 258 of the Guards, the French upwards of 4,000. With the Reserve there were only subalterns to superintend the guns, and when the ammunition in the boxes and limbers was used, there was no supply for some time. The musket ammunition was also too far away at the rear and took hours to arrive. He also thought that the artillery, which had previously been one of the best British corps, had degenerated badly; there was a want of military spirit among the officers, who Moore thought seemed to prefer comfortable positions than 'those which lead to distinction'.

Then came the bad news: the ball that had struck Abercromby was stuck in the bone and could not be removed. After several days when he seemed likely to recover, gangrene set in and on 28 March he died, mourned by all on the field and at home. The Duke of York issued a general order giving him as an example to the British army and a monument to his memory was erected in St Paul's Cathedral.

Hutchinson's first act on taking over the command was to fortify the British position in front of Alexandria. Heavy guns and ammunition had been brought up and strong redoubts were built. His main objective was to isolate Alexandria and effectually blockade it so that it could be controlled by a relatively small force. Once able to do that, he could take some troops to the lower part of the Nile, take possession of Rosetta and perhaps Ramanieh as well, thus gaining control of the resources of the fertile delta while he waited for reinforcements which would allow him to commence larger scale operations against the French elsewhere in Egypt.

At the beginning of these works, Hutchinson summoned the defenders of Alexandria, sending Sidney Smith in with a flag of truce on 23 March. He was refused admission to the French lines, and had instead to hand over his letter proposing that the garrison should be evacuated to France. This was summarily refused in the reply from Friant who declared that they would defend Egypt to the last extremity. He also stated that Menou was not in Alexandria, which the British did not believe. While he was waiting for the reply, Smith had talked to the French outposts, who wished the British luck in their dealings with the inhabitants of this wretched land. Over the next few days, conversations of officers who galloped across while visiting their own outposts confirmed that the French were, with only the exception of what they described as 'this haughty stubborn corpulent man' (Menou), anxious to go home.

The next step in isolating Alexandria and preventing, or at least considerably impeding, its garrison from communicating with Cairo, without using the long and difficult route across the desert, was to cut the dyke between the two lakes of Maadieh and Mareotis, which was no stronger than was necessary to carry the canal that brought fresh water from the Nile at Ramanieh to the cisterns of Alexandria. Cutting the dyke also involved cutting this canal. It only took two days, 12 and 13 April, to complete this work and the salt water began to pour through the gap. The bed of Lake Mareotis was considerably lower than that of Lake Maadieh and within two weeks the lake was full, forming a body of water of more than 1,200 square miles. Numerous gunboats moved in, further securing the position of the British troops.

Moore was not seeing any of this first hand, being confined to his bed; first on board *Diadem* in Aboukir Bay and then, when the surgeons recommended it, on land in a cool house at Rosetta. The bullet had passed between the two bones of the lower leg without touching any bone, but the wound was giving him trouble, especially after *Diadem* had to put to sea with the fleet to seek out an enemy squadron. What had been a comfortable situation turned into being tossed about at sea, and this, as well as the natural progression of the wound, had caused considerable inflammation and his temperature was up. The surgeons probed the wound several times without finding anything, but at one point Moore became so desperate that he suggested amputation but the surgeons were sure the leg could be saved and applied fomentations and poultices and the inflammation went down. Then another inflammation broke out further down the leg, and this time when the surgeons opened it up and probed they brought out some pieces of cloth from Moore's breeches; pus was discharged and the leg began to heal. He wrote to his father on 28 May and reported that the original wounds where the ball had entered and exited were healed up; those made by the surgeons to open the sinus lower down would probably be closed in three or four days and the leg was resuming its usual colour. He was able to get up and move about with crutches, but the leg was wasted and weak after so many weeks of inaction, and as a result of contractions did not reach the ground by about an inch and a half; this would get better with gentle exercise. Moore had also been weak from his illness but said his health was good otherwise and that he hoped to be able to rejoin the army in a fortnight. Anderson's wounded arm was also nearly closed, but it would probably be some months before he had the full use of his hand. While on *Diadem*, Moore received visits from various people including Hutchinson, who dined with him and brought him up to date on his intentions.

On 29 March Hutchinson had learned from a captured French vessel that there had been a change of government at home: Pitt had resigned, to be replaced by Henry Addington, and Dundas had been replaced by Lord Hobart. They had inherited Dundas' view that the numbers of French in Egypt were much lower than was the case. Hobart may also have inherited Dundas' opinion of Hutchinson, Captain Cochrane having written to Dundas stating, 'Neither army nor navy have confidence in General Hutchinson, who tho' possessing many good qualities has not those necessary for the commander of an army'. He went on, 'Moore [was] our principal hope, and it will be well for General Hutchinson if he follow his advice.' It was not only the senior officers who disliked Hutchinson. He was not a great leader, lacking both charm and presence, this latter not helped by his slovenly dress. He had a violent temper and was rude; his views were provocative and his aggression prominent; he had a hurtful tongue which he used on anyone who disagreed with him. Strangely, at about the time when Hutchinson took over, Moore thought him accomplished and 'a man of sense' which was not entirely wrong. He may have lacked the usual attributes of a leader, and was indecisive when planning, but he did have the good strategic judgement needed after the Battle of Alexandria.

On 6 April news arrived that a French squadron of six or seven battleships had sailed from Toulon full of troops and was heading for Alexandria. They had met up with Sir John Warren's squadron off Sardinia but managed to escape him in the night and were last seen, in a crippled state, heading back to Toulon. Keith had gone to join Warren and the combined squadron off Alexandria in case the French made another attempt by sea. They had already managed to strengthen their troops at Alexandria and Rahmanieh, but the British also had help on the way: the Grand Vizier was moving closer to Cairo across the eastern desert, and Admiral Blankett with 5,000 or 6,000 troops was almost at Suez, having brought them from India up the Red Sea. Having done all that he could to defend his forward lines and keep the French in Alexandria, Hutchinson turned his attention to his next objective, the navigation of the Nile. This required taking over the various towns and forts about the mouths of the river; the first of these was Rosetta, and the forts of St Julien and Stone Fort. He sent Colonel Spencer to Rosetta with about 1,200 British and between 4,000 and 5,000 Turkish troops, who had arrived with the Capitan Pacha shortly after Abercromby's death. On his approach, the French left the town; Fort St Julien held out for several days, then the hastily erected British batteries breached the walls and the garrison surrendered on 19 April.

Captain Stevenson started up the Nile with a strong division of British and a flotilla of Turkish gunboats, heading for El Hamed to join the troops that Hutchinson had sent there under Major General Cradock and Brigadier General Doyle. By the end of April General Coote was left at Alexandria with no more than 6,000 men after Hutchinson had gone to El Hamed himself. When they had reached El Aft, the main French position eight miles from Rahmanieh, the enemy was gone. Hutchinson sent the 89th Regiment and 20 dragoons across the river with 1,200 of the Albanians brought by the Capitan Pacha, all under the command of Colonel Richard Stewart. By the morning of the 9th the British came up to the French position at Rahmanieh, and after a desultory action that lasted until nightfall, the French retired to the south.

News came of the first reinforcements from Malta: the 1/27th and recovered invalids from other regiments, about 1,200 men in all. Hutchinson promptly announced his intention of continuing south to Cairo. This caused a near mutiny among some of his officers: the heat was building, flies and scorpions were everywhere, the sirocco was blowing and plague was raging. Of course they criticised his decisions, but what it really came down to was that he was not their beloved Abercromby, and they disliked him. They even went so far as to write to Moore and Coote, inviting their agreement to a plan which basically intended to deprive Hutchinson of the command of the army. Moore's response to this is not known; he did not mention it in his journal or letters home, but it would almost certainly have been the same as his response in Corsica to Admiral Hood's suggestion that they should attack Bastia contrary to General Dundas' orders: that it was mutiny they were suggesting and that he did not wish to be involved.

Moore was advised by his surgeons that a change of air would be good for him, so on 10 May he left *Diadem* and set out for Rosetta, arriving there before dinner. He had a house on the banks of the Nile, 'agreeably situated' and cool. He had written to Hutchinson as soon as he got there and on the 12th he received a reply, bringing him up to date with the general's intention to move on to Cairo but finding it difficult if not impossible at that time. The troops were succumbing to the heat, they were not prepared for a long march and lacked many essential articles. Having concluded that it was necessary to make a show of following the enemy in order to drive them into Cairo rather than turning off to cross the delta and attack the Grand Vizier's army, Hutchinson decided to follow the retreating French for a couple of days, then return to Rosetta. They would be able to purchase fresh food in the delta, where various crops were grown on the fertile soil: wheat and barley, maize, tobacco, melons, cucumbers and other salad crops. They would be welcomed there by the local inhabitants, glad to be rid of their oppressive rulers who lived like kings while the peasants had only mud-walled hovels. To avoid infection in these squalid dwellings, the British soldiers were forbidden to enter the villages and the huts left by the French were burned down.

Moore had news: on 14 May Hutchinson's army had intercepted a large convoy of boats carrying ordnance and military supplies from Cairo to Ramanieh and its escort of 150 French soldiers, and another which had been sent out from Alexandria to collect supplies, as well as its escort of 570 men and 500 camels. More important news was that a corps of French had marched out of Cairo to attack the Grand Vizier. Hutchinson changed his plan of returning to Rosetta and instead moved across the delta to Bilbeis to support the Vizier and also to facilitate the junction with the British army from India, some 5,000 men. There had been some 500 French in Fort Illisbe, near Damietta, but they had spiked the guns and retired on Burlos, then left in a small vessel which was later taken by one of the British cruisers. A detachment was sent to occupy Burlos, and the Turks occupied Illisbe; the whole coast was now in the possession of Turks or British.

Hutchinson wrote to Moore from his camp at Algam with news of a battle at El Hanha between the advanced corps of the Vizier's army and some 7,000 French, Greeks and Copts from Cairo.[3] Hutchinson had previously written to the Vizier asking him not to risk an action until the British were close enough to give support. The Vizier had intended to wait, but his army of 5,000 cavalry and 3,000 infantry did not care for this idea, and fought and defeated the French contingent. Hutchinson had not yet received details of the action, only that it had occurred and was successful. As a consequence, Hutchinson changed his plan to cross the Nile and carried on to Cairo; on 15 June he sent in a summons to General Belliard to capitulate. This was indignantly refused but on 22 June, with the British at Giza and the Turks at the city walls on both sides, Belliard sent out an invitation to negotiate. This took several days until on 27 June a convention was signed for the surrender of all places in Egypt held by the French (including Alexandria) and the repatriation of the French with their arms and artillery, such of the women as they wanted to take, and the body of their beloved General Kleber. There were some 13,000 men in Cairo, of whom only 8,000 were fit for duty.

Shortly after this, Hutchinson and Cradock fell so seriously sick that the command of the British army devolved on Moore. He had taken his first steps on 16 June, and moved to Cairo in a *djerm* (small river boat), sending his horses by land and joining the army on 29 June. Anderson's wounded arm had healed but was not very functional, and he was advised to go back to England, this being the best chance of recovering its full use, and he did so. Moore had very little to do, so he rode out to see the pyramids, but was not particularly impressed by them, as he later was by Pompey's Pillar. He had little opinion of the town of Cairo, which was, he thought, 'very bad: the streets unpaved and narrow, the houses sad and the heat intolerable. A great part of it is in ruin, the consequence of frequent revolutions and plague. The latter carried off this year 30,000 people.'

Moore had the task of escorting the French from Cairo over the 200 miles to Rosetta: the 8,000 fit French troops, their arms, baggage and artillery, with an escort of a few hundred Turks and Mamelukes and 3,500 British troops. There were 500 British soldiers left to guard the sick French officers in Cairo, which was otherwise given over to the Turks. Leaving on 15 July, the march to Rosetta took two weeks, without any trouble en route, but there was one little problem, in that the French resisted all formal efforts to ascertain their numbers. This was necessary to calculate the tonnage of shipping required. Moore waited until they reached a defile between Lake Edku and the Nile then halted his troops and made them face the French as they filed through. As they passed, two officers of the Quartermaster General's staff counted them, arriving at a total of over 8,000. There were another 2,000 on the river boats which carried the baggage and assorted miners and sappers, sick, auxiliaries, seamen and guides. Adding some civilian employees from the mathematical school, library and press bureau, and the printing press, the final number embarked was 13,754, not counting women and children; by the middle of August they had all sailed for France and Moore could join the rest of the British army outside Alexandria.

Menou had rejected the capitulation signed by Belliard and declared death was better than surrender. He had been strengthening the French lines on the heights facing the British as well as the forts on his rear; meanwhile Hutchinson had received large reinforcements from Minorca. The troops from Bombay did not arrive until several weeks after the capitulation of the French in Cairo. These had suffered a series of mishaps and complications, not least of these being in the matter of command. The force was made up of two contingents, the first of these from Trincomalee under Arthur Wellesley who arrived at Bombay first; the second was from Calcutta under Major General David Baird. Wellesley was to be second-in-command under Baird, but fell ill with a severe fever and as soon as he recovered was recalled to Mysore; his illness was genuine, but he was certainly reluctant to serve under Baird.

Baird arrived at Bombay on 31 March, the last of his troops sailed two days later and he followed on 6 April; he arrived at Mocha on 25 April and found that two divisions of his army had already sailed. What they had not realised was the difficulty of navigating the Red Sea, or even of reaching it. The fleet was partly dispersed even before they had reached the straits of the Bab–el–Mandeb, some of the smaller vessels were lost and many of the transports, fighting against the northerly winds, gave up and returned to India. Baird's third division came into Mocha and spent some days taking in water, then he sailed with it for Jeddah before going on to Cosseir, the previously arranged rendezvous. At Jeddah he found that the first two divisions had not received his orders and carried on for Suez. Meanwhile Admiral Blankett, who was not connected to Baird's expedition, had arrived at Suez with a detachment of the 80th Regiment on his flagship; it was this that had made Hutchinson think that the Indian troops would shortly be with him. Then Commodore Sir Home Popham arrived at Jeddah from the Cape with two battleships, and some of the transports that he had met en route, having brought with him the 61st Regiment, some of the 8th Light Dragoons and a company of field artillery. He had called at Mocha but had no news of the fourth division or the provision ships from India. On 26 May Baird sailed with Popham for Cosseir, arriving on 8 June. Over the next three weeks more of the missing transports arrived in twos and threes.

At Cosseir Baird found two divisions of troops had been waiting for him for six weeks, and that the Quartermaster General had obtained some camels. Blankett arrived a week later with a letter dated 13 May from Hutchinson to say he would not leave the vicinity of Cairo until the Indian contingent had safely crossed the desert. Blankett informed Baird that it was hopeless to attempt to sail to Suez during that season; Baird then prepared to march his column of over 5,000 men across the 100 miles of desert to the Nile at Keneh. The plan was complex: Colonel Murray went all the way to Keneh to organise water and provisions at the various stopping points along the route, sending much of this back from Keneh, while parties of Sepoys went out from Cosseir to find springs and dig wells at those same stopping points. There were seven of these, and the army was to march in small divisions, expecting to find water at the first, third and fifth stops. When the first group reached the Nile, they were to send their camels and water bags back to the fifth stop, the second was to send its camels and water bags back to the third stop when it reached the fifth and the third was to do the same at the third stop, sending its camels and water bags back to Cosseir, with subsequent groups following the same reverse leapfrog pattern.

This would have worked better, had the water bags, which were made of skin, not leaked and almost emptied themselves between stages. Fortunately some water was found by digging halfway between the third and fourth stages. Finally, on 8 July, Baird brought the 10th and 88th regiments and a few companies of Sepoys to Keneh where he waited for orders from Hutchinson; at last he heard of the fall of Cairo and then received a letter from Hutchinson who gave him instructions to move down to Gizeh. Baird then had to obtain boats to take his men to Cairo, and then, soon after, took them all back down the Nile to Rosetta.

Having seen off the French from Rosetta, Moore took the reserve to Alexandria, arriving on 13 August. Hutchinson, who was still very weak from his illness, had been resting on *Foudroyant*, but was expected at Alexandria any day. The British position before Alexandria was, said Moore, formidable. Lake Mareotis was full, and the Guards, General Ludlow's, Lord Cavan's and Finch's brigades, some 5,000 men, under the command of General Coote had embarked on boats to land 7 miles west of Alexandria, effectively completing the investment. This movement was delayed for a day when it was realised that the boats had come with no provisions. In order to distract the defenders while this manoeuvre was in progress, two lodgements were ordered, the one on the left under General Cradock, the one on the right under Moore.[4] Stewart's regiment and the Lowenstein Rangers were selected for this, and they drove in the enemy's outposts and pushed forward to a commanding hillock some 900yd from the enemy's works. This gave them a perfect view of the enemy's position, but the fire was too great to retain it and they were too distant from their own lines to be supported, so they retired to a previously selected position where entrenchments were being dug. They had never really intended to try and retain the hillock, just use it as a reconnoitring device.

Coote landed opposite Fort Marabout on 17 August and moved over the isthmus to take it. The fort was built on a rocky island connected to the mainland by a fordable underwater ridge, with a high rock which commanded the island. There was a long limestone ridge at the northern edge of the isthmus. There were also numerous quarries to the south of this, and Coote settled in among them, his troops carrying in stores and dragging his two 12-pounders and two 8in howitzers. He sank two French gunboats which were lying under the fort and sent another scuttling back to Alexandria and began to bombard Marabout, but soon realised that heavier guns were needed to breach the walls of the fort. While he waited for 24-pounders to arrive, his infantry took over the siege, and sharpshooters of the 54th Regiment were positioned on the high rock and as the French guns were on open platforms it was not long before the gunners had retreated to better cover. On 20 August the heavy guns began battering the walls of the fort, bringing down a tower, and by daybreak of the 21st the defenders had retired to the rocks on the north of the island. Preparations were made by four companies of the 54th to storm the remains of the fort while a summons was sent in; the commandant surrendered with 168 men. This not only removed the threat to Coote's rear while he moved forward, but also opened the Old Harbour to British shipping. In the meantime Coote was moving forward: 2 miles by the 21st, another 4 miles on the following day and then to his final position just short of Alexandria.

On the eastern side of the city, Hutchinson had brought up the rest of his troops in preparation for the attack. From the Roman Camp he intended to approach with heavy guns to play on the French fieldworks, thus forcing Menou to move men forward to defend them. The Roman Fort was already occupied by Moore's three brigades; their task was to drive in the enemy's outposts and dislodge them from a small sand hill known as the Sugarloaf Hill. As before, it was not intended to retain this, but it did give Moore the opportunity to view the enemy's main defences. As he withdrew his men from the Sugarloaf, the enemy, thinking that the Green Hill which had been captured by Cradock was now unoccupied, pushed forward 500 men. The British had not departed, merely retired below the crest to shelter against the enemy's cannon fire. Although only 250 strong, Colonel Lockhart quickly formed his men, fired several volleys and charged the French with bayonets; the French broke and ran. Moore's force halted at a halfway point where entrenchments were already being dug but he was not happy at the prospect of a siege of the Heights of Nicopolis, remarking that the enemy's position on the Heights was 'very formidable. Nature had made it strong, and they have added to it much by art'. The following night he sent forward a party of 300 men to strengthen the battery and trenches, but when he inspected them the following morning he found them 'still extremely defective'. On 22 August Moore received orders to give a false alarm to the French, who were suspected of being about to launch an attack on Coote, so at 4 o'clock the next morning he drove in their picquets and moved the Turks forward; as hoped, this made the enemy open all their batteries and continue firing until after daylight. The only British casualties were one Turk and two horses.

Hutchinson, having visited Coote's force on the west side of Alexandria, decided to concentrate the attack there and sent Blake's brigade of 1,300 men round to assist. Aided by fire from British and Turkish sloops in the Old Harbour, Coote began his attack on 24 August. The French response was somewhat desultory, on this and on the eastern side of the city; by occupying the western approaches to the city, the British had cut off their food supplies. They had some rice but had no meat except horses and camels; they were slaughtering seventeen horses a day. Moore also paid a visit to Coote on the 26th and having seen the situation from that side agreed that it was the best side to concentrate their attack; it would be easier for Coote to get into the city from the west than for the troops on the east, as the latter still had several strong lines of fortifications to cross.

There was no need to do so: on that same evening Menou sent out an aide-de-camp to Coote under a flag of truce to ask for a three-day armistice to draw up terms of capitulation; he did the same on the eastern side to Hutchinson. Firing was suspended, and Hutchinson, mindful of the negotiations for a peace under way in Europe, immediately sent a despatch to Lord Elgin to pass on to London, to the effect that the French were about to capitulate. Just 7 hours short of the expiry of the armistice, Menou sent an aide-de-camp to Hutchinson demanding a 36-hour extension, at the end of which, said Menou, he would be ready to receive commissioners to negotiate a convention. Hutchinson was furious at this, and sent a reply that stated that he wanted terms for a capitulation, not negotiations for a convention, and that he would resume firing at midnight, giving the order for this in the hearing of Menou's representative. The aide-de-camp departed and was back at 9 o'clock with a promise that the terms would be sent by 2 pm the following day. When these arrived, it was found that Menou's terms included the return of all French shipping to France, including warships, the retention of all Egyptian public property currently in French hands, and to Hutchinson's greater fury, a further extension of the armistice for nineteen days, when Menou would be free to recommence hostilities if reinforcements reached him from France.

Hutchinson rewrote the terms and sent them back, declaring that unless they were immediately accepted he would resume hostilities and storm the town. At this Menou gave in and sent back a messenger to Hutchinson as late as he dared (11 pm). He would accept Hutchinson's terms: repatriation to France with personal arms, private property and ten artillery pieces, but surrender of the public property and shipping. Hutchinson sent General Hope in to sign the capitulation. At 11 am on 2 September the grenadiers and detachments of guards and dragoons marched into the town with drums beating and flags flying.

Moore wrote to his mother, reporting the surrender and commenting on a letter he had received from his father with the news that brother Charles had been made a commissioner of bankrupts, a position that should soon lead to better things. He enclosed a couple of shawls for his mother and sister, which he had been given by the Capitan Pacha, explaining that while they might not be of any value they would keep them warm, 'and you will wear them for the sake of the donor'. He hoped to be home to eat his Christmas dinner with them: 'begin to fatten your turkey'.

And after that all but a few of the British left Egypt, some via Minorca where they recovered their wives and discovered the cheap wine, soon becoming scandalously drunk. Of the others, 7,000 went to Malta with General Cradock, 4,000 to Gibraltar and then on 'a particular service' with General Coote, and the remaining 4,500 to England with General Ludlow. Moore was appointed to command the British garrison which was to remain at Alexandria with 6,000 men; an appointment which did not please him: 'It has never been my object to remain in garrisons anywhere', he wrote. He had received a letter from the Duke of York, written in June, pressing him to return home for the better recovery of his wound, which had been reported as being very bad, and he appealed to Hutchinson on the grounds of that letter and that he had heard from England that his father had been very ill, and that he 'had been very little with him since the comencement of the war; that I knew it would be a great comfort to him as well as to my mother that I should be with him, which I also said was of importance to my family affairs'. Hutchinson agreed and Moore sailed for Malta on the 23rd in *Termagant*. Before he left, when there was an opportunity of a fast delivery through Constantinople, he wrote to Colonel Brownrigg telling him that he was on his way home and thus would not upset any plans the Duke might have for him. He also added that he felt hurt that he was not given an active command as others had been, but was to be left in command of a garrison.

On 29 September they met up with Keith's fleet of nine battleships, and Keith invited to him to go on board, as he was also bound for Malta. They arrived there on 8 October and after paying a visit to General Fox, the new Commander-in-Chief in the Mediterranean, Moore left for England in the *Morgiana* brig. Pausing briefly at Gibraltar to deliver some letters for the garrison, they received the news that peace had been signed with France before continuing to England, arriving at Portsmouth on 10 November.

Chapter 9

Shorncliffe

In the summer of 1801 negotiations for a peace were conducted in Paris and on 30 September a preliminary agreement was signed. The terms of this agreement required Britain to restore most of the French colonial possessions it had acquired, to vacate Malta which was to be handed back to the Knights of St John, and to withdraw from other Mediterranean ports. France was to restore Egypt to the Ottoman Empire (the news of the British victory in Egypt had not yet reached Europe), to withdraw from most of Italy and to preserve Portuguese sovereignty. Ceylon was to remain with Britain, and Britain was to recognise the Seven Islands Republic which France had established in the Adriatic. Both sides were to be given access to the Cape of Good Hope which was to be restored to the Batavian (Dutch) Republic and there was a secret clause leaving Trinidad with Britain.

King George III announced the cessation of hostilities on 12 October. In November Marquess Cornwallis was sent to Paris with plenipotentiary powers to negotiate a final version of the agreement. This was much as above, but also required the release of prisoners and hostages, most of the Dutch islands of the West Indies were to be returned to the Batavian Republic, France was to withdraw its forces from the Papal States and the Kingdom of Naples, the borders of French Guiana were to be fixed, the islands of Malta, Gozo and Comino were to be returned to the Knights and declared neutral, while the islands remained under the British Empire, the island of Minorca was to be returned to Spain and the House of Orange-Nassau was to be compensated for its losses in the Netherlands (but not by the Batavian Republic; this last item being the subject of a separate agreement between the Dutch and French representatives). All this was to be incorporated in the Treaty of Amiens which was signed on 25 March 1802.

What came to be known as the Peace of Amiens did not last very long. Buonaparte spent much of the peace time consolidating his power in France and reorganising its administration at home and in some of its client states. He sent troops into Helvetia (modern Switzerland) and annexed the Cisalpine Republic (a substantial portion of north-east Italy). He demanded that the British government censor the anti-French press and expel French expatriates from Britain. Buonaparte also sent a naval expedition to regain control over Haiti and to occupy much of Louisiana. The British government saw his demands as a threat to its sovereignty, and his actions in the Caribbean and Louisiana as first steps in enlarging his empire. There were many other examples of Buonaparte's unwillingness to adhere to the terms of the treaty. But equally, Britain had not removed its troops from Egypt and Malta, and also had not, as was usual, demobilised its army, keeping a peacetime army of some 180,000 men.

Seeing a return of hostilities as inevitable, on 8 March 1803, King George sent a message to Parliament that it was necessary to prepare for war. On 17 May, the British

navy was ordered to seize all French and Dutch vessels in British ports or sailing round the
British Isles. Buonaparte retaliated by ordering the arrest of all British males between the
ages of 18 and 60 in France and Italy; this was denounced by all the major powers as an
illegal act but Buonaparte ignored this, instead announcing that he had taken some 10,000
prisoners. This was a gross exaggeration; the true figure was closer to 1,800, but these men
were kept in France until Buonaparte abdicated in 1814. As a result of this and other acts
by Buonaparte, Britain declared war against France on 18 May.

* * *

At the beginning of February 1802, Moore was given command of a brigade in
Brighton, but had to return to Richmond at the end of the month when his father
sickened and died.[1] Dr Moore had left an annuity for his wife, and John immediately
offered to purchase an additional annuity to boost her income; she would not accept
the full sum he offered, but did accept half. John's share of his father's estate was just
over £3,300.

He spent several days answering letters of condolence before returning to his
training duties at Brighton. Brother Graham, who was suffering from rheumatism,
joined him there to take warm salt baths; these did not seem to do him any good and
he left after a month to return to Richmond and then to Liverpool to visit his friend
James Currie.

In April, Moore was presented with a sword by Edward Paget on behalf of the
commanding officers of the corps who had served with him in Egypt. An elegant
letter accompanied it:

> From Colonel the Hon Edward Paget to Major-General Moore. April 1802
>
> Sir, the commanding officers of those corps who had originally the good
> fortune to be placed under your command in the reserve of the army in Egypt,
> have commissioned me to present a sword to you in their name, and to request
> that you will accept and consider it as a token of their unbounded esteem.
>
> It would be presumptuous, Sir, in me to attempt to point out in you what
> are those rare talents which you possess, the application of which has rendered
> you the object of so much veneration to the corps which had the honour to
> serve under your immediate command. I must therefore content myself, Sir,
> with alone entreating you to believe that, whatever these are, they have not been
> less successfully exerted in promoting the interest of His Majesty's service
> and in confirming the glory of our native country throughout an arduous and
> memorable campaign than they have been in fixing on a basis never to be shaken
> the affections and admiration of those in whose name I have the honour to
> subscribe myself, with every sense of respect, Sir - -Yours &c.,&c.,

It is easy to see army officers of that period as simple fellows, interested only in
their duty and politics, but John Moore was not of that type. His wide education, his
father's erudition and his habit of reading had given him the ability to respond to this
letter with an equally elegant letter of his own:

Sir, I had the honour to receive your letter to me, in the name of the officers commanding the corps which composed the reserve of the army in Egypt, together with the sword which they have done me the honour to present to me. Such a present, from men themselves so respectable and whose conduct had merited so much praise, cannot fail to be equally flattering and pleasing to me, in whatever light I consider it – as a mark of their approbation or a token of their friendship or regard.

I beg that you and those gentlemen will accept of my warmest thanks. Be assured that I shall be proud of wearing their sword upon every occasion; and when it becomes necessary to draw it, I hope it may be at the head of men like them and those they commanded, who leave little else to their General than to emulate their example and second their ardour in the road to fame and honourable distinction.

By September 1802, Moore was at Canterbury, where he received a request from James Currie who was writing an account of the Egypt expedition and wanted to borrow his journal. Moore replied that while he would send the journal, he thought it would be little use as it was written mainly to help him recall events. He added that he would try to get Currie a sight of Abercromby's and Hutchinson's papers. He also remarked that he approved of Currie's advice to Graham about his latest inamorata; Graham was somewhat prone to falling in love, and was about to become engaged to this lady. Moore agreed with Currie that 'A Lady is not known, particularly if she is handsome, in ten or twelve days, and a Lady in the countryside is not always what she is in Town'.

In 1802 Colonel Coote Manningham and Lieutenant Colonel William Stewart sent a memorandum to the government suggesting a permanent rifle corps. This resulted in what was known at first as the Experimental Rifle Corps. In July 1803, just three months after Britain had declared war on France, Moore was appointed to command a brigade made up of the 4th, 52nd, 59th, 70th and 95th regiments which were encamped at Shorncliffe, near Folkestone. This was to be a training camp for light infantry, and the newly conceived Rifle Corps. At the beginning of October, Moore sent orders to Stewart to march the Rifle Corps to Shorncliffe, adding 'I hope you will find the station at Shorncliffe adapted to both your target practice and field movements'.

The firearm used by the British army at that time was the British Land Pattern Musket, affectionately known as 'Brown Bess'. Smooth bored and muzzle loading, and fired by a flint lock, the barrel was 42 to 46in long. Fired in a volley at an approaching mass of the enemy, it could inflict heavy damage, but was woefully inaccurate when fired at specific targets except at very short range. The Board of Ordnance had been trialling German rifles since 1775 and purchased 200, then sent some of these to British gun-smiths to copy, finally purchasing another 800 from this source. In 1800, a London gun-smith, Ezekiel Baker, had produced a rifle with seven grooves with a quarter turn inside the barrel and this was found to be more accurate than other patterns with a three-quarter turn. Baker was given an order for his rifles and the 95th Regiment was equipped with them.[2]

Many of his contemporaries (and historians) have praised Moore's method of training at Shorncliffe, but none have given much, if any, detail of his method. Unfortunately, no full account of his system survives, if, indeed, such a thing ever existed but the historian J.C. Fuller has extrapolated the training given at Shorncliffe from other written accounts of the time, which he believes Moore would almost certainly have studied.[3] His method was to adapt existing methods according to his own experiences; although drill was taught, his great contribution was moral discipline rather than discipline designed to create blind obedience, it also created the confidence with which every soldier should look up to his officers.

Moore appointed Lieutenant Colonel Kenneth MacKenzie, who had served with him in Egypt, as his second in command; MacKenzie's first action was to weed out all the officers he thought would not make good trainers and instructors. He also introduced new drill, march and platoon exercises; Moore was doubtful about these at first but later came to see that they were useful and supported them.

When one reads accounts of battles, it is obvious that troops should be familiar not only with the standard manoeuvres but also the bugle calls that ordered them. New recruits also had to get fit, as even country men would not have the necessary fitness to run and jump obstacles when necessary, let alone march for many miles a day for many days on end. It was also desirable for light infantry to be able to swim, as they might have to cross rivers (with their arms and uniforms on a little raft which they pushed in front of them) or swim ashore or back to boats to re-embark. And of course they had to be taught how to march before learning the movements of wheeling, advancing and retiring.

At the beginning, each recruit would ideally be taught these basics individually, and then in squads and finally in companies and battalions. Instructors were enjoined strictly not to move on from one lesson to the next without express orders from a field officer or the superintendent of drills. The first lesson was how to stand to attention and at ease, and then an 'extension' movement was taught to improve carriage and develop the chest: arms were raised to the front, then circled over the head and down to the line of the shoulders. Marching instruction included the various steps: oblique, stepping out, stepping short, marking time, changing feet, the closing step, the back step and quick march; once these were perfected in squads, they moved on to battalion drill: lines, columns and forming squares.

However, before the rank and file soldier could be taught, it was first necessary to teach the young officers. When they joined their regiment, these ensigns started in the ranks to learn the drills and to become acquainted with the men they would later command. They learnt to march and perform the manual exercises from the Sergeant Major, and the sword exercises from the Adjutant. Colonel Coote Manningham gave a series of lectures for young officers at Shorncliffe; these dealt mainly with advanced or outpost duties and reconnoitring, and emphasised the need to treat local inhabitants humanely. This last was also a necessity for sentries, especially those locals who supplied food!

In 1805, having seen the value of Baron de Rottenburg's musketry training system, Moore used it as the basis of his own musketry and rifle training. The first lesson was familiarity with and care of firearms, then practising the movements of handling them: secure arms, shoulder arms, order arms, fix bayonets, shoulder arms, present arms, shoulder arms, port arms, charge bayonets, shoulder arms, advance arms, shoulder arms, support arms, carry arms. There were seven movements to loading: push open the pan, seize a cartridge, bite and twist the end off the cartridge, bring the cartridge close to the pan, shake the priming into the pan and close the pan, bring the musket/rifle to the ground with the barrel up then insert the cartridge and seize the ramrod. Draw out the ramrod from its holder and push it down 1in into the barrel, then use both hands to force the cartridge home and remove the ramrod, return the ramrod to its holder. They then practised firing at a target (of at least 5ft in diameter) starting at a range of 50yd, then gradually increasing this to 300yd.

With all this systematic and consistent training, it is little wonder that Moore's system of training earned so much praise.

When he wasn't directly involved in the training programme, Moore spent much of his time on administrative duties. His letters to Brownrigg, now a general, and his successor as Military Secretary at Horse Guards, Lieutenant Colonel James Willoughby Gordon, show that much of this was concerned with moving officers around, usually because they wished it, occasionally when Moore and his other senior officers thought they were unsuited to the position they were in. In January 1803, he remarked that in each of the two battalions formed of the 53rd and 96th regiments, 'there are sixty or seventy men who ought to be discharged, under the Heads of Old, Short, and Weak'. He went on to say that the 'Light Infantry does not so much require men of stature, as it requires them to be Intelligent, Hardy, and Active. And they should, in the first instance, be young, or they will neither take to the Service, nor be easily interested in it.' He even lent money through the Army Agents Cox and Greenwood to one young officer who could not afford to recruit the thirty men he needed in lieu of the money to purchase his commission.

A major concern throughout 1804 and 1805 was the possibility, if not the certainty, of an invasion. Buonaparte had assembled a Grande Armée of 175,000 men on the heights above Boulogne, plus numerous other workmen building forts and batteries, quays and jetties; some 2,000 assorted vessels waited to carry the army across the Channel, escorted by a squadron of naval ships. Buonaparte declared, 'Let us be masters of the Straits [of Dover] for six hours, and we shall be masters of the world.' He also declared, 'I want only for a favourable wind to plant the Imperial Eagle on the Tower of London.' However, while he might have such grand plans, Buonaparte had little practical knowledge of nautical matters and this whole scheme was impractical. The work on harbours at Ambleteuse, Etaples and Boulogne to hold the landing craft could not provide viable harbours: that at Boulogne could hold 1,000 landing craft, but only at high water. It would take five to eight days just to get the whole army into the boats and the calm seas needed to row across the Channel were rarely forthcoming. He did attempt a trial crossing, but the weather was blowy and thirty vessels were overturned and several hundred men were lost. Admiral St Vincent addressed the House of Lords on the subject: 'I do not say, my Lords, that the French will not come. I say only they will not come by sea'.[4] And of course the Channel was permanently patrolled by the British navy.

Even before the Treaty of Amiens had been signed, the Adjutant General had published a set of instructions for the various commanding generals around the south coast. These required them to draw up a plan of defence for their district, including moving troops to likely landing places, with the intention of harassing the enemy, not least by depriving them of any source of provisions or transport. This was known as 'driving the country', which meant removing to a safe distance all horses, wagons and farm livestock and removing or destroying stocks of foodstuffs. Moore did not care for this; it sounded like an excellent idea in theory, but he thought it was impracticable as the roads would soon be blocked with cattle and sheep, and would take more than a week to complete. He had a better plan, which was to attack the enemy as soon as they came within musket range of the shore, and charge them with infantry as they attempted to leave their boats and assemble on the shore.

He also spent some time inspecting the defences of the Kent and Sussex coast against the expected invasion. To Brownrigg he remarked that it was a long line from Deal to Dungeness but that Dover and the castles of Deal, Sandown and Walmer should be defensible; the forts from Hythe to Dungeness were not defensible and would have to be abandoned as soon as a landing was made. A further visit to Dungeness let him see how faulty the works there were. They needed at least five towers, and there wasn't time to build them, but they could repair the stockading and some of the towers and move some guns into better positions. The other area that was seen as giving easy access to the French on their way to London was Romney Marsh; little thought had been given to its defence because it was thought that flooding it would create such a morass that it would become impassable. The problem with this was the same as with driving the country: it would take too long after closing the sluices for the full benefit of the flooding to build up. Lieutenant Colonel John Brown, Commandant of the Royal Staff Corps, saw this and suggested that instead of flooding the marsh, a canal should be dug from Seabrook (near Folkestone) round the back of the marsh to the River Rother near Rye, some 19 miles. Water could enter the canal from the Rother and the sea. It would be 20ft wide at the surface, 15ft wide at the bottom and 10ft deep. The soil from the excavation would be used to make a parapet on the northern edge; troops would be able to hide behind this.

In September 1804 Brown reported to the Duke of York, who consulted the prime minister (William Pitt was again in this post); both liked the idea and John Rennie, the famous engineer, was appointed as consultant engineer. The proposed canal was extended to 28 miles, from Rye to Cliff End (East Sussex), of which over 5 miles would consist of a part of the River Brede. It was going to cost £200,000 and would be completed by June 1805; this date was wildly optimistic, as was the cost. Completion, of a shorter canal, was in April 1809, and the cost was over £234,000.[5] By this time, the threat of invasion was long since gone; Buonaparte had already moved most of his Grande Armée from Boulogne before the end of September.[6]

Moore's social life suffered during his time at Shorncliffe; there were very few people of his sort living close enough for regular visits. He did receive visits from his friend Creevy and his family, and hired a house by the beach at Sandgate for his mother and sister; Pitt lived at Walmer Castle when he was not in London, and Moore dined with him frequently. Pitt was single, and his niece, Lady Hester Stanhope, lived with him and ran his household; she was one of London's renowned beauties and was particularly proud of her milky white skin. Moore was clearly taken with her and enjoyed her company (in one of his letters to her from Spain he remarked that it was a pity she was not there as she would have cheered them all up) but whether he had any idea of marrying her, as she thought he did, is another matter. After Pitt died she moved to London; when Moore was also in London in 1806, he visited her frequently, usurping George Canning (who was at that time Treasurer of the Navy) in her affections. As to the precise nature of this relationship (and that with Canning), there is a little story which she told her biographer which may shed some light: her brother Charles, who was one of Moore's aides-de-camp, asked her if she did not think Moore was a handsome man, and went on to remark 'Oh, but you should see him in his bath; he is like a Greek god!' Hester reported that she did not say anything, but thought 'How naive', in other words, she knew exactly what Moore looked like without clothes. The modern saying 'Why buy the cow if you are getting the milk free?' comes to mind, and quite apart from Canning and Moore, she is known to have had several lovers. Not quite the most suitable wife for Moore, certainly not in the eyes of his family.[7]

One event which made Moore an even more desirable 'catch' for any lady was the King's bestowal of a knighthood in September 1804. Although it naturally pleased his mother immensely, he made light of this honour himself, telling people who addressed him as 'Sir John' that he preferred to be known as 'General Moore'. However, when considering the design for his coat of arms, he chose a Highlander for one of his 'supporters' in memory of the two soldiers of the 92nd who picked him up after his facial wound in Holland. His other supporter was a Light Infantry soldier.

In October 1804, brother Graham had enjoyed a major success. Patrolling between the Rock of Lisbon and Cape St Vincent, as commodore of a squadron of four frigates, word came that four sail were seen in the west heading towards them. Although Spain was not at war with Britain at that time, it was imminent and if these were Spanish ships it would be wise to prevent them getting into Cadiz where they would become part of an aggressive fleet when war was declared. Graham Moore wanted, at the very least, to speak these ships; if they would not suffer themselves to be examined or detained, then it must come to a fight. This is what happened and a fierce fight took place; one of the Spanish ships blew up and three were captured. They turned out to be carrying vast amounts of treasure, and Graham Moore gained much kudos from the action, not to mention a considerable amount of prize money.

There were two major events which broke the boredom of John Moore's time at Shorncliffe, both taking him to reconnoitre potential military targets on the northern Spanish coast and the French coast opposite Dover. The first of these was in November 1804, and at this point he resumed his journal. He was called to London to meet with Pitt and Lords Camden and Viscount Melville (formerly Henry Dundas); another letter from Gordon informed him that the Duke of York also wished to see him. When he arrived at his lodgings in London he was met by Mr Huskisson, one of the secretaries at the Treasury, who gave him a bundle of papers containing some correspondence from a reconnaissance of Ferrol at the beginning of the year; these probably did not contain anything useful for Moore's mission, but Huskisson said he had been directed to give them to Moore. The reports stated that it would be easy to destroy the Spanish fleet and arsenal at Ferrol. Unfortunately no one had thought to send an army officer ashore, although at that time it would have been easy enough to land anywhere on the adjacent coast or even go into Ferrol itself.

At the meeting, Pitt and the two lords were strongly of the opinion that a sudden attack would carry the town of Ferrol or destroy the fleet and arsenal by bombardment from the south side of the harbour, and they were willing to spare 15,000 or 20,000 men for the expedition. Moore told them that he had no personal knowledge of Ferrol and that the practicability of such an action would depend on the town's situation, its harbour and its garrison. None of this was in the reports he had read, nor anything about the batteries which defended the harbour, whether they could be taken by an assault or would need heavy artillery. Such a bombardment would take several days and that would allow enemy troops to be gathered from the neighbourhood; it was therefore essential to know to what extent the isthmus on which Ferrol stood would allow a British force to cover the bombardment until it had completed its objective, and then to allow that force to re-embark its men and guns.

Melville remarked that Admiral Sir Edward Pellew, Admiral Cochrane and the officers of the squadron then off Ferrol, not to mention Admiral Gambier who was known to be difficult to convince in such matters, all recommended the attack on Ferrol; there was a general conviction that the place was weak. Moore replied that it might well be the case and he knew nothing to the contrary, but since it appeared that he was to have the command of such an expedition, he wished that the attempt, if practicable, should be made. But he did not know on what grounds the gentlemen mentioned had formed their opinions as in the reports he had seen they did not state the information on which they had reached these conclusions. He then offered to go himself to Admiral Cochrane's squadron and talk to him and his captains to hear the extent of their information, and he would take the opportunity of seeing Betanzos and Arres Bay and the land on the isthmus. This suggestion was approved and his brother's frigate, the *Indefatigable* was decided on to take him, under the pretense of carrying despatches to Cochrane. The orders for taking the despatches would be given publically and Moore, whose presence on board was to be kept secret, would achieve the rest by writing privately to his brother.

Moore dined with Pitt, Melville, Camden and Lord Harrowby, then spent the next two days with the Duke of York discussing the particular troops, officers and ordnance he would need. Moore recommended they consult General Congreve of the Artillery on the subject of the ordnance for the bombardment and also recommended him as the best person to command the artillery on the expedition. If chosen, Congreve could be trusted with some, if not all, of the objects of the expedition; two other officers, Hadden and MacLeod, were definitely not to be recommended, as Moore suspected them of 'carrying on a kind of underplot at the Ordnance, to serve their friends and to be courted by them'. He left London that afternoon in a post-chaise for Plymouth, where *Indefatigable* had been undergoing some minor repairs, but when he arrived two evenings later and met Graham, he learnt that the ship was at Hamoaze at the top of the estuary of the River Tamar, and although it was hoped to be able to warp her out the next morning, the wind was blowing right in that evening. It continued to do so for six days before they were able to leave on 5 December. Since Moore had been pretending to be a Mr Williams, he had had to keep out of sight in the inn, in case anyone saw and recognised him, a situation which he found extremely boring.

The contrary strong winds delayed their journey and instead of the two days it should have taken to reach Ferrol, it took nine. Cochrane's squadron was at anchor in Betanzos Bay but the wind failed and prevented *Indefatigable* getting in. The next day the squadron came out and a boat was sent with the despatches. Moore wrote to Cochrane to tell him that he was on board and although he had offered to go to Cochrane, the admiral came to see him when *Indefatigable*'s boat returned, as there were officers on the flagship *Northumberland* who would have recognised him. Cochrane's latest information was that the Spanish had taken an alarm about Ferrol and were marching considerable numbers of troops to the town. He continued to have correspondence with Ferrol and Corunna, but boats were no longer allowed to land in Arres Bay or on the peninsula. He suggested that *Indefatigable* should anchor a good way up in Betanzos Bay, where Moore would have a good view of Arres Bay, the batteries which defended it and the ground near it. In the meantime, Cochrane would keep the squadron cruising to prevent anyone seeing Moore.

On 17 December, Cochrane joined the two Moore brothers, and dressed in blue jackets, carrying fowling pieces and accompanied by some gun dogs, they went ashore with a small escort of sailors on the pretence of shooting. Cochrane suggested they land on the east side of the bay and walk the 2 miles up to the top of a hill where they could have a good view of Ferrol and the surrounding country; he said he often shot there, the inhabitants of the country were used to the English and there were no troops on that side. From the top of the hill they could see the peninsula of Arres and the town, arsenal and shipping at Ferrol, about 5 miles away. Then Moore saw a party of soldiers in a boat heading towards the place where they had left their own boats and realised that they had been spotted. They sent a sailor down to the boat to tell it to go round to a sandy bay some distance from where they had landed; telling him that if he was stopped and questioned he was to say they had gone to the village of Hiume. It was about 3 miles to where the boats should be, but when they got there the boats had not arrived. They tried to persuade a fishing boat to take them a little way off shore but despite offering a generous price were unable to do this. At last their own boats arrived and they embarked rapidly. The sailors told them that the soldiers from Reddes had just told them to go away, but before they had collected everyone a larger party of soldiers appeared. They pushed off immediately but two of the men from Cochrane's boat and a young midshipman were left behind and promptly taken prisoner. Moore thought at the time that they would probably be released when asked by Cochrane, but that this would not have been the case if they had got hold of the admiral himself. What he did not know at that point was that Spain had declared war three days earlier, but he did realise that if he had been captured and his name discovered he could have been treated as a spy.

Unfortunately, since they were only able to stay on the hill for less than half an hour, the view Moore had had did little more than satisfy general curiosity. From such a high point, he was not able to judge the ground or to see whether there were favourable positions for covering the artillery during a bombardment, or judge the distance from the peninsula to the arsenal and shipping and thus form an opinion of the effect of a bombardment. He then learned from the Admiral that the Spanish had marched a considerable number of troops to the area, that the fort was very strong and the other batteries which defended the entrance to Ferrol were in such positions that they could only be taken by land, so British ships could not get into the harbour. The land defences were not quite so strong but were still impossible to assault as their bastions were solid with several heavy guns each; the curtain walls were from 15ft to 25ft high and 3ft thick.

The Moore brothers had intended to depart for home almost immediately, but the weather prevented this with gales and they did not get away until 23 December, reaching Plymouth on 3 January, once again having been delayed by adverse winds and gales en route. Back in London, Moore's report to Pitt was the end of the planned expedition. The Spanish were now on their guard so a surprise attack was out of the question, and the seasonal weather made naval activity even more difficult.

Moore's second reconnaissance was to Boulogne on the *Antelope* with Sir Sidney Smith in September 1805. With most of Buonaparte's army gone and the camp broken up, the government wanted to know what the true situation was over there. Moore was back by 1 October and reported to the Duke of York on what they had seen. It would be possible, if strict secrecy was maintained, to land to the north of Boulogne, but without direct observation of the country it was not possible to say whether such an attack would succeed. Although he had been able to see that some 5,000 or 6,000 men were still in the camp, he could not see enough from the sea to ascertain whether a force could be landed, carry what was left of the enemy's lines, destroy the flotilla in the harbour and re-embark. Given the volatility of the weather, it might not be possible to re-embark the troops; a considerable force would be required. As with the proposed expedition to Ferrol, this one was also abandoned.

At the same time as his letter to the Duke of York, Moore wrote a private letter to the Military Secretary, Gordon, in which he expressed his opinion of Sir Sidney Smith, who he would encounter later in the Mediterranean:

I witnessed Sir Sidney's manoeuvres during three days, and as a certain degree of cleverness is required to be perfect any way, it is impossible to deny that he has talents, for undoubtedly he is the most finished mountebank I ever saw. I am sorry to see that Government place confidence in him – had anything been practicable at Boulogne – he was one of the least capable in the Navy to have had the conduct of it. He will jump about, talk and take a posture and often risk his person, for he is brave - but believe me he is not capable of understanding any solid operation. God forbid we should ever have to depend on him, for landing me on an enemy's coast – it is quite interesting to see the pains he takes to keep up the humbug – had I been with Owen in the *Immortalite* with anybody but Sir Sidney I might have seen everything on Saturday, or early on Sunday, and been back at Sandgate that night, but we were delayed hours after hours for his conferences – his dispatches, with Captains, cutlers, & guards all in attendance. I never saw such a man, talking on all subjects superficially, but fluently, even on science, of which he is ignorant, but turning the subject with great address whenever pushed by those who understand it better. He must, I think, think most meanly of himself for he cannot humbug himself nor believe his own lies.

At the end of October that year, Moore was promoted to Lieutenant General, perhaps as a reward for the Boulogne trip, as he remained at Shorncliffe for a further seven months. As always when he found himself in a static situation, Moore had become bored, and was looking for a more interesting post. He wrote to Gordon, 'I am now 44, and may therefore consider myself as having still eight or ten years of my best service in me. These I should wish to employ in circumstances where I had a chance of raising my character, and of being of use to my country.' He had hoped to be sent as Commander-in-Chief to India. This would be a three-or four-year posting, where, as he wrote to his mother he would 'be employed in the direction and management of a large army, and in the defence of the most important colony any nation ever had'. This would not only be a most useful professional exercise, but he would return 'with an independent fortune. As Commander-in-Chief, independent of the chance of prize money, from my appointments alone, I shall be able to save, yearly, from £8,000 to £10,000'.

But it was not to be. In May 1806, he was notified that he was to go to Sicily, as second in command to General Fox (brother of the statesman Charles James Fox) who was Commander-in-Chief in the Mediterranean. Fox, although a good soldier, was not in the best of health and thus unable to take an active part in army activities; he was also, as Moore remarked, so fat he looked like statues of the Buddha. Moore was not best pleased with this, feeling that he should have had a more senior command, but, as he remarked to Gordon, 'I ... know my duty too well to hesitate, and shall go and do my best, wherever I am ordered'.[8]

Chapter 10

Sicily

The Kingdom of the Two Sicilies comprised Naples and the surrounding area and the island of Sicily. It was strategically important that Britain should retain some control of Sicily, as in French hands it would effectively block Britain's route to the eastern Mediterranean and the countries which surrounded it. Sicily was a poor and backward country, with a privileged aristocracy, numerous clergy and impoverished peasants; there was virtually no middle class.

Buonaparte had already seized Naples and created his brother Joseph King; King Ferdinand and Queen Maria Caroline had fled to Sicily and set up their court at Palermo. They were an unprepossessing couple: Ferdinand was mainly interested in hunting rather than ruling his kingdom, a task which he left to his wife. He had low tastes which made him popular with the common people of Naples and he had a nasty sense of humour: he thought nothing was so funny as emptying the contents of his chamberpot over the heads of his guards. His queen, Maria Carolina, the sister of the unfortunate French queen Marie Antoinette, was superstitious and religious to the extent of scribbling prayers on little pieces of paper and keeping them in her clothes; although she could be charming when she chose, she was devious and scheming and her main interest was regaining the kingdom of Naples. It was thought she would even treat with Buonaparte for that end.

* * *

After pausing at the beginning of January 1805 Moore started his journal again as his ship, the *Chiffone*, prepared to sail from Portsmouth. He briefly reported on the changes of command in Sicily: Sir James Craig had returned home in bad health after taking possession of the citadel at Messina and then giving up the command to Major General Sir John Stuart. Major Generals Mackenzie, Fraser and Sherbrooke and Edward Paget were also ordered to Sicily where the force was to be increased from 7,000 to 12,000. They sailed on 14 June and arrived off Cadiz on 20 June where they saw Admiral Collingwood's fleet; Moore went across to meet Collingwood, dined with him and remained until the evening. Moore's impression of Collingwood was that he was 'a respectable-looking sea-officer of the old school, simple and unaffected in his manners ... a man of sense'. It took a further eight days to reach Gibraltar, where to his irritation Moore found that he had missed Fox by 3 hours, particularly annoying since Moore had letters for him which he should have received before he reached Sicily. They included Fox's appointment as Minister Extraordinary and Plenipotentiary to the court of Naples, which he was to hold simultaneously to the command of the troops, as well as letters of recall for the present Minister, Hugh Elliot (brother of Sir Gilbert, who had caused Moore so much trouble in Corsica).

Easterly winds kept them in Gibraltar for a further eight days before they sailed as part of the escort for a convoy of nineteen transports, with victuallers and merchantmen. Moore spent three days on shore, where he was sorry to see how Gibraltar had deteriorated since he was there before: the inns were bad, hot and dirty and the garrison was in a bad state while the troops off duty were dirty and slovenly and the regiments undisciplined.

It took another thirty days to reach Messina, partly due to adverse winds and partly because it was thought dangerous to go through the narrow Straits of Messina with a convoy, so instead they went south and east of the island and northwards up to Messina. He arrived on 5 August, ten days after Fox. The frigate which had brought him to Sicily returned the next day and he took the opportunity to write to his mother, telling her that he had arrived safely and also telling her about the British victory at Maida in Calabria; all the troops from that action were in Messina, and General Stuart who had commanded them was about to go home. Moore reported that he had got a great house, but it was 'without any one convenience'. His servant Francois was perplexed by the lack of furniture. The next letter to his mother, a month later, enclosed a locally made silk shawl, remarking that although she could probably get one just as good in London, she would be able to tell her friends that this one was a present from her son in Sicily.

By the end of the month, General Fox was receiving daily demands for men, arms, ammunition and money from Sidney Smith, who was operating off the coast of Calabria. Unable to see from Smith's letters exactly what was going on, or why men were necessary, Fox sent Moore to go and see Smith, find out what he was doing and if possible meet with the 'capi' (the chiefs in the interior) and report back on the true state of matters. He gave Moore powers to make decisions and give directions as he thought necessary. Moore found Smith in the Bay of Salerno with a small squadron consisting of his own ship, the *Pompee*, 80, the *Thunderer*, 74, the *Hydra* and *Aurora* frigates, four transports and several gunboats and avisos. When Moore went on board the *Pompee* he found that Smith had taken the squadron under a French battery at Cape Licorna which had struck the *Pompee* thirty-two times and killed or wounded forty-three men, including a lieutenant and a midshipman among the dead. He had then ordered the marines to land and get in the rear of the battery, which they achieved without loss and took forty prisoners. Moore reflected that if he had done this first he would have saved his men and not risked his ship.

During the conversation which followed, Moore reported that Smith spoke as though he was directing a considerable force under distinguished leaders, 'and that nothing but the want of money and arms, which were denied him, had prevented his driving the French from lower Italy and placing Ferdinand upon the throne of Naples'. Moore then explained that Fox had not been able to come himself, but that he considered that the Calabrese who did not side with the French and called themselves 'banditti' or 'briganti' were intent on plunder and murder rather than a love of liberty; their leaders were mostly adventurers from other countries. Given that little dependence was to be placed on these Calabrese 'massi', General Fox did not consider it safe to risk a small corps of British in their defence and did not believe it to be the policy of England to tie up a large one in such a venture; the defence of Sicily was the main object. He also felt that frigates and gunboats would be best employed in preventing warlike stores moving along the Calabrian coast; some Neapolitan troops had already moved into lower Calabria, to be stationed at Monteleone. Fox was trying to obtain information about the country and its inhabitants and intended to send British officers over; if the Calabrese could be organised to provide a useful resistance they would be supplied with the necessary means, but in the meantime he wished Smith would refrain from interfering with the affairs of Calabria and not give promises, or direct measures, which when done without his (Fox's) knowledge and sanction, would be likely to counteract the plans he might adopt. Gordon later informed Moore that Smith had been reprimanded by the Admiralty for accepting the command in Calabria.

Moore then paid a brief visit to Lieutenant Colonel Lowe at Capri, who was stationed there in command of a Corsican Corps. Although the island gave a good view of the bay of Naples, there was no anchorage in the winter and few landing places; as these were difficult to access, it was a safe post. There were two regiments in transports under Brigadier General Acland, which Moore ordered him to take to Messina. On returning to the Bay of Salerno he found Smith in almost the place where he had left him, 'floating in search of adventures for no earthly use'. Moore gave him a written version of what he had told him before, and Smith commenced a long discussion on what had lead him to take a lead in the affairs of Calabria. 'There was much falsehood and misrepresentation in what he said,' wrote Moore, 'but he did not know how much I already knew of all that had passed previous to my arrival in Sicily.' He told Smith that Fox was satisfied that everything had been done with the best intentions, but now it was time for more order and regularity, and that much inconvenience would result if everyone acted independently.

On his way back, Moore looked in at several places on the Italian coast, where he found that 'The magistrates and persons in authority ... are a set of weak, pusillanimous men' who were incapable of protecting themselves and that those who wanted support from the British army merely wanted to be relieved of the French and to take revenge on their countrymen who had joined them. Moore remarked:

> It seems therefore to me to be cruel and very unbecoming the British nation to encourage this kind of insurrection, which tends to the ruin of both parties, and, if we do not mean really to defend the Calabrese, we should leave them to make the best peace they can, and not, by encouraging the revolt, subject them to more severe punishment.

While he was away, Moore received a letter from Fox enclosing one from Stuart pressing him to send troops 'to make demonstrations' on the coast; Fox was averse to frittering away his force and said in his letter that he would wait for Moore's return or until he heard from him before doing anything, but when he did return it was to find that Fox had yielded to Stuart's importunity and had sent Brigadier General Cole with his brigade to Pizzo. Acton had gone with some infantry and cavalry to Monteleone and Stuart had gone over to Calabria at Scilla with a troop of cavalry and some companies of light infantry. On Moore's advice, Cole was ordered to return immediately, and, he hoped, Stuart would be too. Moore was convinced that they should either take their whole force into Calabria or leave the Calabrians to themselves, not risk small corps without providing real protection. Such small forces would only serve as bait to the French who would not fail to cut them up. He thought that the troops at Messina and some transports stationed at Milazzo would make the French cautious of further actions in Calabria; they would do better to concentrate their efforts on the immediate defence of Sicily and to get their troops and departments into order so that they would be ready to defend Sicily if it were attacked or go on some other service if ordered. Meanwhile Fox had written a strong letter to Smith telling him to desist from interfering with the inhabitants of Calabria.

The news came that peace had been signed between France and Russia; the terms included the withdrawal of French troops from Germany, an agreement that Swedish Pomerania was not to be attacked by the French, and a guarantee that the dominions of Turkey were to remain as they were. The most unfortunate effect of this treaty for Britain was that it released French troops for an attack on the Iberian peninsula or Sicily. This latter possibility threw the Court of Palermo into a panic, and letters from Elliott said that the Queen intended to go to Messina. Her chief minister Sir John Acton had resigned and was replaced by the Marquis of Circello. General Fox had yet to present his credentials to the Court at Palermo, and decided this was a good time to do that. While he was away, Moore sent all the official letters on to him; one of these was from William Windham, Secretary for War and the Colonies, stating that he intended to send a further 6,000 troops to Sicily.

Fox wrote to Moore that Maria Carolina was pressurising him to take troops to Naples, he was resisting this but feared she would then press him to occupy Maida which he thought he would have to do unless he received orders from home to the contrary. Moore replied that no doubt he would be instructed from home, but if not, his advice to Fox was that he should do neither. Landing at Naples would do no permanent good to their Sicilian Majesties without the assistance of other powers, and Maida was not a position of advantage but one from which the British could easily be driven. He thought it best to wait and see the development of the British government's views on the long-term occupation of Sicily without concerning himself with the wishes and opinions of the Neapolitan Court, certainly not those to the effect that if all the British intended to do was preserve Sicily they would be better off on their own.

When Fox returned to Messina he told Moore that he had received no orders from home but hoped to have these before the reinforcement arrived. He was disgusted with the Court of Palermo, saying he had seen more childishness, wickedness and folly than he had seen in any other part of the world. Smith was also at Palermo, paying private visits to the Queen twice a day; it was said that she was going to make him Viceroy of Calabria, or to give him the island of Lampedusa to hold as a fief from the King of Naples with the title of Duke; he was encouraging her to invade Naples and regain her throne there.

Moore had received some information about the French in Calabria from a merchant who had marched with their army from Salerno to Melito before he moved on to Scilla. He said they had forces totalling 14,000 men; then some later news said that reinforcements had arrived at Naples; Moore took it for granted that these would be sent to join the others. This meant they were not committed to any activity but would be ready to act against the British if they landed at Naples or Calabria. He paid a brief visit to Milazzo to see whether it would be a suitable location to place the incoming troops. It was, he wrote, different from any other country he had seen in Sicily: below the village of Gisso it spread into a plain of different breadths between the mountains and the sea. The Bay of Milazzo offered a good anchorage for even large ships, but was exposed to winter winds which prevented the British fleet from using it in winter; although those winds rarely reached the shore ships could ride safely there. The plain seemed to Moore to be a good location for the disposable British force; they could leave a garrison at Messina with the rest camped on the plain with their transports in the bay. This would be better than dispersing them in the villages around Messina, keep them healthier and better prepared for service.

At the end of September, Moore set out on a tour of the northern part of the island but was recalled before he got any further than Taormina. Fox wished to consult him on despatches he had received from the Marquis of Circello. These included a letter with a plan for an attack on the city of Naples; the letter stated that the King received daily requests from the people of Naples, and their discontentment, with other reasons, had determined him to use all his resources to execute the plan. However, Ferdinand needed assistance from the British to ensure success, so he wanted troops and the aid of a naval force; Circello had already received orders to apply for the latter from Sir Sidney Smith. The plan stated that the total force available to the French was no more than 20,000, only half of which consisted of French troops. There were fewer than 2,000 in the garrison of Naples. There was, said the plan, a disposable force in Sicily of 27,000, 12,000 of which was British, the rest Sicilian; a corps of 8,000 could be picked and sent with the Prince of Hesse to land near Naples. Twelve-thousand of the French army were with General Massena some fifteen days forced march from Naples and thus could not offer resistance. Once success at Naples was known, the British would land in Calabria to follow and harass Massena on his way to Naples.

Moore found the whole plan absurd, and the facts on which it was formed false. It was full of impertinence, and the language and general tone suggested strongly that it had been produced by the Queen and Smith. Fox was concerned that a torrent of abuse would be sent to the British government if he refused to assist; since the subject was purely military, he wished for Moore's opinion. This was that he knew of nothing new to induce Fox to change his mind on the subject and that he thought the position taken up by Massena was one in which he could not be hurt, and being half way between Naples and Calabria he could quickly move to either one. Instructions from home should soon arrive, and there should also be news of the negotiations which were currently under way; if the coalition which was talked of in Northern Europe was formed they would then be able to act effectively in Italy, but in the meantime prudence required them to remain quietly and not allow themselves to be led by what he termed 'the folly and wickedness of the Court of Palermo and its advisers' into measures which they disapproved.

He recommended that Fox should respond to Circello by positively refusing to concur in the proposed measures while assuring him that it was the wish of the British Court to see their Sicilian Majesties restored to their throne and former dominions. He would be happy to use the force under his command in whatever manner would lead to that desirable end, but had to hold himself the sole judge of when and how that could be done. It was his opinion that this was not the right moment and that the plan submitted was so faulty that he could not believe it had been drawn up with the advice of any man with military experience. He would thus decline to have any share in it, and would regret it if His Majesty was sufficiently ill-advised to attempt it on his own. As to naval assistance, Sir Sidney Smith had already received orders from his Commander-in-Chief, and as he (Fox) believed these were to protect Sicily and act with the British land forces he could not believe Smith would take the fleet and transports under his command and employ it in ways in which the British army took no share and with which the British commander of that army did not agree.

Moore also advised Fox to write to Smith and in plain terms inform him that his conduct was no secret, that his intrigues with the Queen and the Court of Palermo were well known, and that he had been sent to command his squadron with the specific purpose of acting in concert with the British army and not to intrigue with the Sicilian Court. If Smith had any ideas to discuss, he should do this direct with Fox not through Circello. He (Fox) understood that Smith was to be appointed to escort the Neapolitan forces to Italy but since Fox disapproved of this and refused to co-operate with this plan, he trusted Smith would think carefully before he joined in any enterprise which might prevent his co-operation with the British troops. Unfortunately Fox did not write to either Smith or Circello in as forcible terms as Moore advised him to, believing that both needed to be dealt with in very plain language. Moore remarked in his journal that he would not have hesitated to tell Smith that he was fully acquainted with his intrigues, so it seems that Fox did not do so. Moore also remarked that since the British paid a subsidy to the Court of Palermo, and had a force that could command the island, that they should be informed, though respectfully, that it was for the British to dictate and not to be dictated to.

At the end of October, Brigadier General Campbell, the Adjutant General for the army in Sicily, arrived after an adventurous journey. His ship, the *Athenian* packet, had been wrecked on the reef of Skerki (a shallow area between Sicily and Tunisia) and Campbell had been one of the lucky few who escaped alive. He brought confirmation of Charles James Fox's death; he had been succeeded by Lord Howick. If there had been any public despatches for Fox they had been lost. However, Campbell said that the reinforcements had sailed from Plymouth a week before he left and should arrive any day. Negotiations were continuing in Paris, but Buonaparte had left there to assemble forces in Westphalia. Moore hoped that there was a good chance of peace, as otherwise the government would have sent Fox instructions. There was no reason for sending reinforcements unless they were intended for some offensive action; Fox, however, would not make any such move until he had instructions. Perhaps, thought

Moore, the Ministers were not able to give such instructions at the current stage of negotiations.

Three weeks later, Fox received a letter from William Drummond, announcing that he had been appointed Minister Plenipotentiary to the Court at Palermo, together with a copy of his instructions. He also received letters of recall as Minister from Lord Howick. Drummond's letter mentioned the hope of the Court at Palermo for a military enterprise against Naples but added that it would be unbecoming for him to offer an opinion, especially one which might be contrary to Fox's intentions. However, since he had to report home the various statements which had been made to him, and since he did not wish to appear biased, he wished to know Fox's views on the expediency of such an enterprise.

Fox thought it would be better, rather than writing, for Moore to go to Palermo and explain everything to Drummond in person. Fox felt that whoever was sent to take over the diplomatic part of his functions should remain subordinate to him or whoever was the military commander, as had been Charles James Fox's principle. He had already stated his wish to give up the diplomatic part of his function in preparation to also giving up the military command. It seemed that his brother's view on the matter of who was subordinate had not been adhered to, and Drummond had no such instructions. Fox had, however, been given leave to give up the command in Sicily whenever he pleased and to return to Gibraltar or England as he thought best. He had not yet decided on these points.

Moore landed at Palermo on 29 December and went straight to Drummond's house where an apartment had been prepared for him. In their first conversation Moore explained Fox's reluctance to take troops into Calabria or Naples. His force was not large enough to engage the French until they were recalled elsewhere, and thus any such landing would depend on events in Northern Europe rather than close to hand. They discussed the Court of Palermo and Smith, and Moore wrote that Drummond, who he found to be a sensible, well-informed man, was prepared to agree with him on all subjects. Drummond had been Minister to the Court of Naples and thus was acquainted with the Court and the people who composed it. For the years when Sir John Acton was Minister and had charge of affairs, the Queen had little to say but she had contrived to get rid of him and brought in Circello instead, since when she had had control of the government. King Ferdinand was indolent, hated business and was happy to let the government go on without him as long as he could carry on with his hunting and fishing. Moore remarked that he did not know what degree of intellect Ferdinand possessed, but that he was good-natured and popular with both the populace of Naples and Sicily, as well as some of the Sicilian noblemen.

Queen Maria Carolina, although generally considered clever, meddled and intrigued, more like a man than a woman. Like the late Empress Catherine of Russia she had a lover, but Catherine's lover had been rewarded with riches and titles whereas Maria Carolina was governed by her lover Circello. She had given him a post for which he had no ability, but was much influenced by him, and since he was French, he was probably betraying her. Moore considered she was not clever except in conversation and intrigue, and wrote that 'She is a violent wicked bitch with a most perverted understanding, led by her passions, and seldom influenced by reason. She is attached to nobody but as far as they can be of use to her.' She let herself be led by those who flattered her and agreed with her views, and despite being incapable of managing affairs was only happy when dabbling in them. Her current passion was to return to Naples; she was not prepared to listen to any obstacles and was prepared to sacrifice every man in Sicily in the process.

Soon after Moore had arrived, Ferdinand returned from one of his hunting trips and Moore and Drummond had a private meeting with him. He said that although some persons had given the impression that he was not satisfied with the English, this was not true; he wished to be on good terms with England and was satisfied that they were acting fairly towards him. He would ensure that nothing was transacted that had not passed through his hands and of which he approved. The King's manners, remarked Moore, were those of a good-natured country gentlemen. He invited them to dine with him on 11 January; twelve sat down to the meal, including Drummond, Moore, Smith, the Russian Minister and ministers and officers of the Court. It was not a ceremonial meal; the King was in good spirits, telling some ridiculous anecdotes; the conversation was mostly about hunting. Moore thought that if he had £3,000 a year and a pack of hounds he would be suited to his place but as a king in difficult circumstances, it was a little disgusting to see him totally occupied with his amusements. After dinner, they moved to another room for coffee with the Queen, the princes and princesses. She introduced the latter to Moore and paid many compliments to the British troops but he knew that she liked neither. Although it was the only territory she had, she disliked Sicily, considering it unworthy of her attention and she had no thought for improving it or its inhabitants. She would not accept that the British had been sent to Sicily for its preservation and only to give aid in the reconquest of Naples when the time was right. The Sicilian generals did not think that time had arrived, but no matter how they argued their position, she hated them and the nation, placing her confidence in Frenchmen who encouraged her in her views, especially when these would serve their personal interests.

Moore continued:

It is difficult to describe a Court more debauched, more mean or more weak. Their only talent is intrigue; it is the Queen's but they counteract each other, and everything is known, all intrigue and are intrigued against. The Queen has spies in every family, but they all have spies equally on her and on each other. It is a scene quite painful to witness and I never was more pleased than when I was able to come away from it.

He advised Drummond that if he were to use bold and firm language with them that this might overawe them, given that he was supported by a military and naval force and represented a nation which paid them subsidies but Drummond replied that his instructions were to maintain good relations with the Court.

After dinner, Drummond closed his despatches to go home by the packet. He had written in strong terms on the behaviour of Smith, stating the impossibility of dealing with a man who seemed to have forgotten the honourable position of a British admiral and had dwindled into a mere Neapolitan courtier. Otherwise, he repeated Fox's statements and asked for permission to use language better to control the Sicilian government. Moore then returned to Messina. At the end of the month Admiral Sir John Duckworth arrived with a squadron of large ships; he brought despatches from the Secretary of State and Admiral Collingwood (Commander-in-Chief of the Royal Navy in the Mediterranean). Duckworth's mission was to go to the Dardanelles and Constantinople, consult with Mr Arbuthnot, the British Minister, on the situation with the Turks, and if necessary to commence hostilities against them, including sending a corps of 5,000 men from Sicily to Alexandria. Duckworth had called at Palermo on his way to Messina and although Drummond had not been able to see him, he had sent a message warning Duckworth about Smith, who if trusted with information would almost certainly pass it on to Maria Carolina. Drummond added in a letter to Moore that there was strong reason to believe that Maria Carolina had, at one time, been negotiating with the Russians to send a corps of troops to Sicily, but was then negotiating with Buonaparte.

When Fox learned that he had missed Duckworth, he directed Moore to go to Malta where he would be able to see Duckworth and explain matters to him, something which could be done more fully in person than by letter. Delayed by the winds, Moore arrived at Malta just as Duckworth was leaving, but they were in time to make a signal that Moore wished to speak to the admiral and the ships bore up for him to go on board the flagship. Duckworth told Moore that he had sent a vessel to inform Fox that the Russian Minister at Constantinople had managed to escape to Malta, where he reported that the Turks had declared war against Russia and that since Duckworth considered a war with Russia to be equivalent to war with England, he had suggested to Fox that he should send the troops to Alexandria straight away. Moore replied that he was not sure what Fox would do, but that it might be better to wait for the reaction to his appearance in the Dardanelles; they could take Alexandria any time they chose, but when the Court at Palermo were suspected of negotiating with Buonaparte for its surrender it was important not to reduce the British force there until the last moment. Duckworth agreed with Moore on this, and showed him his instructions, which were that if the Porte did not cease its hostilities with Russia he should demand that they surrender their fleet; if they did not do so within an hour, he was to destroy the city of Constantinople and take or destroy their fleet.

Whatever the result of Duckworth's visit to Constantinople, Moore was not enthusiastic about the possibility of an expedition to take Alexandria. He thought that attacking the Turk's distant provinces would not affect them much, and it would have been better to use the men which the Alexandria expedition would require to accompany Duckworth to Constantinople, secure his passage through the Dardanelles and enable him to destroy the Turkish fleet and arsenal. He was, once again, unhappy about his position as second in command to Fox, who although not fit enough to command himself, was fully aware that if any service was required it could be done by Moore. Moore had written to Brownrigg and Gordon, asking them to mention to the Duke of York that it was hard to be detained in Sicily merely for Fox's convenience when he had permission to go home. If Fox was well enough to command in all aspects, there was no reason for Moore to continue and in that case he would prefer to be recalled in the hope of getting a chief command elsewhere.

One bright spot in the general gloom which Moore felt was that Smith had been superseded in the command of the squadron in the central Mediterranean by Captain Hallowell; he had called at Palermo and finding that Drummond wished to see Fox had brought him to Messina. Drummond reported that the Queen no longer had any influence over affairs, which were dealt with between the King, Circello and himself, as a result of which he had agree to continue paying the subsidy which he had been withholding. Moore thought, and told Drummond, that this was merely a ruse by the Queen to get the subsidy; her character was such that she would not have meekly given up the power, and her hold over Circello was such that he would have told her everything. Drummond announced that he was perfectly satisfied, but Fox having left the conversation mainly to Moore, the latter did what he often did in such situations and told Drummond exactly what he thought: 'I did as I always shall do on such occasions, gave my opinion fully, both with respect to what he had done and what he should do, without troubling myself whether it was agreeable to him or not. I consider truth and plain dealing as most fit for public business.' Moore seemed to think that having unburdened himself of his opinion, the recipient would think the matter at an end, as he did himself, never realising that it would rankle for a long time. This conviction did not make him popular with those who were on the receiving end of such pronouncements, and it certainly did not make him popular with Drummond.

On 18 February the brig *Delight* came in with despatches from Duckworth. He had passed through the Dardanelles and was at Tenedos, the small island close to the Sea of Marmara just short of Constantinople. The British Minister Mr Arbuthnot had managed to escape from Constantinople and was also at Tenedos; Duckworth took this as being tantamount to a declaration of war and gave notice that the expedition could sail for Alexandria. Meanwhile, he had been joined by Sir Thomas Louis and together they intended to force their way through the Bosporus to Constantinople. The corps for Alexandria was assembled: 5,300 troops, consisting of two battalions of the 35th, the 31st, De Rolls', the Chasseurs Britanniques, the 78th, the 20th Dragoons and the Royal Sicilians, with a detachment of artillery, commanded by Major General Fraser, with Major General Wauchope, Brigadier Generals the Honourable William Stewart and Meade. They were ready to go in three days but had to wait for Captain Hallowell who had been delayed by contrary winds and did not arrive until 1 March.

On 13 March Moore set off on a tour of the island. In every town and village that he passed through he found the magistrates and inhabitants very civil, but all complained about the government. The towns themselves consisted of a few reasonable houses, many peasant's huts and many convents and churches. He paused at Girgenti on the 25th and stayed at the house of the British Consul, Mr Sterlini, where he received a despatch from Fox, enclosing a letter from Drummond, urging him to take an expedition to Naples. Drummond, he remarked in his journal 'seems to be completely in the hands of the Sicilian Court, at the same time that he is flattering himself that he is directing them'. Once again, Fox asked for Moore's opinion which was as before: that it was absurd. Since over 5,000 troops had been sent to Alexandria, they no longer had a force equal to the task, and it seemed, he thought, that the British government had given up all idea of acting in Italy.

By 6 April he had arrived at Syracuse, where Colonel William Clinton, who commanded the flank battalion of the Guards, rode out to meet him with Moore's old friend and relation, Mr Leckie, and escorted Moore to Leckie's house in the town where he stayed overnight. While he was there, he inspected the fortifications. These were in good repair and made the town very secure, but they needed more casemates and magazines. Once again Moore received letters from Fox enclosing two notes from Circello, and as before Circello relayed the King's desire to retake his kingdom of Naples and wanting to know what support he could expect from the British. Fox asked for Moore's opinion, which was unchanged. Although it was said that the Russians had had some successes against the French, and that there was only a small number of French troops in Naples, the time to consider such action would not be until the position and actions of the French were confirmed. Even then, he thought Ferdinand should attempt to take possession of Naples with Neapolitan troops only, he certainly would not allow any British soldiers to leave Sicily, especially not as auxiliaries to Ferdinand. Moore went on: 'I should certainly not go there unless we had command of the King's person, that the Queen and all her emissaries were removed and that we had the complete direction of the Government.' He remarked that the notes from Circello were identical to those which were sent every day while the Queen was in command, and proved that her influence had not changed; Drummond ('poor man' said Moore) was clearly under her influence.

He wrote a long letter to Brownrigg, bringing him up to date with events; these included a comment on the unfortunate ending to Duckworth's expedition to Constantinople, where he had fallen victim to the huge guns. These damaged several of his ships, including the *Windsor Castle*, which was struck by a marble shot weighing over 800 pounds.[1] Moore also took the opportunity to express his opinion of Drummond: 'though a good scholar and possessing remarkable talents, [he] proves in point of character to be one of the weakest and silliest of men'. His opinion of General Fraser's activities in Egypt was considerably better: '[he] seems to have conducted his operation well, and he has succeeded at Alexandria with little or no loss'. His only criticism of Fraser was that instead of sending 1,400 men to Rosetta and Rhamanie under Brigadier General Wauchope, he should have left a few hundred men to guard Alexandria and Aboukir and gone himself to Rosetta where he would have had easy access to plentiful supplies.

The next news from Egypt was not good. Wauchope had marched his men into Rosetta before he had obtained permission from the garrison or inhabitants; these flew to arms and fired on Wauchope's force from their houses, driving the British troops out of the town with a loss of some 500 killed and wounded. Wauchope was killed and General Meade wounded. Fraser then sent a further 2,500 men, including artillery and dragoons, under Brigadier General Stewart; these invested the town and opened fire on it with cannon and howitzers in hopes of forcing it to surrender. A large body of Turks came down the Nile to support the inhabitants of the town and forced Stewart to raise the blockade. He retreated to Aboukir with a loss of about 1,000 men killed and taken. Fraser's reaction to this was to call for reinforcements of men, money and provisions. Moore realised Fraser had been misled by Major Misset, the British consul in Egypt, as to both numbers of the enemy's force and the military position; neither Rosetta or Rhamanie were places which could be held by small forces and with only 5,000 Fraser could not have done other than hold Alexandria.

When Fox returned from Catania it was decided to send two victualling ships to Alexandria immediately, to be followed by a reinforcement of 15,000 men as soon as a naval escort could be arranged. This was accompanied by specific instructions to the effect that all he was expected to do was hold Alexandria; if it was found impossible to obtain provisions and water from within Egypt, then they must evacuate. Fox wrote home to explain the position at Alexandria when it was cut off from the rest of Egypt, pointing out that to conquer Egypt and hold it would require an army of at least 15,000 or 20,000 men. While they waited for a response with instructions, a further despatch from Fraser gave news of a further disaster. In order to defend his rear, Stewart had sent a force to El Hamed, then a further 800 men to reinforce it. A large force of Turks arrived from Cairo, including a large body of cavalry. They surrounded the British troops, killing or taking about 750 men, upon which Stewart had destroyed his ammunition, buried his guns and retreated.

A further defeat had occurred in Calabria. The Prince of Hesse, with about 2,000 Neapolitan troops, had sailed for Reggio where he expected to find a further 1,000 troops and expected 5,000 cavalry to arrive from Palermo. They had found only an advanced force of French which retreated, but this was a ruse to draw the Neapolitans forward, followed by an attack which totally defeated them. They dispersed and fled, losing all their cannon, but the Prince managed to escape, arriving back in Sicily on 1 June. The Prince said he had left Colonel Nunciate with a garrison in the castle. Moore felt uneasy about Reggio and sent Lord Proby, the Deputy Adjutant General to go over and gave him a letter for Nunciate. When he returned, he reported that he had found Nunciate and all the troops from the town had escaped to the gunboats where they were firing on the French in the town. They had left a captain and 130 men in the castle; the Prince, remarked Moore, had shown them the way by not taking pains to collect his broken army before leaving. He went to see the Prince and told him in no uncertain terms of Nunciate's shameful behaviour and the disgrace they would all suffer if Reggio was allowed to fall into French hands. This had the effect of making Nunciate go back into the castle to defend it. 'The Prince was', said Moore, 'drunk, which is generally his situation after dinner' but he did, under pressure from Moore, send some men to reinforce Reggio, and started collecting his people who were arriving in boats. Moore wrote 'I do not believe there ever was such a rout; both officers and men seem to be panic–struck. I am certain that if the French made a show of coming here they would all run away.'

A despatch had arrived for Fox from Lord Castlereagh (now the Secretary for War and the Colonies) stating explicitly that the Government did not intend to pursue the war against the Turks any further, but to employ the British force in Sicily in active operations against Naples or some other part of that coast, just leaving sufficient garrisons to secure their return. Castlereagh had computed the available force, including the Neapolitans, at 20,000 men; he appreciated that the Neapolitans were inferior soldiers, but since numbers were important they must be 'encouraged, improved, and made the most of with a view to this important object'. Moore remarked that it was difficult to believe that Castlereagh had read Fox's correspondence with Ministers since he took the command in Sicily, for although these had not always been as explicit as Moore would have wished, they were sufficiently so to have prevented such orders.

Moore wrote to Brownrigg and reported this, remarking that what could be done with the British force alone might be attempted, but that he believed that anything communicated to the Sicilian Court would be passed to the enemy. Fox, he said, had never had any command over the Sicilian troops who after their recent debacle were reduced to 7,000 or 8,000, 'without spirit as without discipline, ill-officered, ill-paid, and disaffected'. The British force, after leaving 2,000 men to garrison Messina and Syracuse, were no more than 8,000, including the Corsican Regiment at Capri, and supposing a regiment to be taken from Malta. This totalled a force of 15,000 for active operations, over half of which Fox had no command, and even if he did, he would probably be more embarrassed by them than helped. Although it could not be verified, Moore believed that the French force in the Kingdom of Naples was not less than 20,000. Fox replied immediately to Castlereagh, stating his reasons for doubting the practicalities of carrying the orders into execution, but adding that the British troops would be held in readiness and he would seize the opportunity to act if one presented itself. He also wrote to Drummond, asking him to apply to the Court for assurance that, if they should go to Italy, he would have their command; if not, he said, he would undertake no service in which they were involved. To Brownrigg, Moore remarked that he feared that the British ministers had been misled by Drummond.

On 9 July despatches were received from Castlereagh ordering the evacuation of Egypt, the troops from there to return to Sicily. A private letter from the Duke of York to Fox accompanied the despatches, notifying him of his recall and desiring him to give up the command to Moore. The letter was perfectly polite, but said that as Fox's health did not permit his exerting himself as would be necessary if there was service in Italy, King George thought it proper that the command should be in the hands of the officer to whom that service would be entrusted. This came as a surprise to Fox as he had not intended to give up the command. Fox asked Moore to send the appropriate orders to Fraser to evacuate Alexandria. Sir Arthur Paget was on his way to Tenedos to try and negotiate a peace with the Porte, and it was thought that Alexandria should be held for a short while in order to aid these negotiations by offering the evacuation of Alexandria as an inducement to making peace. In view of this, Moore's instructions to Fraser were to make his plans for evacuation quietly, taking care to keep them secret. While he waited to hear of the outcome of the negotiations at Tenedos, and for Fox to leave for home, Moore wrote a long and confidential letter to Castlereagh explaining all his thoughts on the situations in Sicily and the steps he intended to take as soon as the command was his.

Fox departed for home on 3 August, taking his family with him. As well as his wife, he had two daughters, Louisa (who married Henry Bunbury) and Caroline (who later married William Napier, the historian). It seems that Moore was enamoured of Caroline, although she was only just 17; he told Anderson that she was the only woman he had ever thought of marrying, but had not pursued the match as he was so much older than her (45) and he thought that it could only lead to unhappiness for her to later find her husband was an old man. The only evidence for this is a third-hand report: Anderson told Charles Napier who told his brother William.[2] Although it is not unknown for middle-aged men to fall for very young women, it is perhaps a little odd that Moore never mentioned it in writing, not even to his brother Graham.

Moore's first task as Commander-in-Chief was to pay a formal visit to Palermo, taking three days on the road along the coast between the sea and the mountains. The road was typical of Sicilian roads, unformed and bad, but lined quite a way up the mountains with corn, olives, mulberry trees and vineyards. He dined with Drummond then paid a visit to Circello and then the Queen. Circello told him he had orders from the King to direct Brigadier Fardelli, chief of the *État Major*, to wait on him with full details of the state of the Sicilian army and answer any questions Moore had. Moore responded that this would give him information on the size of the army and on its discipline and state of preparedness, but did not give him any command of it and was no answer to Fox's letter. Circello replied that the command would certainly be given to him if he would undertake to act against Naples. There was no one else, he said, to whom it could be given but the British General. Circello paid Moore many compliments, but nothing was decided.

The visit to the Queen was merely formal and nothing much was said; Moore wanted a private meeting with her in order to explain the reasons he and Fox had acted as they did, and he hoped to remove the unfavourable impressions she had gained from reports. He asked Sir John Acton how he should go about getting a private meeting with her and Sir John said he would write to her; on receiving this letter she made an appointment for Moore to see her the next afternoon. She received him politely, listened patiently to what he had to say and then said she was satisfied with his explanations. She believed him, she said, to be a man of honour and character who would not say or do what he thought wrong in order to agree with anybody and esteemed him for it. Moore felt easier for having had the chance to make these explanations to the Queen, but it led to a row with Drummond who said he felt hurt for Moore having asked for a meeting with the Queen without him, expressing himself in a way Moore thought improper.

Moore told Drummond in plain terms that as Commander of the Forces in the island he thought himself different to ordinary subjects; that he was to a certain extent accredited to the Court as much as the Minister and had a right to ask for an audience whenever he thought proper, but as he did not wish to deviate from ordinary rules, nor to disoblige Drummond, he would in general prefer to arrange such meetings through the channel of the Minister. Moore then wrote:

This matter being settled, but both [of us] a little heated, led to further discussions. He complained of the contemptuous manner in which I had always spoken of him. I told him that I thought his conduct had been weak and pusillanimous; that with common fairness, when he first came, he might have gained an ascendancy at this Court which at present he does not possess. He harped a good deal upon the asperity of my expressions with regard to him, until I lost patience. I believe he wanted me to retract them; so I told him that if he had heard of my speaking harshly of him, we had also heard of his not speaking very respectfully of the Generals, that for my part I thought he should for ever hide his head. 'Hide my head!' he exclaimed. 'For ever hide your head,' I repeated, 'for having encouraged the reports of us which were made to the Court, for having betrayed conversations which had passed in confidential communications between yourself, General Fox, and me; for having at all times spoken slightingly and disrespectfully of us.' [Drummond said that the Queen had regained her influence since Fox's letter about command of the Sicilian troops.] I do not believe Drummond to be such a ninny as to credit this; but it suits his purpose to say so, to cloak his weakness, and a lie is at all times preferable to truth with him.

One of the issues which Moore took up with Drummond was that the latter had passed on to Maria Carolina a casual remark of Moore's to the effect that 'she should be shipped off to Trieste'.

When Moore saw Fardelli and saw the state of the troops which he brought with him, after much conversation he arranged to see the infantry the next day and the rest of the Sicilian army in the course of the following few days. The cavalry, he thought, was tolerably good, the reserve of about 1,500 infantry was passable, a few hundred artillery were said to be good and well-equipped with horses and drivers, but all the rest were very bad. The troops lacked confidence, were badly commanded and generally bore the marks of long neglect. Moore asked for an audience with the King and Queen, at which he told them of the inefficient state of their army and the unprepared state of the country for any kind of war, whether offensive against Naples or to defend Sicily. He told them he regretted the lack of confidence shown to England by their government; she had not sent flatterers and intriguers but fleets and armies with proper generals and admirals, who kept away from their Majesties except when necessary for business. Surely if the English were bad, they would flatter their Majesties by encouraging their attempts to recover Naples; by advising the opposite they gave strong proof that their prosperity was the most important.

The Queen said she could see the reasoning of this argument, but that it was fear, not distrust that drove her actions. The King denied that he had either but it was obvious to Moore that the actions of the government clearly showed distrust. The day after this meeting, Circello (who Moore described as an old goose) sent a formal letter repeating what the King had said about the command of the Sicilian army and asking for his recommendations on how to make it more effective. This letter started with some thoughts on the past and Fox's conduct; Moore found this improper and told Circello so in his answer. He enclosed some headings on how the Sicilian army could be improved: all the troops should be assembled near Palermo and divided into brigades under good officers, the whole under the command of General Bourcard, whom the King had already named as Commander-in-Chief, and whom Moore thought a very good honest man.

On the day that Moore saw the King and Queen he was seized with a fit of the fever, which kept him in his quarters for a week and lingered for several more days. During that time news came of the successes of the French army on the Vistula, the fall of Dantzig and Konigsberg, followed by the signing of peace between France and Russia at Tilsit. This news caused the Queen and the court to despair; she wanted to see Moore before he went back to Messina and he went on the evening of 8 August during an interval in the fever. She was in tears over the peace of Tilsit, and said she supposed she would have to give up Naples to Joseph Buonaparte and would be given Dalmatia or some small islands in compensation. She kept Moore talking for an hour and a half, during which he began to change his opinion of her, thinking that perhaps she was not herself a wicked woman but was too much guided by those around her; if she could see herself as others did the things her counsellors made her do, she would disapprove of them as others did. Unfortunately she lacked the capacity to involve herself in public affairs and her weaknesses led her to be violent, absurd, cruel and unjust.

Moore was not well enough to go back to Messina overland so he sent his horses back and embarked on a transport which was in the bay, arriving back in Messina on 16 August. The fever had left him and he was gradually regaining his strength. He spent the next week catching up on the business which had accumulated while he was away. All was quiet for some time, although he did receive news that the Russians were giving up Corfu and the Ionian islands to the French; masters of merchant ships reported that French troops were going from Otranto to Corfu in small vessels. Although he put the fortresses into a state of defence, there was no movement towards Sicily from the French.

Then on 15 September he received despatches which had been sent direct from England on a fast-sailing cutter. They were actually addressed to Fox, and they instructed him to embark with the Guards, 20th, 52nd, 61st, Watteville's, 2nd Battalion 35th, and 78th regiments, and go with them to Gibraltar, where he would receive further instructions. The generals named to serve under him were Major Generals the Marquis of Huntley, Wynyard, Oakes, Fraser and Paget. It was expected that the troops from Alexandria had arrived back in Sicily, but if they had not, he was not to leave until they did. In the meantime, all this must be kept a strict secret. Moore decided not to change any of the officers named in the despatch, and intended to leave the command in Sicily with Major General Sherbrooke, the senior general officer of those not named to go with him. In the meantime the troops from Alexandria had not arrived, and they were not expected until the middle of October; they actually arrived on 16 October. Moore immediately embarked on the *Chiffone* frigate and sailed for Syracuse, where Admiral Collingwood had directed the convoy of transports to assemble. Reaching there on the 26th, Moore transferred to the

Queen with the Quartermaster General Major General Oakes, the Adjutant General Lieutenant Colonel Lord Proby and their aides-de-camp. Two men-of-war and fifty-four transports set off for Maritimo where they expected to meet the *Windsor Castle* which was to accompany them to Gibraltar. They had 7,258 rank and file, 445 sergeants and 178 drummers with them, including sick, who Moore had ordered to be taken in the expectation that they would recover on the voyage, or if not, they could be left at Gibraltar.[3] They were accompanied by Dr Franklin, the Inspector of Hospitals and head of the Medical Department in the Mediterranean; he returned to Sicily after they reached Gibraltar.

After a tedious rough passage of five weeks, they arrived at Gibraltar on 1 December, where he received two dispatches from London. The first, dated 8 October, required him to leave two regiments at Gibraltar to reinforce the garrison and proceed to England with the rest. The second dispatch, dated 8 November, said that an order had been sent to him at Sicily requiring him to remain there with the whole force if this missed him, and assuming that he would not have got any further than the Straits of Gibraltar, his force would be available for several of the purposes for which it was called to Gibraltar. This dispatch then went on to explain the British relationship with the Court of Portugal, and told Moore to correspond with Lord Strangford, the British Minister at Lisbon. If the Portuguese royal family had decided to go to Brazil, they were to be accompanied by seven sail of the line under Smith's command with the aid of a corps of British troops. Moore was to land with those under his command, but not until the forts of St Julian and Bugio had been handed over to him.

When the royal family had embarked, he was to accompany them as far as Madeira, of which he was to take possession. If the royal family decided not to go to Brazil, but to enter an agreement with France to close Portugal's ports to British ships, Moore was to send a force to take possession of Madeira. If Lord Strangford, as a result of a Portuguese-French alliance, was obliged to return to England, and Rear Admiral Smith wished it, Moore was to take his force to rendezvous with him off the Tagus and to proceed jointly with such measures as they both agreed necessary for His Majesty's service. He was not able to leave Gibraltar immediately, as the transports had to be re-victualled and watered; some also required considerable repairs. This was expected to take up to ten days. While this was being done, Moore decided to take the *Chiffone* frigate off Lisbon to seek Smith. En route, they met some of Admiral Purvis's squadron which were blockading Cadiz and Captain Fleming Elphinstone told him that Smith was off the Tagus, and that he understood Lord Strangford had already sailed for England. The Portuguese had refused to allow the squadron into Lisbon, where French and Spanish troops had arrived. He had received information at Gibraltar that the Portuguese Government was hostile towards Britain, that the Court had no intention to go to Brazil and had completely deceived Lord Strangford. All their troops had been recalled from the frontier with Spain and gathered round Lisbon, where they had been employed in improving the defences of the Tagus. Sir Hew Dalrymple, who was the Governor of Gibraltar, had introduced Moore to some British merchants who had recently left Lisbon, who confirmed the situation in Lisbon. It seems Strangford was, in Moore's words 'a very young man, one of those who upon leaving college without any intermediate intercourse with mankind became statesmen and diplomatists'.

On 8 December, *Chiffone* met up with *Foudroyant*, whose captain informed Moore that he was part of Smith's squadron. They had been uncertain of what the Court of Lisbon would decide, when on the morning of 29 November eight sail of the line came out of the Tagus, carrying the Portuguese royal family. Moore's brother Graham, with four ships, was named to accompany them, and they all sailed off for Brazil; Smith accompanying them. Smith was expected to return to his squadron. He had ordered *Foudroyant* to return to the Tagus, which she was doing; Moore decided to go with her in hopes of meeting Smith there. The French troops had arrived at Lisbon the day before the royal family left; the Portuguese had not strengthened the defences as the merchants had reported, but had instead destroyed the batteries at Belem in the mouth of the Tagus. Strangford was with Smith, and the Consul, M. Gambier, had gone back to England.

Moore rethought his decision to go to the Tagus but went instead went back to Gibraltar where he expected Smith or Strangford to communicate with him. He arrived back in Gibraltar on the 10th, having met Admiral Purvis off Cadiz and told him what had happened at Lisbon. There were no letters from Smith waiting for him at Gibraltar, which he considered unaccountable behaviour. He concluded that there was no longer any need for his assistance in taking possession of Madeira and decided to take his troops home to England. In fact Lord Hawkesbury had written to him to tell him that since the Madeira matter was urgent, they had sent 3,500 men under Major General Beresford direct from England, if Moore had not yet sent a force to Madeira when he received that letter, he should not do so, and if he had already done so, he should recall it. Beresford had been ordered, if he arrived at Madeira and found Moore's force there already in possession, to send two regiments to the West Indies and join Moore with the rest of his expedition.[4] Moore left Gibraltar on 15 December and after a pleasant passage of thirteen days arrived at Spithead on the evening of the 28th; in the morning it was blowing too hard to weigh anchor and go in to Portsmouth, but a telegraph was sent to announce his arrival. After three days in quarantine, the troops were landed in Portsmouth and sent on to Kent by road, while the general officers and their staffs were allowed to go to London. In view of the uncertainty of his arrival, Major General Spencer had already sailed for Gibraltar with 8,000 troops; on arriving there, if he found that Moore had gone, he was to continue to Sicily.

In London, he found that some members of the Cabinet, influenced by Drummond's correspondence, disapproved of his conduct in Sicily, and concluded, from the strong language which he had used in his official letters that he was violent in his conduct. In view of this, he thought it necessary, when he first saw Castlereagh, to explain himself. He had, he said, wanted only to tell the Government the truth of matters, it was his duty to hide nothing from them, this being the only way they could frame proper instructions. It was, he thought, unjust that because he did not disguise his sentiments from Ministers, they should conclude that he did not know the respect due to the princes and public authorities with whom he had to deal. He told Castlereagh exactly what sort of person Drummond was, giving several examples of his falsehood and meanness, and said that since he (Moore) had been employed in the King's service for so long, and had held numerous public situations, he thought that his character should be well known and that Castlereagh, and the rest of the world, must have gathered whether he was wrong-headed or not.

Castlereagh spoke kindly of all Moore had done and said he hoped there would soon be an opportunity of advantageous employment. Soon after this interview, Castlereagh sent for Moore to consult him on various matters relating to Sicily and the Mediterranean. The Duke of York had stood by him through all the attempts to blacken his name, and Moore was told that the King had refused to be influenced. Moore believed he had only two or three enemies in the Cabinet, and they were men whose character did not make him concerned whether he was approved by them or not.[5]

Chapter 11

Sweden

Sweden was Britain's last ally on the Baltic, the sea which was important not only as the route to Pomerania, Prussia and Russia for exports of British manufactured goods, but also for imports of ship-building supplies and of grain from those countries. At a time when changeable weather conditions had led to a series of disastrous harvests in Britain, this grain supply was essential to feeding the British populace. The only entrance to the Baltic was through The Sound, a narrow stretch of water between Sweden and the Danish island of Zealand. It might have been possible to have held this large island and its city of Copenhagen the previous summer, when a British army of 27,000 men under General Cathcart had occupied the island, bombarded Copenhagen and seized the Danish fleet. There had been much discussion at the time on whether to retain control of the island but it was concluded that it could not be done even with 27,000 men and eventually Cathcart's army went home. At the time these events were declared a great British victory, but it had offended the Danes so much that they had signed an alliance with France, more than doubling their defence force. That year had also seen Napoleon's inexorable advance through northern Europe with the loss of Swedish Pomerania, Russia's annexation of Finland, and its alliance with France, formalised at the Treaty of Tilsit. The fear of both the Swedish and British governments was that French troops could easily cross The Sound from Denmark, invading Sweden and thus cutting off that single entrance to the Baltic.

Sweden itself was not entirely politically stable. Its merchant class was predominantly pacifist, but its king, Gustav IV, saw himself as a great military leader, a view certainly not shared by most of the officers of his army. A faction of those officers, led, it was strongly rumoured, by his uncle the Duke Charles, had assassinated his father in 1792, leaving Duke Charles as Regent until Gustav came of age in 1799. A similar faction of young officers was still active; their principal complaint against Gustav was that he was unfit to rule because he was insane. Whether this was an accurate description is a matter of argument among modern historians, but his behaviour during Moore's visit to Sweden was certainly less than rational.

Like many militaristic rulers, Gustav's military ambitions were not matched by the state finances, and so he turned to Britain for funds to support his army. A subsidy based on a set amount per soldier was paid; the norm was £12 10s per annum per soldier, but in 1805 Gustav had pushed this to almost double by threatening to exclude Russian troops from Swedish Pomerania, where they were essential to repel Napoleon's advance. After the failure of this strategy, followed by Russia's new alliance with France and the loss of Swedish Pomerania in 1807, the subsidy was renegotiated, to £100,000 a month for as long as Sweden used its army and navy 'in the most effectual resistance to the common enemy'. In addition to the subsidy, some specific military supplies were sent (although these *were to be paid for out of the subsidy) and military assistance was promised. This originally consisted of a substantial augmentation of the Royal Navy's Baltic fleet, together with specific orders for that fleet to help defend Sweden from a threatened French invasion in addition to its usual trade protection duties in those waters. Gustav had also asked for an auxiliary military force, but at the time of the negotiations Britain had no troops to spare. When Moore returned from the Mediterranean with his corps of almost 8,000 men, the Cabinet saw a way to keep their promise to Gustav, and also to solve another problem which was exercising them, that of choosing a general to command a proposed expedition to Portugal.*

According to a strong rumour, the King had promised this command to the Earl of Chatham; alternatively he might give it to his son, the Duke of York.[1] Both were tainted by their involvement with the disastrous Helder expedition of 1799, and thus would have been a very unpopular choice. The Cabinet's preferred commander was the well-connected General Arthur Wellesley but he was junior to Moore. Although he was the obvious candidate for the Portugal command, Moore was distrusted by many of the Cabinet members for his Whiggish politics. Sending him to Sweden (where the Cabinet thought his troops would serve as an auxiliary force to the Swedish army) would get him neatly out of the way so that Wellesley could be appointed.

* * *

Although Moore had arrived back in London early in January 1808, and had been promised by Castlereagh that an advantageous opportunity for service would soon be found for him, it was not until April that it was decided to send Moore to Sweden.

While he waited for new orders, Moore served on the Court Martial of General Whitelocke, who had commanded the disastrous expedition to Buenos Aires, eventually having to surrender and losing 3,000 of his 10,000 men in the process. (Found guilty of all but one of the charges against him, Whitelocke was dismissed the service.) Moore meanwhile renewed his relationship with Lady Hester Stanhope, to the chagrin of George Canning, the Foreign Secretary, whom Moore had supplanted in her affections. This may have been a contributory factor in Canning's dislike of Moore.

After Pitt's death, Canning had attempted to prove his claim to be Pitt's political heir. There was some foundation to this, as Canning had unquestionable ability and leadership qualities but these were marred by ambition. As Pitt's protégé, he had served briefly as under-secretary for foreign affairs but he had a fondness for intrigue and a lack of steadiness which destroyed Pitt's confidence in him. In his last years, Pitt preferred to rely on Castlereagh. While Castlereagh was Portland's secretary of war, the two men would have to work together, but mutual distrust prevented them from being genuine partners; however, both worked on changes to Britain's war policy under the Portland government. There were problems which the new Cabinet had to address. Recent military expeditions to South America and the Mediterranean had proved costly failures; the war on the Continent mainly consisted of Prussia and Russia trying to hold back France.

Moore's wait for a call to service finally came on 17 April when he was called to meet Castlereagh and the Duke of York, where they told him that he was to take a force of 10,000 men to Gothenburg. They believed that his arrival would free the Swedish troops in that area. There was no intention that he would ever put himself and his troops under the command of the Swedish King, or engage in any enterprise which would lead him from the coast or risk his re-embarkation or the power of withdrawing if he thought it was proper to do so, or he was so ordered from England. All this seemed rather vague, and he wrote, 'It was plain from the whole of Lord Castlereagh's conversation that the government had no specific plan and had come to no determination beyond that of sending a force of 10,000 men to Gothenburg.'

His written instructions were equally vague. They admitted, in the second paragraph, that:

> It would certainly have been desirable before this Force proceeded on Service, that His Majesty's Government had been more fully apprized of the Military views as well as the means of Sweden, and that a more precise and definite object could have been determined on, to which the services of this Corps should, on its arrival be applied. But the anxious desire His Majesty feels to afford to His ally the King of Sweden, the most prompt support, and the experience He has had of the great delays which attend communications between this country and Sweden, have prevailed over all other considerations in determining His Majesty in complying with the pressing solicitations of the Swedish Minister at this Court, to send the troops as soon as they can be embarked, to Gothenburg; Mr Adlerburg having pledged himself in the name of his Government that they shall experience on their arrival at that place, the most friendly and cordial reception.[2]

The other fifteen paragraphs of instructions were equally unclear, typical of the tortuous ramblings which were known to mar Castlereagh's speeches and writings.[3] It takes several readings to see that these instructions do indeed state that the main objective was to free up Swedish troops and that Moore should stay close to the coast and not be drawn into the interior or merge his army with Swedish troops, and that in order to keep his corps in contact with the fleet at all times it should always be under the command of its own officers. They repeated that the force should not go far from the coast, as King George reserved the right to recall them if he needed them elsewhere, but then they said: 'if circumstances require that the troops of the two nations should act together with a view to any particular service you will concert the necessary arrangements in that spirit of conciliation and confidence which so happily prevails between the courts of London and Sweden'.[4] They went on to say that Moore was to 'at all times pay the utmost deference and attention consistent with the principles above stated, to the suggestions and wishes of His Swedish Majesty'. Moore commented in his journal that he found these instructions 'inexplicit and contradictory'. What was clearer was the requirement to work with the British fleet under the command of Admiral Sir James Saumarez, an experienced and competent naval officer who had had some notable successes in the Mediterranean just before the Peace of Amiens. Moore was given a copy of Saumarez' orders and instructed to 'cultivate the most perfect understanding with that officer and co-operate with carrying out those orders so far as they relate to joint operations'.

While Moore was to put the security of Sweden first, he might consider the necessity of conducting offensive operations against Norway in order to achieve this. However, since the Government was not in possession of enough information to make an immediate decision, Moore was to examine the possibility of such operations in concert with the Swedish Government. He should ensure that the Swedes realised the difficulties of taking possession of Norway and of holding it afterwards; since they could not count on the permanent aid of an auxiliary British force they should consider how the garrisoning of Norway would weaken their ability to defend against invasion from the opposite coasts of the Baltic or of an attack by Russia.

The troops assigned to Moore were 6,631 Germans, including 597 Dragoons, the rest being infantry, and 4,233 British, made up of the 4th, 28th, 79th, 92nd and company 3 of the 95th, a total of 10,864.

On the same day as his letter to Moore, Castlereagh gave detailed instructions to Lieutenant Colonel George Murray, who was appointed Quartermaster General to Moore's force. He was to precede Moore to Sweden and meet with the British minister Edward Thornton, who would present him to King Gustav, and assist in obtaining nineteen listed pieces of military information. These related to various aspects of the strength and disposition of not only the Swedish army but also of the Russian and Norwegian armies, to the size of force needed to achieve specific objectives such as taking possession of Bergen, what plans the Swedes had for using the British troops, and the arrangements for the reception of British troops and their heavy baggage; all this in addition to any other enquiries Moore wanted him to make. When he arrived in Gothenburg, it was thought advisable that Colonel Marsheim, who had lived in Sweden for some time, should go to General Armfelt's headquarters to collect the desired information on Norway, while he should go himself direct to King Gustav's residence. Finally, he should meet with Mr Lutyens of the Commissary General's department and give him instructions on preparing the necessary supplies for the troops. After completing all these tasks, he was to return to Gothenburg to meet Moore and report back to Castlereagh.

On 1 May, Castlereagh wrote a separate set of instructions for Moore regarding the island of Zealand. Strongly defended, there was considerable doubt as to whether Sweden could raise a force strong enough to reduce the island, but it was believed that Gustav was disposed to concentrate on Zealand in preference to engaging in offensive operations against Norway. The information available from Thornton was only general, so the Government could not arrive at a judgement on the expediency of operations in Zealand but they wanted to bring it to Moore's attention as he was likely to find himself importuned on the subject by the Swedish Government immediately on his arrival.

All in all, these letters demonstrate just how little the British Government knew about the country and the administration of the country into which they were sending over 10,000 of their troops.

After receiving his written instructions, Moore went first to Deal to see his troops embark, then sailed on ahead to Yarmouth where Saumarez' fleet and the troop-ships were assembling. He was disconcerted to find that the troop- and store-ships provided were very small, requiring as many as seven or eight ships for a single regiment. With eighty-eight troop-ships, forty-three horse-ships and twenty-seven store-ships, he thought this an unwieldy number and wrote to Castlereagh to request larger ships; twenty or twenty-five would be sufficient to carry the whole expedition, he suggested. Castlereagh replied that the small ships were more suitable for the shallow waters of the Baltic; although he didn't mention it, Castlereagh would have known that it was too late to change the ships. The government did not own such ships and the process of finding, surveying and hiring merchant ships for such tasks was notoriously time-consuming; some of them had to be altered internally to fit them out for carrying troops and horses. Even with the ships that they did have, it was a full month after receiving his orders, delayed first by adverse winds and then by three days of fog, that Moore finally arrived at the Flemish Roads just outside Gothenburg on 17 May.

His first action, after reporting that he had arrived, was to report on the local state of affairs. 'I am inclined to consider an attack on Zealand as out of the question', he wrote, 'it is defended by 28,000 Danes and 44,000 French, Spaniards and Dutch, under [the French Marshall Jean-Baptiste] Bernadotte'.[5] A few days later he was able to add the news that Murray had brought on his return to Gothenburg, bringing back not only information on the Swedish troop strength but also the King of Sweden's plans for the employment of the British troops and his strong objections to the conditions attached to their use, in particular that of landing British troops in his realm. Gustav refused permission for the troops to land, declaring that Adlerberg, his Minister in London, had exceeded his instructions by promising on-shore accommodation for the British. This meant that the unfortunate British troops had to remain in the cramped conditions on their tiny troop-ships for several weeks, apart from a few days when groups of men were landed on small islands off Gothenburg for exercise, and, according to an unsubstantiated report, at least once in Gothenburg itself.

There was worse news. Gustav had no intention of allowing the British troops to defend his country while his own departed to fight elsewhere. He wanted Moore to take his troops and attack Sweden's enemies but even working as a joint force, Gustav's plans were unrealistic. His own army consisted of fewer than 29,000 men, of whom 8,000 were already facing 30,000 Danes and Norwegians on the Norwegian frontier, with another 10,000 facing an even greater force of Russians in Finland. 10,000 were guarding Stockholm and the southern Swedish coast. This count did not include the depot garrisons or the Lévé en Masse. None of these could be moved without risk to their current missions, although those in Finland had already been forced to retreat. Gustav's first plan, to invade and hold Zealand, would require a much larger force than Moore had available. Regardless of such considerations, Moore could not contemplate such an operation when his orders required him to remain on the Swedish mainland within easy reach of the coast. Gustav's alternative plan was equally unrealistic: to join General Armfelt and invade Norway. This plan required a further 10,000 Swedish troops to join the 8,000 already on the frontier – but where were those men to be found? To take them from Finland would immediately expose that flank to Russian invasion; to take them from the garrisons on the southern and eastern Swedish coasts would be equally risky. And even if those troops could be spared from their current duties, by the time they had been gathered and moved to the Norwegian frontier, the brief northern summer would be over and they would all be trapped there by winter.

Feeling that it would be best if full information on Sweden was delivered in person, Moore sent Murray back to London, remarking that he had had the opportunity of obtaining knowledge of the country and that he knew Moore's opinions. He closed this letter with a comment that he had consulted General Hope, but 'I see the difficulty of withdrawing the corps but at the same time I see no useful service it can render here.'

There was another major problem. Whether Gustav had been misled about the conditions attached to Moore's mission, or whether he had chosen to misinterpret them is not certain, but he took exception to three of those conditions: the right to withdraw the British troops if they were needed elsewhere (Gustav wanted at least two weeks' notice of such a withdrawal, and also wanted the right to withdraw his own troops or order the British to leave); the requirement for the British troops to act independently and always remain in close contact with the British fleet (he felt this would restrict the operations of both army and navy); and the fact that the British troops would remain under the immediate orders and disposition of Moore as the British general in command, stating that this was contrary to general custom 'as the entry of any auxiliary corps into the territory of an independent State necessarily supposes the chief command to be in the sovereign who reigns'. All this was stated in a letter from Gustav which Murray brought with him; Moore replied that he was honoured by the letter and that nothing could be more gratifying to him than to be employed in whatever manner Gustav thought best, but that the conditions communicated to Gustav by the British Minister, Edward Thornton, were those stated in his (Moore's) instructions, from which he could not depart. He had therefore sent Gustav's letter by Murray to London and hoped that amended instructions would be sent which would be more acceptable to the Swedish King.

In a letter to Gordon, Moore remarked, 'It would have been fortunate had Government waited to be informed of the real state of this country before they determined to send this force … now I believe they had better avail themselves of the excuse given them by the King of Sweden's demands to withdraw it'.

Moore had been given a paper describing the current state of Sweden by what he described as 'a gentleman who has resided some time in this country'; he felt it was in some respects a just representation of the facts, and therefore passed it on to Castlereagh. It gave a brief history of the military state of the country, including the fact that Sweden had always needed subsidies for military purposes but had not spent this money on its intended objects; it never kept up the quotas of troops or proper stores and arsenals, instead using the money for other things. The King did not know the true state of things, gave orders and made plans but was 'not possessed of the necessary discrimination and judgement [and] was surrounded by persons, either incapable or untrustworthy, who are more alive to their individual interest and party machinations than to the public good and welfare'. It did not occur to Gustav that his servants might be capable of treachery and corruption, or that his subjects did not wish to join in the current struggle. He was of the opinion that 'Sic Volo, Sic Jubeo'.[6]

The paper then went on to give opinions on Gustav's advisers. General Tibell, the Quartermaster General was clever but sympathised with France and had served with Buonaparte in Italy; the King was much under his influence. General Felt Tygmastaire directed and superintended the Ordnance, he was a German who had risen from the ranks, well-informed but disliked as a foreigner. The Swedes said he was a charlatan who kept the King amused with new inventions such as gun-carriages and firelocks. General Armfelt was 'a most superior man' but opposed by Tibell and Tygmastaire and a powerful clique led by the Duke of Sudermania. Field Marshal Toll contrived to observe and steer a middle course, but like all the others was mainly out to secure his own advantage.

By this time Moore and his immediate staff had been given permission to move to a comfortable house in the town where he could deal with his administrative tasks undisturbed, and take himself out of Saumarez' and Keats' way on *Victory*. Because the troops remained on board their transports in the roads outside Gothenburg, their officers and the four subordinate generals with their staffs had to stay with them, and this created an administration problem of peculiar social delicacy: that of the cost of feeding them. The rations for troops on board transports and the method of paying for this was laid down and dealt with by the Navy's Victualling Board, but this did not cover officers. Junior officers, whether on transports or Navy ships, would have dealt with it by joining the ship's officers' 'mess' which paid for its food by contributions from the mess members. But senior army officers, who were always accommodated on naval ships, ate at the captain's table, which he paid for himself. The generals who were on *Audacious* and *Ranger* would have been perfectly willing to reimburse the captains themselves, but the captains' dignity would not allow them to accept money for this. Moore wrote to Castlereagh explaining that he had dealt with this delicate problem by giving warrants for £200 each to the two captains, drawn on the 'extraordinaries' of the army. For himself, to cover the period when he was living on *Victory*, he remarked that he intended to give Saumarez 'a present'.[7]

There was another, rather more urgent problem to deal with. Moore's Deputy Commissary General needed £50,000 to pay the troops, but the Treasury, which should have known about this, had clearly not been told, and had instead instructed the consul Mr Smith that any money he held was to be retained for paying Gustav's subsidy. This was a matter for Canning's department to organise, so Moore wrote to Thornton to ask him to sort it out.[8] Even this was not as simple as it might have been: the Commissary General had been paying for provisions in paper money, but this was not suitable for paying the troops, who should be paid in Spanish dollars, unless it was settled that they were going to remain in Sweden. A few days after this, he wrote again to Thornton to tell him that the value of the Spanish dollar had fallen by nearly sixpence sterling, as a result of collaboration between local tradesmen. He asked Thornton to apply to the Swedish government to issue an order to fix the exchange rate for the Spanish dollar, as it was, he said, most unjust that the soldiers should be imposed on just to enrich a few speculators.

He wrote a calm letter to his mother, describing the town as 'small but cheerful, with water running through the middle of the streets. The country is more rugged and rocky than any I have seen; but the inhabitants are more like ourselves than any foreigners I ever met.' The peasants, he added, were like the Scots one met in Kilmarnock, resembling them in face and dress. He mentioned that there was a twice-weekly packet from England and vice versa; brother Frank had obviously not yet realised this as he had not sent the newspapers.

He summed up the situation he found himself in by remarking that he had found things

> very different to what I had been led to expect; the military force so small, and the government in such weak hands, that it was in vain to hope the aid I was directed to offer could enable the Swedes to resist for any length of time. At the same time, in spite of this weakness, moral and physical, their King's views were of the most magnificent kind.

He was rather more forthright in his journal: the King of Sweden, he said, was:

> without ability, and every now and then proposes measures which prove either derangement or the greatest weakness of mind. He has no minister, but he governs himself, and as he has neither the habits nor the talents requisite, Sweden is in the state of a country without a government, or of one that is only governed by fits and starts. The King is perfectly despotic; whatever he orders must be done, and unfortunately, when he gives orders he depends entirely on himself and on his own impressions as facts. He does not see the perilous position he is in, and nobody dares represent it to him. He is speculating on conquests when he has already lost one province, and has not the means to defend the next. In such a state of things we can do him no permanent good, he will not follow our counsels, and our force alone is not sufficient. I am therefore quite satisfied that we should take advantage of the objections he had made to the conditions upon which the force is offered and withdraw it.

Murray returned to Gothenburg on 11 June, bringing with him a letter from Brownrigg, now the Duke of York's Quartermaster General, with some 'inside' information:

> Ministers, I hear, would have been better pleased had you acted on your own responsibility; here they are like all other ministers that I have ever known, always backward in giving specific directions and endeavouring to get rid of the responsibility which properly belongs to them.

Brownrigg then passed on the latest news on Spain: 'a more encouraging scene … where the army and people have shown a disposition to make a struggle for their independence'. With troops from England and Ireland, and some already in Gibraltar, an effective army of some 12,000 men would be available 'which report says is to be commanded by Sir Arthur Wellesley. It is needless to say I wish it were you.'[9]

Murray also brought three letters from Castlereagh, one of which related to the 15,000 Spanish troops in Denmark: it was thought possible that they might be persuaded to return to Spain, but in that case they would need transports, hopefully those which had brought Moore's troops to Sweden.[10] The second was a formal letter with further instructions to Moore for dealing with Gustav's objection to Moore's original orders, which Castlereagh had put before the King. Those points dealing with combined operations were acceptable as were the time scales for withdrawing troops, but the last point, on Gustav's right to have direct command of the British troops, was less so. It was clearly a matter which Gustav saw as being of great importance. This should not have come as a surprise to Castlereagh and King George, as it had been the subject of an earlier letter from Canning to Edward Thornton. Writing at the beginning of March, Canning remarked that sending an army to Sweden without stipulations 'as to the objects and the mode of its employment would be attended with infinite inconveniency' then went on 'it must give rise to a renewal of those discussions respecting command which have been so often provoked by His Swedish Majesty'. No attempt appears to have been made to reach proper agreement with Gustav before the troops left England, nor does it appear to have occurred to the Cabinet that Gustav's objection to taking his own army abroad while allowing British troops to defend his country was perfectly reasonable: any king, not just one who was known to be paranoid, would have seen this as the first step to a full-scale invasion. Canning was aware that Gustav would react that way, but failed to convey that knowledge to Castlereagh. Perhaps this failure to clarify matters was a product of the beginning of the breakdown in relations between the two ministers, but even so, Castlereagh's vague instructions, which he did little to clarify when the problems started, put Moore in an invidious position.

In the second letter Castlereagh wrote that he had consulted the King and that while George was not overly concerned with the concept of Gustav's having command of the British troops in Sweden, Moore was to be the judge of the acceptability of Gustav's orders, and if in doubt should check with London before carrying them out.

The third letter from Castlereagh was a separate formal order on that last point: if Moore received orders from Gustav which he considered to be at variance with his instructions 'and to be in their nature sufficiently important to justify such a step on your part' he was authorised, after explaining his reasons for disagreeing, to tell Gustav that he could not comply without specific orders from home. If Gustav insisted on his orders being obeyed, and tried to force compliance, Moore could withdraw his troops immediately, although he should try and give the requisite notice. This letter ended 'I thought you should have precise instructions on this'.

Moore concluded, after reading these letters, that he should go to Stockholm to meet Gustav himself. When he got there, he called first on Thornton, who made the necessary formal introduction to Gustav on 17 June. Little was said at that meeting, but immediately after Moore and Thornton left the King's presence, Moore was called back in on his own. In his letters reporting this and the following day's meeting to Castlereagh, Moore remarked that Gustav had stated that his first objective was for Moore to take his troops to attack Zealand, which he could not do if he was only to act under Gustav's orders while in Sweden. Moore pointed out that it was the British government's opinion that even with a joint force such an attack on Zealand could not be successful. Gustav enquired how it could be asserted that the combined British and Swedish forces were not sufficient to take Zealand, 'when I have already told you that if you will not assist me, I will take it with my own'. Although surprised at this example of illogicality, Moore gave a lengthy explanation of the strength of Zealand, what would be needed to force a landing and the stores necessary for a siege of Copenhagen, and that with the large force the Danes had on such a small island, they could distribute their troops in such a manner to oppose a landing with superior troops, wherever it was attempted. Gustav said he had quite sufficient force, being able to apply 16,000 or 18,000 men without weakening his armies in Norway or Finland, then forgetting that the British were not going to cooperate, said that his troops and the British would make an army of 26,000 men, quite enough to beat the Danes 30,000.

Moore asked whether the peasants he had seen exercising in the villages he had passed through were to form part of Gustav's army for the attack on Zealand, and whether Gustav considered them fit to take the field against regular troops; he did, saying that his army was perfectly formed, organized, sufficiently numerous and ready to act. He was, he said, surprised to hear Moore advising him not to attack, as it was well known that all those who had been satisfied with defence only had been beaten. He clearly had not listened to Moore's reasoning, merely repeating what he had said previously.

At their next meeting, Gustav read a paper which he said contained a plan for Moore to conduct an aggressive operation against the Russians occupying Finland and produced a chart showing the Gulf of Finland and the places where he intended Moore and his troops should land, asking sarcastically if that, too, was contrary to Moore's instructions. Moore replied that he believed there was a misunderstanding between the two governments. Gustav interrupted several times; there was, he said, no misunderstanding on his part, he had only asked for troops for offensive operations, Sweden had no other use for foreign aid, was perfectly capable of defending herself and would never to submit to 'the disgrace' of receiving foreign troops in its own country for that purpose. Moore saw that it was pointless to continue and shortly afterwards the meeting was concluded. He confided in his journal, 'I soon discovered by the King of Sweden's answers that reason has no weight with him when opposed to his own opinions. He generally answered either by something which did not apply or by a simple assertion or repetition of his first observation.' His comments to his friend Gordon were even more forthright:

> I should think I had acted a dishonourable part, if after what I have seen and heard of the person who directs this government, I were capable of committing the safety of the corps I command to his management. Everybody here sees the weakness and absurdity of his actions. He is jealous of being governed. He

will not suffer the least advice.... On the least remonstrance, he speaks harshly, sends [the remonstrator] to inferior situations in the provinces.... It is difficult to say whether it is madness, or infinite weakness, [or] want of capacity but no child of ten years has a more troubled intellect.

Moore then received a visit at his lodgings from Tibell, the Swedish Quartermaster General with a new plan to attack Norway. This plan was so absurd and sketchy that it had obviously been produced in haste and at Gustav's dictation. It was soon evident that Tibell was embarrassed by the absurdity of the plan, and observing that he was having difficulty in keeping a straight face, Moore suggested that having played their parts by giving the necessary gravity to examining the plan, they should leave it and speak of other things. Tibell was happy to agree and they chatted amicably until bedtime. One of the things Tibell told Moore was how Gustav had reacted furiously to the news that Adlerberg had promised accommodation on shore for the British troops: he had raged so much for three days that no one had dared to approach him. However, he added, Moore was going to have to tell Gustav personally that he could not agree to being involved in the plans to attack Norway.

Gustav did not receive Moore's opinion of the Norway plans well, complaining bitterly that Moore would do nothing he desired. What use, he asked, was Moore's force if they would not act? Moore replied, perhaps less than tactfully, that they had acted promptly enough in sending troops when they were requested, but had found, when they arrived, that no arrangements had been made for their reception. If his king had known what they were wanted for, Moore continued, he probably would not have sent them. But now that they were there he would carry out any operations his king would approve, but he knew such approval would not be given to any of the King of Sweden's current plans. 'I might as well not have spoken', wrote Moore in his journal. 'His Swedish Majesty answered me by saying that he had no use for British troops in Sweden, had never asked for them and would never admit them.'

Again Gustav asked Moore to invade Norway for him, again Moore refused. When he reported all this to Murray and Thornton, he told them he thought it was impossible to work with the King of Sweden. They agreed with him that it was time to withdraw and take the troops back home. This decided, Moore wrote to Gustav to tell him of this decision, and was promptly summoned to a further meeting on 23 June.

When he and Murray arrived for this meeting, they found that General Tibell, Admiral Riolia and Gustav's secretary Baron Wetterstedt were also there, to serve as witnesses. Moore had already remarked in an earlier letter to Castlereagh, that he wondered if some of the King of Sweden's convictions had originated with anti-British elements in the Swedish court. In his report to Castlereagh, Moore described this meeting as 'a most painful interview' and said he soon realised that the purpose of the meeting was to shift the blame for Gustav's inability to achieve his military objectives onto Moore and the British government's restrictions on the use of its troops.

Gustav, Moore reported to Castlereagh, 'wounded my feelings most severely, for [he] did not scruple to assert that I had misrepresented what had passed at the former conference, [and that] it was for this reason and lest I should misrepresent him to my government that he had now chosen to explain himself before the gentlemen present'.

Moore was starting a very bad cold at this time and thus would not have been feeling at his best. It was probably as a result of this, and the injustice of such accusations, feeling 'provoked and irritated', he made a hasty promise to consult the British government again before taking his troops home.

On returning to his lodgings after the meeting of 23 June, Moore spent some time thinking through what had happened and concluded, after re-reading Castlereagh's instructions, that he should not have promised to seek further instructions from home before withdrawing his troops. Those instructions were 'pointed and leave me no option'. Having reached this conclusion, and now worried about what he had said to the King of Sweden, he decided to consult Thornton. He had intended to leave Stockholm on the following day (the 24th), but instead he spent the day with Thornton discussing the situation. They decided that Moore should write a formal letter to Thornton asking for him to write a formal letter to Baron d'Ehrenheim, the Swedish chancellor with responsibility for foreign affairs and the first point of diplomatic contact with the Swedish court, explaining that on rereading his instructions Moore had found them clear on the point and thus had to retract his promise of writing to England for instructions and remove his troops immediately, and asked d'Ehrenheim to inform Gustav of all this. In this letter to Thornton, Moore stated that he had already mentioned his conclusions to General Tibell, who had visited him on another matter, and asked the General to make them known to the King of Sweden, so it would not come as a complete surprise to him.

Thornton remarked in his subsequent letter to Canning that Moore, from 'that character of openness and candour which has distinguished the whole of his conduct throughout the whole of this delicate and painful discussion' felt that the letter should be sent to d'Ehrenheim while Moore was still in Stockholm, rather than leave himself open to accusations of 'disengaging himself of a promise when he was out of reach of representation or remonstrance'. Reading between the lines of this letter, one suspects that Thornton had suggested to Moore that he should wait until he was at least well on his way to Gothenburg before his letter to Gustav could be delivered. If that was the case, Thornton was undoubtedly correct. The letter written and sent off, Moore ordered horses for his departure the following day and went to bed, only to be disturbed by the Swedish Adjutant General just before midnight with a message from Gustav that he was not to leave Stockholm without the King's express permission.

Although there was no physical constraint, nor any form of guard at Moore's door, this was effectively an arrest, as Thornton agreed when Moore called on him the next day.[11] Their first action 'while still able to communicate with the fleet' was to send a special messenger to Admiral Saumarez and General Hope, Moore's second in command at Gothenburg, 'to put them on their guard, and if all intercourse with me was stopped, I directed General Hope to return with the troops to England'.

Thornton wrote, in separate letters to Hope and Saumarez, that 'yourself and every part of His Majesty's service under your present orders should be placed out of the reach of any event which should occur'.

Moore expressed his indignation to Castlereagh:

> sent by the King of England, commander of a body of his troops to Sweden, I am prevented from joining them - unless in the annals of French anarchy, there will not, I believe, be found elsewhere among civilised nations, an example of such an act of violence as that now perpetrated upon my person by orders of the King of Sweden.

This, strong though it is, is quite mild when compared with Thornton's letter to d'Ehrenheim. Although the document in the Foreign office papers is a clerk's fair copy, his outrage radiates up off the page at the reader:

> The undersigned Envoy Extraordinary and Minister Plenipotentiary of his Britannic Majesty to His Majesty the King of Sweden, has learnt with an astonishment which he cannot find language to express that General Moore, commander-in-chief of His Majesty's troops in the port of Gothenburg, after having taken leave of His Swedish Majesty, has been detained at Stockholm by His Swedish Majesty's order, and has been prevented from returning to the command of the troops entrusted to him by the King his master. Without entering into any discussion of the motives which have produced such orders, the undersigned thinks it sufficient to state to d' Ehrenheim, the simple fact, to demand their immediate retraction, and to represent that the persisting in them for an instant cannot fail to be regarded as an outrage of so insulting a nature to His Majesty's person and government, and to the British nation, as must immediately produce the most injurious consequences to the alliance and friendship which have hitherto subsisted between the two countries ...

The first response to Thornton's protestations was a summons for Murray to see Gustav. This was the first of three meetings over three consecutive days, and they must have been a great trial to Murray. Moore had asked Murray to make a detailed report of the meeting of 23 June, thinking this would be best done by a spectator. It is on reading Murray's reports of this meeting, and the following three meetings which Murray had on his own with the King of Sweden, that one gains a clear impression of that king's character and mentality. Whether or not Gustav was deranged, as has been suggested, during this episode he certainly comes across like a spoilt child who is used to being immediately given whatever it demands. Gustav appears to have been incapable of grasping the possibility that he could be refused. At all these meetings, he would state what he wanted, seem to listen to the reasons and logic for refusal, make a couple of irrelevant remarks, then go back to the beginning of his demands and repeat them. This happened several times in each meeting, almost as though Gustav was stuck in a behaviour loop which ran to the end and then repeated itself. The only difference in successive performances of this 'loop' was that he became more and more aggressive, accusing Moore first of trying to misrepresent him, then of deliberately thwarting him, then of deliberately making a promise with the specific intention of insulting Gustav by retracting it. He said several times that the troops could go if Moore stayed, and at other times that Moore could go if the troops stayed (although it does not seem to have occurred to him that he could not enforce such an edict when the troops were in ships escorted by a large naval force). He also threatened to close Swedish ports to British shipping; Murray forbore to mention that such an action would deprive Sweden not only of its desirable British imports, but also its ability to export its goods to Britain.

Gustav also accused his own minister, Adlerberg, of acting without instructions in promising accommodation for the troops at Gothenburg; he had never, Gustav said, told Adlerberg to offer this, a statement which Canning had anticipated of him, stating in a letter to Thornton: 'We fully expect His Swedish Majesty to disavow his minister's engagement at the moment he is violating it.' This was never openly challenged, as it was a diplomatic face-saver but Gustav carried it through by recalling Adlerberg soon afterwards. Gustav also took a strong dislike to Thornton at this time, and asked for him to be recalled and replaced. Again one is reminded of the spoilt child, declaring that it hates the person who is refusing to give it what it wants.

By the second of those meetings, it should have occurred to Gustav that he might be putting the subsidy at risk, but he was not sufficiently alarmed to prevent him from making further ridiculous demands on Moore, including one that he should write a personal letter of apology in terms which Gustav wanted to dictate. This was clearly impossible, as Thornton remarked to Canning, 'that which an officer can never make in any form whatever without violating the dignity of his own sovereign and the honour of the British nation and without irretrievably sacrificing his own character and the unimpeachable consciousness of having never by any intention or act done anything of which he can accuse himself to His Swedish Majesty'.

On the third meeting Murray did manage to slip in a neatly veiled threat: he remarked that Moore's continued detention would become a matter of public debate and dissatisfaction at home, then added that Admiral Saumarez and General Hope were now aware of the situation and thus would be most anxious, an anxiety which would be best allayed by Moore's instant arrival. One can easily imagine other means which an army of 10,000 men and a battle fleet might consider to ensure the well-being of a popular general!

A final example of Gustav's weak grasp on the realities of this whole situation came at the end of the third meeting: having again spent over an hour ranting at Murray, Gustav then remarked that he assumed Murray would be going back to London to seek further instructions, in which case would he be so obliging as to carry Gustav's despatches to Adlerberg. Murray does not report how he responded to this.

The other line of communication was between Thornton and d'Ehrenheim. Thornton does not seem to have had a response to his letter of 25 June until the evening of the 28th when d'Ehrenheim asked him to call. The purpose of this was a repetition of Gustav's demand for a personal letter of apology from Moore. In his report to Canning on this meeting, Thornton remarked dryly, 'You will note that there was no mention of recalling the order for detaining the General at Stockholm, or of any satisfaction or answer to my note complaining of this outrage on an officer of high rank acting under the immediate orders of his sovereign.' Thornton told d'Ehrenheim that he had heard no mention of such a proposal, and remarked that Murray would not have agreed to carry such a demand; he also commented that since he had already reported events to London it was too late to receive such propositions.

There were two things which Thornton did not tell d'Ehrenheim at that meeting: that Moore had already left Stockholm, and that he carried with him a letter to Admiral Saumarez asking that the silver to pay the next two months subsidy, which was due to arrive any day, should be retained on board ship until further notice. The consul at Gothenburg was also warned that he should put his cash funds on a ship for safety.[12]

Moore's departure from Stockholm was arranged by Thornton. On the afternoon of the 27th, he had driven out, as though just taking the air, in the curricle of Mr Oakeley, the British Secretary of Legation. Oakeley took him a short way beyond the first stage (i.e. point where horses were changed) where they were overtaken by Mr Johnston, an English messenger carrying despatches to Gothenburg, who took Moore on with him while Oakeley returned to Stockholm. Such messengers were not merely people who carried mail, but officials employed specifically to carry despatches and diplomatic correspondence, and occasionally to escort prisoners, for which they were remunerated at different rates according to the importance of the prisoner. They travelled whenever possible by post-chaise, with an allowance of two or occasionally three horses when the roads were bad and they used sledges in snowy winter conditions.

Johnston arrived late at the rendezvous, but he and Moore then drove non-stop to Gothenburg, although they did have trouble with one set of horses which were so bad that one of them actually fell down before they had gone a mile. There are two usual causes of this: either the horse is ill or too weak to proceed, or it is badly trained and does not pick its feet up properly and stumbles. However, it is possible that the carriage was unbalanced from an uneven load, as Moore remarked in a letter to Thornton that 'Mr Johnston could not help his weight ...'. This incident could easily have been the end of Moore's escape, leaving him exposed to recapture but they were able to get the horse on its feet and back to work, and the carriage was not damaged, so despite this setback, they arrived in Gothenburg late on the 29th and Moore went straight to *Victory*, where he wrote a long letter to Thornton, ending with one of his elegant paragraphs:

> Our acquaintance has begun in trouble and therefore a shorter time has made us better known to each other, than had the times been quieter. I shall be glad to cherish it and always be happy in the reflection that I had a colleague of so much judgement and candour as yourself, and who had patience and made allowance for my exuberances and unmilitary impetuosity ...

Contrary to a much repeated story that Moore was disguised as a peasant, and amazed everyone on *Victory* when he arrived in the middle of a party given for the ladies of Gothenburg, this is not the case.[13] The morning after his arrival, Admiral

Saumarez took the whole fleet of warships and transports to the Varga Sands, a bleak group of islands known to the British as Wingo, some 14 miles from Gothenburg. Murray, who had left Stockholm a few hours after Moore, having first arranged for their baggage and papers to be sent on, left Sweden with despatches on a fast packet ship on 2 July, arriving in London on the 9th. Moore followed with his army on the 3rd, arriving at Yarmouth on the 15th.

The final twist in this convoluted story of events in Sweden is that on 30 June, Gustav appointed a regency to act in his absence and sailed off on his yacht to visit his fleet in Finnish waters, unaware or uncaring that Moore had gone. The Swedish military commanders, who had already failed in a previous attempt to have Gustav declared physically and mentally unfit to rule, continued their plots and succeeded in having him dethroned in March 1809, to be replaced by Jean-Baptiste Bernadotte, who had been one of Napoleon's marshals.[14]

Chapter 12

Portugal

As well as the friendship between the rulers of Britain, Spain and Portugal, the strategic importance of the Iberian Peninsula's coasts and ports and the threat from French warships emerging from those ports, and their ability to prevent British shipping entering the Mediterranean gave it priority for British military assistance. By the end of 1807, as French troops invaded both countries, the Portuguese royal family and their court had fled to Brazil with the aid of British warships, and the Spanish king Ferdinand had been forced to abdicate, to be replaced by one of Napoleon's brothers. After pleas for help, British troops were sent in 1808, to help eject the enemy, starting what came to be known as the Peninsular War, which continued until Napoleon himself was forced to abdicate in 1814.

* * *

Moore's return to England from Sweden brought him to the anchorage at The Downs on 15 July 1808. He sent for his letters but there were no official ones. The senior naval officer at The Downs, Captain Owen, had received orders to complete the transports in provisions and water as soon as possible. Moore sent express letters to London for the Duke of York and Castlereagh to announce his arrival, and during that night orders were received for the troop transports to go to Portsmouth and for Moore to go to London. The transports were already weighing anchor when he set off in the morning, arriving in London in the evening. The following day was Sunday, so none of the ministers were in town, but he was able to see his friend Gordon, who told him he was to go to Portugal or Spain with the troops he had had in Sweden, where they were to be joined by others embarking at Portsmouth, some from Cork under Sir Arthur Wellesley, and more under General Spencer, making 30,000 in all, to be commanded in chief by Sir Hew Dalrymple with Sir Harry Burrard as second in command. Moore understood from Gordon, and other friends, that there had been much intriguing about the command. Ministers wanted to give it to Wellesley, but he was so young that the Duke of York had objected. Ministers had not wanted the command to go to Moore, so Burrard was named as second.

Moore saw Castlereagh the following afternoon; their conversation was entirely on Sweden. Castlereagh said that the Cabinet realised the difficulties of the situation Moore had found himself in, having to deal with a mad and impractical king, with only vague instructions; government was perfectly satisfied with the way he had conducted himself. The only point on which there was difference of opinion was the propriety of his having removed himself from Stockholm without Gustav's permission; some thought he should have remained and left the situation for the

Government to resolve, others that he should have told the Swedish officer who brought him the message of arrest that he was not under Gustav's command and left Stockholm immediately. Castlereagh told Moore that he was not mentioning this officially, or as implying the slightest blame, but merely informing him of the opinion of some members of the Cabinet. Moore told Castlereagh that he felt no uneasiness from such opinions; they were only speculative, and he thought that he had acted for the best with the agreement of the British Minister; after much discussion they had concluded that his departure would leave the Government at more liberty to act as they thought proper without being embarrassed by considerations of his safety. Castlereagh then asked some questions about Moore's troops and when he thought they would be ready to proceed; as Moore was leaving Castlereagh said he would probably see him again the next day, to speak on another subject.

After leaving Castlereagh, Moore went to see the Duke of York, who received him with his usual kindness and assured him that he and the King approved all he had done in Sweden, and that it was fortunate that he had been given command of the army and was able to withstand Gustav's importunity and not allow that army to be wasted in unnecessary service. He asked if Moore had seen Castlereagh, Moore told him he had just come from there and that they had discussed Sweden, and Castlereagh had told him the Cabinet approved of his actions there. The Duke then asked if any other subject had been discussed. Moore replied that it had not, and noted that the Duke seemed somewhat embarrassed and realised that what was going on was none of his doing. Moore went back to his lodgings and later that night, after he had gone to bed, a message arrived from Brigadier General Charles Stewart (Castlereagh's brother currently acting as his secretary) that Castlereagh wanted to see him at three the following afternoon, and that he should make arrangements for leaving London as soon as possible after that meeting. On reading this, Moore began to be a little indignant; he had not been told what he was to do next, yet he was required to leave London that evening. Fortunately all his baggage was still in the ship in which he had come from Sweden, so he had little to do in the way of preparation; he ordered a chaise for 4 o'clock.

Castlereagh began the meeting by saying that Sir Arthur Wellesley had sailed from Cork on the 12th and was expected to be off the Tagus on the 20th. His instructions were that having ascertained the number of enemy troops, he should land and attack them if his numbers were strong enough or wait for Moore's force and the others which had been ordered. It was assumed that Sir Hew Dalrymple would not yet have arrived from Gibraltar, so the operation would be undertaken under Sir Harry Burrard. At this point it was not stated, but merely inferred, that Moore would serve as a Lieutenant General under Dalrymple and Burrard. Moore found this extraordinary, feeling that when he had returned from a command-in-chief with the troops he had commanded in that capacity, and it was thought necessary to send him and those troops in an inferior position, that some sort of explanation or excuse should have been given. He thought it evident from Castlereagh's manner that he was ashamed of himself and could not bring himself to state plainly what Moore's position was to be.

Moore was determined to go on the expedition, but felt it became him to express his feelings on the way he was being treated, so when Castlereagh had finished speaking, Moore said

> My Lord, the chaise is at my door, and upon leaving your Lordship's I shall set out for Portsmouth to join the troops with whom I perceive it is intended I shall proceed as lieutenant-general. It may perhaps be my lot never to see you again. I, therefore, think it right to express to you my feeling of the unhandsome treatment I have received from you.

Castlereagh replied that he did not understand what treatment Moore was referring to, so Moore summed up all that had passed since his arrival in The Downs, and continued:

> Had I been an ensign it would hardly have been possible to treat me with less ceremony. It is only by inference at this moment that I know I am to be employed, for your Lordship has never told me in plain terms that I was appointed to serve with the army under Sir Hew Dalrymple as a lieutenant-general, and, coming from a chief command, if it was intended to employ me in an inferior station I was to expect that something would be said to me. You have told me that my conduct in Sweden was approved, but from your actions I should have concluded it was the reverse. I am at a loss to conceive the cause; for if there is an officer in the service who has steered a straight course, who without intrigue or detracting from the merit of others has endeavoured by his own exertions to establish his reputation, I think it is myself.
>
> Why I should be the object of such obloquy I cannot guess; but, my Lord, I have been treated unworthily and in a manner which no part of my conduct could justify. His Majesty's Ministers have a right to employ what officers they please, and had they on this occasion given the command to the youngest General in the army, I should neither have felt or expressed the feeling that the least injury was done to me; but I have a right, in common with all officers who have served zealously and well, to expect to be treated with attention, and when employment is offered to me, that some regard should be had to my former services.

In this last comment he was referring to Dalrymple and Burrard, neither of whom had Moore's experience in active service. All Castlereagh had to say in response to this was that he was not aware of having given any cause for complaint; Moore rose abruptly and retired.[1] He reflected in his journal that he understood that several of the Cabinet had taken a dislike to him, despite his having seldom seen them. They clearly wanted to give the whole of the command in Spain and Portugal to Wellesley; he was the youngest of all the lieutenant generals, and the King and Duke of York objected to him. This provoked the Cabinet, and added to their general dislike of Moore this had driven them to attempt to mortify him by placing him in the same position as Wellesley. They had been forced to approve his actions in Sweden, but reluctantly, for Moore had made no attempt to conceal his opinion of the ignorance which had sent him there, when they should have known that it would be impossible to do anything given the character of Gustav and the weakness of his army.

He set out for Portsmouth immediately after leaving Castlereagh, pausing to visit his brother Frank and then his mother en route, arriving on the evening of Wednesday, 20 July. When he arrived, he found that the fleet had just come on from The Downs and immediately occupied himself in getting everything ready to proceed. On the 23rd, he received a letter from Castlereagh:

> Sir, I think it right that you should not leave England without hearing from me, that I have communicated to the King's Ministers (as I felt it my duty, and conceived it to be your purpose that I should do) the complaint which you made to me in our last interview, of 'unhandsome and unworthy treatment' received by you, on the part of the King's government, and on mine, in the mode of carrying their measures into effect.
>
> At the same time that the complaint is felt by them, as it is by me to be unfounded, I have to assure you, that had not the arrangements of the army been so far advanced, as that they could not be undone without considerable detriment to His Majesty's service, there would have been every disposition on their part, humbly to have advised His Majesty to relieve you from a situation in which you appeared to consider yourself to have been placed, without a due attention to your feelings as an officer.
>
> I am further to add, that it is thought proper, that His Majesty should be apprized of the complaint which you have made, together with the sentiments of His Majesty's confidential servants thereupon.

Moore thought this letter was intended deliberately to irritate him and provoke an intemperate response which would give them an excuse to recall him; probably because as he was senior to Wellesley they thought he would be in Wellesley's way. He sent a calm reply designed to disappoint them:

> My Lord, I am this instant honoured with your Lordship's letter by messenger of yesterday's date.
>
> As I have already had the honour to express my sentiments to your Lordship fully at my last interview, it is I think unnecessary to trouble you with a repetition of them.
>
> I am about to proceed on the service on which I have been ordered, and it shall be my endeavour to acquit myself with the same zeal by which I have ever been actuated when employed in the service of my country: the communication which it has been thought proper to make to His Majesty cannot fail to give me pleasure.
>
> I have the most perfect reliance on His Majesty's justice and shall never feel greater security than when my conduct, my character and my honour are under His Majesty's protection.

He then sent copies of both letters to Gordon for the Duke of York, with a narrative of everything that had passed since he had returned to England. He hoped that he would thus be allowed to go off quietly without further aggravation and indeed he heard no more on the matter. Setting out from Portsmouth on the 27th, they were still no further than St Helens a week later. The wind was from the eastward when they departed, but soon changed round to the south-west and they had to anchor and wait. On the 29th Burrard received a despatch from Castlereagh reporting that Wellesley had arrived at Corunna and communicated with the Spanish patriots. They had offered facilities for the transports at Vigo, encouraged the attack on Portugal, and offered to send a corps of Spaniards to assist. They reported that the French force under Junot consisted of a total of 15,000, 12,000 of whom were at Lisbon. Wellesley left for Oporto on the 21st.

They left St Helens on the 31st, but winds continued to be adverse and it was not until 16 August that they saw the land of Cape Finisterre where they met a frigate which informed them that Wellesley had landed with his troops in the Mondego River. Burrard moved into the frigate and went on ahead of the transports to Oporto, where he hoped to obtain information which would aid him in deciding his next move. Unable to receive orders from Burrard because of the north-east winds, Moore carried on to Oporto, arriving there on 18 August. Burrard had moved on the previous evening to Mondego, and there was news that Wellesley had been joined by General Brent Spencer with a force from Cadiz, and they were marching towards Lisbon. Moore's little fleet then moved on towards Mondego, arriving there on 20 August. There he received orders to land his troops at Mondego and move on to Leiria, to provide some backup for Wellesley if needed.

Moore went on shore on the 21st and fixed the ground for the troops to hut on; he did not intend to use tents. It was extremely difficult to land at Mondego and only possible when the weather was calm and at certain times of the tide. There was a bad bar at the entrance to the river. The rest of the ships came in during the night and arrangements were made to land the cavalry, artillery and first division of the infantry. Moore met a captain of the 45th when on shore, who told him that Wellesley's army had had a brush with about 8,000 of the enemy, driving them from the far side of a ravine where the road lay. Wellesley's army had lost some 500 men killed and wounded, including 2 lieutenant colonels.

The disembarkation of Moore's troops began at 8 o'clock on the following morning; Moore had just got into a boat to land himself when a letter arrived from Burrard. He had seen Wellesley who told him that Junot had advanced with all his force from Lisbon and was then at Torres Vedras. Burrard thought Moore should join him there immediately with his troops, sailing immediately with those who had not yet disembarked, and leaving some general officers to re-embark the rest. A great portion of the infantry, much of the cavalry and more than 150 horses were already on shore, but most of them were back on board ship before dark.

Moore went on ahead, arriving at Marriere on the morning of the 25th, where he found some of the transports at anchor. He was told that the army had marched towards Torres Vedras, and on the 21st the enemy had attacked them at Vimeiro and been completely defeated. On that same day the French General Kellerman came with a flag of truce from Junot, and a suspension of arms had been agreed.

Moore went on shore with General Hope and went to headquarters with him, where he found 'the greatest confusion and a very general discontent'. After the action, Wellesley had been all for pursuing the enemy and making their defeat a complete rout, but Burrard who had landed during the action and Dalrymple who arrived the day after refused him permission to do this, on the grounds that they did not know what other enemy troops might be waiting for them. Moore, like the other senior officers who had been in the action, thought that Wellesley was right; several of the British brigades had not been in action and their spirits were high. There was little doubt that they would have been successful if they had continued. But the two senior generals were adamant: they were negotiating terms with the French for what came to be known as the Convention of Cintra. The French tried to include the Russian fleet (then in the Tagus) in the Convention, but this was refused on the grounds that they were thought not to have any right to negotiate for them. For themselves, the French were not to be prisoners of war, but were to be sent back to France in British ships complete with their arms and baggage. Much of what they claimed to be their personal property was actually valuables which they had plundered from the Portuguese. The whole Convention was disliked in England, to the extent that a major enquiry took place, but it was the French being allowed to take their plunder with them that caused the biggest scandal, one which was taken up by the newspapers.

One popular cartoon, by G.Woodward, consisted of a series of drawings accompanied by an extended rhyme. Like 'The House that Jack Built', each line builds on the last:

This is the City of Lisbon
This is the gold that lay in the City of Lisbon
These are the French, who took the gold that lay ...
This is Sir Arthur (whose valour and skill began so well but ended so ill), who beat the French who took ...
This is the Convention that nobody owns, that saved old Junot's baggage and bones, although Sir Arthur ...
These are the ships that carried the spoil, that the French had plundered with so much skill, after the Convention which ...
This is John Bull, in Great Dismay, at the sight of the ships which carried away, the gold and silver and all the spoil, that the French ...

In due course, Wellesley and Dalrymple were summoned to give evidence at the enquiry. Moore remarked in his journal that 'It is evident that ... seniority in the Army List is a bad guide in the choice of a military commander'. Moore magnanimously waived any right to take over from Wellesley as senior, saying, 'I considered this as his expedition ... it was but fair that he should have the command of whatever was brilliant in the finishing'.

The army moved on to Lisbon, leaving Torres Vedras on 1 September and arriving on the 8th at Papo Dos Arcos (about 6 miles from Lisbon) where they stayed for a few days and reorganised themselves. The troops were generally in a single line, extending along a rugged steep ravine, with intervals between the four new divisions, each commanded by a lieutenant general, plus a Light corps commanded by Major General Paget and a Reserve commanded by Major General Spencer. The cavalry was commanded by Brigadier General Charles Stewart and Wellesley's division was on the other side of Lisbon. The tents had been landed and at last the troops could be under cover. Dalrymple had never had the experience of command in the field and did not know how to work with the heads of departments; this caused great confusion, and the troops suffered as a result. Dalrymple was busy with his correspondence with the British government, and with the Portuguese and the French, who were giving the commissioners sent into Lisbon to oversee the fulfilment of the treaty a great deal of trouble, 'from bad faith and the tricky disposition which, if it was not natural to them before the Revolution, has been characteristic of them ever since' said Moore.

Dalrymple spoke to Moore on what they might do next and showed him a dispatch from Castlereagh, proposing operations on the flank and rear, as he called it, of the French at Santander, while the Spanish pushed them from the front. This was, said Moore, Castlereagh's 'usual verbose nonsense … the sort of gibberish which men in office use and fancy themselves military men, but without knowing how far it is susceptible of being carried into practice'. It seemed that the British ministers were not in contact with the leading men in Spain, or knew of their means or designs, without which it would not be possible to decide where or how the British army could act.

News came from Madrid on the 12th that the French had collected some 40,000 troops near Burgos, commanded by Soult and Ney. An insurrection had been attempted by the Spanish at Biscay but had been crushed by the French. Various corps of Spanish troops were at Madrid, and generals Blake at Leon, Cuesta at Salamanca, Palafox at Saragossa and Llamas at Valencia. It was expected that General Castaños would be declared Generalissimo. One division of the departing French was embarked, and the Russian squadron of seven ships, which had been detained in the Tagus, was about to sail for Portsmouth under Admiral Tyler and seven British ships of the line. British headquarters moved to Belem that morning and six days later Fraser's and Moore's divisions marched to make camp at Quelus; it was intended that the whole army should assemble there, with Burrard commanding the camp.

The night before, Moore had received a letter from Wellesley, saying he wanted to talk to him about the discussions which he understood Moore had had with Ministers before leaving for Portugal:

> It appears to me to be quite impossible that we can go on as we are now constituted; the Commander-in-chief must be changed, and the country and the army naturally turn their eyes to you as their commander. I understand, however, that you have lately had some unpleasant discussions with the King's Ministers, the effect of which might be to prevent the adoption of an arrangement for the command of this army which in my opinion would be the best, and would enable you to render those services at this moment for which you are peculiarly qualified. I wish you would allow me to talk to you respecting the discussions to which I have adverted, in order that I may endeavour to remove any trace which

they may have left on the minds of the King's Ministers, having the effect which I have supposed.

Although I hold a high office under Government, I am no party man, but have long been connected in friendship with many of those persons who are now at the head of affairs in England; and I think I have sufficient influence over them, that they may listen to me upon a point of this description, more particularly as I am convinced that they must be as desirous as I can be to adopt the arrangement for the command of this army which all are agreed is the best. In these times, my dear General, a man like you should not preclude himself from rendering the services of which he is capable by an idle point of form. Circumstances may have occurred, and might have justified the discussions to which I have referred; but none can justify the continuance of the temper in which they are carried on: and yet, till there is evidence that it is changed, it appears to be impossible for the King's Ministers to employ you in the high situation for which you are most fit, because during the continuance of this temper of mind there can be no cordial or confidential intercourse.

In writing thus much I have perhaps gone too far, and have taken the permission for which it was the intention of this letter to ask; but I shall send it, as it may be convenient for you to be apprised of the view which I have already taken of these discussions, as far as I have any knowledge of them, in deciding whether you will allow me to talk to you any further about them. If you should do so, it would probably be most convenient to us both to meet at Lisbon, or I can go over to you, if that should suit you better.

Arthur Wellesley[2]

Moore replied saying he would be happy to see Wellesley if he were able to come to Quelus, which he did. Moore told Wellesley that he thought of their present commander as Wellesley did; 'it was impossible not to see how unfit he was for the station [in which] he was placed, and not to regret that he was every named to it'. But, he continued, he could not enter into any intrigue on the matter. He went on to tell Wellesley of the events before he left England, and said that he had heard nothing from anyone connected with the Government since he left England and couldn't see how he could open the subject with them, but if Wellesley chose to approach Castlereagh on his behalf he would not object. Wellesley seemed of the opinion that what Moore had taken as deliberate neglect was merely omission and forgetfulness, and seemed anxious that Moore should allow him to make a stronger advance than he felt he could himself. Wellesley was to sail for England on the following day and promised to say no more to Castlereagh than Moore had authorised him to. Moore confided in his journal that if Wellesley was sincere, and he had no reason to think that he was not, his conduct was very kind; if not, he was no worse off than before, as he had said no more to Wellesley than he would have done to anybody.

On the 23rd, Moore was invited by Dalrymple to join him and the other lieutenant generals at the first visit from the Regency of Portugal since they had been reinstated, and also to attend him when he returned it. The whole Regency did not attend, but had deputed the Marquis de las Minas; it seeemed more like a private visit but when the visit was returned Dalrymple, the generals and their aides-de-camp all attended, and were greeted by the whole Regency. It had not occurred to Dalrymple that he would be expected to make a speech and he had nothing prepared. Bows were exchanged and then there was a pause, the Regency obviously expecting to be addressed; Dalrymple, rather confused, muttered something which Moore could not hear and after some more awkwardness the British party retired to visit General Beresford, who had been appointed Commandant of Lisbon.

At the beginning of October they received newspapers from England; it seemed that the British public were not at all pleased with the terms of the Convention, especially since it came after the despatches relating Wellesley's defeat of the French. Moore reflected that Wellesley had been superseded at a fortunate time for him, just after a successful action but before any difficulties began; after the negotiations began the French had been allowed to recover from their initial panic and collect their force at Torres Vedras and the surrounding countryside. The difficulties arising from this included the necessity for all supplies for the army to come from the fleet. This was at anchor on an open coast where it was difficult to land anything even in good weather; as the season advanced, it might be impossible for those ships to remain at anchor. He thought that these difficulties were obvious to Wellesley because he had approved and signed the preliminary articles of the Convention. Moore remarked again on Dalrymple's conduct: 'confused and incapable beyond any man I ever saw head an army ... a very foolish man. I had always before given him credit for some degree of sense and understanding, but I see I was mistaken.' Dalrymple had received orders to return to England to explain, giving up the command to the next most senior officer, Burrard.

Letters arrived from Lord William Bentinck, who had been sent to Madrid and seen the President of the Junta (the Spanish government), Mr Florida Bianca. He was waiting to see General Castaños, but said that the joint wish of the civil and military leaders was that the British army should go into Spain. This, however, would have to wait until orders arrived from England, as Burrard's command was merely temporary.

Those orders arrived on 6 October, and to Moore's surprise they appointed him Commander-in-Chief of all the troops to be employed in Spain, leaving Burrard in charge of 10,000 men in Portugal as a completely separate command. He was to have a total of not less than 30,000 Infantry and 5,000 Cavalry, these to be employed in the north of Spain, to co-operate with the Spanish armies in the expulsion of the French from that kingdom. 20,000 of the infantry and the 18th and King's German Light Dragoons, with a proportion of artillery, were to come from those already in Portugal, and a further 10,000 were assembling at Falmouth and would come out to Corunna under the command of Lieutenant General Sir David Baird. This force would include some cavalry and artillery, which would be sent as soon as the horse transports returned from the Tagus, and were expected to arrive before the rest of the troops could be assembled and equipped to take the field. The total force under Moore's command would be some 40,000. 'There has been no such command since

Marlborough for a British officer. How they came to pitch upon me I cannot say, for they have given sufficient proof of not being partial to me', he remarked in his journal.

It was thought that it would be best to assemble this force in the north of Spain, this being the place where they could be most speedily brought together, and the part of the country where the enemy seemed to be principally focused; for that reason it was thought best that the troops which were to come from England should go to Corunna rather than try to join the army currently in Portugal or anywhere else closer to the enemy. It was left up to Moore to decide where in Galicia, or on the borders of Leon, the troops could be best assembled and equipped for service; it was also left to Moore to decide whether the whole of the infantry and artillery should go from Lisbon to Corunna by sea, or whether a proportion should be marched through Portugal to that destination. Obviously the cavalry would be best going overland, and if the artillery did the same, the horse transports could be returned to England more quickly, and thus accelerate the arrival of the rest of the cavalry.

The matter of Moore deciding to send his troops by land has been criticized by various parties, from officers present at the time, and historians since. Castlereagh's letter did not say Moore could move the whole army by land, but he chose to interpret it that way, writing in his journal 'It is left to me to embark the army and go to Corunna by sea or march the army by land', and replying to Castlereagh's letter:

> It is my intention, as it was that of Sir Harry Burrard, to move with the troops from this on Almeida and Ciudad Rodrigo. This movement your Lordship will observe by Wm. [*sic*] Bentinck's letters of the 2nd inst, is recommended by the Spanish generals and I think it preferable for many reasons, to a movement by sea to Corunna … the march from this will be by three routes, Coimbra, Guarda and Alcantara …

One of those reasons was the difficulties of embarking the troops through rough surf, followed by the distinct prospect of a very rough passage at that season. Another was an almost complete lack of maps or any knowledge of the condition of the roads. It seemed there was only one route which was suitable for artillery, the southern-most route through Elvas and Badajos, though even that was not as good as could have been desired.

A newly appointed Commissary General, Mr Erskine, was being sent out (this was a surprise to Robert Kennedy, who was already doing that job) and the Cabinet felt that he would be the best person to organise an adequate supply of horses and mules to render the army moveable, and in order that this, and the purchase of other supplies could be done quickly it would probably be best to draw these from different parts of Spain and not to depend on Galicia which had already been considerably drained of its resources by the equipment of General Blake's army. A Deputy Commissary, Mr Azziotti, was on his way with Colonel Hamilton of the Wagon Train into the Asturias to procure such horses and mules as that country could supply and he had been directed to report his progress in these purchases. Once he knew how many draught cattle would be needed to make the army moveable, he would be able to regulate the purchases being made by the various agents. The new Minister, Mr Frere, who was on his way to the Central Government in Madrid, might be helpful in this respect, and Moore was authorised to contact him or any other of the British civil or military agents now employed in the respective Spanish provinces.

As far as provisions were concerned, three months' provisions were being sent in victuallers with every corps being sent; there were also provisions in the transports which could be averaged at about ten weeks additional consumption. A large proportion of biscuit had been sent in the victuallers to eliminate the inconvenience of baking when the troops were in motion. This supply, with the cattle which would be procured for the troops when on shore should considerably exceed a six-month supply; sufficient provisions for 20,000 men for three months were being embarked on ships in English ports and constantly kept as a depot, so there would be no difficulty in sending them at short notice if it was thought prudent not to depend on the resources of the country.

With respect to the plan of operations for employing the troops when assembled and ready for service, there would be plenty of time before all the equipment could be sent to agree this plan with the commanders of the Spanish armies. Castlereagh would send whatever information he was able to collect, and recommended that Moore should immediately open communications with the Spanish authorities for the purpose of agreeing such a plan of the campaign.

The King had directed that the command on which Moore was re-employed should be considered as a distinct and separate one from that of Portugal but Moore should continue to communicate with the Commander-in-Chief at Lisbon.

A separate letter informed Moore that Major General Broderick, who was with General Blake's army, had been ordered to go to Corunna to speed preparations for the reception of Moore's force; Moore could send any specific orders to him direct.

Castlereagh also sent an informal friendly note to accompany the formal orders:

> I cannot allow the official notification of His Majesty's determination to reach you unaccompanied with an assurance of my personal desire to render you every aid in my power in the execution of His Majesty's commands, and I beg you will correspond with me unofficially and without reserve on all points in which my interference can contribute to promote the public service.

Moore responded with two letters, formal and informal, acknowledging their receipt and asking that Castlereagh would convey to the King 'the high sense I have of the honour he has thus conferred upon me ... I have nothing more at heart than the good of his service, that my best exertions shall not be wanting to promote its success ...'. He said he would be replying in full on some of the details mentioned in the letters of 25 and 26 September, but that he intended to move the troops to the north of Spain by land rather than by sea. This had been Burrard's intention, and was recommended by the Spanish generals; the movement by sea would be tedious and uncertain. He would be marching his army by three separate routes, to Coimbra, Guarda and Alcantara; one regiment would be setting out in two days to Coimbra, and all the others should be on their way in eight or ten days. When they would be able to move on, or pass the Portuguese–Spanish border he could not say, as it depended on a knowledge of the country they would pass through and on the arrangements to be made by the Commissariat. He was, however, anxious to get the whole army on its way before the rains set in.

This was his main object, but his army lacked any vehicles or draft animals to carry regimental light baggage, artillery stores, provisions, or 'other appendages of an army'. No magazines had been forwarded on any of the routes to be used. The few days Burrard had been in command had allowed him to see what was needed, but not to do anything about obtaining them; Moore mentioned this, he said, not only because it was the truth, but to prevent Castlereagh being too sanguine about his reaching the north of Spain.

A further letter from Castlereagh arrived, dated 30 September, saying, among other things, that there were more enemy to be transported from Portugal than had been expected, which meant that Moore's option of moving north by sea was not available.

Moore wrote again to Castlereagh on 10 October, reporting that he was still in Lisbon. All his departments were operating with zeal, but in some of the important ones there as a lack of experience and, alas, even ability. This was especially prevalent in the Commissariat, where few of the personnel had ever seen an army in the field, only on short maritime expeditions. He damned Mr Erskine with faint praise: he 'is a man of strict integrity, but still his habits have not been such of late as to prepare him for a situation [which required] so much activity, ability and energy'.

Erskine's career had included a stint as a master at Oxford, a filazer* at the Court of Common Pleas, and he had a law degree. His appointment as Chief Commissary General in the Peninsula was only intended to be temporary. He was actually one of the Comptrollers of Army Accounts; he had been consulted on the choice of a suitable man for the job but no one could be found in the short time available and eventually Erskine agreed to go himself until someone else could be found. Spencer Perceval (Chancellor of the Exchequer at that time) when explaining this to Castlereagh referred delicately to Erskine's health, and agreed that Moore could replace him if he wished, but should take care not to hurt his feelings. As it happened Erskine took to his bed in Lisbon with severe gout soon after he arrived and was still there at the end of November, by which time Moore and his army were long gone. Even Erskine's aides were insufficient in both number and quality; what was needed, said Moore, was not men from government departments, but men of business and resource.

Moore was still waiting for wagons; he was unable to take more than the light baggage, the ammunition immediately necessary for the artillery and a small supply of medicines. He had hoped to establish a depot at Almeida, but had been unable to do so. Money and stores were urgently needed, and he asked that what was sent should be carefully inspected before despatch, as what they had was generally bad.

---

* A court officer who filed writs.

One thing which was giving him some concern was the practice of putting British officers in the provincial Spanish armies, especially those who were not British. He had ordered Major Cox, who had been at Seville, to return to his regiment at Gibraltar and intended to call in others in the same situation. A Lieutenant Colonel Doyle had already received the rank of Brigadier General from one of the provincial Spanish governments, and was now given the ranks of Marechal de Camp and Major General in General Blake's army. Moore felt it lacked propriety in a British officer to accept rank in a foreign army without the King's permission, and also that it risked a temptation to forget their duty as British officers.

He wrote a further letter a week later, including copies of Castlereagh's instructions to Baird, letters to Bentinck, and a report from the Marquis de Romagna (who had brought his troops back from Denmark) on his march from Corunna into Castille. Moore had written to Baird and told him not to send his empty transports from Santander or Corunna as he was going north by land, but remarked that if he had wanted to send some men by sea he could have done so as there were still enough ships for 12,000 men after the French had gone.

He had recently received letters from Bentinck, mentioning that the Spanish Government had been extremely alarmed at the content of an intercepted letter from the Governor of Bayonne to Marshal Jourdan informing him that between 16 October and 15 November some 66,000 infantry and up to 7,000 cavalry would enter Spain. Bentinck felt this alarm was salutary, as it had replaced the former lassitude of the central council towards this danger. Troops from Madrid had been ordered to the north by double marches, General Castaños had been ordered to the army, and it had been decided to appoint General Cuesta as the Minister for the War Department. Letters had also been written to Bentinck and Mr Charles Stuart, the chargé d'affaires, urging them to press for the junction of the British army with those of Spain.

Moore had written to Stuart and Bentinck informing them of the assistance coming from England, and of his progress, but warning them that while he was doing what he could to speed matters, he was still dependent on supplies. It was, he said 'needless to take forward troops without the means to enable them to act'. He had decided on the lightest of equipment, but even this was difficult to obtain. He was leaving the conduct of the separate marches in the hands of their commanding generals and intended to go direct to Almeida himself to decide the next move. He had sent two staff officers to Corunna to assist Baird, but had not yet heard from him.

He wrote to Castlereagh on 27 October to bring him up to date. The last few regiments would march from Lisbon the next day, while Moore himself was leaving in a couple of hours. He had sent Lieutenant General Hope with the artillery, cavalry and a corps of infantry, some 6,000 men in all, by the road to Badajoz and then to Madrid, this being the only road suitable for artillery or cavalry. It was a long way round, and would separate Hope's troops from the rest of the army for a while, but there was no alternative. Just short of Madrid, the road turned north for Espinar from where the troops could move on to Valladolid or Burgos or wherever else it was desirable for the army to join up. The other troops had been sent by two routes, two brigades of infantry by Coimbra and Almeida, and two by Abrantes and Castel

Branco. He had issued a general order about women and children accompanying the army: as no carts were to accompany the march, they would be exposed to hardship and distress, and general officers were to prevent as many as possible from following the troops, especially those with young children. Those who did not go would be left with the heavy baggage, an officer would be appointed to draw their rations, and they were to be sent home at the earliest possible opportunity; once there, they would be given an allowance to enable them to return to their homes.

A further general order reminded the troops that it was for their honour and advantage that they endeavour to maintain the high opinion and cherish the goodwill of the Spanish people. They were 'a grave and orderly people, extremely sober but generous and warm … [but] easily offended by any insult or disrespect offered to them'. Moore hoped that the British soldiers would respond with equal kindness and not shock the inhabitants by intemperance and disorderly behaviour. On crossing the border into Spain, as a compliment to the Spanish nation, they would wear a red cockade as well as their own.

Sir David Baird had been in Ireland; Castlereagh wrote to him at the beginning of September telling him that he should tell the naval officer who would be escorting his convoy of transports that they were to go first to Falmouth to wait for further orders. If the artillery horses were not ready to leave when he did, he was to go on without them. Baird replied on 8 September that his seven battalions would embark the following day, but that he had not been aware that two companies of artillery were also going. There were no transports yet for them or the artillery horses or those of the general and regimental staff officers; he intended to wait a few days for them. Castlereagh wrote to him again on 28 September with orders: he was to be under Moore, and should go to Corunna with his troops, where Major General Broderick was making provision for his reception. He was to buy cattle for regimental baggage, commissariat and military stores from Galicia or North Portugal; the Commissary would pay for them. Baird was to get his troops landed and into cantonments to make room for any troops sent round by Moore; he was to let Moore know when he arrived and hold his transports in case Moore wanted them. On 30 September, Baird wrote to Castlereagh from Falmouth, where five of the transport ships were missing, thought to have gone to Plymouth. His next letter, the following day reported that he should be ready to leave in a couple of days. The general officers had arrived on a warship which departed as soon as she had seen the convoy into port, but not before her captain had told Baird that he had asked Castlereagh to order that these officers (and Baird himself) should be accommodated on one of the warship convoying them to Corunna. However, the senior officer of the convoy said he had received no such order. Apart from himself, there were three Major Generals (Manning, Warden and MacKenzie) and Brigadier General Craufurd. There seemed to have been neither paymaster nor commissary appointed.

He received a sharp reprimand from Castlereagh for all this:

In the hurry of my last dispatches addressed to you at Falmouth, I ommitted to take notice of your having taken upon yourself to postpone your sailing of your corps from Cork until the transports for the artillery horses arrived from England – not-with-standing my express order to the contrary of 3rd September repeated in my letter of the 28th in both of which you are directed to sail without loss of time, leaving orders for the artillery horses to follow to your rendezvous.

I am to desire that you will not hereafter take upon yourself to disobey an order which you could not suppose was given under an ignorance of the mode in which the public service would be affected by its execution and for the reasons for which it was not in your provision to consider yourself as competent to judge.

Baird wrote on 3 October to say that he hoped to depart in the next two days if the wind was favourable. There were not enough provisions on some of the transport and he had ordered this to be corrected from the victuallers which were to accompany them. He had told the local transport agent to make arrangements for the general officers who would not be coming on warships. An assistant commissary, J. Dickens, had reported to him but lacked orders on whether or not he was to be attached to Baird's force, as had some other commissaries who had arrived; Baird intended to take them all with him unless they received other instructions. He was still awaiting a paymaster. He left Falmouth on 9 October, and finally arrived at Corunna on the 13th.

However, his problems were only just starting. Expecting to be able to disembark his troops immediately, he found that permission for this was denied. The Provincial Junta, which should have been able to give permission, felt that it could no longer do so, since supreme power had been handed over to the Central or Supreme Junta in Madrid. Until that body had agreed, there was nothing to be done, although they did allow Baird to disembark his artillery horses. He had heard nothing of Mr Aziotti or his success in buying draft cattle, and he had been unable to obtain a supply of money. Castlereagh replied that money had been ordered ($500,000) and should be with him soon. Castlereagh had intended this money to be for the whole British army in the Peninsula, but Baird took the whole amount for his purposes when it did arrive.

Baird's next letter stated that he thought it would help if Moore went to Corunna to push forward preparations (a strange idea, wanting the Commander-in-Chief to leave his much larger body of troops to travel several hundred miles to sort out the problems of an inferior officer), but he had written to Moore asking if he would do this and also asked for some money. He had, meanwhile, managed to get £6,000 and sent an assistant commissary to Oporto to try and get more, but doubted this would be successful. A few days after this, the new Minister, John Hookham Frere (a friend of Canning), arrived with Romagna, and informed Baird that rather than approach Bentinck, he should have dealt with Stuart, who was the only British person in Madrid with a diplomatic position. The Provincial Junta had finally heard from Madrid with permission for Baird to disembark his army, but not all at once; they were to leave their ships in divisions of 2,000 or 3,000 and move on south straight away rather than collect in cantonments near Corunna.

Baird's first division was to land on 26 October and would push eastwards towards Leon, where they would wait for horses and mules. There was to be a large fair of horses and mules at Leon on 1 November; he had sent an assistant commissary to attend it and purchase as many as he could, but without interfering with Aziotti if he was there. He had not been able to obtain any bread or other provisions until they were landed from the victuallers. 'The Junta', he said, 'offers much but does not fulfill its promises.' He also remarked that he thought it was his duty to give a warning that although the Spanish government said it felt much obliged to Britain, and showed every attention and civility, it was his distinct impression that the British army was not wanted. This was the first, but by no means the last time this comment was uttered by British officers.

In a further letter to Castlereagh, Baird passed on the news which had just reached him that a column of about 1,500 Spanish troops, en route from Oporto to Burgos to reinforce the army there, received a sudden order to go to Ferrol. There was no real garrison there, and he thought it was just jealousy caused by Baird's arrival. And in yet another separate letter he reported that he could not get draft cattle, just a few mules. He was unable to get much of anything else either; the person who was to have supplied provisions had withdrawn, and the Provincial Junta although liberal in their professions of help were totally devoid of ability and energy. By this time heavy rains were setting in; the villages on their route were too small to provide cover for the troops, and Baird expected much sickness as a result. He intended to occupy Lugo and 'St Jago' (Santiago), then continue until he heard from Moore.

Moore had been notified that Baird had arrived at Corunna on the 13th, had not heard from him but understood that he had landed and had written to tell him to march to Astorga as soon as his troops were equipped. Moore did not intend to march any of his troops further than Salamanca until Baird and Hope had arrived at Estorga or Espinar. He hoped that they would arrive there before the first rains fell. These usually lasted some six or eight days, and fell so heavily that troops could not move until they stopped.

He had told Baird to form a small provisions depot at Astorga and was trying to do the same himself at Almeida, but the difficulty of transporting supplies through Portugal meant it would not hold sufficient stock to be any use to them as they passed through Portugal. He now thought that any supplies from England must be sent to Corunna. He had, however, asked Admiral Cotton not to send the transports home unless ordered to do so from England. In this case, some ordnance and supply ships should be kept at Lisbon to carry supplies to Corunna if required.

An officer sent from Madrid, Colonel Lopez, had remained with him for three days then went to assist Hope on his march. He was sure they would not want for supplies, and it was on this general assurance Moore was taking his army into Spain without establishing magazines first. What he really needed was money, and he had been able to obtain very little. Baird had arrived without any and his troops had only been paid until 24 September (since the army only supplied troops with basic rations of meat and bread, they needed at least subsistence money, if not all their wages, to buy additional food for themselves); Moore had only been able to send him some £8,000. Erskine had written home about this and it was hoped more was on its way.

As soon as the necessary arrangements had been made for the troops at Almeida, Moore intended to go to Madrid for a few days. No Spanish Commander-in-Chief had been named, and Moore was concerned of the consequences if more French troops arrived while the different Spanish armies were directed by a council of civilians in Madrid. By 27 October he had reached Villafranca and three days later had arrived at Abrantes. He reported that he had been well entertained at gentlemens' houses whenever he stopped; the road thus far was good, but the country through which he passed was generally neither beautiful nor fertile. The only crops were grapes and olives. At Castelo Branco he stayed with the bishop who received him kindly but was, said Moore, small, dirty, completely lacking dignity and spoke such bad French it was impossible to carry on any conversation with him.

The next letter from Castlereagh, dated 2 November, informed Moore that Bentinck had ordered Major Roche, who understood Spanish affairs, to attend Moore's march. Castlereagh had ordered large quantities of specie to be sent to Corunna, and also sent instructions to Erksine for procuring Bills of Exchange; there was another tranche of money being sent to Lisbon. He also said that if there was any difficulty in obtaining supplies in Spain, he could send flour, biscuit, salt meat, spirits, oats and pressed hay to Corunna or wherever else Moore wanted. He also mentioned that lots of provisions, arms and camp equipment had been sent to the Deputy Commissary General Mr Azziotti at Santander for Romagna's and General Blake's armies; this was to be distributed by Major General Leith's orders and was intended to subsist them for two months. There was also camp equipment, camp kettles, haversacks and canteens for 50,000 men, 10,000 stand of arms, 50,000 greatcoats and 50,000 uniforms for the Spanish army, whose current clothing was not suitable for a winter campaign.

He did not yet, Castlereagh continued, feel able to say anything officially on the matter of relative command, as until Moore's army was completely assembled the matter did not arise. He had been waiting to see if the Spanish intended to appoint a Commander-in-Chief of all their armies, who was the only person who might be thought superior to Moore. 'None of the officers placed at the head [of the distinct corps], whatever might be their nominal rank, could reasonably pretend to command a British general at the head of an army of 40,000 men', he wrote. He saw the possibility of a Spanish commander over Moore as nominal only, to satisfy Spanish pride 'but the safety and movements of the British army must [remain] in your personal determination, and the cooperation result from concert rather than obedience'. He finished this section of the letter with a comment on how pleased he was with the good relations between Moore's army and the Spanish people. It was necessary that the men did not arouse their sensibilities, especially in the matter of the differing religions, and also of the British soldiers' propensity for intoxication.

He added that he had told Burrard that he should return home to give evidence at the inquiry into the events leading up to the signing of the Convention of Cintra, and since it was not thought wise to leave the command in Portugal in the hands of such a young officer as Brigadier General Stewart, was sending out Sir J. Cradock to take the command. He would take care to let that officer know that in the event of Moore's having to fall back into Portugal, his superior rank was not to interfere with Moore's command of the army in the field. Since it would be some days before Cradock could arrive, Moore should send some other dependable officer to take the command temporarily, perhaps General Beresford.

While on the subject of having to fall back into Portugal, Castlereagh would be pleased to know Moore's opinion of the defensibility of Portugal with the British army currently in the Peninsula with the assistance of the Portuguese army against the French; if such an attempt to hold the country against the French was not advisable, where Moore would see as the best place for retiring (Lisbon or Peniche); and finally what precautions would be necessary in such a case for provisioning the frontier garrisons or strengthening the positions on the coast to aid a re-embarkation of the army. Castlereagh hoped such eventualities would not arise, but felt it was wise to make preparations if the Spanish were to succumb to the French.

A separate letter of the same date announced the assembling of the inquiry into Cintra, and mentioned that it would be necessary for some of the officers with Moore to give evidence. The two he thought most likely to be called were Brigadier General Clinton and Colonel Murray; he did not wish to give orders for their return until he was sure they would be needed, but felt Moore should give some thought to how he would deal with their absence.

There may have been major problems with moving the army by sea, but there were also several relating to the march overland. Not least of these was that of moving supplies. The only wagons available were those belonging to the locals, and they would not go any further than from their own village to the next, meaning that the contents had to be unloaded from one lot of wagons and reloaded onto another. The drivers could not be persuaded to go any further, deserting if pressed; they also tended to do this if they thought the French were close, taking their oxen with them. They refused to cross the border into Spain. The wagons themselves were slow (no more than 2 miles an hour) and crudely made, often being no more than rough planks nailed to a central shaft, and with sides made of wicker. The axles passed through two roughly rounded blocks and rotated with the fixed wheels which were made of solid wood with an iron binding.[3] Accompanied by an awful creaking and squeaking from the ungreased wheels of these wagons, Moore's army moved on into Spain.[4]

Chapter 13

Into Spain

The Spanish army was not a single entity, being divided into the Army of Galicia, commanded at the end of October by General Blake; the Army of Aragon, commanded by General Palafox; the Army of Estremadura, commanded by General Galluzzo (later by the Conde de Belvedere); the Army of the Centre, commanded by General Castaños; the Army of Catalonia, commanded by General Vives; and the army of Granada, commanded by General Reding. These regional armies were reported to consist of a total of over 151,000 men. There were also armies of Reserve: the Galician, the Madrid, commanded by General San Juan; of Estremadura; of Murcia and Valencia, and of Andalucia. These reserve armies were reported to consist of a total of over 65,000 men. Both sets of numbers later proved to be extremely optimistic. The Spanish army did not have a national commander.

Administratively, Spain was divided into provinces, each ruled by a Provincial Junta, and, by the time Moore moved into Spain, these were overseen by a Central (or Supreme) Junta; this was made up of two members from each province, making a total of thirty-six. Established at the prompting of Charles Stuart who passed on his government's concerns at having to deal with the provinces in such matters as subsidies, its priorities were not always what the British might have wished. When it first met in September 1808, it spent several days on the case of one of the deputies who had been arrested by General Cuesta on the grounds that he was infringing the general's prerogatives. It then moved on and spent several more days on deciding how it should be addressed, jointly and singly, finally deciding that since all members were councillors of state individual members should be addressed as 'Your Excellency', the President as 'Serene Royal Highness' and the group as 'Your Majesty'. The next important matter to be considered was the uniform and regalia to be worn, the salaries to be paid (annually $5,000 per individual and $25,000 for the President, who also had the privilege of living in the Royal Palace at Aranjuez). It planned a grand occasion when it moved into the Royal Palace at Madrid, with a general amnesty for all crimes, a reduction in the tobacco tax and a distribution of silver coins to the admiring populace as it processed to the Palace.

To no one's surprise, one of the new Junta's first acts was to ask Britain for an annual subsidy and arms and equipment for 300,000 troops. They had already received over £1 million, plus 200,000 muskets, 17,000 pikes and clothing for 100,000 men. Now they wanted (they said 'it is absolutely necessary that the British government should supply ours with') £10,000,000 in specie; 500,000 ells of broadcloth for soldiers' coats, mostly blue and white and some other colours for facings to distinguish regiments; 4 million ells of linen for soldiers' shirts, and for hospitals; 300,000 pairs of shoes; 30,000 pairs of boots; 200,000 cartouch [sic] boxes and swordbelts; 200,000 muskets complete with bayonets;

12,000 pairs of pistols; 50,000 sabres; 25,000 pounds of rice; and great deal of salt meat or salt fish. This was closely followed by a further request for $3,000,000 to meet urgent expenses. Other 'requests' were to follow.

The foreign secretary appointed John Hookham Frere as his envoy to the Junta, and explained the policy he was to follow. The money and arms already sent to Spain would be considered as a gift, although future British aid must be on a somewhat different basis. Frere was given £650,000 in silver to help the Junta, pending the conclusion of a formal subsidy agreement.

* * *

Having previously discussed using three routes into Spain, Moore finally used four. Hope, with some infantry, all the cavalry and all the artillery except a battery of light guns which went with Fraser, took the southernmost of these, passing close to Madrid and then turning north-west to Salamanca. Paget crossed the border at Arronches, turned north at Aliseda through Alcantara and Ciudad Rodrigo, Fraser went through Abrantes, Castello Branco, Guarda and Ciudad Rodrigo to Salamanca, while Beresford marched almost due north then north-north-east through Coimbra to Vizeu, then east to Ledesma and into Salamanca from the west. Hope and Beresford had comparatively good roads, Paget had the worst, many of them steep and rocky. Moore accompanied Fraser, whose route was mountainous and difficult, especially when moving the guns downhill; they had to be 'braked' by soldiers hanging on to ropes behind them, an activity which wore out their shoes in days. Many ammunition carts were smashed, despite having been supposedly built for such conditions. Pack mules would have been better, but so many would have been needed that this was out of the question. And now it was raining heavily, and the miserable villages through which they passed provided little in the way of overnight accommodation for the wet and weary troops and their women and children, who, despite Moore's general order that they should not accompany the army, did so, adding gypsy-like trains in wagons and on foot.

Letters began to arrive for Moore with news of the situation in Spain. Some of the Spanish armies had been grouped together, to form the Army of the Right, the Centre and so on. A council of war had been held at Tudela at which it was determined that as soon as the Army of the Centre had crossed the Ebro, it, and the Army of the Right should attack the French at Caporosa; however, these two armies together consisted of no more than 66,000 effectives. The French had pressed a number of mules and carts and reinforced their forces round Caporosa. The Army of Estremadura had been ordered to Burgos, but a greater number of French reinforcements marched against Blake. Blake's army had already suffered defeats at Bilbao and Durango, and was then was routed at Burgos. A French officer, Count Phillipe Segur, who arrived at Burgos at daybreak, reported that he saw the high road and fields covered with the bodies of dead Spaniards. 'As for Burgos itself ... the doors of the houses had been battered in, the streets were strewn with torn clothing and broken household items and furniture ... [due to] our pressing need for food ... nothing escaped this destruction'. The remains of Blake's army fled towards Santander, and Blake was shortly thereafter removed from his command by the Central Junta and replaced by the Marquis of Romagna.

The Army of the Centre, made up of the armies of Aragon (Palafox), Estremadura (Galuzzo), Castile and Andalucia (Castaños) had finally taken up a position facing the French at the River Ebro, having taken an inordinate length of time to get to that point. Part of the delay was a lack of money, which had been solved by the intervention of Colonel Doyle and Major Cox (appointed to liaise with the Supreme Junta by Dalrymple), but Castaños had lingered in Madrid, possibly because he hoped to persuade the Junta to appoint him as Commander-in-Chief of all the Spanish armies. Another of Dalrymple's liaison appointees, Captain Samuel Whittingham, reported Castaños's army as consisting of 11,000 men, but having seen it he described it as 'a complete mass of miserable peasantry, without clothing, without organisation, and with few officers that deserve the name. The General and principal officers have not the least confidence in their troops; and what is yet worse, the men have no confidence in themselves.'

Two days before Moore reached Salamanca, there had been a court martial on a soldier (Rogers of the 6th Regiment) accused of marauding and stealing. He had been found guilty and sentenced to death, and appealed to Moore for mercy. Moore responded by issuing a general order:

> Nothing could be more pleasing to the Commander of the Forces than to shew mercy to a soldier of good character under his command, who had been led inadvertently to commit a crime but he should consider himself neglectful of his duty, if from ill-judged lenity, he pardoned deliberate villainy. The crime committed by the prisoner now under sentence, is of this nature, and there is nothing in his private character or conduct which can give the least hope of his amendment, were he pardoned. He must therefore suffer the awful punishment to which he has been condemned.
>
> The Commander of the Forces trusts that the troops he commands will seldom oblige him to resort to punishments of this kind and such is his opinion of British soldiers, that he is convinced they will not, if the officers do their duty, and pay them proper attention.
>
> He therefore takes this opportunity to declare to the army that he is determined to show no mercy to plunderers and marauders, or, in other words to thieves and villains.
>
> The army is sent by England to aid and support the Spanish nation, not to plunder and rob its inhabitants and soldiers who so far forget what is due to their own honour, and the honour of their country, as to commit such acts, shall be delivered over to justice. The military law must take its course, and the punishment it awards shall be inflicted.

Moore arrived at Salamanca on 13 November, and immediately sent two officers forward to reconnoitre. Lieutenant Colonel Lord Proby got as far as Tordesillas, a distance of 45 miles, and stayed overnight before returning. Captain Gomm went 70 miles to Valladolid, returning on the 16th. Neither had seen any signs of the enemy. A few days later, fleeing soldiers from Blake's army began arriving after travelling over a hundred miles without seeing more than a few French cavalry patrols. Although this would have allowed Moore to advance without opposition, he did not do so, but remained at Salamanca for three weeks, waiting for Hope's, Beresford's and Paget's divisions to join him. He had considered moving on to Madrid to join the Spanish armies, but they were long gone, either far to the north or defeated and scattered.

He had not reported back to Castlereagh since 27 October, but wrote two long letters to him on 24 November, one formal and one personal. The formal letter reported that he had reached Salamanca on the 13th and that the regiments had started to arrive, by corps, in succession. One brigade of infantry had not yet arrived, being employed in escorting the ordnance and other stores. The troops were fitter than when they left Lisbon and they had behaved well on the march. Hope had not yet joined, and was expected to arrive at Arevola on the 25th; Moore had ordered him to halt and close up there. The first of Baird's troops reached Astorga on the 13th and the whole, including the 7th, 10th and 15th Dragoons, should be there about 5 December. If they were not interrupted by the enemy, the whole army should be together early in December. However, the French were at Burgos and Blake's army had been 'defeated, dispersed, and its officers and soldiers are flying in every direction' and the armies of Castaños and Palafox were too far away to assist Moore's army. He began to think the junction of his army exceedingly precarious, requiring much care; if the French advanced upon them before the junction was complete, he thought Baird would have to retire on Corunna, and the rest would be forced to fall back on Portugal, or join Hope and retire on Madrid.

This said, he moved on to the general situation in Spain.

The information which your Lordship must already be in possession of renders it perhaps less necessary for me to dwell upon the state of affairs in Spain so different from that which was to be expected, from the reports of the officers employed at the headquarters of the different Spanish armies. They seem all of them to have been most miserably deceived; for until lately, and since the arrival of Mr Stuart and Lord Wm Bentinck at Madrid, & of Colonel Graham at the Central Army, no just representation seems ever to have been transmitted … The Spanish Government do not seem ever to have contemplated the possibility of a second attack, and are certainly quite unprepared to meet that which is now made upon them. Their armies are inferior even in number to the French. That which Blake commanded … did not exceed 37,000 men, a great proportion of their men peasantry. The armies of Castaños, & Palafox united, do not now exceed 40,000, and are not, I suspect, of a better description and until lately they were much weaker. In the provinces no armed force whatever exists, either for immediate protection or to reinforce the armies. The French cavalry from Burgos, in small detachments, are overrunning the Province of Leon, raising contributions to which the inhabitants submit without the least resistance. The enthusiasm of which we heard so much, nowhere appears, whatever goodwill there is and I believe, amongst the lower orders, there is a great deal, is taken no advantage of.

He went on to say that he had had no communication with any of the Spanish Generals, except for General Castaños who was deprived of his command at the moment Moore had begun to correspond with him. Castaños had had very little influence, complaining that his subordinate generals intrigued against him, and the civil servants sent by the Supreme Junta had no plan of their own, and did nothing except stir up dissention, and control his actions. Romagna, who had succeeded Castaños, was still at Santander. Moore knew nothing of their plans or that of the Spanish government.

Given this state of things, Moore felt it difficult to form any plan beyond assembling his army. He would then be able to undertake something and if the Spanish became more enthusiastic and determined there might still be some hope of expelling the French. He saw no point in giving Castlereagh (and the British government) a false picture of the situation since there was no good purpose to represent it otherwise. He stated that he did not feel despondent, and did not wish to excite any despondency in others but he thought their situation would soon become arduous and not necessarily completely successful. He was confident that his army would always do its duty but ultimate success would depend more upon the Spaniards themselves than on the efforts of the British, who without such aid were not sufficiently numerous to resist the armies which would immediately be opposed to them.

Moore's private letter to Castlereagh was rather more pessimistic. He started by saying that he had been so busy with his army and its administration that he had trusted to Frere, Stuart and Bentinck to convey the civil and military state of the country. He went on to say that he thought his army risked being forced into action before it was united and all its stores had been brought forward.

I never understood the meaning of the Spanish generals in [positioning] their armies, beyond communication, on each flank of the French. But I gave them credit, that their plans were calculated upon their strength, and framed by a knowledge of Country and other circumstances of which I was ignorant, and as they proposed Burgos, I certainly thought I was perfectly safe in assembling the army at Salamanca, but if I had had, sooner, a conception of the weakness of the Spanish armies, the defenceless state of the country, the apparent apathy of the people, and the selfish imbecility of the government, I certainly should have been in no hurry to enter Spain, or to have approached the scene of action, until the army was united, and every preparatory arrangement made for its advance.

By the time he had arrived at Salamanca and Baird's troops had landed at Corunna it was too late to retire, although that now looked like the wisest thing to do. He saw no chance of resisting the enemy, given its numbers. The Spanish seemed to lack an army, generals or a proper government. If the people were enthusiastic and determined, and proper leaders were appointed there might be some chance, but without this there was none.

We are here by ourselves, left to manage the best way we can, without communication with any other army, no knowledge of the strength or position of the enemy but what we can pick up, in a country where we are strangers, and in complete ignorance of the plans, or wishes, of the Spanish Government – indeed, as far as I can learn, the Junta, alarmed at this intention which they might have foreseen, and obviated, are incapable of forming any plan or of coming to any fixed determination. I have, of course, communicated my sentiments to Mr Frere, and in a late letter have plainly told him, that the ruin of the Spanish cause seemed to me so inevitable, that it would very soon become my duty to consider alone the safety of the British army, and withdraw it from a contest which risked its destruction without the prospect of doing the least good.

In the meantime, he reported, he was in constant communication with Baird and Hope, and that everything they needed was on its way from Corunna and Lisbon. 'But your Lordship must be prepared to hear that we have failed, for situated as we are, success cannot be commanded by any efforts we can make if the enemy are prepared to oppose us.'

He had no money to pay the army their subsistence, and was concerned that without it their supplies will be stopped. Baird had kept and already spent the $500,000 Castlereagh had sent. It was impossible to obtain anything but trifling amounts of money from Madrid or the other towns of Spain, which had put them into an extremely embarrassing situation:

nothing but abundance of money & prompt payments, will compensate, when we begin to move, for the want of experience and ability of our commissariat. Mr Erskine is still at Lisbon, confined to his bed with the gout. There must be a change in the Head of this department. I doubt if money, to any considerable amount, can be procured in any part of Spain and your Lordship must be prepared to supply it from England. Provisions can be of no use to us, unless we are acting upon the coast – it would be impossible, when at a distance, to have them conveyed to us.

It was his intention to make the troops find their own meat, and to call upon the commissary for bread, wine and forage only but in order to do this he had to be certain of money to pay them.

He was not happy with the officers seconded to the Spanish armies; Major General Leith, although a good man, seemed to have mistaken the purpose of his mission, so he had ordered him to join Baird. He did not agree with the character ascribed to Lieutenant Colonel Doyle; he was good natured, but Moore felt he could not rely on his reports. He was not well thought of by the Spanish army. As for the Spanish officers, he understood that the Duke of Infantado was a very silly young man; and Palafox, although spirited, was very weak. In general he thought that the British officers employed with the Spanish armies should confine themselves to their duties, and send faithful statements of all that passed, but should keep aloof from all cabals, or intrigues.

He said he felt no uneasiness about the relative rank he would hold when serving with the Spanish armies, but did think it would be best if the British government made some stipulation on this. He remarked that being at the head of such a large British force would always give him sufficient influence, and that in his letters to Castaños he had emphasised that he wanted to follow Castaños's wishes and asked for these to be communicated to him; he intended to adopt the same tone with other Spanish officers. He felt that as the commander of an auxiliary force, he had the power to depart from any place he disapproved, but that this need not be invoked unless required. It was, he pointed out, only natural that the commander of the Spanish army should be considered as the Commander of the whole.

He closed by saying that he had passed letters for Charles Stewart (Castlereagh's half-brother who was with Hope) to him, and that he was hearing good accounts both of him and of the cavalry.

Castlereagh had already mentioned the matter of relative command in a letter of 14 November, but this did not reach Moore until 4 December. It directed him generally to conform to orders received from the Commander-in-Chief of the Spanish armies, but went on to add that if any such orders hazarded the safety of the British army, he was authorized to suspend the execution of that order until he had reported to Castlereagh for the King and received a response, but that in such a case he was to inform the Spanish Commander-in-Chief of his reasons for doing this. He went on to say:

> But as it is of the utmost importance that any measure which might interrupt the harmony and good understanding which happily prevails between the two states, should be studiously avoided, you will consider this as a discretion entrusted to you to be exercised only in a case of urgent necessity, and as it is hoped that none such may arise, you will consider this instruction as of the most confidential nature.

Castlereagh added that two regiments of Light Cavalry were marching to Falmouth (to avoid delays caused by adverse winds up the Channel) and that two regiments of heavy cavalry would follow; in addition two troops of Horse Artillery, 300 artillery horses, and a proportion for the remount of the German Cavalry would embark in the course of the week at Portsmouth. A supply of shoes and flannel waistcoats, and about 150 Commissariat wagons were embarked or embarking. He would wait for Moore's information on what more supplies would be needed before sending more. He then went on to say that of all future requisitions, those to be supplied by the Ordnance Board needed to be precise: 'you know how much precision of demand is desired in that quarter before they move, [but] when once in motion I know of no department that executes with more rapidity'. He also reminded Moore that his force was intended to act as a field army and should be kept together as much as the circumstances permitted, and that it was not to be separated into detachments, nor to be employed in garrisons if this made a material reduction of its effective field strength, nor to be employed in sieges without Moore's express order.

Another letter from Castlereagh, written a week later, informed Moore that Lieutenant General Sir John Cradock had been given the chief command in Portugal. Among Cradock's instructions was a proviso that if Moore's operations required him to move back into Portugal, his command was to remain separate from Cradock's. Castlereagh also sent Moore a copy of a letter which he had received from Baird suggesting that he should receive his instructions direct from London in case he did not manage to join Moore's force. This seemed like a minor takeover bid from Baird, but Castlereagh nipped it in the bud by telling Baird that he would not receive any instruction which might interfere with those given by Moore, and that if it had not proved possible for the two armies to join up, or for Moore to send instructions, Baird was to take measures to place his corps where they could act on instructions received from Moore. He did, however, point out that the security of Ferrol was important if he did have to fall back and asked for a report on what the Spanish were doing to secure it. It was possible he might end up there; if he needed help with garrisoning it, Baird was authorised to send 3,000 men and let them have some provisions, all this of course if it did not conflict with Moore's orders.

Soon after arriving at Salamanca, Moore received information that the French had advanced and entered Valladolid, a mere 20 leagues from Salamanca and a distance which could be marched in three or four days. He did not expect the rest of his army to reach him before the 25th, and feared that if the French continued to advance, he would have to fall back on Ciudad Rodrigo and perhaps even into Portugal. He ordered the troops already with him to be ready to march with three days' provisions, but did not stop the other corps which were marching to join him. He did, however, write to Baird and Hope, telling them to use their discretion and act according to circumstances.

Three days later he heard from the officers he had sent out to reconnoitre that 1,000 French cavalry with 2 cannon had advanced to Valladolid after the action at Burgos but then returned to Palencia. He had also heard that Blake's army had been defeated and dispersed; this made him think that his junction with Baird was dubious. He had received Castlereagh's letters, brought by a King's Messenger, and was concerned that people at home had been cheered up by the false information sent back by the British officers seconded to the Spanish armies 'who had neither sense to see nor honesty to tell the truth'. As well as his responses to Castlereagh, Moore wrote to Frere at Madrid, complaining of the conduct of the Spanish government. 'I understand they are in great confusion, are frightened and know not what to do.' he remarked in that letter. The French cavalry were everywhere, extracting 'contributions' from the Spanish people, who could do no other than submit; they had no arms and no one to command them, but they were sympathetic to the British. Lord Proby was at Fordillas when a French cavalry patrol arrived, they stayed some time and despite everyone in the town knowing that Proby was there, no one betrayed him. When the French had gone and he went into the streets the locals declared that though they had no weapons, they would have died rather than allow him to be taken prisoner.

Life at Salamanca was pleasant enough; in the early evenings the Spanish assembled on the Plaza Mayor for the daily promenade round the square, often joined by the British officers. Many friendships were made, especially that of Surgeon Neale, who met Dr O'Leary, an amusing companion who had lived in Spain for many years. O'Leary warned Neale that he should not trust too much to the Spaniards:

> I believe they always mean well but they bluster, and after much bragging and many big words, like a passionate child, they scold themselves to sleep … their army [is the same]. During the last thirty-five years, I have watched its progress, and know it well; when they have muskets, they generally want cannon; if they have powder, they are often without flints; if they are well fed, then they are naked; if they get shoes, they want a loaf of bread; if the soldiers would fight the officers are unwilling; and when the generals wish to have an engagement, the men are sure to run away.[1]

Baird had been informed that the French were assembling at Medina de Rio Seco to stop him joining Moore, and was preparing to retreat. This turned out to be false information and Moore wrote to tell him so and tell him to continue towards a junction. Colonel Graham had been at Castaños' headquarters for some days and wrote to Moore on 9 November (a letter which Moore received on 15 November) that Castaños, having received information that the French were moving towards him, decided that he would move some of his troops to support those left from Blake's army at Calhona. He hoped that the Aragonese army would come over and reinforce Castaños, but this was complicated by the necessity for orders to go to them from Palafox (one of the members of the Supreme Junta) and then for its commander, General O'Neill, to obey that order without waiting for one from his immediate commander, the Captain General of Aragon. This would lead to a delay of up to 24 hours, meaning a difference of some 18,000 men ready to join battle against the French. Graham had then been called into a council of war, with the two Palafox's (one Junta member and one General), Don Carlos Doyle and Captain Whittingham, the Junta Palafox's assistant Montijo and Lieutenant General Consigni. Graham stayed only a quarter of an hour, 'enough' he wrote, 'to be quite satisfied of the miserable system established by this Junta'. He went on to express his opinion of Montijo ('a whippersnapper') and Consigni ('who I believe [to be] a thorough intriguer'). Not only was Castaños threatened by French movements, it was clear that he would either be beaten or have to retreat. The French were also threatening Madrid and the Supreme Junta was preparing to leave the city. It was believed that Napoleon was at Vitoria.

On the night of the 28th Moore received an express letter from Stuart at Madrid containing one from Lieutenant Colonel Doyle, announcing the defeat of Castaños' army near Tudela on the 23rd; they had made little resistance and were, like the remnants of Blake's army, flying for their lives. Castaños had hoped to attack Lanne's French troops with his own army mounting a frontal attack and the Army of Aragon making a simultaneous attack on the French left flank. Then came news that Marshal Ney had reached a position only 30 miles from Castaños, who changed the alignment of his army from east to west to north to south. This was not the best move, as it stretched his line over more than 22 miles. The Aragonese army arrived at Tudela in the evening of the 22nd and there was another council of war, this one very tumultuous and ending with no definite plan being adopted. On riding up to the heights to see the position of the enemy, who were now very close, Castaños was approached by one of José Palafox's aides-de-camp asking for a cavalry escort for the general, who was returning to Zaragossa, explaining that the general's presence was required there 'to make certain dispositions'.

This left Castaños in command of both armies and knowing practically nothing about the Army of Aragon. They were on the extreme right of the line and, at that moment, bearing the brunt of the French attack. Castaños felt he should go to them, but if he did this he would barely have any control over his own men who were stretched out over a 14-mile front. He sent a message to General La Peña, who was immediately next to him, to move to the right and support the Aragonese, but received a reply from La Peña that this was impossible as he was currently engaged with 8,000 French infantry and 2,000 cavalry. This wasn't quite true; he was actually pinned down by 1,200 dragoons while the French infantry was attacking the Aragonese at Tudela. The Aragonese began to disperse, so Lannes turned his troops towards La Peña's division which promptly gave way, as did the Spanish troops to La Peña's left. What had been a retreat rapidly turned into a rout, with the French cavalry under the command of General Lefebvre-Desnouettes in pursuit, using their sabres on the fugitives. At Borja, 46 miles south-east of Tudela, the remains of the two Spanish armies separated, the Aragonese retreating to the east and the remains of Castaños' army to the south. When it arrived at Catalayud it was in a state of complete disorder, with the soldiers accusing their general of treason. On the following day, 26 November, Castaños received a letter written six days previously telling him that the French were close to the Somosierra Pass and only 70 miles from Madrid; not knowing what might have happened in the interim, he set off to follow the Junta's instructions to go to the assistance of the troops defending the Pass. Before he got there he received a letter telling him he was relieved of his command; as ordered he turned the army over to General Cartaojal, who received orders a day later to turn it over to La Peña, who marched the disorderly and often mutinous troops as far as Guadalajara, where he received orders to march as quickly as possible to the defence of Madrid. He did so, but the French cavalry caught up with them and attacked them mercilessly with their sabres. On 8 December the Spanish troops accused La Peña of treason and refused to follow him. The command was then given over to the Duke of Infantado, who led the exhausted, demoralised and completely undisciplined remains of the joint armies to Cuenca; of the original 30,000, only 12,000 were left.

The Supreme Junta were aware that Napoleon might view them as having usurped his brother's throne and would be seeking revenge. They prepared to flee from Madrid and in the meantime had ordered General San Juan to take some 13,000 men to defend the pass of Somosierra. When he arrived there, he detached General José Sarden to take 4,000 men north of the pass to form an advanced position at Sepulveda. Napoleon sent General Savary to take a force to reconnoitre; this was driven back by Sarden, who reported to San Juan that having been attacked by 4,000 infantry,

1,500 cavalry and four artillery pieces, he had 'repulsed the enemy with great glory to the arms of King and Country'. However, more like a defeated general than a victorious one, instead of retiring to join San Juan's force at the pass, he took himself and his troops south-west to Segovia, allowing the French to advance unhindered to the pass. Although San Juan had been there for ten days before the French arrived, he had done very little to strengthen his position. He could have dug trenches, created earthworks and palisades by or across the road, and made fieldworks on the hills either side of the road; all he did was put four guns behind each of three light breastworks and four more at the summit. On the morning of 30 November, Napoleon moved to force the pass, sending light infantry up the mountain either side of the road, and a squadron of 150 Polish light horse straight up the road. They speedily captured the guns and dislodged San Juan's army, which like Sarden, moved off to the west, leaving the road to Madrid open. San Juan was subsequently thrown out of a window by his soldiers, hanged and his body was fastened to a stake and used for target practice.

These two incidents demonstrate the quality of generals, officers and soldiers of the Spanish armies with whom Moore was meant to co-operate; fortunately the Supreme Junta never did appoint a national Commander-in-Chief of their armies, so Moore did not have that problem to deal with.

After the news of Tudela, Moore wrote in his journal on 30 November:

> This renders my junction with Baird so hazardous that I dare not attempt it, but even were it made, what chance has this army, now that all those of Spain are beaten, to stand against it? The French have 80,000 in Spain and 30,000 more are to arrive in twenty days from the 15th of this month. As long as Castaños' army remained there was hope, but now I see none. I therefore determined to withdraw the army. I have written to Sir David Baird to fall back on Corunna, embark, and go round to the Tagus. I have ordered General Hope, the head of whose column was arrived at Villa Castin, to push by forced marches for Penaranda and Alba de Tormes. When he gets there he will march on Ciudad-Rodrigo, to which place I shall also retire as soon as he is safe at Alba. There is considerable risk that he may be intercepted or be forced to fall back by the Guadarama on Madrid. I am making every preparation to retreat, and to enter the frontier of Portugal, where at first I shall find great difficulty in subsisting, and which I cannot long defend; but perhaps for a sufficient time to cover the embarkation of the stores, etc., from Lisbon. Portugal must be evacuated if the French get Spain. If the Spaniards still hold out, by taking this army to Cadiz and landing it there it may still be of some use. I have written so to Lord Castlereagh.

Hope had arrived at Alba on 4 December, and the following day Moore wrote to Castlereagh again.

He reported first that Hope was within 4 leagues of Salamanca, and his junction with Moore's force was thus assured. Moore was preparing to fall back on Ciudad Rodrigo and since the enemy were concentrating their whole force on reaching Madrid, thought that he should be able to reach Portugal unmolested. It was, he said:

not without much reflection, and extreme reluctance that I determined to
withdraw the army from Spain and to abandon a cause for the success of which
the government are so much interested and the publick mind so highly exalted.
My letters to your Lordship of the 25th & 26th Nov [*sic*] containing a just
representation of the state of affairs in this country, would tend to shew how
much the government and the people of England, had been deceived, and would
prepare your Lordship for the reverses, which have since taken place.

As long as there remained an army, and any hope of resistance on the part
of the Spaniards, I was determined to persevere, at all risks, in the junction of
the army, and then if General Castaños had received a check, or been forced to
retreat, it was my intention, if nothing better offered, to march upon Madrid,
from whence, getting behind the Tagus, we should have given the Spaniards
an opportunity of rallying around us, and have shared their fortunes. But the
sudden defeat of General Castaños's army, so complete, and yet accomplished
after so little resistance, shewed with what little ardour the Spaniards are
inspired in their country's cause, it left nothing either to aid me, or to prevent
the further progress of the enemy.

He pointed out that the British Army could not be united before the 13th or 14th,
and it would be even later before it would be ready to make an offensive movement
towards the enemy. He commented that his experience showed him the Spanish
Government lacked energy and ability, the people were apathetic and the country
unprepared. 'It may fairly be said that the British Army never reached Spain, it
cannot, in the true sense be called an army until it is united, and prepared to act …'.

And then, seeing that there were many people who would place the blame for
events on his shoulders, he finished this letter by saying:

I feel the weight of the responsibility which has fallen to me; I had nothing but
difficulties to chase; whether I have chosen the least, and that which will be the
least disapproved of by His Majesty and my Country, I can not determine. My
wish has been to decide right, I reflected much upon the different duties I had
to discharge; and if I have decided wrong, it can only be because I am not gifted
with that judgement which was imputed to me when I was entrusted with this
important command.

On 5 December Moore received an appeal, written on the 2nd, from General
Tomás Morla and the Prince of Castelfranco on behalf of the Junta. This stated
that San Juan's army of 10,000 and Castaños' army of 35,000 were falling back on
Madrid, where they would be joined by a third army of 40,000 raised in the city;
they hoped that Moore would join these defenders or fall on the enemy from the
rear. The statements about Spanish troops were obviously false, and Moore could
not reach Madrid. However, with Napoleon's troops to his south and Soult's smaller
force far to the north he would be able to strike at the rear of the enemy, and this had
probably already occurred to Moore and his staff. As an opportunity to escape from
the difficult position he was in, Moore took the decision to attack the French rear.

That same day Moore had had two visitors: Brigadier Charles Stewart who was one of those who did not relish the idea of a retreat, and did not hesitate to say so later, and the French emigré Colonel Venault de Charmilly, who brought what turned out to be two letters from Frere. Moore was not pleased to see Charmilly, as he had encountered him in the West Indies and was not impressed. Charmilly was considered a rapacious adventurer, who after much lobbying managed to obtain permission to raise his own regiment to serve in the West Indies, then tried to do the same in Spain. He had visited Moore ten days previously and proposed that he should be taken onto Moore's staff; this was refused and he went on to Madrid and then Aranjuez, where he stayed for three days, dining with Frere before he and the Central Junta left for Aranjuez which they thought would be safer. Charmilly went back to Madrid, staying for no more than 3 hours on a dark winter night; most of this time was spent indoors, meeting with the Duke of Infantado and another (unnamed) Spanish nobleman who thought the command of the Spanish army should be given to Moore. He then went on to catch up with the Junta, which had reached Talavera de la Reina where he saw Frere again, giving him an enthusiastic account of the situation in Madrid. Based on this, Frere gave Charmilly two letters for Moore, the first of which recommended Moore to listen to Charmilly's account of the preparations for the defence of Madrid which:

so much exceeds everything which I had ventured to say of the spirit and resolution of the people, that I cannot forbear representing to you in the strongest manner the propriety, not to say the necessity, of supporting the determination of the Spanish people, by all the means which have been entrusted to you.

I have no hesitation in taking upon myself any degree of responsibility which may attach itself to this advice; as I consider the fate of Spain as depending absolutely for the present upon the decision you may adopt. I say <u>for the present</u> [*sic*], for such is the spirit and character of the country, that, even if abandoned by the British I should by no means despair of their ultimate success.

Frere instructed Charmilly that if Moore did not abandon his plans to retreat, Charmilly was to give him a few hours to consider his attitude, and then deliver the second letter:

In the event, which I did not wish to presuppose, of your continuing the determination already announced to me of retiring with the army under your command, I have to request that Colonel Charmilly, who is the bearer of this, and whose intelligence has been already referred to, may be examined before a Council of War.

Charmilly's version of these events is that Moore was rude and aggressive to him and forcibly ejected him from headquarters. It is tempting to accept that Moore threatened Charmilly by standing very close to him, and using bad language (indicated in Charmilly's account by several sets of asterisks), but this is not typical of Moore's character, and since one part of Charmilly's version, that Moore tore up Frere's second letter, is certainly not true, it puts doubt on the whole of Charmilly's 'refutation'.[2] In fact that second letter is still extant, and written on the back of it, in Moore's hand, is the note:

> Received from Colonel Charmilly the morning of the 6th December. He arrived at Salamanca on the evening of the 5th, and delivered to me a letter of the 3rd, but said unless he saw it necessary he was not to deliver this. He had attempted the evening before to speak confidentially to me, but having no opinion of him, I avoided entering on any subject with him, Madrid or other, and wished to avoid letting him guess my design. I was surprised at the confidence put in him by Mr Frere, and to find he knew the contents of the letters.

Moore wrote a calm but firm reply to Frere, explaining his decisions: if the army had been united and ready to act when Castaños was defeated, it had been his intention to have marched to Madrid, or if he could not obtain supplies, to retire behind the Tagus, thus giving the broken Spanish armies the chance to assemble close to him and then march with them to Madrid. This was well known to both his own officers and to Castlereagh, and if Frere had disagreed with this plan, Moore would have valued his thoughts. If Frere had been with him on 28 November, when he learned of Castaños's defeat he would have informed Frere of his decision, 'but should never have thought of asking your advice or opinion, as that [decision] was founded on circumstances with which you could not be acquainted, and was, besides, a question merely military, of which I should have thought myself the best judge'. Moore explained a little more of his plans and made a mild complaint of the behaviour of the Spanish armies and finally attempted to mend their relationship:

> I wish anxiously, as King's Minister, to continue on the most confidental footing with you; and I hope, as we have but one interest, the public welfare – though we may occasionally see it in different aspects – that this will not disturb the harmony that should subsist between us. Fully impressed as I am with these sentiments, I shall abstain from any remark upon the two letters from you delivered last night and this morning by Colonel Charmilly, or on the message which accompanied them. I certainly, at first, did feel and express much indignation at a person like him being made the channel of a communication of that sort from you to me. These feelings are at an end, and, I dare say, they will never be excited towards you again. If Mr Charmilly is your friend, it was perhaps natural for you to employ him; but I have prejudices against all that class, and it is impossible for me to put any trust in him. I shall, therefore, thank you not to employ him any more in any communication with him.

The ending of this letter does two things: first, it is an example of Moore's tendency to tell people off, then say that now he's got it off his chest he will forget about it in the hopeful but often erroneous knowledge that they will do the same, but secondly it offers a less than subtle (and perhaps unintentional) insult about Frere's choice of friends.

In a second letter on the same day Moore mentioned that he had received a visit from two elderly generals, Escalente and Bueno. He remarked that they seemed to him to be:

two weak old men, or rather women, with whom it was impossible for me to concert any military operation had I been so inclined. The persons with whom such operations can be concerted at present, are the generals who command the armies, not men like these two, who have no information upon which such plans can be formed except the official papers, always incorrect, which have been given to them from public offices. Their conference with me consisted in questions, and in assertions with respect to the strength of different Spanish corps, all of which I knew to be erroneous and they neither knew that Segovia, or Somma Sierra, were in possession of the enemy.

At about this time, Frere received a letter from Romagna which had been passed it on to him by General Escalente. The only version available of this letter is a translation, which has a note at the top saying 'The expressions which might be offensive to General Moore were suppressed and others substituted.' It included details of what it called 'the extravagant project of Sir John Moore for retiring and marching into Portugal'. Romagna said that the division which was in Astorga was doing the same, and that he was tired of writing to them to delay for a few days, and had 'at last told them that for what they are doing, they might as well return to England'.[3] He went on to say that he had now 20,000 men of 'excellent troops' and was only waiting for clothing and shoes before they could march before urging Escalenta to prevail on Moore to stop his retreat. As was the case with the other commanders of Spanish armies, Romagna's statements of the size and standard of his army was seriously exaggerated; he had certainly not told Moore he might as well go home.

On 9 December Moore wrote in his journal that after defeating Castaños, the French had marched for Madrid, where the inhabitants barricaded the streets and swore to die rather than submit. This, he remarked, was 'the first instance of enthusiasm shown; there is a chance that the example may be followed and the people be roused, in which case there is still a chance that this country may be saved'. In the hope that this was true he stopped Baird's retreat and hoped to join up his army while the French were occupied with Madrid: 'we are bound not to abandon the cause as long as there is hope; but the courage of the populace of Madrid may fail; at any rate they may not be able to resist'. Things would be no better unless the whole country roused and went to the aid of the capital, and he saw no evidence of that where he was. That same day he had sent Colonel Graham to Madrid to get up to date information, having found it difficult to get people to bring it to him. He continued his preparations for retreating to Portugal if it proved necessary. Lord Paget and the cavalry from Baird were close to joining him; they would be at Zamora on the 10th and he planned to move a division of infantry to join them to be close to Baird, who had been ordered to send his troops on by brigades as they came close to Benavente.

On that same day, Canning had written to Frere and Castlereagh sent a copy of this letter to Moore.[4] It was not quite a reprimand, but it did inform Frere that he should be firmer with the Spanish government on the matter of communication between the Junta and Moore, especially relating to their plans for engaging the French army, pointing out that neither Moore nor Baird had 'received the slightest intimation of any such plan'. He then went on:

> The British government has most cautiously and scrupulously abstained from interfering in any of the counsels of the Junta, or presuming to suggest to them, by what plan they should defend their country. But when the question is as to the cooperation of a British force, they have a right, and it is their duty to require, that some plan should have been formed, and being formed, should be communicated to the British commander in order that he may judge of, and (if he shall approve) may be prepared to execute the share intended to be assigned to him.
>
> You will recollect that the army, which has been appropriated by His Majesty's Government to the defence of Spain and Portugal, is not merely a considerable part of the disposable force of this country. It is in fact the British army. The country has no other force disposable. It may by a great effort reinforce this army for an adequate purpose. But another army it has not to send.

He then went on to remind Frere that the terms upon which the British army was sent to Spain was that it was only to act as a single body and not to be split up into smaller units and attached to this or that unit of the Spanish army 'as the exigencies of the moment happens to press'. The British army would, he continued

> decline no difficulty, it will shrink from no danger, when thro' that difficulty and danger, the Commander is able to see his way to some definite purpose.
>
> But in order to do this, it will be necessary that such purpose should have been previously arranged; and that the British army should not again be left as that of Sir John Moore and Sir David Baird have recently been, in the heart of Spain, without one word of information except such as they could pick up from common rumour, of the events passing round them.

Although he was not receive this letter for several days, Moore wrote on the 12th to Frere complaining that he had failed to reply to the two letters he had written to him. As a result, he was 'disappointed of his cooperation, or of knowing what plans he proposes'. He understood from intercepted letters that the French force in the north of Spain was already from 80,000 to 90,000 men and since many of those letters mentioned seventh and eighth divisions, it seemed that more were on their way.

There was much correspondence between Moore and Baird, mostly on the action to be taken if either should be forced to retreat; this was not because either was indecisive, but because it was sensible to investigate the likelihood of things going wrong and planning how to deal with this. Although they discussed retreat, and some stores and small groups of troops were moved to the rear, Baird did not leave Astorga nor Moore leave Salamanca until he moved northward. They both understood that if either force was attacked, and communications between them broken, the other was free to look after itself as best it could. On 23 November, Baird had not heard from Moore for several days and, worried that he had been forced back to Ciudad Rodrigo, called Generals Paget, Coote Manningham, Henry Warde and Robert Craufurd, and

Colonel Bathurst, to a council of war. They decided that if the French got to within three days march of Astorga, or if joining Moore seemed impossible, Baird's corps would retreat.

By the beginning of December, it seemed wise to move some of Baird's corps back to Villafranca, but he sent forward his cavalry, and the new detachments of cavalry coming from England. On 6 December Moore wrote again, instructing him to return to Astorga, and on the possibility that they might yet have to turn and run for the coast, he told him to establish one magazine at Villafranca and one or two more further back, stocking them with salt meat, biscuits, rum or wine and forage, all from Corunna. A further supply base was to be established at Zamorra and commissary Schaumann was instructed to bake a large quantity of biscuit. Meanwhile, Moore prepared to move north to meet Baird halfway.

Moore was also in constant communication with Hope. Most of this was concerned with Hope's progress towards a meeting, or reports on supplies, but there was one little triumph which Stewart had reported to Hope and Hope passed on to Moore. The French General Junot had come across a large quantity of bales of cotton at Rueda and seized it as plunder with the intention of sending it to Bayonne via Lisbon. Brigadier General Charles Howard had acquired information on this and sent Lieutenant Colonel Jones with eighty men to prevent it. Not hearing from Jones as soon as he had hoped, Howard followed himself with another fifty men, to find that Jones 'had executed my orders with the same ability and zeal he observed on all occasions'.

Graham returned from his reconnaissance to Madrid without managing to get into the city, which had capitulated on 3 December. The people had insisted on keeping their arms and said they had been betrayed by the Prince of Castelfranco and Monsieur de Morla, the two who had written to Moore on the 2nd asking for help, 'and the next day it appears they capitulated! I cannot think the inhabitants could have been very determined, or those gentlemen could not have capitulated.' He could not get any accurate reports of the situation in the city but did know that the French had the gates, the Retiro and the Prado, two areas in the centre of the city. He decided to move his troops to the Duero and assemble them at Valladolid without waiting for Baird. This movement would threaten French communications and make a diversion for the Spanish if they could take advantage of it, but he thought they would not move, instead leaving him to fight by himself.

Before Moore's army left Salamanca, there had been a clash between Stewart's dragoons and a group of 400 French cavalry at Rueda. Although he had strict orders not to risk losing any of his men, when Captain Dashwood, one of his aides-de-camp, who had gone into the town disguised as a Spanish peasant, returned with news that the French dragoons had posted advanced picquets, Stewart sent some of the 18th Light Dragoons into Rueda under Major Otway on the night of the 13th to cut off the French with the cotton. There, assisted enthusiastically by the inhabitants, Otway's men succeeded in taking the enemy's post after a few minutes brisk fire; they killed eighteen and captured thirty-six of the enemy, returning with French helmets and other accoutrements, to the envy of those who had not gone with them. The

French arms and cartidges were distributed to the peasants and the cotton, valued at £1,500 was removed; Stewart asked Moore for instructions on its disposal. The incident, though successful, was unfortunate but inevitable, and Moore then had to assume that the French knew he was advancing.

The reserve left Salamanca on the 11th, Fraser's division on the 12th and by the 13th all his troops would have left Salamanca. Moore left that day, moving his headquarters to Alaejos, where he saw an intercepted letter from General Berthier, Prince of Neuchatel, to Marshal Soult who was at Saldanha. It stated that Madrid was quiet, that the troops were on the march, and encouraged Soult to clear the country between the Galicias and the Duero; there was no Spanish army to oppose his two divisions, and that the British had retreated into Portugal. Moore changed his plan to move to Valladolid and went instead to Toro as being the quickest way to unite his army. The day after he left Salamanca he reached Alaejos where he received a letter from Berthier (at Napoleon's headquarters) to Soult. This had been carried by a French courier who had arrived at Valdestillas (close to Tordesillas); the courier had been so rude to the postmaster that the villagers had killed him. Shortly after this, Captain Walters, who had been sent forward to get information, arrived and the villagers told him what had happened. He gave them $20 for the dispatch, which said, among other things 'Take possession of Leon, throw the enemy back into Galicia, [and] seize Benavente and Zamora. His Majesty feels sure that you will use every effort to subdue the country between the Duero, Galicia and Asturias.' He went on to assure Soult that he would encounter no resistance, as all available information pointed to the British having retreated into Portugal. 'Our advance guard', he said,

> is today at Talavera de la Reina on the road to Badajos and will shortly be in that city. You will understand that this movement will force the English to retreat hastily to Lisbon, if they have not already done so. At the moment, Marshal, you can be certain that everything justifies the presumption that there are no English on your front, and that you can march ahead with confidence.

Moore sent a copy of this letter to Castlereagh on the 16th, with one of his own bringing him up to date. He hoped his position there would be able to protect Baird's arrival, although he did not expect the whole of his corps to have arrived before the 20th, when, 'If then Marshal Soult is so good as to approach us I shall be much obliged to him, but if not, we shall march towards him. It will be very agreeable to give a wipe* to such a corps ...' He wrote of Romagna and his talk of attacks and movements 'which are quite absurd'; but he had not, as Moore had requested, destroyed the bridge at Mansilla, instead posting some troops there; these were taken prisoner by the French on their march from Majorga.

While at Toro Moore received a letter from Romagna (who Moore had described to Stuart as 'a shuffler') stating that he had 22,000 men and would be happy to co-operate. However, Baird had already passed on a letter he had received from Romagna,

---

* A pencil note in the margin of this letter defines this word as 'a blow'.

written at a later date, which stated that he was retiring into the Galicias. Moore's letter had been carried by an aide-de-camp, and Moore sent him back with a reply asking him if he was indeed about to retire. In his journal he wrote 'In truth I placed no dependance on him or his army, and was determined to persevere in moving up to Soult at all events.'

Moore's opinion of Romagna's army was confirmed by a report from Lieutenant Colonel Michael Symes who Baird had sent to check the strength and condition of Romagna's army, which was at that time at Leon. En route, he had encountered a brigade of Spanish artillery with two howitzers, and six field pieces; they were proceeding to Ponteferada, for what precise object Symes could not learn; perhaps to defend the passes of the mountains. He also came upon another brigade of Spanish guns, about a league north of Astorga, drawn up on rising ground. These guns had only three or four men to guard them, and no regular sentinels. Symes was told that the gunners and draft cattle* were in the neighbouring village. He examined the state of the guns and the ammunition as closely as he could without giving offence, and found them very defective. The men said they had come from Leon fifteen days ago, and didn't know whether or when they were to proceed. At Orbigo, 4 leagues from Leon, he found the place occupied by some 4,000 troops under Major General Don Jenaro Frigador. There were five regiments; three of the line and two of militia.

The equipment and appearance of these troops was miserable. He was able to inspect the arms of the General's guard, which were extremely poor; the springs and locks did not often match; either the main spring was too weak for the feather-spring, or the feather-spring too weak to produce certain fire from the hammer. He tried sixteen of these; only six had bayonets, and these were short and bad. The ammunition-pouches were not rainproof, some of the men were half-naked and some of the others wore what could only be described as motley. They were in general stout young men, but without order or discipline, and not at all ferocious; they were at least not drunk. Soon after leaving Orbigo, Symes met the regiment of Vittoria marching from Leon to Ponteferada; as with the others, the men were wretchedly clad and armed.

Arriving at Leon early in the evening, Symes waited on Romagna; he had not heard of the capitulation of Madrid; was vague on his future movements and stated his force at 22,000 infantry and 300 cavalry. He complained that he had too few officers; he had intended to form his army into five divisions, but could not do so without officers to command them so he intended to divide his army into wings; one under General Blake, the other under himself. He said that his army was daily increasing with fugitives. He hoped that the British had light troops to oppose those of the French, and added that he was training 6,000 of his men as light troops. There was to be a general review the next day, Symes asked to attend this with Romagna. In the morning he pressed Romagna as far as he felt he could on when he thought he might join Moore's force but got no more than general assurances. Romagna did not think

---

* Probably mules.

the enemy in the north numbered more than 10,000 men in all; and that there was no danger of their penetrating into Asturias. He recommended breaking down the five bridges between Toro and Aranda; that Zamorra should be fortified and made a depot; and that magazines should be formed at Astorga and Villafranca. He regretted that he had no cavalry and expressed a wish to procure 2,000 English muskets, and shoes for his army. Symes asked him for 100 draft mules for General Baird's army but was told this was impossible; he had not one to spare.

Symes attended the review. The troops were drawn up in three columns; each consisting of about 2,500 men. The Marquis, on horseback, reviewed each column separately then the troops formed into lines, The right wing was badly armed, and worse clothed; the left was better, being chiefly provided with English firelocks; and a corps of 1,000 men in uniform, who, Symes was informed, were light troops, were respectable. Their movements from column into line were badly performed, and the officers were comparatively inferior to the men; there was only one brigade of artillery in the field; Symes doubted there were any more in Leon. The guns were drawn by mules. No ammunition wagons were brought into the field for inspection.

Symes' conclusions, from his observations and his conversations with Romagna, were to doubt the latter's inclination of moving forward to join Moore, instead looking to secure his retreat into Galicia, unless matters changed for the better. If he did join Moore's main force, Symes doubted whether his aid would be found useful. He stated his reasons for these conclusions: if the Marquis meant to advance, why send his artillery and troops into the rear? And why, as he was assured of the time when Moore intended to be at Benevente, decline to fix any precise day to make a movement? Symes's reasoning for doubting Romagna's usefulness was based on the inefficient and undisciplined state of his army. He felt it was impossible that they could stand up to a line of French infantry. At least one-third of the Spanish muskets would not fire, and a French soldier could load and fire his piece with precision three times before a Spaniard could fire his twice. However brave, he said, men could not stand against such odds; as to charging with the bayonet, even if their arms were fit for the purpose, the men had no collective confidence to charge, nor officers to lead them; they were more likely to disperse, probably on the first fire, and would never be rallied, unless they voluntarily returned to their General's standard; this was unlikely as Romagna's army was almost wholly composed of fugitives from the defeats in the North. This was evidenced by what Romagna had told Symes: that the Spaniards did not lose above 1,000 men in their late actions with the French. This was not, said Symes, a proof of the weakness of the French, but of the incapacity of the Spaniards to resist them; in fact the Spaniards fled before a desultory fire, saving themselves, and then claimed merit for having escaped.

At Toro, Moore had a visit from Stuart who had been sent by Frere, accompanied by a member of the Junta, to request him to join up with Romagna. He was, he told them, about to do that, having written to Romagna from Salamanca. He told Stuart how surprised he was at Frere's extraordinary conduct towards him, and showed him two of Frere's letters. These were so optimistic that Moore described them to Stuart as 'really equal to any of the visions of Don Quixote. The windmills were not less giants than his representations to the real state of Spain'.

There had been an attempt by the Cabinet to place Moore under Frere's orders, and it was with great difficulty that Moore's friends at Horse Guards had prevented this. Supported by the Duke of York, Gordon had insisted that 'it must be explicitly defined that the British General cannot be placed in any manner under the control of the British Minister (Frere) or receive any orders from him'. Frere may have been told of the first part of this but perhaps not the latter, as he did attempt to give Moore orders later. This may have been exacerbated by Moore asking him for his opinion on part of the army's movements, on the grounds that he would probably have a better idea of how the Cabinet would react; this was certainly not intended as an invitation to dictate tactics.

Moore continued to move his headquarters up and by the 22nd they were at Sahagun, where he learned of a splendid action by Paget and the 10th and 15th Hussars. Soult was aware that Moore was moving, but not in which direction nor that Baird and Moore had united; he expected them to join up at Valladolid and wrote for reinforcements. While he waited for these, he sent his two divisions of infantry to concentrate on Carrion and Saldanha while two cavalry brigades covered Sahagun and Majorga. He was not aware that Paget and his two dragoon regiments were only 12 miles from him. Learning where the French were, Paget marched with the 10th, 15th, Captain Thornhill and twelve men from the 7th, and four pieces of horse artillery. It was a bitterly cold and dark night, with heavy frost and some sleet; in some places the road was covered with sheets of ice, in others with deep snow drifts. The men had to dismount and lead their horses, but even so several fell. Early on the morning of the 21st, Paget's advance guard came up to a French patrol and took five prisoners, the rest gave the alarm and galloped off. The rest of the French cavalry were sleeping next to their ready saddled horses, woke, mounted and formed up on the plain outside the town, with a steep ravine at their backs. Paget soon came up and was checked by the ravine but soon found a way round it and fell on the French; their force numbered no more than 450 while Paget had at least 500. The French leading regiment, the 1st Provisional Chasseurs, fired carbines from the saddle at Paget's charging men but the 15th crashed into them, broke their line and that of the 8th Dragoons and drove them back. In the confusion their general, Debelle, was thrown and trampled. The action then turned into a melee with both sides using their sabres or swords; eventually about half the French escaped and made off to Saldanha. As well as those killed, Paget captured 12 officers and 145 men, for a loss of 2 men and 4 horses killed, 2 officers and 18 men and 10 horses wounded, and 26 other horses lost, having shed their riders and galloped off after the French. This was all the work of the 15th Hussars, as the 10th arrived too late to do more than join the pursuit; they did, however, manage to seize the French baggage and transport.

For the rest of the British troops, it had been necessary to halt that day after the hard marches in the very cold weather, over ground covered with snow. It had been Moore's intention to leave at 8 pm on the 23rd and march overnight in two columns to Carrion where he believed there were some French troops, arriving to attack at daylight, but about an hour before the march was due to begin he received a letter from Romagna reporting that the French were marching from Madrid towards them. This was verified by information that in the villages before Palencia, the inhabitants were preparing provisions for the enemy; he also knew that the French march on Badajos had been stopped. With no doubt that all the disposable French troops were being turned against him, Moore had to give up his idea of an attack on Soult and return to secure his communication with the Galicias. That evening he received a report that Carrion had been reinforced by troops from Palencia and abandoned his plan to atttract the enemy's attention from the armies in the south and hopefully to strike a blow at a weak corps while it was still thought that he was retreating into Portugal. He knew that had been a risky strategy but thought it was worth it for the honour of the service.

He sent an update to Frere on the 23rd, saying that he was on his way to Saldanha to attack Soult. Romagna might be of use in this operation, but Moore did not expect him to move until it was too late, and did not intend to wait for him. He went on:

> The movement I am making is of the most dangerous kind. I not only risk to be surrounded, at any moment, by superior forces, but to have my communication intercepted with the Galicias. I wish it to be apparent to the whole world, as it is to every individual of this army, that we have done everything in our power in support of the Spanish cause, and that we do not abandon it, until long after the Spaniards had abandoned us.

On 24 December, Hope and Fraser retired to Majorga. Baird was to take his division to Valentia and Moore would himself follow Hope and Fraser with the reserve and two light corps to Benavente. Paget would follow him with the cavalry. He confided to his journal that he hoped to steal two days marches on the French which would allow them a quiet journey, but if they were closely followed he would have to close up and halt and offer them a battle. 'At this season of the year,' he wrote, 'in a country without fuel, it is impossible to bivouac; the villages are small, which obliges us to march thus by corps in succession, our retreat, therefore, becomes much more difficult.' Although he continued to write letters to his normal set of correspondents, these were the last words he was to write in his journal.[5] He had concluded that he had to retreat.[6]

Chapter 14

Retreat and Battle

Intending to commence his march the following day, Moore wrote to Romagna on 24 December, telling him of his plans. He intended to march in two divisions on Valencia de Don Juan and Benevente, and asked Romagna to keep a strong corps at Mansillia to guard the bridge. Baird would go with the division to Valencia de Don Juan and he would himself command that going to Benevente. He repeated his request that Astorga and its neighbourhood, together with the passage of the Galicias, would be kept clear for the British troops and not occupied by Romagna's. He received a reply not from Romagna but from Symes, dated 25 December, reporting that it was impossible for any of Romagna's troops to move into the Asturias as there had been an exceptionally heavy snowfall, blocking the roads. Romagna did intend to retire to Astorga, but leaving some 2,000 troops at Leon to boost and give some training to the inhabitants and students, a number estimated at between 1,200 and 1,500. Leon was a large city, surrounded by a high wall, but this was broken down in several places and there were no gates in the gateways. There was no high ground close enough to allow the enemy to command the city; instead there was a vast plain extending for several miles with nothing to oppose advancing troops. Romagna's army was moving to Leon that same day.

Moore had received a letter from Romagna, when he had reached Leon, stating that the enemy 'when they shall have assembled all the forces which they have scattered about at all points in the surrounding parts', would have no more than 8,000 to 9,000 infantry, and 1,000 cavalry, with 8 to 10 pieces of artillery. It would be, he said, 'of great importance to surround this corps and destroy it'. If Moore agreed, Romagna would make a movement with from 9,000 to 10,000 men, 'of those which are best clothed and armed, all the rest being nearly naked and very ill-equipped'. He was persuaded that the enemy were not strong, and that all the disasters they have witnessed were due to the failure of their armies to unite.

Another letter from Symes dated 27 December reported that Romagna's army did not move from Mansillia as planned on Christmas Day as the weather was tempestuous, and there was no pressing necessity. Romagna did not think there was any point in destroying the bridge at Mansillia; Symes saw it as the only way the Spanish could secure their retreat as there was no other way to defend the town. Before returning to Leon, Romagna left 3,000 men and 4 field pieces at Mansillia. Symes thought that Romagna should have organised a defence of Leon three or four weeks previously but he had failed to do so and it was now too late.

A letter from Royal Engineeer Captain Carmichael-Smyth to Paget gave news of the terrain around Astorga. Much like that of Leon, the country was perfectly open and would give no advantage to a small corps to enable it to oppose a large force with any prospect of success. However, about 2 leagues from Astorga towards Villafranca the hills closed in, offering some strong ground, in particular behind the village of Rodrigatos which looked to offer a most advantageous position. But until they reached that point, the ground would give more advantage to the French and there there was a possibility that such a position could be forced from the Fonsevados road. Carmichael-Smyth thought the strongest position between Astorga and Villafranca was about a league in front of Villafranca, but hastened to add that these were only observations rather than direct recommendations.

By 28 December Baird was at Valencia de Don Juan and Moore was at Benevente, where he wrote again to Castlereagh. The army had, he reported, been marching through snow and extreme cold; then in the last few days it rained, rendering the roads almost impassable. Hope and Fraser had already moved on towards Astorga; Moore and the Reserve would be following the next day. The French, who had been marching towards Badajos, had stopped and were now turned in Moore's direction. Moore had ordered the supplies at Benevente to be sent back to Astorga, and those at Astorga to Villafranca. The roads were very bad and there was little transport available and he feared that if he were close pressed by the enemy he would lose some of those stores. He might be forced to a battle but would avoid this if possible; it was reported that Napoleon was coming himself with 10,000 of his guards and that the whole force approaching was not less than 50,000. The British force, when at Astorga, would total some 27,000; Romagna's force, Moore concluded from the fact that he had brought no more than 6,000 to Mansillia, could not have more than 8,000 fit for action. His intention was to stop at Astorga for no longer than it took to secure his stores, then move on to where he understood there was a fortress, but if the French were pursuing, he felt he would have to move on towards the coast where there was a good route to Vigo. He assured Castlereagh that he would retreat no further than absolutely necessary, but added that once he was forced into the mountains the lack of provisions would make it necessary to make for the coast where they could re-provision from ships. He reminded Castlereagh that it was necessary to send transports immediately to Corunna and Vigo to re-embark the army.

A memorandum from the Transport Office dated 15 December shows the numbers of transports available:

	Troops No.	Cavalry No.	Store No.	Total No.
Corunna	67	29	50	146
Lisbon	38	27	60	125
With French troops	29	1	–	30
	134	57	110	301
Under orders	48	130	60	238
(to sail from home)	182	187	170	539

By this time, possibly partly due to the troops' disgust at having to retreat while there was a chance to have a real fight with the French, discipline was breaking down. Moore issued a General Order:

The commander of the forces has observed with concern the extreme bad conduct of the troops at a moment when they are about to come into contact with the enemy, and when the greatest regularity and the best conduct are the most requisite. He is the more concerned at it as until lately, the behaviour of that part of the army at least which was under his own immediate command, was exemplary, and did them much honour.

The misbehaviour of the troops in the column which marched by Valderas to this place, exceeds what he could have believed of British soldiers. It is disgraceful to the officers; as it strongly marks their negligence and inattention.

The Commander of the Forces refers to the General Orders of the 25th of October and the 11th of November. He desires that they may be again read at the head of every company of the army, he can add nothing but his determination to execute them to the fullest extent. He can feel no mercy towards officers who neglect in times like these, essential duties, or towards soldiers who disgrace the country they are sent to protect.

The Spanish forces have been overpowered; and until such time as they are reassembled, and ready again to come forward, the situation of the army must be arduous, and such as to call for the exertion of qualities the most rare and valuable in a military body. These are not bravery alone, but patience and constancy under fatigue and hardship, obedience to command; sober and orderly conduct, firmness, and resolution, in every different situation in which they may be placed. It is by the display of such qualities alone, that the army can expect to deserve the name of soldiers, that they can be able to withstand the forces opposed to them, or to fulfill the expectation of their country.

It is impossible for the commander of the forces to explain to his army the motives for the movements he directs. The Commander of the Forces can however assure the army that he has made none since he left Salamanca, which he did not foresee, and was not prepared for; and as far as he is a judge, they have answered the purposes for which they were intended. When it is proper to fight a battle he will do it and he will choose the time and place he thinks most fit, in the meantime he begs the officers and men of the army to attend diligently to discharge their parts and to leave to him and with the general officers, the decision of measures which belong to them alone.

The army may rest assured, that there is nothing he has more at heart, than their honour, and that of their country.

This Order was evidently not entirely successful, as after reaching Astorga Moore found it necessary to issue another:

The present is a moment when the Army is necessarily called upon to make great efforts and to submit to great privations, the bearing cheerfully with which is a quality not less estimable than valour. The goodwill of the inhabitants will be particularly useful to the Army, and can only be obtained by good conduct on the part of the troops. The Commander of the Forces cannot impress too strongly on the whole Army the necessity of this, and he trusts that the generals and commanding officers will adopt such measures both on the march and in the cantonments, as will ensure it. It is very probable that the Army will shortly have to meet the enemy and the Commander of the Forces has no doubt that they will eagerly imitate the worthy example which has been set them by the cavalry on several recent occasions, and particularly in the affair of yesterday; in which Brigadier-General Stewart, with an inferior force charged and overthrew one of the best corps of cavalry in the French Army.

The generals will immediately inspect the baggage of the brigades and divisions. They are held responsible that it does not exceed the proportion fixed by the General Orders.

The incidents which led to these orders were plundering and drunkenness: in some villages, the troops tore down anything which would burn, including doors and windows from the houses, and anything which could be drunk, including large casks of wine, and this inevitably led to straggling. This word, sounding comparatively innocent, described behaviour which was closer to desertion: drunks lying around unconscious or wandering off; many of these men were captured or killed by the enemy. Much has been made of these incidents, but they were not specific to the retreat, nor to Moore's army. To a large extent it was associated with specific regiments, and at the end of the day, that came down to the commanders. Even Napoleon and Soult complained of the high number of stragglers in their armies. A few tried to cut off corners by leaving the road and then got lost. Most stragglers were ill, exhausted, hungry or footsore from bad shoes; many were drunk, looking for plunder, or just bad soldiers. Much of the plundering was done by the baggage guards, and there is a suggestion that they also took care of officers' plunder.

Much of the plundering was done in the search for drink, or food. Food was short, and when he arrived at Astorga, Moore had been surprised to find Romagna was there with part of his troops, despite his promises that he would go elsewhere and leave the town clear for Moore. Not only had Romagna cluttered the town and the road with troops and much abandoned equipment, they had brought typhus with them. Every day that they were there, some sixty or seventy Spanish soldiers were admitted to the hospital, and the disease soon spread to the British troops.[1]

He moved on to Benevente, and from there he wrote to General Broderick at Corunna. They were continuing their march, he wrote, and the lack of food in the mountains meant that he had to go all the way to the coast and embark the troops. He asked Brodrick to pass this information on to the Admiral, and remarked that he had already asked Castlereagh to send transports to Portugal and Vigo. He hoped to be able to write with more detail in a couple of days, but took the opportunity to tell Broderick that while he did not wish to fight a battle: 'the force coming against me is so superior that if it presses me, I must retire'.

He also wrote to Gordon on the same day, giving a brief outline of his situation and enclosing a 'diary' of his march from Toro on 17 December.

On 27 December Charles Stuart had written to Moore from Seville. This letter was not received until 11 January, but does outline the general situation in Spain, which was basically 'no change'. The Junta, having arrived at Seville, had relapsed into its former apathy. Its president had died, leading Stuart to hope briefly that the Junta would take the opportunity to make some changes in their government, but to no avail.

Moore's next letter to Castlereagh reported that his position with the British force

> had come to that point which I have long foreseen. Abandoned from the beginning by everything Spanish, we were equal to nothing by ourselvs. From a desire to do what I could, I made the movement against Soult. As a diversion it has answered completely, but, as there is nothing to take advantage of it, I have risked the loss of the Army for no purpose.
>
> I have no option now but to fall down to the coast as fast as I am able.

He had found no provisions at Toro; the small amount that had been collected there had been eaten by Baird's troops as they passed.

> There is no means of carriage. The people run away, the villages are deserted, and I have been obliged to destroy great part of the ammunition and military stores. For the same reason I am obliged to leave the sick. In short, my sole object is to save the army. We must all make forced marches to the coast, from the scarcity of provisions and to be before the enemy, who, by roads upon our flanks, may otherwise intercept us ... once the rear has passed I do not expect to be molested.

He hoped that transports would be waiting for them on the coast, but if they were not, he hoped to be able to take up a position which he could maintain until they arrived. 'It is only while retreating that we are vulnerable.' He then went on to report that the cavalry had had 'one of the notable skirmishes of the campaign': on the morning of 18 December as they marched from Benevente, some squadrons of French guards attempted to cross the river at a ford. Stewart, with the picquets of the 18th Regiment and the 3rd German Dragoons attacked them and drove them across the ford. The French general, Lefebvre-Desnouëttes, with about seventy officers and men, was taken. Moore had sent Desnouëttes to Corunna to be sent on to England. He was young for his rank and Moore thought he might be one of Napoleon's favourites.[2]

Moore moved on to Bembibre; arriving there on 1 January, they found Baird's division still there, many incapable of movement from excessive drinking. The 28th Regiment were ordered to stack arms and clear the houses, an exercise which took until noon the following day. Romagna's army, the Light Brigade and the King's German Legion took a separate route, much rougher than that taken by the others, and one on which they were pursued by Franceschi's cavalry. That morning, Franceschi had been informed of this column moving towards the pass at Foncebadon, and managed to get ahead of them to the pass. In 2 separate attacks, the French took a total of 2,900 Spanish prisoners and killed about 30.

On the morning of 3 December, the German Light Dragoons were attacked by Franceschi's French cavalry; later that morning Colbert's cavalry harassed the rear guard. There were many similar attacks, followed by what seemed to be preparation for another but this one was on ground which offered a good position, just east of the town of Cacabelos close to the junction with the Camino Real. The Reserve had to remain there until the rear guard were past, and the Third German Dragoons had joined. Moore rode past and went on before returning to survey the ground at Cacabelos; having seen the damage done, he was not in the best of tempers when Brigadier General Slade arrived to ask for assistance at the meadow where Anstruther's men were repelling repeated attacks by Colbert's cavalry. Moore asked him how long he had been Colonel Grant's aide-de-camp; then informed him coldly that the proper position of a general officer was at the head of his men when in the presence of the enemy.

After the men were halted, Moore had them formed up in close lines, then rode up and addressed them on lack of discipline and their outrageous behaviour, ending by saying:

> And if the enemy are in possession of Bembibre, which I believe, they have got a rare prize. They have taken or cut to pieces many hundreds of drunken British cowards – for none but unprincipled cowards get drunk, nay, in the very sight of the enemies of their country; and sooner than survive the disgrace of such infamous misconduct, I hope that the first cannonball fired by the enemy may take me in the head.[3]

Paget then had the regiments formed into a square and each held a drumhead court martial. Two men who had been caught in the act were brought into the centre of the square and nooses put round their necks. Just as they were to be executed, an officer galloped up and reported to Paget that the rear guard was under attack and being forced to retreat; Paget replied as Moore had done, that an officer's place was with his men. He then spoke to the square, saying that it was lamentable that instead of preparing his troops to receive an attack, he should have to be executing two robbers. He then remarked that even though the attack might come on one corner of the square, there was another corner where the executions could take place; then, after a pause, he said he was prepared to forgive those robbers if the regiments promised to behave well in the future 'Say Yes in an instant'. With a little prompting by their officers, all the men shouted Yes three times, and Paget had the square broken up, the regiments formed into columns, and they retreated to Cacabelos. Behind them the rear guard came over the hill and down the gentle slope to the town. Colonel Barclay took the 52nd Regiment through the town in double quick time and took possession of the vineyards over the river; the 95th covered the rest of the Reserve while they crossed the bridge. They formed on the hill behind the 52nd, the riflemen of the 95th took cover behind walls and the 15th halted on the open ground to their front.

When the enemy came to the top of the hill, with Colbert's cavalry on one side of the road and La Houssaye's on the other, Colbert could not see the bridge on the western side of the town as it was hidden by a bend in the road; nor could he see the riflemen south of the bridge. He suspected the riflemen were there, and hesitated to charge; waiting for nearly a hour until he saw the British begin to form up for a retreat before he gave the order to charge. There was fierce hand-to-hand fighting, and the inhabitants rushed to escape, blocking the bridge for the retreating riflemen. Major Colborne shouted for them to run into the houses; some were able to do so, and some were able to cross the bridge but many were captured. Colbert's men tried to cross the bridge into the town but were stopped by the firing of the 52nd and those of the 95th who had managed to cross the bridge; Colbert paused again, waiting for Merle's infantry to come up. In his magnificent uniform he was clearly visible from the vineyards, and rifleman Tom Plunkett of the 95th killed him with a shot in the head. The French continued their attempt to cross the river but were driven back by the riflemen and retired, leaving the British to fall back on Villafranca.

On the night of 3 January the Reserve arrived at Villafranca, Hope and Fraser's division having been there and continued on their way westwards. Although these two divisions had not been able to get as much fresh meat as they would have liked, they had, to a certain extent, found ample supplies of everything else. Hope complained that Fraser had taken all the bread, and that he would have to make do with salt beef as there were no bullocks. Both, however, found plenty of shoes and Hope took 1,200 pairs when he left the city; this should have left enough for Baird's division, but when the stores were mobbed the provost chased the soldiers off and many were not able to get shoes, despite their sore and often bleeding feet. Provisions were issued in an orderly fashion at first, and Commissary Schaumann wrote that they had large stocks of flour and he and his staff spent all night and all day baking bread. They also had large quantities of salt fish and biscuits, and there were more in a convent across the bridge. However, after a while the stores were violently raided and the commissaries had to abandon their attempts to issue provisions properly.[4] Unfortunately, this meant that the rear guard and Reserve got nothing when they arrived, and were treated to the sight of smashed houses and drunken soldiers lying about. Moore issued another reprimand, this time through General Clinton (the Adjutant General) who wrote to the divisional commanders, repeating the orders as before, and adding that some non-commissioned officers had been left in charge of 'a description of baggage which is not allowed'; frequent inspections of soldiers' packs should be made, and any items found in them 'beyond what they are directed to carry on light service order is … to be destroyed'.

By midnight on the 3rd, the three leading divisions were over the summit of the Picos de Ancares and well on the way to Lugo. The Reserve and Moore's headquarters were 12 miles west of Villafranca, at Herrerias, while the rear guard was some 4 miles behind them and there were still many stragglers still in Villafranca. Moore stayed at Herrerias for only a few hours, but it was during that time that he decided he would embark his men at Corunna rather than Vigo or Ferrol, although several days before he had ordered Craufurd and Alten to go to Vigo. They arrived unmolested but much tried by the weather, but Romagna's men, who followed them, were attacked by Franceschi's troopers, and some 3,000 of them taken prisoner.

After making this decision, Moore immediately sent a courier to Admiral Samuel Hood[*] at Vigo, asking for the transports to be sent round to Corunna, and also sent a dispatch by his aide, Captain George Napier, to Baird. This was to be passed on to Hope and Fraser, who were to wait at Lugo for further instructions. Baird was at Nogales, some 16 miles from Herrerias, and was still in bed when Napier arrived. He offered to carry the dispatch on to Hope and Fraser, but Baird refused, saying he would send it on with a dragoon. The dragoon managed to get drunk on the way and lost the dispatch; it was found and returned to Moore, who sent it out again. By the time it caught up with them, Hope was close to Lugo and Fraser had passed Lugo and was well on his way to Orense. He wasted 24 hours on the unnecessary march back to Lugo, losing some 400 stragglers on the way.

The bridge at Villafranca was blown as the British left the town. A sapper officer had ridden through the town at 4 a.m, shouting that the bridge would be blown in two hours, so everyone had to be across. Most heeded this warning, but many were drunk and either didn't care or didn't hear. Soult reported to Berthier that they had brought in over 900 of these drunks, found in wine cellars or lying comatose in the roads. An attempt to blow the bridge at Nogales failed, as had a mine in the roadway; these failures have been blamed on the inefficiency of the Royal Engineers, but Baird's military secretary, Colonel Sorrell, reported that an order given by Moore at Astorga to destroy the entrenching tools was over-enthusiastically carried out and made it difficult for the Engineers to place their explosives properly. Paget asked Moore why they did not destroy more bridges after they had crossed, and Moore replied that since the bridges were constructed of heavy stones and took time and much effort to destroy and that the mountain streams they spanned were rarely far from a ford. As often as not, the time and effort needed to destroy these bridges was not compensated by the minimal delay they caused the enemy. Such observations of matters which other officers often missed were part of the reason Moore was held in such high regard by his staff.

Moore's headquarters left Nogales on 5 December, having, just before they left, the good fortune to encounter a Spanish convoy of clothing; this was promptly seized, the clothing handed out to the British troops, and the oxen taken to pull British wagons. The oxen pulling British wagons were failing, and near the village of Cerezal two wagons of money were found stopped in the road, their oxen having collapsed from exhaustion. Rather than delay the march while the inevitable plundering of this treasure took place, the barrels of silver coin were thrown over the cliff, although Lieutenant Hugo of the 3rd Light Dragoons arrived with twenty-five men and was given permission to try and save some of the money. They filled the empty grain bags which they carried, and duly delivered them to the Commissariat at Corunna. When the leading French division came up, they did exactly what Moore had feared his troops might do, filling their

---

[*] This was the son of the Admiral Hood who Moore had encountered at Toulon.

pockets and whatever bags they had. This actually had a good effect, as the weight of the silver slowed the pursuit and the rear guard was not as badly harassed as they had previously been, although the French were still closing in.

After they got close to Lugo, Moore paused. He did think of making a stand there, as his army was on the hills on one side of the valley and the French on the other. Neither could make the first move without being exposed to withering fire, so the two armies spent three days watching each other, with no more activity than some desultory skirmishing. Once again, Moore felt the need to issue a General Order:

> Generals and Commanding Officers of corps must be as sensible as the Commander of the Forces, of the complete disorganization of the Army.
>
> The advanced guard of the French is already close to us, and it is to be presumed that the main body is not far distance; an action may, therefore, be hourly expected. If the Generals and Commanding Officers of the regiments (feeling for the honour of their country and the British army) wish to give the Army a fair chance of success, they will exert themselves to restore order and discipline in the regiments, brigades, and divisions which they command.
>
> The Commander of the Forces is tired of giving orders which are never attended to: he therefore appeals to the honour and feelings of the Army he commands; and if those are not sufficient to induce them to do their duty, he must despair of succeeding by any other means. He was forced to order one soldier to be shot, and he will order all others to be executed who are guilty of similar enormities: but he considers that there would be no occasion to proceed to such extremities if the officers did their duty; as it is chiefly from their negligence, and from the want of proper regulations in the regiments, that crimes and irregularities are committed, in quarters and on the march.

And, on the following day, another, this one more encouraging:

> The Army must see that the moment is now come when, after the hardships and fatiguing marches they have undergone, they will have the opportunity of bringing the enemy to action. The Commander of the Forces has the most perfect confidence in their valour, and that it is only necessary to bring them to close contact with the enemy in order to defeat them; and a defeat, if it be complete, as he trusts it will be, will, in great measure, end their labours.
>
> The General has no other caution to give them, than not to throw away their fire at the enemy's skirmishers, merely because they fire at them; but to reserve it till they can give it with effect.

On the morning of 7 January, pipe-clayed and polished, the British troops marched into their positions, waiting until the afternoon until Soult ordered a probing attack by Merle's infantry on the British centre, and another on the British left by Franceschi's cavalry, more infantry and five guns. Some of Hope's division did give way but were soon checked; some of the French infantry did manage to get into the village of Villanova which was between the opposing forces, but were soon driven out. Despite the French army expecting to be given the order for a general attack, they were not. Soult, explaining this to Napoleon, said that he was waiting for more infantry, artillery and cavalry to come up, and would then advance. 'From what I have seen' he said 'it will be a large scale battle, since I do not think the enemy will abandon his position without a fight, but the morale of the troops is so high that there can be no doubt of the outcome.' He expected to be ready to launch the attack at noon the following day 'unless I discover that the enemy has such large forces that I am outnumbered'.

Another day passed, while the troops of both sides waited in the miserable rain. Finally, with only one day's bread ration left, Moore decided to move on, issuing another General Order to his divisional commanders:

It is evident that the enemy will not fight this Army, notwithstanding the superiority of his numbers; but will endeavour to harrass and tease it upon its march.

The Commander of the Forces requests that it may be carefully explained to the soldiers, that their safety depends solely upon their keeping their divisions, and marching with their regiments; that those who stop in villages, or straggle on the march, will inevitably be cut off by the French cavalry; who have hitherto shewn little mercy even to the feeble and infirm, who have fallen into their hands.

The Army still has eleven leagues to march, the soldiers must make an exertion to accomplish them; the rear-guard cannot stop, and those who fall behind must take their fate.

As well as the bread shortage, there was a danger from the French cavalry. The country through which they would be passing was good for cavalry, and while the French had several divisions of cavalry, the British were down to a few squadrons. They moved out during the night of 8 January and the early morning of the 9th. Bundles of burning straw were placed on the secondary roads to mark the route. This was not a success, as some were blown away and others extinguished by the rain; this caused some delays and confusion, but there were no serious consequences. Some men were left behind to keep the camp fires alight to deceive the enemy, a tactic which did work, as despite Soult having informed Napoleon that if the British withdrew, he would follow immediately and force a battle, he did not realise they were gone until too late. And gone well ahead, for the British did not see Soult's troops between Lugo and Betanzos.

Getting close to the embarkation point, many stragglers rejoined the column, only to be replaced by the sick, many of whom dropped out suffering from dysentery and opthalmia. Captain Gordon reported in his journal that Brigadier General Stewart and Paget were both afflicted, the former with a white handkerchief bound over his eyes and his horse led by Colonel Elley, the Adjutant General of the cavalry. Exhaustion also took its toll, of officers as well as men; some almost falling off their horses when they went to sleep in the saddle. Some regiments arrived at Betanzos with less than fifty men behind the colours, one had colours but no men following. The 9th regiment waited outside the town to gather up its stragglers and then marched into town with sixty men. But as always, even though cold, wet and miserable, the British soldiers still managed to joke about their situation.

By noon on 10 January, all the regiments had arrived at Betanzos, where there was food, but the 28th Regiment, especially General Moore Disney's brigade, which had arrived close to last, had little. They remedied this by sending out a party to search the stragglers as they came up, taking part of what each man carried in his pack or haversack, and soon had enough flour, bread, potatoes and bacon to serve out a portion to each man. Realising that it could only have been acquired by plunder, they also took all the money from these stragglers and distributed it among the men who had maintained discipline. Lieutenant Blakeney listed some of the different items of plunder which they found: 'brass candlesticks bent double, bundles of common knives, copper saucepans hammered into masses, every item of domestic utensils … without any regard to value or weight …'.

Moore had thought of embarking his troops from Betanzos Bay, at the head of the estuary of the Rio Mino, but Major Fletcher of the Royal Engineers, who had gone on ahead to survey the ground, reported back that he had heard from Admiral de Courcy who had been at anchor in Betanzos Bay. Although it was a good anchorage, it was within gunshot of both shores and would be even more difficult to get away from than Corunna; the latter would be better as an embarkation point. Fletcher had also heard from his collegue Captain Charles Lefebvre, who had walked round the peninsula at Corunna between the citadel and the sea. He reported that there were well-screened places for the troops to camp, both in valleys and on rising ground; there were also two small sandy coves which would be useful for maintaining communication with the fleet. These were Playa de St Anajo on the eastern or harbour side of the bay, with a smooth sandy beach some 100yd long; despite a gale blowing when Lefebvre visited it, there was no swell or surf. The second was Playa de la Lafa, on the western shore, with the same type and length of beach, with no surf but a little swell. He planned to speak to General Brodrick that evening about getting a naval officer to visit the bays and give an opinion. There was plenty of water available from wells and running down the side of the hill during the rain.

Fletcher passed all this on, then remarked that as Corunna was fortified, revetted and flanked by defensible places, although the ground was not itself favourable, it could not be carried by the enemy if properly defended. It had plenty of cover for men and could even hold out for several days against artillery. Moore accepted this recommendation and decided to move on to Corunna.

From his headquarters in Betanzos, Moore issued another General Order and a memorandum for General Officers:

A great deal of irregularity has arisen from the practice of some Commanding Officers allowing soldiers, who pretend to be bad marchers, to precede their corps. Men of this description, whom Commanding Officers may think expedient to send forward, must be placed under an officer, who is held responsible for their conduct.

Memorandum for General Officers

To prevent the renewal of the same scene which the march of last night presented, the Commander of the Forces directs that, previously to the march tomorrow morning; the General Officers will see their divisions and brigades properly formed; that they wheel them by sections; and that, during the march, they pay constant attention to the preservation of that order.

Soult arrived at Lugo on 9 January; he too had many stragglers and wrote to Marshall Ney at Astorga asking for them to be gathered up and sent on, forcibly if necessary. He arrived at Rabadé in the afternoon and was stopped by the bridge which the British had blown after they crossed; this was not a complete demolition, having only blown up one of the piers and damaged two arches, and Soult's Engineers managed to repair it enough overnight for the infantry and cavalry to cross, completing their work on the 11th so the artillery could cross.

Moore's army marched the last 14 miles from Betanzos to Corunna, destroying three bridges as they went. Soult's army entered Betanzos soon after Moore's Reserve left. The blown bridges delayed them a little, but they were settled opposite the British lines by the 13th.

Despite the good weather, when Moore's army arrived at Corunna, there were no transports waiting for them in the bay, although there were two warships and twenty-six storeships and hospital ships. Leaving the Reserve, which was now serving as rear guard, Moore rode ahead to examine the ground; he also wanted to be at the port when his army arrived. Achieving this, he reviewed them as they arrived, Captain Robert Arbuthnot, an assistant adjutant general, with him. Moore pointed out to him a body of men in the distance: 'they are the Guards by the way they are marching'. With drums beating, the drum-major flourishing his stick at the front and drill-sergeants on the flanks keeping the men in step, they marched smartly into the town.

It was not only the troops who suffered from the poor conditions. William Napier, who later became a historian, crossed the mountains between Orense and Vigo in charge of the sick, wounded and military stores, reported that he had marched several days with bare feet and only a jacket and trousers for clothing; his feet were swollen and bleeding and he thought he would have died had he not been lent another officer's spare horse. His brother George, wrote to their mother:

> We have made a most <u>rapid retreat</u>; & the General most richly deserves the thanks of his Country, for saving this army, by his own Superior talents, for he received not the slightest assistance from the Spaniards, on the contrary, they seemed to wish for the success of the French; damn their Souls, the Ships are not yet arrived from Vigo where they had been sent, the army is <u>outside</u> the Town on the Heights, & the French are on the opposite & some on this side of the river, the Bridge we have destroyed; but I think we <u>must lose</u> some men before we get off, for they have an immense force, & every day brings them more men & artillery; however we all have the greatest confidence in our General, the Whole Army look up to him as their preserver, Oh my dear Mother, what fatigue of Mind and body he has and does now undergo; I can assure you that for these

last seven days & nights, he has never closed his eyes, constantly has he been on horseback, I fear his health will suffer, but as yet he is well but much pulled down; besides the bad behaviour of the army in general had much <u>annoyed</u> him, & he has made some severe examples; however, they are now behaving well again, which will be a great gratification to him; would to God the French would come over the river and give us <u>one</u> day, before we Embark, & then; Eternal Glory will be his lot … tell Dick that his friend Ferries has joined, his servant was killed a day or two ago, & all his baggage taken, poor fellow, poor me too for he had 3 pairs of Boots for me which would have been most acceptable as at present I am bare footed.[5]

This at least could be remedied at Corunna, where there were stores of boots, arms and ammunition. Having supplied the troops with these, the rest was destroyed, and the ammunition store blown up. They also had to destroy most of the horses as there were only sufficient horse transports for 950; rather than let them fall into French hands, almost 2,000 horses were shot or driven over the cliff. Meanwhile, 227 more transports and warships had assembled at Vigo, and these left for Corunna on the 13th and arrived at Corunna on the night of the 14th/15th. The warships consisted largely of the Baltic fleet which had gone home for the winter, and three more from the Tagus. These consisted of *Ville de Paris* (110 guns), *Victory* (100), *Barfleur* (98), *Audacious* (74), *Elizabeth* (74), *Implacable* (74), *Norge* (74), *Resolution* (74), *Zealous* (74), *Endymion* (50), *Mediator* (36), *Minerva* (32), *Champion* (24) and *Cossack* (22). The advantage of the large ships was that they had many boats and the crews to man them during the evacuation.

There was an established routine for embarkation of troops: the army gave the transport agents lists of the strength of each regiment and the agents allocated transports for them. The naval and transport officers were given lists of these and the officers of the regiments were given the names and numbers of 'their' transports. This system worked well in daylight, but after dark and with 250 ships in the harbour, it took too long for the boats to find the right ships, so the ships with space left showed lights at the fore-topmast, and took these down when the ship was full. When it got light, they used an ensign instead.[6]

Stewart, still suffering from ophthalmia, was to go back to England immediately, carrying dispatches, and many others took the opportunity of sending letters home with him. On the 13th, having been busy all day, Moore declared he was too tired to write, and said that Stewart, 'being a competent judge of everything' could tell his brother all he needed to know. Moore's confidence in Stewart was not shared by all his staff, nor, as shown by his behaviour back in London, should it have been given by Moore. George Napier added a postscript about Stewart to his letter to his mother: '… but fine fellow as he is, You <u>must not judge</u> of things by what he says, I mean as to the movements of this Army'.

When he had rested a little, and eaten, Moore found that Stewart had not yet departed, so changed his mind and wrote to Castlereagh:

Private and confidential Corunna 13th January 1809

My Lord,

Situated as this army is at present, it is impossible for me to detail to your Lordship the events which have taken place, since I had the honour to address you from Astorga on the 31st decer. I have therefore determined to send to England Brig-Genl Charles Stewart, as the officer best qualified to give you every information you can want, both with respect to our actual situation, and the events which have led to it. From his connection with your Lordship, and with His Majesty's Ministers, whatever he relates, is most likely to be believed. He is a man in whose honour I have the most perfect reliance - he is incapable of stating anything but the truth, and it is the truth which at all times I wish to convey to your Lordship, and to the King's Government.

Your Lordship knows that had I followed my own opinion as a military man, I should have retired with the Army from Salamanca. The Spanish armies were then beaten, there was no Spanish force to which we could unite; and from the character of the Government, and the disposition of the inhabitants, I was satisfied that no efforts would be made, to aid us, or to favour the cause in which they were engaged. I was sensible however that the apathy and indifference of the Spaniards would never have been believed; that had the British been withdrawn, the loss of the cause would have been imputed to their retreat; and it was necessary to risk this army to convince the people of England, as well as the rest of Europe, that the Spaniards had neither the power nor the inclination to make any efforts for themselves. It was for this reason that I made the march to Sahagun – as a diversion it succeeded: I brought the whole disposable force of the French against this army, and it has been allowed to follow it, without a single movement being made by any of what the Spaniards call armies to favour my retreat. The Marquis of La Romagna was of no other use but to embarrass me, by filling the roads, by which I marched, with his cannon, his baggage and his fugitives.

The people of the Galicias, tho' armed, made no attempt to stop the passage of the French thro' their mountains. They abandoned their dwellings at our approach, drove away their carts, oxen, and everything that could be of the smallest aid to the army. The consequence has been, that our sick have been left behind. and when our Horses and Mules failed, which on such marches and thro' such a country was the case to a great extent – baggage ammunition, stores, and even Money were necessarily destroyed, or abandoned.

I am sorry to say that the army, whose conduct I had such reason to extol on its march thro' Portugal, and on its arrival in Spain, has totally changed its character, since it began to retreat.

I could not have believed, had I not witnessed it, that a British Army, could, in so short a time, have been so completely disorganised. Its conduct during the late marches has been infamous beyond belief.

I can say nothing in its favour, but that when there was a prospect of fighting the enemy – the men were then orderly, & seemed pleased, and determined to do their duty – in front of Villafranca the French came up with the Reserve, with which I was covering the Retreat of the Army. They attacked it at Cacabelos. I retired, covered by the 95th Regt, and marched that night to Herrerias, and thence to Nogales and Lugo, where I have ordered the different divisions which preceded, to halt, and collect. at Lugo the French again came up with us, they attacked our advanced posts on the 6th and seventh, and were repulsed in both attempts with little loss on our side.

I heard from the Prisoners taken, that three divisions of the French Army commanded by Marshall Soult were come up, I therefore expected to be attacked in the morning of the 8th. It was my wish to come to that issue, I had perfect confidence in the valour of the Troops, and it was only by crippling the Enemy that we could hope, either to retreat, or to embark unmolested – I made every preparation to receive the attack and drew out the Army in the morning to offer battle. This was not Marshal Soult's object. He either did not think himself sufficiently strong, or he wished to play a surer game by attacking us, on our march, or during our embarkation. The Country was intersected, & his position too strong for me to attack with an inferior force. The want of provisions would not enable me to wait longer. I marched that night, and in two forced marches, bivouacing for six or eight hours in the rain, I reached Betanzos on the 10th inst. The stragglers of the Army amounted to many thousand, occasioned partly by the length of the marches, which in bad weather, many men were unable to support. The want of shoes, hundreds being barefoot, and many left their ranks who had not so good an excuse but from a desire to plunder. As the Army was followed by the French Cavalry, a great number of the above descriptions fell into their hands.

At Lugo I was sensible of the impossibility of reaching Vigo, which was at too great a distance, and offered no advantages to embark in the face of the Enemy. My intention then was to have retreated to the Peninsula of Betanzos; where I hoped to find a position to cover the embarkation of the Army in Ares or Rodes Bays but having sent an officer to reconnoitre it, by his report I was determined to prefer this place. I gave notice to the Admiral of my intention, and begged that the Transports might be brought to Corunna. Had I found them here on my arrival on the 11th, the embarkation would have been easily effected, for I had gained several marches on the French. They have now come up with us, The transports are not arrived, my position in front of this place is a very bad one; and this place if I am forced to retire into it, is commanded within musket-shot; and the harbour will be so commanded by cannon on the coast that no ship will be able to lay in it. In short, my Lord, Genl Stewart will inform you how critical our situation is. It has been recommended to me, to make a proposal to the Enemy, to induce him to allow us to embark quietly in which case he gets us out of the country soon, and this place with its stores etc. complete, that, otherwise, we have it in our power to make a long defence, which must ensure the destruction of the Town. I am averse to make any such proposal and am exceedingly doubtful if it would be attended with any good effect – but whatever I resolve on this head, I hope your Lordship will rest assured, that I shall accept no terms, that are in the least dishonourable to the Army, or to the Country.

I find I have been led into greater length, and more detail than I thought I should have had time for; I have written under interruptions, and with my mind much occupied with other matters. My letter written so carelessly, can only be considered as Private. when I have more leisure I shall write more correctly. In the mean time I rely on Genl Stewart for giving your Lordship the information & detail which I have omitted. I should regret his absence, for his services have been very distinguished but the state of his eyes makes it impossible for him to serve, and this country is not one in which Cavalry can be of much use. If I succeed in embarking the Army, I shall send it to England – it is quite unfit for further service until it has been refitted, which can best be done there – and I cannot think, after what has transpired, that there can be any intention of sending a British force again into Spain.

I have the honour to remain

My Lord

Your Lordship's

Faithful & Obedient

Servant

John Moore.[*]

This letter, although superficially just a recounting of what has happened and what Moore intends to do next, is worthy of a more careful reading, for it shows a lot of Moore's character: worried at all the bad things that had happened and at finding that the transports were not there to receive them, then becoming more positive, stating that whatever happened, he would do what was necessary to preserve the honour of the British army and the British country. He certainly was not going to surrender to Soult and plead for terms that would allow his army to depart while leaving their stores behind; he had it in his power to make a prolonged defence. He had moved from a series of situations over which he could have no effective control to one where he knew his business and was prepared to engage on it. The wording of the letter is telling enough, but the original hand-written document also shows the stress under which he wrote, his writing getting progressively worse until he arrived at the situation where he could take control again, when the writing improves.

On 14 January, Moore rode out to the lines where his army was drawn up to oppose the French, a couple of miles outside Corunna. The peninsula of Corunna reaches out to the north, with the sea on the north and west and the bay on the east side. To the south of the town there are several ridges of low hills of varying heights; the British army was drawn up about 2 miles from the town and the French army

---

[*] Reproduced with the permission of The National Archives, from WO 1/236.

about 800yd further south. Moore had arranged his force in four divisions, each with two brigades in the line and one in reserve. Hope's and Baird's faced the French: from east to west Hill's and Leith's of Hope's division, then Manningham's and Bentinck's of Baird's division. Nine guns had been retained, and were placed in four positions: three on the front line, between the brigades there, and the fourth further back, between Fraser and Paget's brigades. Manningham's and Bentinck's brigades had the heaviest fighting, with the 4th, 50th and 42nd regiments bearing the brunt. At the western end of that ridge before it dropped into a steep canyon was a hamlet of a few houses called Castro de Elvina (part of the village of Elvina); on the 15th French infantry attacked Castro de Elvina, drove out the British picquets and brought up eleven guns with which they could command the right of the British line. However, Paget's and Fraser's divisions were placed at right angles to the rest of the line where they could outflank the French if they committed themselves against what they thought was the British flank. There was some other minor skirmishing that day and Soult formed a plan to attack the British advanced positions on the following day.

Meanwhile, the transports were arriving; squeezing into the inner harbour. The sick, the dismounted cavalry, fifty-two guns, baggage and the stores of the artillery brigades were loaded throughout the night of the 15th and on the morning of the 16th the horses and men of the cavalry were loaded, with women, the commissariat and other civilian branches of the army. Thirty-six fully loaded ships were sailed out of the harbour to make room for others to load, and waited off-shore under naval escort. It was intended to start loading the infantry at 4 pm on the 16th. Moore had issued another General Order:

> The Commander of the Forces directs that Commanding Officers of Regiments will, as soon as possible after they embark, make themselves acquainted with the names of the ships in which the men of their regiments are embarked, both sick and convalescent: and that they will make out the most correct states of their respective corps: that they will state the number of sick present, also those left at different places; and mention on the back of the return where the men returned on command are employed.

In the event, the final stages of the embarkation became somewhat chaotic; when the system of taking the members of each regiment to its designated ship became impossible in the dark and haste, the loads of many of the ships consisted of men from several different regiments. Many others ended up on the warships, again in mixed regiments.

Soult's army was in three divisions: Delaborde's on the east, Merle's in the centre and Mermet's on the west of their line, with the French cavalry under Lahoussaye and Franceschi to the west of Mermet. Soult decided to start his attack on the British right flank, placing his artillery batteries on the hill opposite Baird's division. Delaborde and Merle were to attack the British left and centre to prevent their moving reinforcements to their right, while Mermet was to attack Bentinck's brigade and try to get round his right flank. There were no roads on the ridges of the hills and the ground was rough, so it took the French until noon to get into their positions.

By this time Moore was concluding that the French would not attack that day and ordered Paget's division to return to Corunna and embark on the transports, but the French attack began soon after 1.30 pm. Moore had set off to visit the lines but had not gone far when word came from Hope that the French were getting under arms. On confirmation of this, Moore set off at the gallop with Colonel Graham, with, as Graham wrote, animation and an expression of 'almost boyish gaiety'.

Four French columns were advancing, one each on the British left and centre, the other two on the right, supported by artillery. The French guns were eight-pounders and they ranged 500 or 600yd behind the British lines. Early in the battle, Baird was struck by a ball which shattered an arm. The British guns were lighter (seven light 6-pounders and one 5½in howitzer), and had a much shorter range. The French moving towards the British right extended beyond the end of the 4th Regiment and the half of this regiment on the extreme right wing wheeled back from the other half, which stood fast, and opened a flanking fire. With Baird badly wounded, Moore had to take personal command of his division; he recalled Paget from Corunna and ordered Fraser to take up what had been Paget's position and guard against the French cavalry.

Major Charles Napier (brother of George and William) of the 50th was standing on a knoll in front of his left wing watching proceedings, able to see most of the field from his elevated position. He reported that everyone was anxious to see Moore: 'There was a feeling that under him we could not be beaten, and this was so strong at all times as to be a great cause of discontent during the retreat wherever he was not.' A firm believer that the most useful place for the Commander-in-Chief was near the point of the greatest struggle, Moore was heading for the hill above Elvina. Napier could hear cries of 'Where is the General?' as he watched his picquets fight skirmishing French 50yd below him. Behind the French skirmishers came a heavy French column, coming down the hill at a run and shouting *'En avant! Tue! Tue!'* ('Forward! Kill! Kill!'); their supporting guns firing from above into the British ranks.

Napier continued with a splendid description of Moore's movements:

Suddenly I heard the gallop of horses, and turning, saw Moore. He came at speed, and pulled so sharp and close, he seemed to have alighted from the air; man and horse looking at the approaching foe with an intenseness that seemed to concentrate all feeling in their eyes. The sudden stop of the animal, a cream-coloured one with black tail and mane, had cast the latter streaming forwards, its ears were pushed out like horns, while its eyes flashed fire, and it snorted loudly with expanded nostrils, expressing terror, astonishment and muscular exertion. My first thought was, it will be away like the wind! But then I looked at its rider and the horse was forgotten. Thrown on its haunches, the animal came sliding and dashing the dirt up with its fore feet, thus bending the General forward almost to its neck; but his head was thrown back, and his look more keenly piercing than I ever before saw it. He glanced to the right and left, and then fixed his eyes intently on the enemy's advancing column, at the same time grasping the reins with both his hands, and pressing the horse firmly with his knees. His body thus seemed to deal with the animal while his mind was intent on the enemy, and his aspect was one of searching intenseness beyond the power of words to express. For a while he looked, and then galloped to the left, without uttering a word.

I walked to the right of my regiment, where the French fire from the village of Elvina was now very sharp, and our piquets were being driven in by the attacking column, but I soon returned to the left, for the enemy's guns were striking heavily there, and his musketry also swept down many men. Meeting Stanhope, I ordered him to the rear of the right wing, because the ground was lower; it was his place. He was tall, the shot flew high, and I thought he would be safer. Moore now returned, and I asked to let me throw our grenadiers, who were losing men fast, into the enclosures in front. 'No', he said, 'they will fire on our piquets in the village.' 'Sir, our piquets, and those of the 4th regiment also, were driven from thence, when you went to the left.' 'Were they! Then you are right. Send out your grenadiers' – and again he galloped away. Turning round, I saw Captain Clunes of the 50th, just arrived from Corunna, and said to him 'Clunes, take your grenadiers and open the ball.' He stalked forward alone, like Goliath before the Philistines, for six foot five he was in height, and of proportionate bulk and strength. His grenadiers followed, and thus the battle began on our side.

Again Sir John Moore returned, and was talking to me, when a round shot struck the ground between his horse's feet and mine. The horse leaped round, and I also turned mechanically, but Moore had forced the animal back, and asked me if I was hurt. 'No, Sir!' meanwhile, a second shot had torn off the leg of a 42nd man, who screamed horribly, and rolled about so as to excite agitation and alarm with others. The General said, 'This is nothing, my lads. Keep your ranks. Take that man away. My good fellow, don't make such a noise; we must bear these things better.' He spoke sharply, but it had a good effect, for this man's cries had made an opening in the ranks, and the men shrunk from the spot, although they had not done so when others had been hit who did not cry out. But again Moore went off, and I saw him no more.

Moore had already ordered the 42nd to advance and sent Captain Hardinge for a battalion of the Guards to protect the left flank of the 42nd; he then sent George Napier for another battalion. Thinking they were to be relieved by the Guards, the commanding officer of the light company of the 42nd began to fall back with his men but Moore checked them. 'My brave 42nd', he said, 'join your comrades, ammunition is coming and you have your bayonets.' He then shouted, 'Highlanders, remember Egypt!' and led them towards Elvina. As soon as they had driven the enemy to the bottom of the ravine, Moore directed Major Stirling, commander of the 42nd, to halt the corps and defend that position. Stirling wrote, 'Turning myself round to him when he gave the order, I saw him, at the moment, struck to the ground from off his horse.' Hardinge had just returned and George Napier set off; as he galloped to fetch the second Guards battalion he looked back to see Moore's horse give a leap as

Moore fell and then Hardinge dismount. He thought of turning back but carried on and delivered his message.

Captain Hardinge described Moore's wounding and removal from the battle ground:

I was pointing out to the General the situation of the battalion & our horses were touching, at the very moment that a cannon shot from the enemy's battery carried away his left shoulder & part of the collar bone, leaving the arm hanging from the flesh. The violence of the stroke threw him off his horse on his back; not a muscle of his face altered, nor did a sigh betray the least sensation of pain.

I dismounted and taking his hand he pressed mine forcibly casting his eyes very anxiously towards the 42nd Regiment which was holly [*sic*] engaged and his countenance expressed satisfaction when I informed him that the Regiment was advancing.

Assisted by a soldier of the 42nd he was removed a few yards behind the shelter of a wall. Colonel Graham of Balgowan & Captain Woodford, about this time came up and perceiving the state of Sir John's wounds, instantly rode off for a surgeon. The blood flowed fast, but the attempt to stop it with my sash was useless for the size of the wound.

Sir John assented to being removed in a blanket to the rear. In assisting him for that purpose his sword (hanging on the wounded side) touched his arm and became entangled with his legs. I, perceiving the inconvenience, was in the act of unbuckling it from his waist, when he said in his usual tone and manner & in a very distinct voice 'It is well as it is; I would rather it should go out of the field with me'.

He was borne by six soldiers of the 42nd & Guards, my sash supporting him in an easy posture. Observing the resolution & composition of his features, I caught at the hope that I might be mistaken in my fears of the wound being mortal and remarked that I trusted that he would be spared to us and recover. He than turned his head round and looking steadfastly at the wound for a few seconds, said 'No Hardinge, I feel that to be impossible'.

I wished to accompany him to the rear when he said 'You need not go with me. Report to General Hope that I am wounded and carried to the rear.' A surgeon of the 42nd & a spare file [of men] were ordered to conduct in case of accident their brave General to Corunna, & I hastened to report to General Hope.

On hearing of Moore's injury, Baird, who was having his own wound dressed, told his surgeons to leave him and go to Moore but he dismissed them and told them to go and attend to other soldiers. He was placed in a position of relative safety against a stone wall and visited by Surgeon McGill of the 3/1 Regiment who had been sheltering with his kit behind a nearby rock; he packed the wound after removing some pieces of lapel and some buttons before Moore was carried to his headquarters in Corunna, stopping several times on the way to observe the fighting; when they arrived he was laid on a mattress and his injuries could be seen properly. They were met by Francois, Moore's valet, who was shocked to see the wound. Moore smiled at him and said 'My friend, this is nothing.' Colonel Paul Anderson, who had served with Moore for twenty-one years, was also at headquarters when Moore was brought in and reported that although it was almost dark, Moore knew him immediately, squeezed his hand and said 'Anderson, don't leave me'.

The wound had almost removed the left arm at the shoulder joint. There had been soft tissue loss over the left chest as well. This exposed ribs and broke some. The chest wall muscles had been shredded. With such a wound, it is surprising that Moore did not bleed out more quickly, but it is probable that the tearing action of the ball would have caused the arteries to restrict down and the packing of the wound would also have slowed the bleeding.[7] Moore spoke to the surgeons while they examined the wound but was in too much pain to say much. There is no record of any analgesic being given.

Speaking at intervals, Moore managed to say to Anderson 'you know that I have always wished to die this way' and then asked 'Are the French beaten?' which he repeated to everyone who came in. 'I hope the country will do me justice. Anderson, you will see my friends as soon as you can, tell them everything. Say to my mother ...' at this point his voice failed him and he became agitated. 'Hope, Hope, I have much to say to him, but cannot get it out. Are Colonel Graham and all my aides-de-camp well?' Anderson signed to the others in the room that they should not tell Moore that Captain Burrard had been wounded. 'I have made my will and have remembered my servants. Colborne has my will, and all my papers'. When Colborne came into the room Moore spoke kindly to him, and turning to Anderson asked him to recommend Colborne for a promotion to Lieutenant Colonel; 'tell [them] it is my request ...he has been long with me, and I know him most worthy'. He then asked Colborne if the French were beaten and on being told they were, said, 'It is a great satisfaction for me to know we have beaten the French.' He asked to be remembered to Paget, adding that he was a fine fellow. After a while he said, 'I feel myself so strong, I fear I shall be long dying. It is great uneasiness. It is great pain. Everything Francois says is right, I have the greatest confidence in him.' At that point two more of his aides, Captains Percy and Stanhope came in, and after a while he said 'Stanhope, remember me to your sister (Lady Hester)', pressed Anderson's hand to his body and, after a few minutes, died. Anderson, who reported all this to Moore's brother James, said that apart from asking occasionally to be placed in an easier position, this was all Moore said.[8]

There was then some discussion on whether Moore's body should be taken home or buried at Corunna. Anderson said that he had often heard Moore say that if he died in battle he wanted to be buried where he had fallen. General Anstruther, who had died of pneumonia, had been buried the previous day on the ramparts of the Citadel, where Colonel Graham had his headquarters, and it was decided to bury Moore next to Anstruther. His body was carried from army headquarters to Graham's headquarters at midnight, and a party from the 9th Regiment dug the grave, the aides-de-camp attending the digging in turns. At 8 am some firing from the French was heard, and as the officers would have to leave if an action commenced, they buried Moore at that time. They had been unable to obtain a coffin, so Moore was buried in his uniform and wrapped in a cloak. He was lowered into his grave on the long red sashes of the four officers attending; the burial service was said by Chaplain Symons of the Brigade of Guards.

With Moore and Baird both wounded, the command devolved on Hope. The French had attacked the British line at several points, driving them out of Elvina, and continued to try to get round the British right flank but were driven back by the 95th and the 51st regiments. The French withdrew from Elvina at nightfall, slackening their fire at 5 pm; at 6 pm the firing stopped completely. At this point, both armies were still in approximately the positions at which they had started the day. French casualties were in excess of 600 killed and wounded; British casualties were never accurately reported but are thought to have been between 800 and 900. Soult intended to resume the battle in the morning, but Hope had carried out the rest of the evacuation as Moore had planned. Detailing sufficient men to keep the bivouac fires burning and to walk about in front of them so it looked as though the British were still in their positions, the rest of the men quietly withdrew to embark on the transports. At 5 am on 17 January, the last few men withdrew. The few guns which had not already been loaded onto the ships were spiked and buried.

Beresford's brigade, as part of the rear-guard, occupied the land in front of Corunna town, Hill's on the promontory behind the town. The French pushed their light troops towards the town just after 8 am, then occupied the heights of St Lucia, which commanded the harbour; however, as there was no concern that the rear guard could be forced, Hill's brigade was embarked by 3 pm. Beresford's brigade and all the remaining wounded, with the aid of the Spanish in the town, withdrew from their position soon after dark and all were embarked by 1 am on the 18th. The last brigade to leave, some 2,300 men, was in danger of being overwhelmed by the larger French force, and since the final transports were forced out of the harbour by French artillery fire on the afternoon of the 17th, took longer to embark with the aid of the navy's small boats; these could only take 500 men at a time. The townspeople helped by assisting the garrison to man and fire their guns from the ramparts, the women of the town bringing up cartridges and wads from the magazines.

The French artillery fire caused a panic among the remaining transports in the harbour and in the dash to get out there were several collisions and nine transports ran aground, drowning nine of the Royal Wagon Train. Two of these transports were hauled off by boats from the navy, but the rest had to be destroyed to prevent them falling into French hands and the navy took the last of the army on board warships, reorganising them (and provisions) once safely out in the offing. The actual destruction of the abandoned ships was done by a midshipman who had been sent on shore with a message to Admiral Hood (who was supervising the embarkation), and then went on board the stranded ships and set fire to them.[9]

Although there were several men who claimed to be the last to leave, it was actually Captain Thomas Lloyd Fletcher of the 23rd Royal Welsh Fusiliers who commanded the last of Beresford's brigades, who had that honour. His command filed through the lower gate of the city wall, then Fletcher and a corporal closed the gate and locked it; the key was stiff and it took the assistance of a bayonet through the key's ring to turn it. Fletcher then took the key from the lock and took it home with him.[10]

Chapter 15

Aftermath

With the exception of two ships which were wrecked on the way home during a wild storm, drowning 296 men, all the ships arrived home safely, although the British public, who had rarely seen troops other than when on parade or marching in full uniform from one place to another, were shocked by the poor state of most of the soldiers. Captain Seton of the Gordon Highlanders reported that he had not had a change of clothes since Lugo on 6 January and that many of his men had typhus. Most were dirty and many others were lousy, and soldiers who were billeted on civilians found they were not allowed to sleep in the beds or even sit by the fire because of the lice. The transport carrying the Royal Artillery were not allowed to land at Portsmouth but had to sail on closer to their usual quarters; their pay sergeants went on shore and bought some slop clothing, but this was soon as lousy as the old clothes.

They suffered from opthalmia, colds, neuralgia, rheumatism, minor wounds and other irritations. Colin Campbell of the 42nd Regiment had to soak his shoes in hot water before he could get them off his feet, to which they had stuck. He cut them into strips and pulled these off, sometimes taking the flesh with the leather. During the next six months 2,427 men from Spain and Portugal were admitted to hospitals in or near Portsmouth; 824 of them had 'continental fever' and 1,053 had dysentery. Over 450 of these men died in hospital.

On 13 February, the Commander-in-Chief (the Duke of York) issued a General Order that all men, on returning to their barracks, should be issued with a complete set of clothes, and that their commanding officers were to pay close attention to their health and personal cleanliness, especially of their feet. They were all to have new shoes and warm socks. He also suggested that a breakfast mess should be established in all regiments, including coffee, the price of which had recently fallen, thus making it affordable.

Following this, politicians began to look for someone to blame. The Whigs naturally blamed the Tory government, stating that the campaign was a national disaster, 'an enterprise without plan, combination or foresight and equally ill-timed and misdirected'. George Ponsonby, the leader of the opposition, called for an enquiry and, after speaking for several hours, ended by laying the blame firmly on the government, 'there is something in the Councils of England, in the application of her military force, that makes it impossible ever to place any reliance upon her military assistance'. The next speaker was Mr Tierny who lamented that Moore knew very well that he was acting under an administration which was not his friend: 'The Government's praise of Spain had led the newspapers to promise great effects. But

Moore had arrived to find his allies a heap of ruins.' He knew that if he did anything wrong he had no hope of support from the British Government. Tierny went on to say that with the exception of officers who were connected to Ministers, he 'had not heard of one [officer] returned from Corunna who did not vent execrations against the authors of their disaster'.

During the debate Canning tried to disown the campaign, laying the blame firmly on Moore, as he had done in a letter to Lord Bathurst (Secretary for War and Colonies) even before the British Army reached Corunna. 'The truth is that we have retreated before a rumour … and Moore knows it … O that we had an enterprising general with a reputation to make instead of one to save'. In the debate he said that Moore was wholly answerable for the campaign: 'glorious or distressing, admired or deplored, it was his own; he had kept the government in ignorance of his proceedings'. The truth of this last statement can be seen in the regular correspondence of Moore to Castlereagh; perhaps Canning thought Moore had failed to keep Frere informed, but even this is untrue.

Canning did later change his tune with a statement which vindicated Moore by confirming the strategy which he had followed in luring Napoleon to the north, at the same time commenting on those who quibbled over the petty details of this strategy. He ended by saying, 'If we have been obliged to quit Spain, we have left it with fresh laurels blooming on our brows … Whatever may be the fruits of Buonaparte's victories in other respects, the spirit of the Spanish nation is yet unsubdued'.

The Whigs seized on the attempts by Canning's friend John Hookham Frere and his 'friend' Charmilly to instruct Moore as being much to blame. Frere was known to be somewhat timid and anxious to please when dealing with people face to face, but used decisive and bold language in his letters to those at a distance. Lord Auckland gave his opinion on Frere's letters to Moore as being, 'Offensively and absurdly arrogant beyond all example and imagination; and in the very act of running from Madrid with all the fears of a hare before the hounds, he insists on Moore's exposing himself and his army to evident destruction; and all this in a tone of epigram and sarcasm, and self importance.' He then added, to make it clear where he thought the blame for this lay 'as if the letters had been brought cut and dry, from Downing Street'.

The Charmilly dossier, including the letters from Frere, which Ministers had tried to deny existed, finally arrived in the hands of Lord Liverpool, the leader of the Tory party in the House of Lords. Lord Grenville, after seeing them, said that Ministers were reprehensible for allowing Frere to interfere, albeit unsuccessfully, in military affairs, but mainly for trying to escape from their responsibility by transferring the blame for 'an ill-equipped and ill-conducted expedition upon General Moore'. Liverpool's final statement in the Lords commented that as a result of Moore's advance, Buonaparte had had to abandon his previous plans for southern Spain, an advance 'which was as a spontaneous result of his own free judgement [and] had saved Spain'.

The motion for an enquiry was narrowly defeated, but Moore still had enemies. General John Stuart's advance at the head of the foreign brigade against Menou at

Alexandria had certainly contributed to the success of the battle but not to the extent that he had won it himself. Moore was clearly the hero of that battle, and Stuart's jealousy rankled for ever after, to the extent that he refused to serve with Moore.

And Charles Stewart, who Moore had trusted to give the true story of the retreat, complained extensively to his circle of friends that he thought Moore 'wanted confidence in himself – he underrated the qualities of his own troops and greatly overrated those of his adversary'.

Stewart was not the only officer who thought he knew better than Moore. Colonel Digby Hamilton wrote from Portsmouth shortly after he arrived there to Lieutenant General Browning, Quartermaster General to the forces:

Having with extreme regret witnessed the great irregularity and disorder that unfortunately, but too generally pervaded the British army during the retreat from Sahagun to Corunna, I am induced to attempt to explain the causes which led to such baneful effects, and to submit for your consideration such remedies as I conceive would materially tend to prevent a recurrance of such evils in any situation and under any possible circumstances in which the army might, at any future period be placed.

There were, he thought, three main causes: first, the 'mal-arrangements' of the commissariat in not providing provisions at the pre-arranged halting points, which gave the soldiers an excuse for plundering; secondly, the lack of adequate transport for the baggage; and thirdly, the 'immense' number of women with the troops. There was, he said, an organised system of men quitting the ranks on the pretext of fatigue, but actually to plunder, groups doing this on alternate days.

He believed that a high-ranking officer should be appointed to 'enforce regularity in the movement of the sick, the baggage and the followers', this officer, taking his orders direct from the Commander-in-Chief, should have control of all the wheeled transport. A branch of the Provost Marshall's department should march with each column of baggage, to make immediate examples of stragglers and plunderers.

The maximum weight of baggage allowed to each officer, according to his rank, should be published in the general orders, and rigidly enforced. Perhaps it would be a good idea to have regulation sized trunks provided for each rank, made to fit on pack saddles.

He also thought that much of the problem of sore feet caused by dirt getting into shoes, or shoes being pulled off by heavy clay, could be avoided by providing 'the same kind of <u>high</u> shoe worn by the staff corps'.

Charles Boothby remarked, '[Sir John Moore] after devoting his life to the service of his country, is praised by some and blamed by others. I know the latter to be ignorant, but consequently the most talkative, and your catchpenny Generals come forward and tell you how they could have done better. All this makes me sick.'[1]

Although many of the stories recounted by survivors of the retreat were undoubtedly true, others were severely embroidered if not purely melodramatic including those referring to dead mothers with babies lying at the side of the road. Colborne wrote to his friend Miss Townsend, 'What unheard of difficulties, hardships and labours! Living on turnips! No sleep! All of this frightens Mama, but do not believe the quarter of what you hear. John Bull is as fond of the marvellous as an Italian or a Spaniard.' James Moore was a staunch defender of his brother's reputation, flying to his defence in writing whenever he thought it was being maligned, and writing two books: *The Life of Lieutenant-General Sir John Moore, K.B.* and *Narrative of the Campaign of the British Army in Spain, commanded by H. E. Lieutenant-General Sir John Moore, K.B.*

There were others who took advantage of Moore's posthumous fame, including Thomas Lawrence who had painted portraits of John and Graham Moore, who found himself in financial difficulties at that time as during most of his life, sought to jump on the bandwagon by producing engravings of his portrait of Moore. He wrote to Lieutenant General Brownrigg asking to borrow his copy of Moore's portrait to have this engraving made, feeling sure, he said, that Brownrigg would prefer this to the results produced by those 'mere publishers of prints, with whom to profit by the moment is the sole motive'.

After the immediate controversy about Moore's conduct of the campaign in the Peninsula, the formal histories took over. Walter Scott thought that Moore was 'a general who is always looking over his shoulder, and more intent on saving his own army than on doing the service on which he is sent'. He thought Wellesley would have done a better job: 'Had [he] been there, the battle of Corunna would have been fought and won at Somosierra, and the ranks of the victors would have been reinforced by the population of Madrid.' One wonders where Scott came by this opinion, for it does not match the facts.[2] William Napier's *History of the Peninsular War* reflects Napier's heroic view of Moore; but Sir Charles Oman, who disliked Napier, automatically took the opposite view: a not untypical demonstration of the way many historians seem primarily concerned with scoring points off each other. One of the features of Moore's campaign which were endlessly argued was the matter of splitting his army and sending it by different routes. Oman thought Moore's judgement was faulty in his choice of route for the artillery, using somewhat dubious arguments to support this view; Sir Frederick Maurice showed that Moore chose the best possible routes under the circumstances.[3] In fact, the choice of roads had no effect on subsequent events.

The other major point of controversy was the length of time Moore spent at Salamanca, seen by some as indecisiveness. In fact, he could not move until his army was united, and until he had knowledge of Napoleon's movements. His main objective at that time was to find and attack Napoleon's supply lines; by the time that information was available, his army was united and ready to move on.

Several historians have stated that Moore's big mistake was his decision to march his army up through Portugal and Spain to the north, rather than re-embark them at Lisbon and sail round to one of the ports on the northern coast of Spain. There are three reasons for this decision: the first being the problematic number of available transports, a great number of which were engaged in repatriating Junot's army to France. Second was the practicality of re-embarking his troops and their stores and baggage. Harbour space was limited and using boats to take troops out to ships through the surf at other places was equally risky; ships en route to Santander would also have been vulnerable to the seasonal gales which batter the western coast of Portugal and Spain and the Bay of Biscay; Moore had already experienced himself that in the abortive attempt to land at Cadiz in 1800, and the British nation knew what had happened to the Allied fleet at Trafalgar the day after the battle in October 1805. Instead of risking the loss of ships and men by sailing to Santander, let alone their arrival with the men in a weakened state from the voyage, he chose to go overland, bringing his troops up to a state of fitness.

But all this is nit-picking by those who do not want to lay the blame where serious consultation of the available original documents shows that blame to lie: in the inexperience and poor judgement of the British government where the Spanish nation and its leaders were concerned, and the intransigence and unwarranted boastfulness of the Spanish generals who failed to back up their promises.[4]

This inability of the British government has been neatly encapsulated by Barbara Tuchman, writing of the:

Persistent gap between observers in the field and policy-makers in the capital. When information is relayed to policy-makers, they respond in terms of what is already inside their heads and consequently make policy less to fit the facts than to fit the notions and intentions formed out of the mental baggage that has accumulated in their minds since childhood.[5]

The modern historian J.M. Black underlines this by writing of 'the implication that the European military force was "fit" for its task and largely challenged by environmental considerations'.[6]

Soult finally entered Corunna on 18 January, when the inhabitants surrendered. He asked where Moore was buried and had a rough plinth erected 'to mark the spot where so worthy an adversary lay'. Romagna later had the body moved to what he considered a more prominent location, on the south-west side of the citadel. Moore's body was reburied for the second time in early 1811, and in 1834 the Military Governor of Corunna had a formal walled garden laid out round the tomb. On marble tablets on the wall are the poem by Charles Wolfe, and another, much longer, in the local Gallego language.

One letter which did not reach Moore, because it was written in London on 11 January 1809 and did not get to Spain until after Moore was dead, was from Castlereagh. It certainly would have pleased him. It started by praising the actions of the cavalry, and went on to say that the King still wanted a British force in the south of Spain if this were possible. If Moore did manage to get into Portugal, Cradock had been ordered to hand over all his troops to Moore, thus making him Commander-in-Chief of all the forces in Spain and Portugal.

Chapter 16

Character Assessment

On 1 February 1809 the Duke of York issued a General Order:

> The benefits derived to an army from the example of a distinguished Commander do not terminate at his death; his virtues live in the recollection of his associates, and his fame remains the strongest incentive to great and glorious actions.

In this view, the Commander-in-Chief, amidst the deep and universal regret which the death of Lieutenant-General Sir John Moore has occasioned, recalls to the troops the Military career of that illustrious Officer, for their instruction and imitation.

Sir John Moore, from his youth, embraced the profession with feelings and sentiments of a soldier; he felt that a perfect knowledge and an exact performance of the humble, but important, duties of a Subaltern Officer are the best foundations for subsequent military fame; and his ardent mind, while it looked forward to those brilliant achievements for which it was formed, applied itself with energy and exemplary assiduity to the duties of that station. In the school of regimental duty, he obtained that correct knowledge of his profession so essential to the proper direction of the gallant spirit of the soldier; and he was enabled to establish a characteristic order and regularity of conduct, because the troops found in their leader a striking example of the discipline which he enforced on others.

Having risen to command, he signalized his name in the West Indies, in Holland and in Egypt. The unremitting attention with which he devoted himself to the duties of every branch of his profession obtained him the confidence of Sir Ralph Abercromby; and he became the companion in arms of that illustrious officer, who fell at the head of his victorious troops, in an action which maintained our natural superiority over the arms of France.

Thus Sir John Moore at an early period obtained, with general approbation, that conspicuous station in which he gloriously terminated his useful and honourable life.

In a military character, obtained amidst the dangers of climate, the privations incident to service, and the sufferings of repeated wounds, it is difficult to select any one point as a preferable subject for praise: it exhibits, however, one feature so particularly characteristic of the man, and so important to the best interests of the service, that the Commander-in-chief is pleased to mark it with his peculiar approbation.

The life of Sir John Moore was spent among the troops. During the season of repose his time was devoted to the care and instruction of the Officer and Soldier; in war he courted service in every quarter of the globe. Regardless of personal considerations, he esteemed that to which his Country called him the post of honour, and by his undaunted spirit and unconquerable perseverance, he pointed the way to victory.

His Country, the object of his last solicitude, will rear a Monument to his lamented memory, and the Commander-in-Chief feels he is paying the best tribute to his fame by this holding him forth as an example to the Army.

The historian J.W. Fortescue had this to say on Moore: '[he] was a man of clear insight into the heart of things, of a high disdain for charlatans, and of a critical faculty which was but too keen … who would put hard questions with a bright searching eye, and who would combat hollow arguments with unsparing contempt'.

And Moore's contemporaries said:

his keen, penetrating eye seemed to look through his brain. The lay of his countenance was very remarkable; expressing alike and without effort, the open, familiar bantering humour with which he greeted those he esteemed and the chilling contempt with which he visited the objects of his dislike. He was thoroughly honourable, just and generous; far above all sordid motives and hardly to be swayed by any person from what he felt to be his duty. When speaking of him as a soldier, it was superfluous to touch upon his intrepidity, of which there was but too evident proof, afforded by the many wounds which he received in battle. As a commander, Moore excelled all others I have seen or known of, in teaching both officers and men their several duties. [Henry Bunbury]

His was the fire that warmed the coldest nature, and urged all who came in contact with him onward on the path of glory along which he strode so mightily himself. No man with a spark of enthusiasm could resist the influence of [Moore's] great aspirings, his fine presence, his ardent, penetrating genius … [Charles Napier]

… the complete command he possessed over his temper qualified him peculiarly for disciplining troops. Towards the officers under his command his conduct was friendly, yet firm; towards the soldiers, kind but strict, and to both impartially just. [James Carrick Moore]

These are all the opinions of those who knew Moore. Today, we can only attempt to read his character from his writings, and even these are incomplete. Although he was a great letter writer, with a wide circle of friends, it is clear that we lack much of this correspondence. The correspondence that has survived is that between him and Gordon; those letters have been preserved because Gordon was also a military contact; some of those letters have been preserved in official War Office files and there is a big tranche of correspondence between the two men at the British Library. There are no available letters between Moore and his closest friend Paul Anderson, probably because Anderson was with him most of the time. There were probably also a lot more letters to his family which have not survived, so we are left with correspondence which is almost exclusively of a military nature, and his war journals.

254 Sir John Moore

Many people, especially those who write their memoirs long after the events they portray, tend to embroider them to give a picture of the person they want others to see. Moore's letters and journals do not come across that way; they seem to be genuine immediate reactions to the situation. There have been a few editings in the published versions of his journals, to suit the attitudes of the day. Caroline Napier (neé Fox), who copied Moore's journals for her husband William, did this in several places, most notably Moore's opinion of Maria Carolina (Queen of the Two Sicilies) substituting 'woman' for Moore's original 'She is a violent wicked bitch'.

It is often the case with documents kept by the families of the original writer, that those letters which express unflattering views of prominent people are destroyed. Certainly James Moore, the staunch defender of his brother, could have done this, which would explain some of the gaps in the letters home.

The historian Barbara Tuchman wrote, 'Selection is what determines the ultimate product', and said that was why she only used material from primary sources (i.e. original letters and diaries). She found secondary sources (i.e. books written after the event) useful reading at the start of a project to outline the general scheme of what happened but did not take notes from them as she did not wish to rewrite someone else's book, nor accept that what the writer of those books chose as material was all that existed and thus missing other material.[1]

There is one major biography of Moore by Carola Oman which is more fiction than fact, often reporting things which do not appear in any of the original sources and thus can only come from the author's imagination. This biographer, although using much original material, tended to rely on the hagiographic books published before her, and her book has unfortunately become one of the source documents for those who have written after her. This is why this author has, like Tuchman, and with only one major exception, used only original material.[2]

The earliest of this was letters from his father and himself to his mother when they were on the Continent with the young Duke of Hamilton. What comes across from these letters is that the lad was quite childish, at least until his father's influence overrode that of his mother. In his earliest letters home, his writing was childish and his father had to rule lines on the paper for him.

Although he was a lively boy with a keen sense of adventure which got him into trouble a couple of times, he was a moral boy, refusing to abandon an invitation from some impoverished friends when another invitation came from a higher social contact. He learned early on from his father that he could not hope to be the equal of the aristocrats and royalty whom he met on his travels, and although this is never mentioned, it was probably at this time that he learned to insist on such status as he did have. This would explain the curious incident with Castlereagh when Moore returned from Sweden. Quite why Castlereagh reacted in the way he did is another matter, perhaps he was overbusy with preparations for the Peninsular expedition, or perhaps he did not care to be told how he should behave by someone who he saw as his social inferior.

Moore was always anxious to please his father, and even more so when something occurred which he thought his father might disapprove of; this can be seen in his letters when he was sent home from Corsica. He was strongly attached to all his family, and was often consulted by them on matters of importance. He does not appear to have been religious, never mentioning attending church and only mentioning God a couple of times in passing.[3] He didn't seem to use bad language. He drank little, and was an abstemious eater (although after his mother sent him some mince pies for Christmas told her that he thought they were the best he had ever tasted, and asked for the recipe); after one early experience he didn't gamble. He liked to dance and to tour the countryside when opportunity permitted; from this, and from his other encounters with the inhabitants of whatever country he was in, usually concluded that they were fine people but badly governed and led. This may have been because all ranks of people met him with courtesy rather than anything which might have given a deep insight into their characters; he was a little naive to think that putting better leaders over them would solve all problems, especially in those countries which were deeply religious and where the population had little experience of thinking for themselves.

He was an enthusiastic reader, often asking his 'family' of staff officers if they had brought him any books, and of course he read his father's books. Certainly when at Shorncliffe, if not elsewhere, he spent his winter evenings reading; he read little fiction, preferring Shakespeare and the poems of Robert Burns, as well as a large selection of works on his profession of arms. These were mostly by foreign officers and in French or German; he regretted that few British officers had written such useful books.

He had a keen sense of humour and liked to play minor jokes on the young officers on his staff, on one occasion creeping up behind one who was walking down the street, clapping a hand on his shoulder and announcing that he had caught him out looking at ugly women.

His relationships with women, as with the rest of his private social life, are rarely mentioned. He did receive a dog as a gift from 'a lady' while in Ireland, which suggests a deeper relationship than a mere passing friendship. He did attend several dances or balls when in a position to do so, and his mother seems to have tried some match-making but he was rather picky: of one young lady he remarked that while she was the belle of the ball, it was a pity about her teeth, and of another that although she was fat no doubt some gentleman would find her acceptable. Other than that, all we have is his relationships with Lady Hester Stanhope and Caroline Fox.

With a very few exceptions, he was loved by all who served with him, officers and men, and considered by his professional peers as a brilliant trainer of men. This last has not escaped the notice of historians: it is difficult to find a book on the Napoleonic wars which does not have several flattering mentions of his abilities, both as a trainer and leader of men. He ensured that his troops were cared for as well as possible, but insisted on proper discipline; believing that poor discipline was the fault of regimental officers, he did not hesitate to replace those he deemed incapable of doing their job. When it came to action, he believed in leading from the front and was always in the thick of any battle, and as a result was frequently wounded. He also preferred to live with his men, being perfectly prepared to sleep on the ground in his cloak rather than seek the better accommodation to which his rank entitled him.

With such a multitude of good points, it is also necessary to look at his bad points as well. Some of his critics have declared him to be indecisive (based on his prolonged stay at Salamanca), others think he was depressive. Certainly he was very concerned with how others might see his actions, especially in Corsica, Sicily and Spain, and this does come across in his writings. He was also rather impatient of being inactive, fussing to do something else at times when the immediate action was over and his role became more administrative than military; this was always attached to his desires to serve his country and advance his career. Finally he was seen by some as acerbic, this cannot be denied, but it was only towards people who he thought stupid or ungentlemanly. He did not suffer fools gladly, and did not hesitate to let them know it.

A controversial hero he might have been, but he was clearly usually a pleasant person, and he can best be summed up with a brief description which would have pleased him – he was a soldier, dedicated to his profession.

Appendix I

Army Structure During the Napoleonic Wars

During the Georgian period, there was no standing British Army. There were a few permanent regiments, such as the Guards and Royal Artillery, but otherwise there were numerous private regiments which could be called on in times of conflict. With the exception of the Royal Artillery and the Royal Engineers, which were run by the Board of Ordnance's Ordnance Corps, and where initial appointment and promotion came on acquiring the necessary level of expertise, these regiments were run by, and actually belonged to, their colonel, being kept at low numbers until needed for war, when they made recruiting drives for rank and file. Before 1750, regiments were known by the names of their founders, after this they were given numbers according to seniority of formation.

Officers in these regiments had to purchase their position, from the colonel when the regiment was first formed, and then from the officer who was vacating that rank. When a senior officer moved up a rank, everyone below him was also able to move up if they could find the funds, and assuming that they were acceptable to their seniors. It was not unknown for the sequence of officers getting together to fund the senior's 'retirement' so they could all move up a step. The cost of commissions varied according to rank and to the status of the regiment; rank in fashionable regiments cost more. Those who came in from the outside as ensigns had to find the whole purchase price, all others only had to find the difference between their current and new ranks. Once the new appointee was approved by the regiment, the financial transactions were handled by their agents. A few officers were promoted for merit and good service in the field by the commander-in-chief with Horse Guards approval, but still had to purchase the new rank. Otherwise, promotion was dependent on seniority; it normally took about twenty-four years to get to lieutenant colonel.[*]

General officers were appointed from the army Commander-in-Chief at Horse Guards; Brigadier General was a brevet rank, awarded for a specific campaign only, high general ranks were permanent. When a campaign was organised, the senior general had a certain amount of choice, first in the general officers beneath him, and second in the regiments he was to command.

---

[*] My thanks to Mick Crumplin and Nick Lipscombe for assistance with these details.

Appendix II

Sir John Moore's Will

Sir John Moore wrote his will[*] while on his way out to Portugal on HMS *Audacious*, it was dated 18 August 1808.

Starting 'It is impossible to foresee what may befall me upon the service in which I am going. I take the opportunity at sea and whilst I have little else to do', he made his brothers James and Francis his executors and attached a list of his property: £20,000 in consols; £1,000 Bond with Scott White giving 5 per cent annually; £29.10.0 left to him by his father and some houses and land in Glasgow, plus a fund in the hands of Messrs Drummond & Co.

There were some small bequests: £300 to Henry Hamilton, and each of the children of his brother Frances. To his servant François, £500 and all his personal clothing, to include those with him and those left in England, as well as the wages owing to him. 'Not too much to a man who has served me so long and so faithfully' he added. To General Oakes the sword given to him by officers commanding the regiments in Egypt; to his brother James his gold watch and chain and his table linen. To his brother Graham his books and maps (most of these were with David Dundas in Chelsea); and to Mrs Harris (whom he described as his sister) a set of tea china.

He left his sister Jane £10,000, with the remainder of his estate to his mother.

---

[*] TNA PROB 11/1493.

Charles Wolfe's Poem 'The Burial of Sir John Moore at Corunna'

Charle's Wolfe (1791–1823) was a young priest of the Church of Ireland, who wrote this poem after reading Robert Southey's version of the events in the Peninsula. This poem was first published in the *Newry Telegraph* in April 1817 but was little known until Byron brought it to the attention of the public after Wolfe's death. It was then reproduced in many anthologies during the nineteenth and twentieth centuries, and learned by heart (and frequently misquoted) by several generations of schoolboys. It was much parodied, including one rather rude poem entitled 'The Burial of Sir John Thomas'.

William McGonagall also wrote 'The Battle of Corunna' – a long poem in his usual rambling style and painful rhyming, making much play on the use of the bayonet and ending with:

> Success to the British Army wherever they go
> For seldom they have failed to conquer the foe
> Long may the Highlanders be able to make the foe reel
> By giving them an inch or two of cold steel*

Although there are several inaccuracies in Wolfe's poem, it is tremendously evocative (and was one of the things which inspired this author to write about Sir John Moore).

The Burial of Sir John Moore at Corunna

> Not a drum was heard, nor a funeral note,
> As his corse to the ramparts we hurried;
> Not a soldier discharged his farewell shot
> O'er the grave where our hero we buried.
>
> We buried him darkly at dead of night,
> The sods with our bayonets turning;
> By the struggling moonbeam's misty light
> And the lanthorn dimly burning.
>
> No useless coffin enclosed his breast,
> Nor in sheet nor in shroud we wound him;
> But he lay like a warrior taking his rest
> With his martial cloak around him.

---

* The full text of this poem can be seen at www.poemhunter.com/poem/the-battle-of-Corunna/.

Few and short were the prayers we said,
And we spoke not a word of sorrow;
But we steadfastly gazed on the face that was dead,
And we bitterly thought of the morrow.

We thought, as we hollowed his narrow bed
And smoothed down his lonely pillow,
That the foe and the stranger would tread o'er his head,
And we far away on the billow!

Lightly they'll talk of the spirit that's gone
And o'er his cold ashes upbraid him, –
But little he'll reck, if they let him sleep on
In the grave where a Briton has laid him.

But half of our heavy task was done
When the clock struck the hour for retiring:
And we heard the distant and random gun
That the foe was sullenly firing.

Slowly and sadly we laid him down,
From the field of his fame fresh and gory;
We carved not a line, and we raised not a stone,
But left him alone with his glory.

Appendix IV

Sir John Moore's Letter, Corunna, 13 January 1809

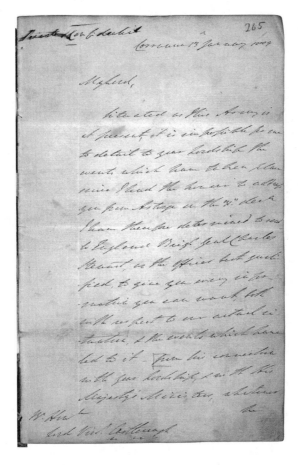

Private and confidential   Corunna 13th January 1809

My Lord,

Situated as this army is at present, it is impossible for me to detail to your Lordship the events which have taken place, since I had the honour to address you from Astorga on the 31st decer. I have therefore determined to send to England Brig-Genl Charles Stewart, as the officer best qualified to give you every information you can want, both with respect to our actual situation, and the events which have led to it. from his connection with your Lordship, and with His Majesty's Ministers, whatever
he

The Honble Lord Vsct Castlereagh

he relates, is most likely to be believed. He is a man in whose honour I have the most perfect reliance – he is incapable of stating anything but the truth, and it is the truth which at all times I wish to convey to your Lordship, and to the King's Government.

Your Lordship knows that had I followed my own opinion as a military man, I should have retired with the Army from Salamanca. The Spanish armies were then beaten, there was no Spanish force to which we could unite; and from the character of the Government, and the disposition

of

of the inhabitants, I was satisfied that no efforts would be made, to aid us, or to favour the cause in which they were engaged. I was sensible however that the apathy and indifference of the Spaniards would never have been believed; that had the British been withdrawn, the loss of the cause would have been imputed to their retreat; and it was necessary to risk this army to convince the people of England, as well as the rest of Europe, that the Spaniards had neither the power nor the inclination to make any efforts for themselves. It was for this reason that I made the march to Sahagun – as a diversion it succeeded: I brought the whole disposable

force

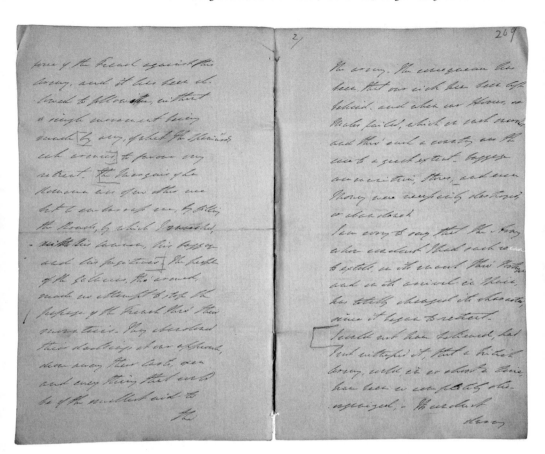

force of the French against this army, and it has been allowed to follow it, without a single movement being made by any of what the Spaniards call armies to favour my retreat. The Marquis of La Romagna was of no other use but to embarrass me, by filling the roads, by which I marched, with his cannon, his baggage and his fugitives.

The people of the Galicias, tho' armed, made no attempt to stop the passage of the French thro' their mountains. They abandoned their dwellings at our approach, drove away their carts, oxen, and everything that could be of the smallest aid to

the

the army. The consequence has been, that our sick have been left behind. and when our Horses and Mules failed, which on such marches and thro' such a country was the case to a great extent - baggage ammunition, stores, and even Money were necessarily destroyed, or abandoned.

I am sorry to say that the army, whose conduct I had such reason to extol on its march thro' Portugal, and on its arrival in Spain, has totally changed its character, since it began to retreat.

I could not have believed, had I not witnessed it, that a British Army, could, in so short a time, have been so completely disorganised. Its conduct

during

during the late marches has been infamous beyond belief.

I can say nothing in its favour, but that when there was a prospect of fighting the enemy – the men were then orderly, & seemed pleased, and determined to do their duty – in front of Villafranca the French came up with the Reserve, with which I was covering the Retreat of the Army. They attacked it at Cacabelos. I retired, covered by the 95th Regt, and marched that night to Herrerias, and thence to Nogales and Lugo, where I have ordered the different divisions which preceded, to halt, and collect. at Lugo the French again

came

came up with us, they attacked our advanced posts on the 6th and seventh, and were repulsed in both attempts with little loss on our side.

I heard from the Prisoners taken, that three divisions of the French Army commanded by Marshall Soult were come up, I therefore expected to be attacked in the morning of the 8th. It was my wish to come to that issue, I had perfect confidence in the valour of the Troops, and it was only by crippling the Enemy that we could hope, either to retreat, or to embark unmolested – I made every preparation to receive the attack and drew out the Army in the morning to offer battle. This was not Marshal Soult's object

He

He either did not think himself sufficiently strong, or he wished to play a surer game by attacking us, on our march, or during our embarkation. The Country was intersected, & his position too strong for me to attack with an inferior force. The want of provisions would not enable me to wait longer. I marched that night, and in two forced marches, bivouacing for six or eight hours in the rain, I reached Betanzos on the 10th inst. The stragglers of the Army amounted to many thousand, occasioned partly by the length of the marches, which in bad weather, many men were

unable

unable to support. The want of shoes, hundreds being barefoot, and many left their ranks who had not so good an excuse but from a desire to plunder. As the Army was followed by the French Cavalry, a great number of the above descriptions fell into their hands.

At Lugo I was sensible of the impossibility of reaching Vigo, which was at too great a distance, and offered no advantages to embark in the face of the Enemy. My intention then was to have retreated to the Peninsula of Betanzos; where I hoped to find a position to cover the embarkation of the Army in Ares or Rodes Bays

but

[handwritten facsimile of letter]

but having sent an officer to reconnoitre it, by his report I was determined to prefer this place. I gave notice to the Admiral of my intention, and begged that the Transports might be brought to Corunna. Had I found them here on my arrival on the 11th, the embarkation would have been easily effected, for I had gained several marches on the French. They have now come up with us, The transports are not arrived, my position in front of this place is a very bad one; and this place if I am forced to retire into it, is commanded within musket-shot; and the harbour will be so commanded by cannon on the

coast

coast that no ship will be able to lay in it. In short, my Lord, Genl Stewart will inform you how critical our situation is. It has been recommended to me, to make a proposal to the Enemy, to induce him to allow us to embark quietly in which case he gets us out of the country soon, and this place with its stores etc. complete, that, otherwise, we have it in our power to make a long defence, which must ensure the destruction of the Town. I am averse to make any such proposal and am exceedingly doubtful if it would be attended with any good effect – but whatever I resolve on this head, I hope your Lordship

will

will rest assured, that I shall accept no terms, that are in the least dishonourable to the Army, or to the Country.

I find I have been led into greater length, and more detail than I thought I should have had time for; I have written under interruptions, and with my mind much occupied with other matters. My letter written so carelessly, can only be considered as Private. when I have more leisure I shall write more correctly. In the mean time I rely on Genl Stewart for giving your Lordship the information & detail which I have omitted. I should regret his absence, for his services have been very distinguished

but

but the state of his eyes makes it impossible for him to serve, and this country is not one in which Cavalry can be of much use. If I succeed in embarking the Army, I shall send it to England - it is quite unfit for further service until it has been refitted, which can best be done there – and I cannot think, after what has transpired, that there can be any intention of sending a British force again into Spain.

I have the honour to remain
My Lord
Your Lordship's
Faithful & Obedient
Servant
John Moore.[*]

---

[*] Reproduced with the permission of The National Archives, from WO 1/236.

Notes

Chapter 1

1. There was a history of tuberculosis in the Duchess' family, the Gunnings.
2. Carola Oman, *Sir John Moore* (London, 1953), pp. 5–6, citing *Intimate Society Letters of the Eighteenth Century*, ed. John, Duke of Argyle (1910) and *Selection of the Family Papers preserved at Caldwell* (Maitland Club, 1854), Vol. 71, iii, pp. 192–4.
3. Possession of Minorca changed several times during the eighteenth century until it was finally ceded to Spain in the terms of the Peace of Amiens.
4. Fortescue says there were nineteen armed ships, Moore said forty altogether, eighteen of which were armed, the rest carrying troops and equipment. J.W. Fortescue, *History of the British Army*, 13 vols (London, 1899–1930) (hereafter Fortescue, *History*), Vol. III, pp. 288–9.
5. There seems to be a gap in Jack's correspondence home; perhaps a batch of letters has been lost.
6. All other references in this chapter have been taken from Dr Moore's and his son's letters home, either at British Library (hereafter BL), Add Mss 57321, or in James Carrick Moore, *The Life of Lieutenant-General Sir John Moore K.B.* (London, 1834) (hereafter James Moore, *Life*).

Chapter 2

1. Desmond Gregory, *The Ungovernable Rock: A History of the Anglo-Corsican kingdom and its role in Britain's Mediterranean strategy during the Revolutionary War (1793–1797)* (London, 1985), passim.
2. Sir Nicholas Harris Nicolas, *The Dispatches and Letters of Vice Admiral Lord Horatio Nelson* (London, 1844) (hereafter *Nicolas*), Vol. I, p. 373.
3. *Ibid.*, p. 380.
4. With the exception of the above, details for this chapter have been taken from Moore's letters (BL Add Mss 57320 and 57321) his journals (BL Add Mss 57324 and 57325), and Fortescue, *History*, Vol. IV, Pt I.

Chapter 3

1. Countess of Minto (ed.), *Life and Letters of Sir Gilbert Elliot, First Earl of Minto* (London, 1874), Vol. II, pp. 235–6.
2. Adhesive 'plaisters' (plasters) were used as an alternative to stitches. Strong linen or cotton strips were cut and spread with a mixture of white lead (i.e. lead monoxide), olive oil and lard shortly before use. I am grateful to Mick Crumplin for this detail.
3. N.A.M. Rodger, *The Command of the Ocean* (London, 2004), p. 433.
4. With the exception of the above, details for this chapter have been taken from Moore's letters (BL Add Mss 57320 and 57321) and his journals (BL Add Mss 57324 and 57325) and Fortescue, *History*, Vol. IV, Pt I, pp. 180–99.

Chapter 4

1. Michael Duffy, *Soldiers, Sugar and Seapower* (hereafter Duffy, *Soldiers*) (Oxford, 1987); Mathew Parker, *The Sugar Barons: Family, Corruption, Empire and War* (London, 2011).
2. Duffy, *Soldiers*, p. 203.

3. *Ibid.*, pp. 54–5, 108–113; WO 1/84, ff. 241–84, 307–15.
4. Abercromby's name is often spelled Abercrombie; however, in his own letters he used the 'y' ending, so that is used here: WO 1/85, passim.
5. This is not an error, a number of East Indiaman were hired as transports for the West Indies campaign.
6. Fortescue, *History*, Vol. IV, Pt I, p. 489.
7. Although not politically correct these days, this and the alternative 'negro' were the terms in use at that time, so I have not altered them.
8. Bark refers to the fact that quinine occurs naturally in the bark of the cinchona tree.
9. In addition to the sources listed above, material for this chapter was taken from: BL Add Mss 57325, 57326, 57327 (Journals), 57320 (letters from Moore to family) and 57546 (letters from Moore at St Lucia to Sir Ralph Abercromby and General Graham).

Chapter 5
1. Tom Wareham, *Frigate Commander* (London, 2004), pp. 165–9.
2. Other information for this chapter has been taken from BL Add Mss 57327, 57328, 57329 (Journals) and 57320 (Letters from Moore to his family), Carrick Moore, *Life*, Vol. II, pp. 334–56; Fortescue, *History*, Vol. 4, Pt 1, pp. 589–98.

Chapter 6
1. Fortescue, *History*, Vol. 4, Pt 2, pp. 684–7.
2. The National Archives (hereafter TNA), War Office document WO 6/20, ff. 137–54.
3. Other information for this chapter has been taken from BL Add Mss 57329 (Journal); 57320 (Letters from Moore to his family), Carrick Moore, *Life*, Vol. II, pp. 251, 356–7; Fortescue, *History*, Vol. 4 Pt 1, pp. 84–113, Vol. 4, Pt 2, pp. 564–7, 671, 688–9; Henry Bunbury, *Narratives of Some Passages in the Great War with France* (London, 1854, facs. edn 2008) (hereafter Bunbury, *Narratives*), pp. ix–xxiv, 2–56, especially 37–56 for Bunbury's opinion of the whole campaign.

Chapter 7
1. Rodger, *Command*, p. 466.
2. Piers Mackesy, 'Most Sadly Bitched: the British Cadiz Expedition of 1800', *Les empires en guerre et paix 1793–1860* (Conference, Portsmouth, 1988), pp. 41–52; Piers Mackesy, 'Cadiz expedition', quoting (p. 41) Lord Cornwallis, State Papers SpP IV, ff. 136–47; Piers Mackesy, *British Victory in Egypt: The End of Napoleon's Conquest* (London, 1995), passim.
3. The Order of St John, the Knights of Malta.
4. Buonaparte had invaded and taken the island in 1798, while en route to Egypt.
5. TNA FO 78/31. 78/31, Elgin to Grenville, Elgin to Abercromby.
6. TNA, WO1/345, Abercromby to Dundas, 21 January 1801.
7. These instuctions were issued on 24 January 1801. Bunbury, *Narratives*, pp. 157–9.
8. These instuctions were issued on 16 February 1801. *Ibid.*, pp. 159–61.
9. Other information for this and the next chapter has been taken from BL Add Mss 57329, 57330 (Journals); 57320 (Letters from Moore to his family), Carrick Moore, *Life*, pp. 368–72; Fortescue, *History*, Vol. 4, Pt 2, pp. 819–23, 827, 832–41, 852, 855; Bunbury, *Narratives*, pp. 83–168; TNA ADM 1/403-4, Keith's despatches to Admiralty, London.

Chapter 8
1. TNA, WO 1/345, Abercromby's report to Dundas, 16 March 1801.
2. HMC Report on the manuscripts of J.B. Fortescue Esq., preserved at Dropmore, Vol. VI, pp. 469–72, Moore to his father from camp at Alexandria, 16 March 1801.
3. Moore refers to Algam as El Kam.
4. A lodgement is the occupation and holding of a position within enemy lines, and the fortifications made to retain it.

Chapter 9
1. Brighton was then known then as Brighthelmstone.
2. It was not until Victorian times that this rifle became known as 'the Baker rifle'; before that it was just known as the British Infantry Rifle. Howard I. Blackmore, *British Military Firearms, 1650–1850* (London, 1962).
3. These include General Dundas, *Rules and Regulations*, simplified by Captain John Cross in *A System of Drill* and *Manoeuvres*, Baron Francis de Rottenburg, *Regulations for the exercise of Riflemen*, expanded by Colonel Neil Campbell, *Instructions for Light Infantry and Riflemen*, and Colonel Coote Manningham, *Regulations for the Exercise of Riflemen*, Robert Jackson, *A Systematic View of the Formations, Discipline and Economy of Armies*, and the regulations of the 95th regiment. Also J.F.C. Fuller, *British Light Infantry in the eighteenth century* (London, 1925) and J.F.C. Fuller, *Sir John Moore's System of Training* (London, 1925).
4. Rodger, *Command*, pp. 529–30.
5. See www.royalmilitarycanal.com/pages/history.asp for more detail.
6. It is often suggested that it was the Battle of Trafalgar, 21 October 1805, which made Bonaparte abandon the idea of invading England, but he moved the Grande Armée further into Europe in September where he won the Battle of Austerlitz at the beginning of December.
7. Martin Armstrong, *Lady Hester Stanhope* (Bath, 1928); C.L. Meryon (ed.), *The Memoirs of Lady Hester Stanhope* (London, 1845).
8. Other information for this chapter has been taken from: Tom Wareham, *Frigate Commander* (London, 2004); BL 57321 (letters from Moore); Cambridge University Library Add 9303 (Graham Moore's journals); Cambridge University Library Add 9340 (John Moore's letter book at Sandgate 1803), Carrick Moore, *Life*, passim; BL Add Mss 49482-49489 (Moore letters to Gordon).

Chapter 10
1. Rodger, *Command*, p. 551.
2. William Napier, *The Life and Opinions of General Sir Charles Napier* (London, 1857), Vol. I, p. 39.
3. TNA WO 1/305, Return of Troops embarked under the command of Sir John Moore KB, 20 October 1807, by Major General H. Oakes, Quartermaster General.
4. TNA WO 1/305, Hawkesbury to Moore, 16 November 1807.
5. Other information for this chapter has been taken from Carrick Moore, *Life*; Piers Mackesy, *War in the Mediterranean 1805–1810* (London, 1957); Fortescue, *History*, Vol. VI, pp. 36, 88, 99, 100–8, 113, 39, 152; BL Add Mss 57331, 57332 (Moore's journals); BL Add Mss (Moore's letters to Gordon); BL Add Mss 57549 (Moore's letters to various), BL Add Mss 37050 (Moore's letters to Fox); BL Add Mss 57550 (Colborne (as Moore's military secretary) and Moore to various); BL Add Mss 57551 (Moore to various); TNA WO 6/56 (Fox to various); WO 1/305 (Fox and Moore to Castlereagh and others, and Admiral Thornborough, Lord Hawkesbury and Castlereagh to Moore); FO 70/29 (H.E. Fox to C.J. Fox).

Chapter 11
1. D.W. Davies, *Sir John Moore's Peninsular Campaign, 1808–1809* (The Hague, 1974), p. 33.
2. TNA, WO 6/42.
3. Christopher D. Hall, *British Strategy in the Napoleonic War 1803–1815* (Manchester, 1992), p. 67.
4. TNA WO 6/42, 24 April 1808.
5. A note in the margin of the original document (TNA WO 1/189) lists these as 25,000 French, 15,000 Spanish and 4,000 Dutch.
6. This roughly translates as 'I wish it, so it will happen'.
7. The 'present' though not specified, would probably have been a substantial quantity of wine.
8. TNA FO 933/35, Moore to Thornton, 8 June 1808.
9. TNA WO 133/13, 31 May 1808.

10. Because of his own situation Moore did not get involved in this, but the Spanish troops were repatriated successfully.
11. One of the many inaccuracies of George Napier's account of Moore's situation in Sweden is that there was a sentinel at the door; Moore states that there was not. General W.C.E. Napier (ed.), *Passages in the Early Military History of General Sir George T Napier, KCB* (London, 1884), pp. 41–2.
12. The British government eventually agreed that the subsidy should continue, but would be paid one month at a time and would be paid 'during the course of the month' not in advance.
13. This story is another from George Napier. There was a ball held on *Victory*, but it was several days after Moore had arrived back in Gothenburg; there is no mention of his arrival on board in the ship's logs, and Saumarez did not mention an unconventional arrival in his letters to his wife. It seems very unlikely that Moore would have so forsaken his dignity as to dress as a peasant, and even if he had, he would have brought his uniform with him to change back into on arrival. Napier's memoirs were produced in his old age, when it seems his memory had become confused about events.
14. Other information for this chapter has been taken from: Carrick Moore, *Life*, Vol. II, pp. 402–5; BL Add Mss 57332 (Moore's journal); BL Add Mss 49482 (Moore to Gordon); TNA 73/45, 48; TNA WO 1/189; Tim Voelcker, *Admiral Saumarez versus Napoleon; The Baltic, 1807–12* (Woodbridge, 2008).

Chapter 12

1. There is a story that Moore paused on his way out from Castlereagh's office, after closing the door, reopened it and said, 'Remember my Lord, I protest against the expedition and foresee its failure'. This is reported in A.G. Stapleton, *George Canning and His Times* (London, 1859), which goes on to say that having said this, Moore 'proceeded to Portsmouth to take command of the expedition'. Stapleton was Canning's secretary. There is no evidence that this story is true, and given that Moore did not go in command of the expedition and that it was written fifty years after the event, it was almost certainly a figment of its author's imagination. See also Davies, *Sir John Moore's Peninsular Campaign*, p. 41n.
2. Wellington, *Despatches*, Vol. III, p. 123.
3. Janet Macdonald, *From Boiled Beef to Chicken Tikka: 500 Years of Feeding the British Army* (London 2014), pp. 46–7.
4. Except where stated, information for this chapter has come from: BL Add Mss 57320, 57321 (letters home from Moore); 57539 (letters in to Moore), 57332 (Moore's journal), 49482-9 (correspondence with Gordon); TNA FO 72/59-61 (correspondence between Charles Stuart, Frere and Canning); Fortescue, *History*, Vol. VI, Charles Oman, *A History of the Peninsular War Vol. I* (London, 1902); D.W. Davies, *Sir John Moore's Peninsular Campaign 1808–1809* (The Hague, 1974).

Chapter 13

1. A. Neale, *Letters from Portugal and Spain* (London, 1809), p. 241.
2. Venault de Charmilly, *To the British Nation is presented by Venault de Charmilly, Knight of the Royal and Military Order of Saint Louis, the Narrative of his transactions in Spain with the Rt. Hon. John Hookham Frere, … and Lt-Gen. Sir John Moore, K.B., Commander of the British Forces with the suppressed Correspondence of Sir J. Moore; being a Refutation of the Calumnies invented against him …* (London, 1810).
3. If he did write such a letter, it does not appear to have survived, but given the veracity of his other correspondence that letter may never have been sent.
4. Canning and Frere were old friends, having been at Eton together, and sharing an interest in literature.
5. Why he did not continue his journal is not known. He often wrote several days of events in one entry, and he may have continued his journal in rough notes, intending to transpose them later; if so, those notes have been lost.

6. Except where otherwise stated, information for this chapter has come from: BL Add Mss 49482 (correspondence with Gordon); 57320, 57321 (letters home from Moore); 57332 (Moore's journal); 57539, 57540, 57541, 57542 (letters in to Moore); 57553 (letters out from Moore); TNA FO 72/59-61 (correspondence between Charles Stuart, Frere and Canning and Moore and Castlereagh); WO 1/230-6 (letters to/from Castlereagh); Fortescue, *History*, Vol. VI, Oman, *A History of the Peninsular War, Vol. I*; Davies, *Sir John Moore's Peninsular Campaign*.

Chapter 14

1. N. Cantlie, *A History of the Army Medical Department*, Vol. 1 (Edinburgh and London, 1974).
2. Lefebvre-Desnouëttes is the subject of another of George Napier's unlikely stories, whereby the Frenchman, about to dine with Moore, lamented his lack of a sword to accompany his formal uniform and Moore took off his own sword and offered it to him.
3. This speech was reported in R. Blakeney, *A Boy in the Peninsular War* (London, 1899).
4. August Ludolf Friedrich Schaumann, *On the Road with Wellington: The Diary of a War Commissary* (London, 1924), p. 113.
5. There is no reason to doubt any of this; it was in later life, when dictating his memoirs to his granddaughters that invention seems to have taken over from strict fact.
6. Michael Duffy, 'The Embarkation of the British Army at Corunna and Vigo in January 1809', in Guimera Ravina and Jose Maria Blanco Nunez (eds), *Guerra Naval en la Revolucion y el Imperio* (Conference in Madrid, 2008). I am grateful to Professor Duffy for letting me have a copy of the English version of this paper.
7. I am grateful to Mr M.K.H. Crumplin (Retired Consultant Surgeon) for this detail.
8. James Moore, *Narrative of the Campaign of the British Army in Spain* (London, 1809), pp. 217–21.
9. Basil Hall, *Fragments of Voyages and Travels* (London, 1832), Vol. 2, pp. 361–6.
10. Except where otherwise stated, information for this chapter has come from: BL Add Mss 49482 (correspondence with Gordon); 57320, 57321 (letters home from Moore); 57332 (Moore's journal); 57539, 57540, 57541, 57542 (letters in to Moore); 57553 (letters out from Moore); TNA FO 72/59-61 (correspondence between Charles Stuart, Frere and Canning and Moore and Castlereagh); WO 1/230-6 (letters to/from Castlereagh); Fortescue, *History*, Vol. VI, Oman, *A History of the Peninsular War, Vol. I*; Davies, *Sir John Moore's Peninsular Campaign*.

Chapter 15

1. C. Boothby, *Under England's Flag: The Memoirs, Diaries and Correspondence of Charles Boothby* (London, 1900).
2. J.G. Lockhart (ed.), *Memoirs of Sir Walter Scott* (London, 1900), Vol. II, pp. 60–70.
3. J. Maurice (ed.), *The Diary of Sir John Moore* (London, 1904).
4. Except where otherwise stated, information for this chapter has come from: Hansard, April 1809; TNA WO 1/230-6 (letters to/from Castlereagh); Fortescue, *History*, Vol. VI; Oman, *A History of the Peninsular War, Vol. I*; Davies, *Sir John Moore's Peninsular Campaign 1808–1809*.
5. Barbara Tuchman, *Practising History* (London, 1980).
6. J.M. Black, 'Wellington in the context of long-term military history', in *Wellington Studies II* (Southampton, 1999), p. 31.

Chapter 16

1. Tuchman, *Practising History*.
2. The exception being Davies, *Sir John Moore's Peninsular Campaign*, which is based on detailed research of French as well as British sources.
3. This is in strong contrast to Nelson, whose letters in the latter part of his life (not to mention his will) were overly effusive on his love of God.

Bibliography

Primary Sources

The National Archives
Admiralty Documents
ADM 1/412-428
ADM 1/3751
ADM 2/1365
ADM 50/58

Audit Office Documents
AO 1/12 (31)

Foreign Office Documents
FO 20
FO 24
FO 28
FO 29
FO 49
FO 72
FO 63
FO 67
FO 70/11-75
FO 72/ 52; 58; 59; 60; 61; 69; 70; 71; 72
FO 73/45; 46; 47; 48
FO 78/31
FO 188/2
FO 933/35

Home Office Documents
HO 28, 50, 51p147

Maps
MFQ 1/133 – map of Aboukir Bay

War Office Documents
WO 1/84, 85; 135; 180; 185; 189; 230-6; 238; 241
WO 1/135
WO 1/180, 185; 189; 229; 261; 262; 267; 280; 281; 285;
    303-315; 345; 638-0; 674; 804-5; 902; 1132
WO 3/34; 598
WO 6/20; 42-3; 48-9; 56-7; 60-1; 87; 133; 156; 208
WO 31/250

British Library Add Mss
14273; 22688; 20107, Vol. 1; 20176; 20190; 34903-5;
34932; 34937; 37050; 37292; 37847; 37852; 38245;
41514; 41516; 49471-512; 57320-21; 57320; 57324–
57332; 57539-554; 59193

National Maritime Museum, Greenwich
Samuel Hood HOO
Minto (Sir Gilbert Elliot) Ell

Nottingham University Library (Department of MSS)
PWF (Portland papers)

Historic MSS Commission
HMC supplementary report on the mss of Robert
    Graham of Fintry: Report on the manuscripts of J.B.
    Fortescue Esq, preserved at Dropmore, Vol. VI

Secondary Sources
Armstrong, Martin, *Lady Hester Stanhope* (Cedric Chivers Ltd, Bath, 1928)
Blackmore, Howard I., *British Military Firearms, 1650–1850* (London, 1962)
Blakeney, R., *A Boy in the Peninsular War* (London, 1899)
Boothby, C., *Under England's Flag: The Memoirs, Diaries and Correspondence of Charles Boothby* (London, 1900)
Brownrigg, B. *The Life and Letters of Sir John Moore* (Oxford, 1923)
Bunbury, Henry, *Narratives of Some Passages in the Great War with France* (London, 1854, facs. edn 2008)
Campbell, Neil (ed.), *Baron Francis de Rottenburg's Regulations for the exercise of Riflemen*
Cantlie, N., *A History of the Army Medical Department* (Edinburgh and London, 1974), Vol. 1
Carrick Moore, James, *The Life of Lieutenant-General Sir John Moore K.B.* (London, 1834)
Charmilly, Venault de, *To the British Nation is presented by Venault de Charmilly, Knight of the Royal and Military Order of Saint Louis, the Narrative of his transactions in Spain with the Rt. Hon. John Hookham Frere, … and Lt-Gen. Sir John Moore, K.B., Commander of the British Forces with the*

suppressed Correspondence of Sir J. Moore; being a Refutation of the Calumnies invented against him ... (London, 1810)

Cross, John (ed.), General Dundas's *Rules and Regulations*, in *A System of Drill and Manoeuvres. And Instructions for Light Infantry and Riflemen*

Davies, D.W. *Sir John Moore's Peninsular Campaign 1808–1809* (The Hague, 1974)

Duffy, Michael, *Soldiers, Sugar and Seapower* (Oxford, 1987)

Duffy, Michael, 'The Embarkation of the British Army at Corunna and Vigo in January 1809', in Guimera Ravina and Jose Maria Blanco Nunez (eds), *Guerra Naval en la Revolucion y el Imperio* (Conference in Madrid, 2008)

Fortescue, J.W., *History of the British Army*, Vols III, IV, Pt I and Pt II, VI

Fuller, J.F.C., *British Light Infantry in the Eighteenth Century* (London, 1925)

Fuller, J.F.C., *Sir John Moore's System of Training* (London, 1925)

Gregory, Desmond, *The Ungovernable Rock, A history of the Anglo-Corsican Kingdom and its Role in British's Mediterranean Strategy During the Revolutionary War (1793–1797)* (London, 1985)

Gregory, Desmond, *Sicily, The Insecure Base: A History of the British Occupation of Sicily, 1806–1815* (London, 1988)

Gurwood, J. (ed.), *The Dispatches of Field Marshall the Duke of Wellington, Vol. III*

Hall, Basil, *Fragments of Voyages and Travels* (London, 1832), Vol. 2

Hall, Christopher D., *British Strategy in the Napoleonic War 1803–1815* (Manchester, 1992)

Herbert, Maxwell (ed.), *The Creevy Papers: A Selection from the Correspondence and Diaries of the Late Thomas Creevy MP* (London, 1903)

Jackson, Robert, *A Systematic View of the Formations, Discipline and Economy of Armies*

Lockhart, J.G. (ed.), *Memoirs of Sir Walter Scott* (London, 1900), Vol. II, pp. 60–70

Macdonald, Janet, *From Boiled Beef to Chicken Tikka: 500 Years of Feeding the British Army* (London, 2014)

Mackesy, Piers, *War in the Mediterranean 1805–1810* (London, 1957)

Mackesy, Piers, 'Most Sadly Bitched: the British Cadiz Expedition of 1800', *Les empires en guerre et paix 1793–1860* (Conference, Portsmouth, 1988)

Mackesy, Piers, 'Cadiz expedition', quoting Lord Cornwallis, State Papers SpP IV

Mackesy, Piers, *British Victory in Egypt: The End of Napoleon's Conquest* (London, 1995)

Manningham, Coote, *Regulations for the Exercise of Riflemen*

Maurice, J.F., *Diary of Sir John Moore* (London, 1904)

Meryon, C.L. (ed.), *The Memoirs of Lady Hester Stanhope* (London, 1845)

Minto, Countess of (ed.), *Life and Letters of Sir Gilbert Elliot, First Earl of Minto* (London, 1974), Vol. II

Moore-Smith, G.C. (ed.), *The Life and Letters of John Colborne, Field Marshall Lord Seaton; Compiled from his Letters, Records of his Conversations, and Other Sources* (London, 1903)

Napier, William, *The Life and Opinions of General Sir Charles Napier* (London, 1857), Vol. I, p. 39

Napier, William (ed.), *Passages in the Early Military History of General Sir George T Napier, KCB* (London, 1884)

Neale, A., *Letters from Portugal and Spain* (London, 1809), p. 241

Nicolas, Nicholas Harris, *The Dispatches and Letters of Vice Admiral Lord Horatio Nelson* (London, 1844), Vol. I, p. 373

Oman, Charles, *A History of the Peninsular War* (London, 1902), Vol. I

Parker, Mathew, *The Sugar Barons: Family, Corruption, Empire and War* (London, 2011)

Rodger, N.A.M., *The Command of the Ocean* (London, 2004)

Schaumann, August Ludolf Friedrich, *On the Road with Wellington: The Diary of a War Commissiary* (London, 1924)

Sherwig, John M., *Guineas and Gunpowder: British Foreign Aid in the Wars with France 1793–1815* (Cambridge, MA, 1969)

Stapleton, A.G., *George Canning and His Times* (London, 1859)

Summerville, Christopher, *March of Death: Sir John Moore's Retreat to Corunna 1808–1809* (London, 2003)

Tuchman, Barbara, *Practising History* (London, 1980)

Voelcker, Tim, *Admiral Saumarez versus Napoleon; The Baltic, 1807–12* (Woodbridge, 2008)

Ward, G., 'Some Fresh Light on the Corunna Campaign', *Journal of Army Historical Research*, XXVII, 110

Wareham, Tom, *Frigate Commander* (London, 2004)

Index